Contents

FROM
GENESIS
TO
CHRONICLES

FROM

GENESIS

TO

CHRONICLES

Explorations in Old Testament Theology

GERHARD VON RAD

Edited by K. C. Hanson

FORTRESS PRESS

MINNEAPOLIS

FROM GENESIS TO CHRONICLES
Explorations in Old Testament Theology

First Fortress Press edition 2005

An earlier edition of this work was translated by E. W. Trueman Dicken and published by Oliver & Boyd, Edinburgh and London, 1966, and reprinted by SCM Press, London, 1984. Translation of *Gesammelte Studien zum Alten Testament,* Theologische Bücherei 8, copyright © Chr. Kaiser Verlag, Munich, 1958. Chapter 6 was originally published in *Interpretation* 15 (1961) 3-13, and reprinted by permission; it was translated by Lloyd Gaston.

Cover art: *Moses Destroying the Tablets of the Law* by Rembrandt von Rijn. Photo © Bildarchiv Preussischer Kulturbesitz/Art Resource, NY

Book design: Zan Ceeley

Library of Congress Cataloging-in-Publication Data

Rad, Gerhard von, 1901-1971.
  From Genesis to Chronicles / Gerhard von Rad ; edited by K.C. Hanson.
    p. cm. — (Fortress classics in biblical studies)
  Includes bibliographical references and indexes.
   ISBN 0-8006-3717-8 (hardcover : alk. paper) — ISBN 0-8006-3718-6 (pbk. : alk. paper)
   1. Bible. O.T.—Criticism, interpretation, etc. 2. Bible. O.T.—Theology. I. Hanson, K. C. (Kenneth C.) II. Rad, Gerhard von, 1901-1971. Gesammelte Studien Zum Alten Testament. III. Title. IV. Series.
  BS1188.R313 2005
  221.6—dc22

                                                              2004030602

Manufactured in the U.S.A.
09   08   07   06   05   1   2   3   4   5   6   7   8   9   10

Acknowledgments

Chapter 1 was first published as *Das formgeschichtliche Problem des Hexateuchs,* BWANT 78 (Stuttgart: Kohlhammer, 1938).

Chapter 2 was first published as "Verheissenes Land und Jahwes Land im Hexateuch," *ZDPV* 63 (1943) 191–204.

Chapter 3 was first published as "Die Anrechnung des Glaubens zur Gerechtigkeit," *TLZ* 76 (1951) 129–32.

Chapter 4 was first published as "Josephsgeschichte und ältere Chokma," in *Congress Volume: Copenhagen, 1953,* Vetus Testamentum Supplements 1 (Leiden: Brill, 1953), 120–27.

Chapter 5 was first published as "Es ist noch eine Ruhe vorhanden dem Volke Gottes," *Zwischen den Zeiten* 11 (1933) 104–11.

Chapter 6 was first published as "Ancient Word and Living Word— The Preaching of Deuteronomy and Our Preaching," *Int* 15 (1961) 3–13, translated by Lloyd Gaston. It was later published in German as "Die Predigt des Deuteronomiums und unsere Predigt," in idem, *Gesammelte Studien zum Alten Testament II,* edited by Rudolf Smend, ThBü 48 (Munich: Kaiser, 1973), 154–64.

Chapter 7 was first published as "Zelt und Lade," *Kirchliche Zeitschrift* 42 (1931) 476–98.

Chapter 8 was first published as "Die Stadt auf dem Berge," *EvTh* 8 (1948–49) 439–47.

Chapter 9 was first published as "Der Anfang der Geschichtsschreibung im alten Israel," *Archiv für Kulturgeschichte* 32 (1944) 1–42.

Chapter 10 was first published in *Deuteronomium-Studien*, FRLANT 40 (Göttingen: Vandenhoeck & Ruprecht, 1947), 52–64.

Chapter 11 was first published as "Das jüdäische Königsritual," *TLZ* 72 (1947) 211–16.

Chapter 12 was first published as "Das theologische Problem des alttestamentlichen Schöpfungsglaubens," in *Werden und Wesen des Alten Testaments,* edited by Paul Volz, Friedrich Stummer, and Johannes Hempel, BZAW 66 (Berlin: Töpelmann, 1936), 138–47.

Chapter 13 was first published as "'Gerechtigkeit' und 'Leben' in der Kultsprache der Psalmen,'" in *Festschrift Alfred Bertholet zum 80. Geburtstag gewidmet von Kollegen und Freunden,* edited by Walter Baumgartner et al. (Tübingen: Mohr/Siebeck, 1950), 418–37.

Chapter 14 was first published as "Aspekte alttestamentlichen Weltverständnisses," *EvTh* 24 (1964) 57–73.

Chapter 15 was first published as "Hiob XXXVIII und die altägyptische Weisheit," in *Wisdom in Israel and in the Ancient Near East: Presented to Professor Harold Henry Rowley,* edited by Martin Noth and D. Winton Thomas, Vetus Testamentum Supplements 3 (Leiden: Brill, 1955), 293–301.

Chapter 16 was first published as "Die levitische Predigt in den Büchern der Chronik," in *Festschrift Otto Procksch zum sechzigsten Geburtstag,* edited by Albrecht Alt (Leipzig: Deichert, 1934), 113–24.

Abbreviations

ANET	*Ancient Near Eastern Texts Relating to the Old Testament.* 3d ed. Edited by James B. Pritchard. Princeton: Princeton Univ. Press, 1969
ANVAO	Avhandlinger utgitt av det Norske Videnskaps-Akademii Oslo
AOT	*Altorientalische Texte zum Alten Testament.* 2d ed. Edited by Hugo Gressmann. Berlin: de Gruyter, 1926
AR	Archiv für Religionswissenschaft
ATANT	Abhandlungen zur Theologie des Alten und Neuen Testaments
ATD	Das Alte Testament Deutsch
BASOR	*Bulletin of the American Schools of Oriental Research*
BBB	Bonner biblische Beiträge
B.C.E.	Before the Common Era
BDB	*A Hebrew and English Lexicon of the Old Testament.* Edited by Francis Brown, S. R. Driver, and Charles A. Briggs. Boston: Houghton Mifflin, 1907. Reprinted with corrections Oxford: Clarendon, 1957
BET	Beiträge zur evangelischen Theologie
BFCT	Beiträge zur Förderung christlicher Theologie
Bik.	*Bikkurim*
BWA(N)T	Beiträge zur Wissenschaft vom Alten (und Neuen) Testament
BZAW	Beihefte zur Zeitschrift für die alttestamentliche Wissenschaft
CBET	Contributions to Biblical Exegesis and Theology
CIS	*Corpus Inscriptionum Semiticarum.* 5 vols. Paris: Republic, 1881

D	Deuteronomic source of the Pentateuch/Hexateuch
DBI	*Dictionary of Biblical Interpretation.* 2 vols. Edited by John H. Hayes. Nashville: Abingdon, 1999
E	Elohist source of the Pentateuch/Hexateuch
EOTHR	Albrecht Alt, *Essays on Old Testament History and Religion.* Translated by R. A. Wilson. Oxford: Blackwell, 1966 [Selections from Alt, *KS*]
ET	English translation
EvTh	*Evangelische Theologie*
ExpT	*Expository Times*
FAT	Forschungen zum Alten Testament
FCBS	Fortress Classics in Biblical Studies
FRLANT	Forschungen zur Religion und Literatur des Alten und Neuen Testaments
HAT	Handbuch zum Alten Testament
HSS	Harvard Semitic Studies
HTIBS	Historic Texts and Interpreters in Biblical Scholarship
Int	*Interpretation*
J	Yahwist source of the Pentateuch/Hexateuch
JSOTSup	Journal for the Study of the Old Testament Supplement Series
JSS	*Journal of Semitic Studies*
KAT	Kommentar zum Alten Testament
KS	Albrecht Alt, *Kleine Schriften.* 3 vols. Munich: Beck, 1953–59
LAE	*Literature of Ancient Egypt.* 3d ed. Edited by W. K. Simpson and Robert K. Ritner. New Haven: Yale Univ. Press, 2003
LAI	Library of Ancient Israel
LXX	Septuagint
m.	Mishnah
MLBS	Mercer Library of Biblical Studies
MT	Masoretic text
OBO	Orbis biblicus et orientalis
OBT	Overtures to Biblical Theology
OTL	Old Testament Library
OTS	Old Testament Studies
P	Priestly source of the Pentateuch/Hexateuch
P^A	earlier redaction of the Priestly Source
P^B	later redaction of the Priestly Source
RB	*Revue biblique*
RSR	*Religious Studies Review*
RSV	Revised Standard Version of the Bible
SBLDS	Society of Biblical Literature Dissertation Series

SBLSymSer	Society of Biblical Literature Symposium Series
SBT	Studies in Biblical Theology
SBTS	Sources for Biblical and Theological Study
SEÅ	*Svensk exegetisk årsbok*
SGK	Schriften der Königsberger Gelehrten Gesellschaft, Königsberg
SGVSGTR	Sammlung gemeinverständlicher Vorträge und Schriften aus dem Gebiet der Theologie und Religionsgeschichte
SHCANE	Studies in the History and Culture of the Ancient Near East
TBl	*Theologische Blätter*
ThBü	Theologische Bücherei
TLZ	*Theologische Literaturzeitung*
TRu	*Theologische Rundschau*
UTB	Uni-Taschenbücher
VF	*Verkündigung und Forschung*
VT	*Vetus Testamentum*
ZAW	*Zeitschrift für die alttestamentliche Wissenschaft*
ZDPV	*Zeitschrift des deutschen Pälastinavereins*
ZTK	*Zeitschrift für Theologie und Kirche*

Editor's Foreword

The impact of Gerhard von Rad on Old Testament studies in the twentieth century persists into the twenty-first. The subtlety of his genius continued unabated until his death at the age of seventy. He stood at a critical juncture of not only biblical studies, but of world history as well. His creative exploration of ancient Israel's traditions marked a clear step forward beyond the atomizing tendencies of German Old Testament scholarship in the nineteenth and early twentieth centuries.

Von Rad was born in Nürnberg, Germany, on October 21, 1901, the year that Queen Victoria died, the Australian colonies became federated into a unified state, J. P. Morgan incorporated U.S. Steel, Marconi received the first trans-Atlantic radio signal, and the first edition of Hermann Gunkel's commentary on Genesis was published. The great jazz musician Louis Armstrong was born and died the same years as von Rad.

Studying theology at the universities of Erlangen and Tübingen, von Rad was ordained to the pastorate in the Bavarian Lutheran Church in 1925; shortly thereafter he returned to his theological studies. He completed his doctorate at Erlangen under the direction of Otto Procksch (1928) and his *Habilitation* at Leipzig under the direction of Albrecht Alt (1930). Alt was a strong, direct influence on von Rad's work; but another major influence was Hermann Gunkel in terms of form-critical method as well as his groundbreaking works on Genesis and Psalms.

Like von Rad, Martin Noth (a year younger than von Rad) also studied at Erlangen and Leipzig; and he too was a student of Alt (who had studied at Erlangen a generation earlier). Von Rad and Noth shared a number of other things in common: von Rad followed Noth in teaching at Leipzig, they were both avid musicians, they were both active in the church, they both served in the German army briefly at the end of World War II, and they both contributed greatly to the analysis of Israelite traditions. But while Noth was drawn more in the direction of history and archaeology, von Rad gravitated toward theological studies.

His teaching career began in Erlangen where he tutored Hebrew. He was Alt's assistant, a *Privatdozent*, then *ausserordentlicher* professor at Leipzig (1930–34), then professor at Jena (1934–44). He served in the German army in 1944–45 and was a prisoner of war for four months (March–June 1945) in Bad Kreuznach. After the war, von Rad was professor first at Göttingen (1945–49) and then at Heidelberg (1949–67). Teaching was vitally important to von Rad, and students came from around the world to study with him. His well-known articulation is "My task as an academic teacher was and is: to learn to read and teach how to read" ("Meine Aufgabe als akademischer Lehrer war und ist: lesen zu lernen und lesen zu lehren"). Numerous students who studied with him went on to prominence in Old Testament studies, including Klaus Baltzer, Rolf Rendtorff, Hans Jürgen Hermisson, Klaus Koch, Rolf Knierim, and Odil Hannes Steck.

As an advocate of the Old Testament's role in Christianity, von Rad fought against the tide of anti-Judaism and theological Marcionism in pre-war Germany. He lectured and preached extensively in churches that identified with the Confessing Church. This led to his isolation at the university of Jena, since "German Christians" (those cooperating with Nazi control of churches) dominated the theological faculty there. Note that von Rad arrived at Jena in the year the Barmen Declaration was issued by the Confessing Church. Brueggemann draws the interesting parallel between von Rad's contrast of Israel's historical credo with Canaanite fertility religion and von Rad's own context of the Barmen Declaration over against the Nazi's focus on "Blood and Soil."[1]

Von Rad is known for several things: the relation of history and cult, the analysis of ancient Israel's traditions, and theological interpretation. His masterwork will always be his two-volume *Old Testament Theology*, which he divided into *Israel's Historical Traditions* and *Israel's Prophetic Traditions*. One of the most interesting turns in von Rad's writing appeared in the publication of his final major work: *Wisdom in Israel*. Throughout most of his career, he had downplayed the role that wisdom played in Israel's traditions. But with the publication of this work he re-examined those assumptions and helped invigorate a whole generation of scholarship on Israelite and ancient Near Eastern wisdom.

He was honored with two *Festschriften*: the first by his former students for his sixtieth birthday (1961) and a second, larger one by a broad range of scholars for his seventieth birthday (1971). Following an international conference in Heidelberg celebrating his importance for theological and biblical studies and the centenary of von Rad's birth, two volumes were published in his honor: one focusing on preaching the Old Testament, and the other on wisdom in ancient Israel (both 2003; see the bibliography at the end of this volume for all four works). Von Rad was awarded five honorary doctorates—from the universities of Leipzig, Lund, Utrecht, Glasgow, and Wales. Furthermore, he was inducted into the Heidelberg Akademie der Wissenschaften and the *Orden pour le Mérite* for Science and Art and made an honorary member of the Society of Biblical Literature and the Society of Old Testament Study.

In addressing the ongoing significance of von Rad, Crenshaw provides an elegant summary:

> His approach to the text emphasized the vitality of competing traditions, the continual actualization of Yahweh's word for each new generation. Moreover, he recognized the role of the cult in shaping religious belief and in transmitting that faith by means of confessional statements. Von Rad thus garnered a theological maximum from a historical minimum. His sensitive reading of the Old Testament enabled many others to span the vast chasm separating them from the ancient text. The sheer beauty of his prose captivated minds, and the passion with which he explored such topics as knowledge and its limits, trust and attack, and divine abandonment came through with enormous force.[2]

The essays in the present collection are some of von Rad's most effective contributions to Old Testament theology and exegesis. It is difficult to read these without seeing his deep understanding of the texts, interesting juxtaposition of passages, creative hypotheses, and subtle tracing of connections between Israel's traditions. While the discussions on these passages have progressed, each one of these gems continues to influence contemporary research.

Von Rad and his wife, Luise, had four children: Christoph (who died of tuberculosis at age nine), Ursula (a theologian), Ulrich (a geologist and oceanographer), and Michael (a professor of psychosomatic medicine). In 1967 he was made emeritus, and on October 31, 1971, he died in Heidelberg.

The reader will note that I have edited the collection in various ways. I have added a few notes (marked by square brackets) and bibliographies, transliterated the Hebrew and Greek, added missing publication information, provided English translations of publications in the notes that were not available earlier, slightly reorganized the sequence of essays, and replaced an essay on 1 Corinthians and the *Testament of the Twelve Patriarchs* with one on Deuteronomy. I am grateful to Prof. Gary Stansell (St. Olaf College) for his careful reading and suggestions; and I am grateful to Prof. Dr. med. Michael von Rad (Munich) for his assistance.

K. C. Hanson

Preface

The reader will readily understand that it is not easy for an author to present in unaltered form studies written over the course of many years. The oldest of the present collection is now twenty-seven years old, and in view of those developments in Old Testament studies, which we all so greatly welcome, much of what has been written ought now to be differently stated. This is particularly true of the first essay, "The Form-Critical Problem of the Hexateuch," which should be read in conjunction with Martin Noth's more recent *A History of Pentateuchal Traditions* (*Überlieferungsgeschichte des Pentateuchs*). The project of amending these studies by making alterations and improvements, if only in certain passages, was soon seen to be impracticable. I must therefore beg the reader to exercise a certain historical discretion in making use of the present volume, and to bear in mind the state of our knowledge of a given topic at the time when each particular essay was written.

The present collection was made at the instance of Professor Hans Walter Wolff. But for him, and for the generosity with which in each case the original publishers have given permission for the articles to be reprinted, this volume would never have appeared. I should particularly like to thank Pastor Hans Jochen Boecker for his kindness in reading the proofs and in preparing the index.

Gerhard von Rad
1958

Translator's Preface

In translating the present work, I have thought it advisable to modify certain minor features of the original in order to conform with standard English practice. In a few places where technical points of Greek or Hebrew grammar or vocabulary were discussed in the text of the original, this material has been transferred bodily into notes. Several paragraphs which were unduly long by English standards have been divided. All biblical references to the Old Testament, taken in the original German text from the Hebrew Bible, are given here according to the numbering of the Revised Standard Version of the Bible, and the text of this version has also been followed wherever possible in biblical quotations. It should be noted, however, that many instances occur in which Professor von Rad's exegesis of a passage precludes the interpretation suggested by the Revised Standard Version. In such cases the text of the translation has necessarily been modified, and a note added to indicate this fact when it is of significance to the main argument.

E. W. Trueman Dicken
Lenten Hall,
University of Nottingham, 1966

Part I

From Genesis to Joshua

1

The Form-Critical Problem
of the Hexateuch

The Problem Stated

No one will ever be able to say that in our time there has been any crisis in the theological study of the Hexateuch.[1] On the contrary, it might be held that we have reached a position of stalemate that many view with considerable anxiety. What is to be done about it? So far as the analysis of source documents is concerned, there are signs that the road has come to a dead end. Some would say that we have already gone too far. On the other hand, in the examination of isolated passages, with regard to both their content and their literary form, we must frankly admit that we have by no means done all that might have been done. But in this field, too, controversy has ceased, and it may be said without exaggeration that scholars, especially the younger ones, are weary of research in hexateuchal studies. The reason for this is not difficult to discover.

Both the lines of investigation mentioned above, despite much diversity of method in their application, led inevitably further and further away from the final form of the text as we have it. A process of analysis, doubtless almost always interesting but nevertheless highly stylized, has run its course, and a more or less clear perception of its inevitability handicaps many scholars today. Indeed, even those who are fully prepared to recognize that it was both necessary and important to traverse these paths cannot ignore the profoundly disintegrating effect that has been one result of this method of hexateuchal criticism. On almost all sides the final form of the Hexateuch has come to be regarded as a starting-point barely worthy of discussion, from which the debate should move away as rapidly as possible in order to reach the real problems underlying it.

It is from this disquieting situation that the present essay takes it origin, addressing itself to a notable gap in hexateuchal studies. There is a question

that, oddly enough, has not yet been asked,[2] the solution of which may perhaps nevertheless lead us to some extent out of the doldrums. It may be
briefly stated at this point.

Let us run over rapidly in quite general terms the contents of the Hexateuch: God, who created the world, called the first ancestors of Israel and
promised them the land of Canaan. Having grown in numbers in Egypt, the
people of Israel were led into freedom by Moses, amidst miraculous demon-
strations of God's power and favor, and after prolonged wanderings in the
desert were granted the promised land.

Now these statements, which summarize the contents of the Hexateuch,
are understood in the source documents to be essentially statements of belief.
Doubtless they have been overlaid with much historically "credible" material,
yet once the basic facts of hexateuchal history are enumerated, it is exclusively
about Israel's *faith* that they speak. That which is recounted, from the creation
of the world and the call of Abraham to the completion of the conquest under
Joshua, is purely and simply a "history of redemption." We might equally well
call it a *creed*, a summary of the principal facts of God's redemptive activity.

Let us now consider this creed from the point of view of its outward form.
It is a truly immense compilation, an arrangement of the most diverse kinds of
material that are all brought into relation with one comparatively simple basic
idea. At once we see that we have here the end-term of a process, something
both final and conclusive. The intricate elaboration of the one basic idea into
this tremendous edifice is no first essay, nor is it something that has grown of
its own accord to the proportions of classical maturity. Rather, as we have said,
it is something pressed to the ultimate limits of what is possible and of what is
readable. It must certainly have passed through earlier stages of development.

In other words, the Hexateuch itself may, and indeed must, be understood
as representative of a type of literature of which we may expect to be able to
recognize the early stages, the circumstances of composition, and the subsequent development until it reached the greatly extended form in which it now
lies before us.

In the absence of much of the firm evidence one would have wished to
find, our investigation will be able to point only remotely to the stages in the
development of this *genre*, and it will have to take account of both constant
and variable elements. The constant element is that of the historical creed as
such. It occurs from the earliest times onwards, and in its basic constituents is
not subject to change. The variable element is the external expression, the
outward form; and not only this external appearance, but above all the degree
of theological penetration and manipulation of the traditional deposit. The
solution of the problems thus raised should have the merit of leading us back
to the final and conclusive form of the Hexateuch by way of an organically

integrated theological process, rather than by the high-handed methods of pneumatic theology.

THE SHORT HISTORICAL CREED

In Deuteronomy 26, two cultic prayers are prescribed which are nowadays generally held to be liturgical formularies. It has been supposed, actually quite unnecessarily, that we are here dealing only with late embellishments; yet the problem of deuteronomic redaction is of small moment beside the fact that we can here clearly discern, from their form and content, two strictly cultic ceremonies.[3] Here we are concerned only with the first of the two prayers, which is to be spoken as the first fruits are handed over at the sanctuary. It runs:

> A wandering Aramean was my father; and he went down into Egypt and sojourned there, few in number; and there he became a nation, great, mighty, and populous. And the Egyptians treated us harshly, and afflicted us, and laid upon us hard bondage. Then we cried to Yahweh the God of our fathers, and Yahweh heard our voice, and saw our affliction, our toil, and our oppression; and Yahweh brought us out of Egypt with a mighty hand and an outstretched arm, with great terror, with signs and wonders; and he brought us into this place and gave us this land, a land flowing with milk and honey. (Deut 26:5b-9)

The deuteronomic phraseology of the latter half of this prayer in particular is quite unmistakable, and there can be no doubt that it is a liturgical formula. Such prayers really were used, and they were certainly not new in the time of the deuteronomist. All the evidence points to the fact that this prayer is very much older, both in form and content, than the literary context into which it has since been inserted.[4] One might even be so bold as to remove the traces of the deuteronomic editor's retouching and to attempt a reconstruction of the original formula; but it seems more important to determine whether the present association of the prayer with the presentation of the first fruits is original or whether it was effected only at a later stage. Jirku held the latter view,[5] but his skepticism was not wholly justified; it is surely inherent in the logic of early Israelite belief that thanksgiving for the harvest should stand side by side with, and indeed be contained within, thanksgiving for deliverance from bondage and for the gift of the promised land.

As to its content, the prayer consists of a quite brief recapitulation of the principal facts of God's redemptive activity: the humble beginnings of Israel in the patriarchal age, the oppression in Egypt. The deliverance by Yahweh and his bringing them into the promised land. The whole might be called a confession of faith, or rather an enumeration of the saving facts that were the constitutive element of the religious community. The speaker divests himself of all his personal concerns and aligns himself fully with the community. Indeed, he identifies himself with the community: at this moment, as he pronounces its confession of faith, he is its mouthpiece.

Deuteronomy 26:5ff. is a creed with all the characteristics and attributes of a creed, and is probably the earliest recognizable example. There must therefore have been a cultic occasion for the recital by the individual of this short confessional statement of God's redemptive activity.

It is interesting to examine the underlying presuppositions of this usage. Such a creed is certainly not an independent feature within the framework of the cultus; it is a derivative one, the subsequent verbal expression of a notion that permeates the whole cultus. In other words, if there is evidence in comparatively early times for the custom of making a cultic confession of this sort, this presupposes the existence of a form of the story of redemption that has already become fixed by usage, and must therefore be older still. Such a summary of the facts of redemption within the cultus cannot be a freely devised meditation based on historical events, but must be a reflection of the traditional form in which the faith is presented.

It might appear unreasonable to examine still more microscopically this admittedly very brief confession, which has in any case been handed down to us only in its deuteronomic recension. Nevertheless, because of its later implications, attention must be drawn to the complete absence here of any mention of the revelation of Yahweh in the events connected with Mount Sinai.

In yet another passage in Deuteronomy (6:20-24) there is a very similar account of the facts of Israel's redemption, also after the style of a confession of faith, which must be assigned to the same category of material as Deuteronomy 26. This short passage is, it is true, firmly embedded in a wider context of paraenetic material, but in the form it nevertheless stands apart from the surrounding homiletic framework. From the words that introduce it, it can be recognized as a direct quotation of more or less stereotyped material.

> When your son asks you in time to come, "What is the meaning of the testimonies and the statutes and the ordinances which Yahweh our God has commanded you?" then you shall say to your son, "We were Pharaoh's slaves in Egypt; and Yahweh brought us out of Egypt with a mighty hand; and Yahweh showed signs and wonders great and grievous, against Egypt and against Pharaoh and all his household, before our eyes; and he brought us out from there, that he might bring us in and give us the land which he swore to give to our fathers. And Yahweh commanded us to do all these statutes. . . ." (Deut 6:20-24)

The summary of the facts of Israel's redemption is almost identical with that of Deut 26:5ff., but here the silence concerning the events of Mount Sinai is even more striking, since the question that was asked, and to which the answer was to be given in the form of the short creed, was expressly concerned with the divine commandments and statutes. Evidently the form was already so rigidly fixed that even in this instance, where they might seem quite essential, these events could find no place. The deuteronomist still has in fact a keen awareness of the lofty sacral significance of this formula that he will have sought to employ for the purpose of religious instruction.

We turn now to another text from a different source that must clearly be ranged alongside those already cited, namely Joshua's oration to the congregation at Shechem. We shall have to deal with this account in greater detail at a later stage; here it is simply the historical excursus that is of interest.

> Your fathers lived of old beyond the Euphrates, Terah, the father of Abraham and of Nahor; and they served other gods. Then I took your father Abraham from beyond the River and led him through all the land of Canaan, and made his offspring many. I gave him Isaac; and to Isaac I gave Jacob and Esau. And I gave Esau the hill country of Seir to possess, but Jacob and his children went down to Egypt. And I sent Moses and Aaron, and I plagued Egypt with what I did in the midst of it; and afterwards I brought you out. Then I brought your fathers out of Egypt, and you came to the sea; and the Egyptians pursued your fathers with chariots and horsemen to the Red Sea. And when they cried to Yahweh, he put darkness between you and the Egyptians, and made the sea come upon them and cover them; and your eyes saw what I did to Egypt; and you lived in the wilderness a long time. Then I brought you to the land of the Amorites, who lived on the other side of the Jordan; they fought with you, and I gave them into your hand, and you took possession of their land, and I destroyed them before you. Then Balak the son of Zippor, King of Moab, arose and fought against Israel; and he sent and invited Balaam the son of Beor to curse you; but I would not listen to Balaam; therefore he blessed you; so I delivered you out of his hand. And you went over the Jordan and came to Jericho, and the men of Jericho fought against you, and also the Amorites, the Perizzites, the Canaanites, the Hittites, the Girgashites, the Hivites, and the Jebusites; and I gave them into your hand. And I sent the hornet before you, which drove them out before you, the two kings of the Amorites; it was not by your sword or by your bow. I gave you a land on which you had not laboured, and cities which you had not built, and you dwell therein;

> you eat the fruit of the vineyard and oliveyards which you did not
> plant. (Josh 24:2b-13)

Here, too, the text is shot through with all kinds of accretions and embellishments that are immediately recognizable as deriving from the hexateuchal
presentation of history. There can, however, be no possible doubt but that this
speech is not an *ad hoc* composition. Its literary *genre* is not that of a more or
less freely compiled account of particular events. Use has once more been
made of a form that is basically unchangeable and allows liberty of adjust-
ment only in insignificant ways.

Here, as before, we have at bottom the major features of the story of
redemption, from the patriarchs to the entry into the promised land. The
minor accretions—details concerning the miracle of the Red Sea, the meeting
with Balaam and so on—are striking only when it is realized that the events of
Sinai are completely overlooked. The revelation of Yahweh and the sealing of
the covenant were, after all, events of such epoch-making significance that
they could certainly have been brought in alongside the story of Balaam or the
mention of the hornet if their inclusion had been regarded as in any way relevant. But the basic pattern seems to have known nothing of these things; and
we are thus faced with the remarkable fact that this *genre* allowed of the interpolation of small details, but not of so fundamental an alteration as would
have been occasioned by the introduction of the events of Mount Sinai.

These texts, briefly as we have discussed them, lead to one provisional conclusion, especially in view of the context in which they stand. In none of the
three cases were we dealing with a casual recollection of historical events, but
rather with a recital in exalted, pregnant form, pronounced in a situation of
lofty significance, in the setting of a cultic ceremony. All three texts were evidently compiled according to the same plan, a fact that was made clear by the
absence of any reference to the events of Mt. Sinai. They follow a canonical
pattern of the redemption narrative long since fixed as to its details. Surely
then it is not unduly bold to conclude that the solemn recital of the main parts
of the redemption narrative must have been an invariable feature of the
ancient Israelite cultus, either as a straightforward creedal statement or as a
hortatory address to the congregation.

At first sight this type of confessional recital of the facts of redemption may
seem very widely removed from our Hexateuch in its present form; yet at the
same time there is in places a surprising similarity of thought-forms. Basically
there is one uniform, very simple train of thought, and Josh 24:2-13 may be
described as already a Hexateuch in miniature. If we stand back to survey the
whole course of the process from first to last we shall have some idea of the
immense power of persistence of Old Testament religion. Weighty as the
embellishments are, and thoroughly as they are worked into the material,

there is nevertheless always one and the same basic idea apprehended as fundamental to the faith that, even in its final form, the Hexateuch did not supersede. It will be our task in the following pages to show at least the principal stages of the process by which this cultic recital developed into the Hexateuch as we have it.

Free Adaptations of the Creed in Cult-Lyrics

Before we pursue further the main problem of the nature and development of the Hexateuch, it will be well to consider a little more fully the literary type which we have discovered.[6]

In the great sentence of rebuke pronounced by Samuel against the people at Mizpah (1 Samuel 12), almost immediately after Samuel's exculpation by the people, there occurs an account of the events of Israel's history in relation to God:

"When Jacob came into Egypt and your fathers cried to Yahweh, he sent Moses and Aaron to them, and they brought forth your fathers out of Egypt, and he gave them a dwelling in this place" (there follows a short summary of the *Book of Judges* from the deuteronomic standpoint) (1 Sam 12:8).

It is to be noticed that this historical digression on Samuel's part is not simply one element of the speech comparable to the others, but is thrown into relief as something standing apart from its context by a solemn introductory pronouncement (v. 7); obviously it is something firmly established and definitive which is being brought to the remembrance of the hearers. The continuation, which concerns the occupation of the promised land, is unquestionably a deviation from the literary type, but a deviation that had authoritative precedent in the deuteronomic *Book of Judges*. The author of this speech needed only to look back to that work in order to establish the complete relevance of the speech for Samuel's hearers.

The litany in Psalm 136 confirms yet again our view of the part played in the cultus by the recital of the saving acts of Yahweh:

> O give thanks to Yahweh, for he is good;
> O give thanks to the God of gods;
> O give thanks to the Lord of lords;
> To him who alone does great wonders,
> To him who by understanding made the heavens,
> To him who spread out the earth upon the waters,
> To him who made the great lights,
> The sun to rule over the day,
> The moon and the stars to rule over the night,
> To him who smote the first-born of Egypt,

> And brought Israel out from among them,
> With a strong hand and an outstretched arm;
> To him who divided the Red Sea in sunder,
> And made Israel pass through the midst of it,
> But overthrew Pharaoh and his host in the Red Sea;
> To him who led his people through the wilderness,
> To him who smote great kings,
> And slew famous kings,
> Sihon, king of the Amorites,
> And Og, king of Bashan,
> And gave their land as a heritage,
> A heritage to Israel his servant;
> It is he who remembered us in our low estate,
> And rescued us from our foes,
> He who gives food to all flesh;
> O give thanks to the God of heaven.

It is a new feature in this psalm that the presentation of the redemptive history begins, not with the patriarchal or Egyptian period, but with the creation itself. The point will call for further discussion at a later stage. The further continuation of the narrative to cover the occupation of the promised land is so devoid of any concrete facts, and speaks in such general terms, that we see plainly the difficulty into which the poet falls when he departs from the traditional pattern. The observation is an instructive one, for the writer feels himself on firm ground as long as he can follow the lines of the canonical story of redemption, but has nothing concrete to say about just those events which are much nearer to his own time. As in the previous examples, there is no mention here of the Sinai revelation.

We add one further instance, the Red Sea Song of Exodus 15, which Hans Schmidt has described as a cultic litany for the feast of the "repayment of vows."[7] In literary type we seem to have departed somewhat from the original form of the creed, it is true; but a glance at the text at once shows that in this poem all the elements of the tradition of the exodus and of the occupation of the promised land have been included, although in a freely adapted form. We begin by extracting from the passage those facts that properly belong to the redemptive history. From a literary point of view, of course, such a proceeding is intolerable, but it may perhaps be allowed on this occasion in order to bring out the individual elements of that tradition from which the poem takes its rise:

> Pharaoh's chariots and his host (Yahweh) cast into the sea; and his
> picked officers are sunk in the Red Sea. The floods cover them; they

went down into the depths like a stone. . . . At the blast of your nostrils the waters piled up, the floods stood up in a heap; the billows surged in the midst of the sea.[8] The enemy said, "I will pursue, I will overtake, I will divide the spoil, my desire shall have its fill of them. I will draw my sword, my hand shall destroy them." You blew with your wind, the sea covered them. . . . You stretched out your right hand, the earth swallowed them. You have led in your steadfast love the people whom you have redeemed, you have guided them by your strength to your holy abode. The peoples have heard, they tremble; pangs have seized on the inhabitants of Philistia. Now the chiefs of Edom are dismayed; the leaders of Moab, trembling seizes them; all the inhabitants of Canaan have melted away. Terror and dread fall upon them; because of the greatness of your arm, they are as still as a stone. So your people, O Yahweh, came in; the people came in whom you have purchased.[9] (Exod 15:4, 5, 8, 9, 10a, 12-16)

It is evident that here, as before, the story is not a free composition, but is recounted according to the accepted pattern with but little variation: it tells of the miracle of the Red Sea, the journey through the wilderness and the occupation of Canaan. Once again there is not a single allusion to the events at Sinai, for "your holy abode" (*neweh qadšekah*) refers, of course, to the "holy land."[10]

These poems now become wider and wider in the scope of their content, and less tied to the traditional pattern. Psalm 105 lays more emphasis on God's covenanted promises to Abraham (vv. 8ff., 42) and then sets out with epic prolixity the story of Joseph, the oppression and the exodus down to the time of the occupation of Canaan. If here we are still firmly within the pattern, Psalm 78 contains an excessively long-winded account of the nation's history right down to the time of the monarchy. The proportion of the material dealing with the time before the settlement is still much greater than that which deals with the history of later times (about fifty-one verses as against sixteen), a fact which enables us to recognize the compulsive power of the *genre* even in a period when much greater latitude was allowable.

Nevertheless there is now something tangible in the second half, too: the worship of the high places, the rejection of Shiloh, the election of Judah and of Mount Zion, and so on. There has been far-reaching relaxation of the fixity of the literary type, and there is obviously a greater willingness to allow all sorts of reminiscences, even secondary ones, to come into their own; yet all this has not led to one reference to the Sinai story, a fact which shows how far removed it evidently is from the tradition preserved in Psalms 105 and 78.

The same is also true of Psalm 135, which, in view of its whole theological content, may be classed as a late compilation. The presentation of the redemption-story is the usual one, from Egypt to the settlement in Canaan (vv. 8-12). The question whether these psalms are loosely attached to the common canonical tradition of the redemptive-story, or whether they draw more directly upon the already extant literary source of the Hexateuch, would require a separate answer in each case. In the event of there being real literary dependence upon our Hexateuch, the omission of the Sinai story would of course be still more striking.

The earlier example of the interpolation of the Sinai story into the canonical story of redemption is found in the great prayer of Neh. 9:6ff.; there at last we find a passage of the kind which hitherto we have everywhere sought in vain:

> You came down upon Mount Sinai, and spoke with them from heaven and gave them right ordinances and true laws, good statutes and commandments, and you made known to them your holy Sabbath and commanded them commandments and statutes and a law by Moses your servant. (Neh. 9:13-14)

This passage undoubtedly depends upon the account of the priestly writer; but the question of its provenance is for us less important than the fact that here at last the momentous Sinai tradition is organically interwoven with the accepted form of the redemption-story. But with this stage we have reached the point at which the *genre* falls apart, for the historical conspectus now includes the creation, the patriarchal history, Egypt, the exodus, Sinai, the desert wandering, the settlement in Canaan, the time of the Judges and the monarchy right down to post-exilic times. Similarly in Psalm 106—a psalm whose historical perspective extends to the exilic or perhaps even to the post-exilic period—we find a mention of the golden calf.

We may sum up the result of our enquiry in the following way: even the more or less free accounts of the redemption-story which follow the canonical scheme do not mention the events of Sinai. These events seem rather to have given rise to a tradition of their own, which remained separate from the canonical pattern and only at a very late date became combined with it.

THE SINAI TRADITION IN THE HEXATEUCH

The conclusions reached in the foregoing section give rise to an important question. If the canonical redemption story of the exodus and settlement in Canaan on the one hand, and the tradition of Israel's experiences at Sinai on the other, really stand over against each other as two originally independent traditions, then there must be more to be said concerning the origin and nature of this Sinai tradition. Above all we must ask whether the hexateuchal presentation of the matter does not contradict our conclusions regarding the independence of the two traditions. We must therefore first examine the place of the Sinai story within the wider context of the hexateuchal narrative.

In so doing we may at once appeal to the long established findings of scholarship:

> Clearly visible behind the work of the Yahwist is a form of the tradition in which the Israelites moved on to Kadesh immediately after the crossing of the Red Sea, without first making the expedition to Sinai. Although we reach Sinai only in Exod 19, we are already at Massah and Meribah in Exod 17, and thus in the area of Kadesh. Hence the narratives which tell of events before the arrival at Sinai brings us back to the same place after the removal from Sinai: the locality is the same both before and after. In other words, the Israelites reached Kadesh, the original goal of their journey, immediately after the exodus, not after an excursion to Sinai.[11]

This simple fact established by Wellhausen really contains the answer to our question. It only remains for us to apply this conclusion to the history of the tradition; for here we are not concerned to elucidate the historical events themselves, nor to investigate an underlying literary stratum that does not yet know of the "excursion" to Sinai. Nevertheless it is highly probably that such a tradition is actually preserved for us in Exod 15:25b and 22b.[12] But even if Wellhausen's hypothesis were not demonstrable on purely literary grounds, this would not affect our recognition of the fact that the Sinai tradition is essentially an independent entity within the hexateuchal tradition.

The problem of the break in the Kadesh tradition between Exodus 18 and Number 10 is not a new one. It was above all Gressmann who showed that Wellhausen's discovery was of more than merely literary interest,[13] and also convincingly established the view adumbrated by Wellhausen that Exodus 18 was originally a Kadesh story.[14] We must therefore distinguish between a cycle of Kadesh narratives (Exodus 17–18; Numbers 10–14) and a Sinai-cycle (Exodus 19–24; 32–34). It is only the former cycle which is closely interwoven with the exodus story proper; the latter cycle is not, as the break between Exodus 34 and Num 10:29ff. shows. The return from Sinai to Kadesh has to be accounted for by an editorial manipulation of the text in Num 10:29ff., since the material of Num 10:29ff. belongs to the Kadesh cycle.[15]

Among the many serious difficulties which have gradually emerged since it was first recognized that the Sinai story is an independent strand of tradition, we mention here only the most important, the observation at Exod 15:25 that "there he made for them a statute and an ordinance, and there he proved them."[16] The sentence is unanimously assigned to the Kadesh tradition, since it undoubtedly contains an etiological explanation of the name Messah. The statement that the divine law was received at Kadesh (for the subject of the verb "made," *śam*, is obviously Yahweh) is nevertheless not striking, for this association of the delivery of the Law with Kadesh runs parallel to the tradition which places the reception of the Law at Sinai.

One cannot plead against this argument the trifling nature of the note in Exod 15:25, for it is only too clear that when the two traditions came ultimately to be edited together one must give way to the other, and the syntactical roughness of the passage also indicates clearly that we have here a mutilated text. Moreover Exodus 18 contains many indications of a Kadesh tradition of sacral law, so that the existence of a twofold tradition at this point is beyond all doubt.[17] But how could this account of the delivery of the sacred law to the congregation be original, in the face of the Sinai story that it necessarily robs of its uniqueness and exclusiveness? A similar problem arises with regard to the revelation of Yahweh which Moses is told to communicate to the people in Exodus 3 and 6: is not this that same revelation which gives the people knowledge of Yahweh and of his saving purpose, and guarantees the success of the exodus and settlement? There is no obvious or easy way of reconciling this with the Sinai tradition.

Let us now, however, direct our attention to the Sinai narrative itself and examine its internal structure as a preliminary step to eliciting some definitive information concerning its situation within the hexateuchal tradition.

The hexateuchal Sinai narrative as we have it is a tangle of strands from a variety of sources. The almost insoluble literary problem barely concerns us, however, for it is the internal structure of the tradition that interests us here, the unity of the material as such rather than its literary unity.

After the arrival of Israel at Mt. Sinai, in E immediately, in P perhaps seven days later, Moses climbs the mountain, there to meet with Yahweh. Here he learns, according to J and E, that the people are to prepare themselves for God's coming on the third day. Moses comes down from the mountain and makes provision for the cultic cleansing of the people. This third day now brings us to the climax of the events in Sinai, the theophany itself. The people are drawn up before the mountain and witness with terror the manifestations of the presence of God—fire, smoke, and the blast of the trumpet. Moses thereupon climbs the mountain a second time and receives the revelation of God's will for the people in the form of the decalogue (E). The sequence of events in J's account is very much the same, the second part of this account being found at Exodus 34,[18] the point to which it was subsequently transferred.

The order of the commandments in J is, of course, no longer ascertainable, for what we now read at vs. 10ff. is a "secondary, composite account."[19] Probably J had its own version of the actual Decalogue, which understandably was obliged to give place to the present one when the sources were conflated. As a necessary sequel to the communication of the divine will to Moses, the people are bound under an oath in the course of a cultic ceremony in which Moses proclaims the commandments to the people and seals the covenant with a sacrifice (E).[20] The same outline of the facts also underlies the much more highly developed account found in the Priestly Code. On the mountains, Moses receives the law of the tabernacle; there follows the proclamation before the people (Exodus 35), the setting up of the holy tent (Exodus 40) and the great sacrifice of Aaron, authenticated by the appearance of the "glory" (Leviticus 9), all these events being re-shaped in a highly individualistic manner to suit P's peculiar theological interests.

Taking a broad view of this tradition, especially as it is presented by E, it appears to be complete and self-contained from the beginning down to the sealing of the covenant in the great sacrifice. Furthermore, all the peculiarities of the individual sources leave us in no doubt that behind the present form of the account there lies one single tradition of a firmly fixed order of events.

There are no elements here that can be omitted without damaging the whole; and if one may infer the inner fixity of a narrative from the fact that the tensions it engenders are resolved in its conclusion, this certainly applies here. The account comes to an end with the binding of the people under oath and the performance of the great covenantal sacrifice; so far as this sequence is concerned, one expects nothing further.

This impression is reinforced by a brief examination of the contents of Exodus 32 and 33, which prove to have much less unity than the passages just discussed. First we have the great narrative of the golden calf. Undoubtedly it is in itself a complete whole. Certainly it is skillfully linked to the preceding passage, in that the events occur during Moses's second sojourn on the mountain, and its conclusion leads on equally skillfully to the following section in which sin has further consequences (Exod 33:1ff.). Nevertheless the tradition must at one time have been independent, and certainly had a long history of its own before it was put into its present context.[21] The sin during Moses's absence, his timely intervention and judgment of the matter, the entrusting of the priestly office to the Levites—as a story it has organic wholeness and a purpose of its own; but it has nothing in common with what precedes and follows it except that these events, too, take place at Sinai.

The material of Exodus 33 also belongs to the corpus of secondary traditions that have become attached to the massive central tradition of the Sinai theophany. Each has its own peculiar history. They contain etiological explanations of various elements of the cultus (the Tent, the "Panim," the Name), and of course each of these aetiologies represents what was at an earlier stage in a separate tradition.

The facts are as follows: in the hexateuchal Sinai narrative, the account of the theophany and the making of the covenant are unquestionably the predominating elements. From the point of view of both content and structure, they form a fixed and complete cycle of tradition. With this are associated various less important traditional elements of an etiological nature, the subject matter of which bore no historical relationship to the account of the theophany and covenant, and whose literary association with each other was indeed only secondary.

With regard to their relationship to the tradition of the exodus and settlement that we have investigated above, it is important to recognize that, considered as traditional material, they were entirely independent. Nor have they been incorporated into the literary version of the exodus tradition with uniform consistency throughout. The material of Exodus 32 and 33 is more closely blended with them (see Exod 32:7ff., 11ff.; 33:1ff.) than is the account of the theophany and the covenant, which offered much greater resistance to such interpolation and redaction because of its own massive importance and the gravity of its particular interests.

We shall search in vain in Exodus 19–24 for even the major elements of that other tradition, the redemptive acts of God in the exodus and desert wanderings. Still less shall we find any mention of the internal dispositions of the tribes consequent upon the settlement in Canaan. There is nothing of the kind here. They have altogether vanished from the scene, and for the time being give place to those momentous events that occupy the interval between the acts of the drama. In each case we are dealing with material of quite a different kind. The exodus tradition bears witness to the redemptive purpose of God revealed to Israel in its travels from Egypt to Canaan; it is a "redemptive history." The Sinai tradition testifies to the divine justice, revealed to the nation and made binding upon it: it is apodeictic law.[22] The exodus tradition, too, contains divine revelation, which from the first authenticated the claim of the entire tradition to be a redemptive history (Exodus 3 and 6). Exodus 3:7ff. shows how closely this divine revelation is bound up with the underlying purpose of the tradition of the settlement in Canaan, and is thus clearly differentiated from Exodus 19ff.:

> I have seen the affliction of my people . . . and have come down (!) to deliver them out of the land of the Egyptians, and to bring them up out of that land to a good and broad land . . .

Thus far our findings have yielded no conclusions with regard to the absolute dating of the two traditions. When Gressmann enunciated the thesis that "the journey of the Israelites to Sinai was wholly unknown to the older tradition,"[23] not only was his method at fault, but he overstepped the limitation of his methods of research. We can say no more than this, that we have two traditions, one of which is incorporated into the other as a subordinate element.

If we hold the account of the theophany at Sinai to be a sacral tradition, it must of course follow that, in the literary form in which it appears in the hexateuchal sources J and E, it must be regarded, relative to the antiquity of the tradition itself, as a late stage in its long history, perhaps indeed the final one. Both the Yahwist and the Elohist rely on a complex of tradition that was already firmly established as an independent entity in all essential features. It may be that here, too, we can postulate a canonical scheme from which both J and P derive, as we so clearly could in the tradition of the exodus and conquest of Canaan.

Let us look around in the Old Testament to see whether it does not preserve some free, poetical variants of this Sinai tradition, similar to those many untheological accounts of the exodus tradition that we found in the Psalms. We take first the opening verses of the Blessing of Moses:

> The Lord came from Sinai, and dawned from Seir upon His people; he shone forth from Mount Paran. . . . Moses commanded us a law, the assembly of Jacob became his possession. (Deut 33:2, 4)[24]

This is, of course, a loosely worded allusion to the Sinai tradition. There is no mention here of the exodus or entry into Canaan, but only a theophany, and the imposition of the divine commandments by which God takes possession of the nation.

> The exodus from Egypt is not taken into consideration in the blessing of Moses. . . . It is mentioned by Moses neither at verse 8 nor anywhere else, a quite incomprehensible phenomenon as seen from the viewpoint of a later age, when the deliverance from Egypt has become the supreme act of God (and of Moses) and on behalf of his people.[25]

The well-known introduction to the Song of Deborah (Judges 5) may also be adduced in this connection, although only in a restricted sense, for the poem, including its opening verses, is concerned with a quite different moment in the history of Israel's deliverance. It nevertheless shows clearly that in this tradition Sinai and the theophany are inseparable associated. The same is true of Habakkuk 3. The constitutive element of the Sinai tradition is the coming of God, not the wanderings of the people.

THE SINAI TRADITION AS A CULT-LEGEND

The next question to be investigated in the case of a tradition which has been transmitted in this way before reaching its definitive form is not whether it is historically credible, but what particular place and function it had in religious life, i.e., its "situation in life." Such material cannot, on principle, be teased out in order to serve as sources for the reconstruction of the historical course of events; but this problem is in any case of quite secondary importance compared with the other problem of the actual circumstances in which it was a living and active thing.

What part in the religious life of Israel was played by this very clearly defined tradition at the time when it was still a living thing? It is evident that such material does not exist in some nebulous sphere of piety, nor is it the creation of a more or less personal religiosity; it belongs to the official worship, and is in fact fundamental to the worshipping community. Its function therefore is to be sought in the public religious activity of the community, that is to say, in the cultus.[26]

The problem has already been both stated and answered by Mowinckel in the most valuable part of his stimulating book on the Decalogue—that dealing with form criticism. Mowinckel sees in the narratives of the events at Sinai none other than an account of the New Year Festival, translated into the language of literary mythology.[27] If the constituent materials of the tradition are considered from this point of view, there can be no possible doubt of the fact that they were originally deeply rooted in the cultus. One can picture the sequence: there is a preparatory hallowing, i.e., a ritual cleansing of the assembly; the assembly draws near to God at the blast of the trumpets; God declares himself and communicates his demands; sacrifice is offered and the covenant is sealed. The whole procedure presupposes a cultic situation.

The recognition of a close relationship between the Sinai narrative and a cultic ceremony carries us a great step forward. Nevertheless, if we come to enquire into the exact nature of this relationship, Mowinckel has left us in some doubt at this point. He calls the Sinai narrative the "description" or "account" of a cultic ceremony. But in what sense are we to understand these terms? For what purpose does one "describe" a ceremony? What purpose could there be in such accounts, closely following the course of a cultic ceremony? They are certainly by no means free poetical versions of the content of the ceremony, nor, so to speak, late transpositions of the constituent elements of the ceremony into literary terms. Quite the contrary. The Sinai narrative in its canonical form (compared with which even J and E must be reckoned secondary!) is itself prior to the cultus and normative for it. Indeed, the whole authority of the cultus itself stands or falls by the Sinai narrative, which is, in other words, the cult-legend of a particular cultic occasion.

One need not at this point take sides in the wider controversy as to whether cult is prior to myth, or myth to cult;[28] but in the present instance we can hardly regard the legend (as we prefer to call it, rather than myth) as the product or outcome of the cultus. That would be to contradict all that is otherwise known to us of the living expression of the faith of the Old Testament, and of its historical background. No, in this case the legend unquestionably preceded the cultus. It gave the cultus its shape in the first place; but we must of course also reckon with a certain reciprocal influence of the cultus upon the legend and upon its formation.[29]

Mowinckel has turned the discussion of this whole problem into particularly fruitful channels by relating it to certain psalms. Let us for a moment consider Psalm 50 from the point of view of the form-categories of its constituent elements. Surprising as it may seem at first glance, we are forced to postulate here a cultic ritual of a similar if not identical kind to that presupposed by the Sinai narrative.

> The god of gods, Yahweh, speaks and summons the earth . . .
> Our God comes and cannot keep silence . . .
> He calls to the heaven above and to the earth,
> that he may judge his people. (Ps 50:1-4)

The assembly stands in anticipation of a theophany, the climax of which is an allocution by God himself. The cultic community had been called together by God and sacrifices have been offered.

> His faithful ones have been gathered together to him,
> > They who made a covenant with him by sacrifice.
> And the heavens shall declare his righteousness;
> > for God himself will be judge;
> "Hear, O my people, I will speak; Israel,
> > I will admonish you:
> > I am Yahweh, your God." (vv. 5-7)

Here we reached the central feature of the rite: the people are summoned to listen, and will hear a voice which will bring them all under judgment. Yahweh reveals himself as the God of the community, and his declaration "I am

Yahweh, your God" points to the first commandment of the decalogue, summing up at this point the revelation of the divine will which is in itself a testimony against Israel.

Admittedly we cannot say that Psalm 50 directly and immediately reflects a cultic ritual; the subsequent verses are themselves evidence to the contrary, since in no uncertain terms they reject material sacrifice in favor of spiritual thankfulness and obedience. The psalm as a whole has thus become detached from the cultus; but in the matter of form it is still firmly tied to the schema of the cultic rite. Verses 18-21 show clearly how deep is the influence of this underlying form:

> If you see a thief, you are a friend of his;
>> and you keep company with adulterers.
> You give your mouth free rein for evil, and your
>> tongue frames deceit.
> You sit and speak against your brother; you slander
>> your own mother's son.
> These things you have done and I have been silent;
>> You thought that I was one like yourself.
> But now I rebuke you, and lay the charge before you.

This is a paraphrase of the decalogue, and is manifestly an integral part of the psalm as a whole. The poet has not included it at this point simply because it suited his particular theological viewpoint, but rather because the fundamental principles of this form made it impossible to leave it out.

A very similar cultic situation is reflected in Psalm 81. Here, too, we are dealing with the residual remains of a liturgy, the occasion of which is expressly said to be a festival—obviously that of the New Year (vs. 4). It is important to notice the words that introduce the divine allocution in the structure of the liturgy; they are set out here with singular clarity: "I hear a voice I had not known . . ." (v. 6).

Now follows the divine allocution itself—we shall return later to vv. 7-8:

> Hear, O my people, while I admonish you!
>> O Israel, if you would but listen to me!
> There shall be no strange god among you;
>> you shall not bow down to a foreign god.
> I am Yahweh your God,
>> who brought you up out of the land of Egypt. (vv. 9-11)

Once again this is the climax of the cultic ceremony, the direct allocution by God and the communication of his will for the people. The divine will is here proclaimed in the words of the first commandment, which, of course, brings to mind the decalogue as a whole.[30]

Psalms 50 and 81 thus confirm and fill out our thesis. We could not perhaps regard either of them in their present state as direct accounts of a cultic ceremony: they are not liturgical manuals, but secondary poetic compositions that retain their characteristics of original *genre* only in their form. Nevertheless, taken in conjunction with the Sinai narrative, they compel us to recognize the existence of a great cultic drama, the distinctive features of which are undoubtedly the divine self-revelation and the subsequent communication of God's purpose in the form of apodeictic commandments. It is not within the scope of our investigation to discuss the problems of the decalogue, but it should be remarked that we are not convinced that the decalogue derives from the rules of holiness to be observed as a condition of joining in the cultus.[31]

A statement of such rules is concerned with what has already happened, or has not happened, as Psalms 15 and 24 clearly show; by its very nature it interrogates the participant in the cultus concerning his past. The provisions of the decalogue, however, as Psalms 50 and 81 show, are set in the middle of a cultic rite, at a time when the question as to who should participate has already been settled. They contain ordinances binding upon human conduct for the *future,* and must therefore be distinguished from the laws governing admission to the rite on account of both their form and their content. Furthermore, with regard to origin of the decalogue, it is to be noted that it is organically bound up with the self-revelation of the deity (understood, of course, only in a cultic sense). This is true of both Exodus 20 and Ps 81:2a,[32] and there can be no serious doubt whatever that these commandments were recited at the very climax and not at some lesser point of the liturgy.

Thus the declamation of divine commandments and the binding of the assembly under obedience to them must have formed a major element of a cultic occasion in ancient Israel. As a recent contribution to this debate, the text of Deut 31:10ff. has been brought into relation with the reading of the law by Ezra: "Every seven years . . . you are to read this law before all Israel" (Nehemiah 8).[33]

In point of fact, this too is an instance of a proclamation of Yahweh's purpose in the presence of the festal assembly. The one new fact that emerges from this text is that Deuteronomy is regarded as a complete and exhaustive definition of the will of God for the congregation, and can thus be proclaimed in this form. But this procedure was certainly not invented *ad hoc,* and goes back to a much earlier date. When Isaiah sees in a vision[34] the nations gathering as pilgrims to Zion, where they will receive instruction on their way of life, it is surely obvious this refers to an actual practice known to the prophet. Feast by feast the crowds would have made their pilgrimage in this way to the Temple, there to hear again the will of God at the climax of the cultic rite, and to return to their homes bound under obedience to God's commandments. It was Alt who taught us in his study on the origins of Israelite law to regard the decalogue as a selection from the abundant store of legislation preserved by the priests, a selection which frankly barely sums up the totality of the divine will for the community.[35]

THE FORM OF DEUTERONOMY

In the light of what has been said, we must now look again at the book of Deuteronomy. We may leave aside the many difficulties currently raised by the problem of *Deuteronomy,* and confine ourselves to a matter that has yet scarcely been touched on by scholars, despite all the controversy about the nature of this book. What are we to say about the *form of Deuteronomy,* with its remarkable succession of speeches, laws, and so on? Even if it be thought that Deuteronomy in its present guise comes straight from the theologian's desk, this does not prevent our asking to what *genre* it belongs. It simply drives the question further back and compels us to look into the history and development of the form of the material used by the deuteronomic theologians. One cannot accept the assumption that these men created *ad hoc* so remarkable a literary form. Various aspects of the matter have, of course, long since been investigated. Köhler has expressed his views on the paraenetic material,[36] the blessings and curses have been the subject of discussions among the form critics,[37] and in this respect the legal provisions in particular have been thoroughly examined.

But all these investigations took as their starting-point the passages that could already be classified as to their *genre,* and studied these as isolated entities. Only then was the field of research broadened to cover the book of Deuteronomy as a whole. The problem of the significance and function of the component elements *in their context in the work* was not, I believe, faced. One might be forgiven for imagining the deuteronomists seated at their desks, hunting round for a diversity of forms into which they could pour a new content, and striving by the most effective combination of the various elements to give expression to their special theological interests. Obviously from the point of view of form criticism no one would accept any such picture of the origins of Deuteronomy: it is precluded by a recognition of the fact that Deuteronomy is, in form, an organic whole. We may distinguish any number of different strata and accretions by literary criteria, but in the matter of form the various constituents form an indivisible unity. The question is thus inescapably raised of the origin and purpose of the form of Deuteronomy as we now have it.

The book falls structurally into four sections:

1. Historical presentation of the events at Sinai, and paraenetic material connected with these events (Deuteronomy 1-11).
2. The reading of the law (Deuteronomy 12:1—26:15).
3. The sealing of the covenant (Deuteronomy 26:16-19).
4. Blessings and curses (Deuteronomy 27ff.).

As we have said, we are here leaving aside all literary considerations. The exhortations, of course, consist of a whole group of paraenetic sermons, and in the same way the sealing of the covenant and the pronouncement of the curses and blessings contain material from several different strata (26:16ff. = 29:9ff.; 28:1-25 = 30:15ff.). But these findings do not preclude the view that in terms of form criticism the main elements of Deuteronomy make up a single whole.

If we now apply what has been said in the previous paragraph, there can be no doubt as to how we must answer the question which we posed: in these four sections we recognize once again the basic features of what was formerly a cultic ceremony, manifestly associated with the same festival which is reflected in the Sinai traditions known to J and E (Exodus 19ff.).

If we look once more at the tradition on which the Exodus version of the Sinai narrative rests, we find the following main elements:

1. Exhortation (Exod 19:4-6) and historical recital of the events at Sinai (Exodus 19ff.).
2. Reading of the law (Decalogue and Book of the Covenant).
3. Promise of blessing (Exod 33:20ff.).
4. Sealing of the covenant (Exodus 24).

This is the tradition known to the Elohist. The particular historical dress which clothes these four elements in the book of Exodus nevertheless cannot disguise the fact that Deuteronomy belongs to precisely the same cultic tradition, with regard both to its form and to its content. It might even be said that Deuteronomy has probably preserved rather better the formal pattern of the cultic rite as a whole. On the other hand, Deuteronomy is doubtless later in date and less close to the actual cultic situation; it has become progressively more detached from those elements that were of particular interest to the cultus in an earlier age. Thus it is certainly not accidental that the residuum of the tradition in Exodus records a solemn sacrificial offering, whilst the deuteronomic account preserves only a spiritualized version of the sealing of the covenant.

There is, however, one feature constantly recurring throughout Deuteronomy, which shows very clearly how intimately its provisions were formerly bound up with the cultus. We refer to the persistent repetition of the word "today," which is the common denominator of deuteronomic homiletic as a whole: e.g. "Today I command you . . ." (Deut 9:1); "Today you have declared concerning Yahweh that he shall be your God" (Deut 26:17); "Today you have become Yahweh's people" (Deut 27:9); "Today I have set before you life and prosperity, death and misfortune" (Deut 30:15); "Today I call heaven and earth to witness against you" (Deut 30:19).

It cannot be maintained that this is merely an effective stylistic device that the deuteronomist has chosen to make more vivid what he has to say. On the contrary, it is a quite fundamental feature of Deuteronomy, reminding us that this is a vivid reconstruction of the events of the redemption story such as only the cultus can furnish. No literary composition, however skillful, could ever bring the events to life in this way. Or let us read from this point of view a passage such as Deut 5:2-4:

> Yahweh our God made a covenant with us in Horeb. Not with our fathers did Yahweh make this covenant, but with us here, who are all of us still alive today. Yahweh has spoken to you face to face out of the fire upon the mountain.

Here the immediacy of the event is still more evident. The divine revelation on Sinai is not something in the past, a matter of history so far as the present generation to whom it is addressed is concerned. It is a present reality, determining the way of life of the very same people who receive it. In a literary presentation of the matter it would be meaningless so to discount the passage of time; such a procedure could carry no conviction with a post-Mosaic generation. But within the framework of the cultus, where past, present, and future acts of God coalesce in the one tremendous actuality of the faith, such a treatment is altogether possible and indeed essential.

This resolute synchronism is a fact that may serve to temper our own strongly marked interest in history and in the passage of time in matters of religion. Later Israel found no difficulty in identifying itself with the Israel of Horeb, and understood itself to be in the most immediate sense the recipient of the promises of Horeb!

The same tendency to actualize the events of Sinai, admittedly in a somewhat different sense, is also to be found in a passage in Deuteronomy 29.

> You stand *today* all of you before Yahweh your God; the heads of your
> tribes, your elders, and your officers, all the men of Israel . . . , that
> you may enter into the covenant with Yahweh your God, and into the
> sworn agreement which Yahweh your God makes with you *today*; so
> that he may *today* make you his people, and that he may be your
> God, as he promised you and as he swore to your father, to Abraham,
> to Isaac, and to Jacob. *Nor is it with you only that I make this sworn*
> *covenant, but with those who are not here with us today as well as*
> *with those who stand here with us before Yahweh our God.*

It is not so much the historical event itself (Deut 29:10ff.) which is actual-
ized here; the case is rather that the validity of the covenant concluded in that
event is extended to the remotest generations, and to this extent the present
relevance of the event is assured.

This emphatic "contemporaneity" for all succeeding generations of what
occurred at Sinai does of course conceal a minor anomaly. How can it be that
at the climax of the cultic action God himself does not address the people as
He did on the first occasion? How could it be explained that the words of a
human mediator were substituted for the unique accents of God? It is not
without interest to observe that this point is already raised in the Yahwistic
account:

> And you said to Moses, "You speak to us, and we will hear; but let not
> God speak to us lest we die." (Exod 20:19)

Here is yet one further proof that this tradition had a cultic setting, for what
is this but an etiology for the function of the cultic prophet? The institution of
a cultic speaker who takes the place of God himself is, moreover, still further
justified in a deuteronomic etiology:

> When you heard the voice out of the darkness . . . you came near to
> me . . . and said, "Behold Yahweh our God has shown us his glory and
> greatness. . . . But why should we die? . . . Go near, and hear all that
> Yahweh our God will say; and speak to us all that Yahweh our God
> will speak to you; we will hear and do it." When Yahweh heard the
> words which you spoke to me, He said to me, . . . "They have rightly
> said all that they have spoken." (Deut 5:23-28)

Among the older scholars, Klostermann adumbrated a theory very similar
to the present one; but he was alone in so doing. Even though we ourselves
were led to the results outlined above by a very different route, by way of cultic

and form-critical considerations, we must not fail to mention his name. It was his belief that chapters 5–11 ought to be understood as "homiletic allocutions introducing and accompanying the recitation of the Law in a public gathering of the congregation."[38] He also held that chapters 12ff. were not a "book of the Law" but "a collection of materials for the public proclamation of the Law,"[39] and that the whole of Deuteronomy was "the fully developed end-product of the actual custom of a public proclamation of the Law."[40] Even he, however, moved straight on from this point to all manner of literary analyses, without first investigating the reason for either the underlying form or the overall structure of Deuteronomy.

At all events our conclusions now marry up with the longstanding problems of the literary composition of the book. Were there at one time various different versions of Deuteronomy, some with historical speeches of Moses, others with paraenetic ones? Our particular statement of the problem would not necessarily preclude such a supposition, for we must certainly reckon with the possibility that, once detached from the cultus, the form of Deuteronomy developed still further and was subsequently adapted to meet particular needs. It might well be that by taking this possibility into account we should shed fresh light upon what has hitherto been felt as a difficulty—the juxtaposition of historical and paraenetic introductory speeches in Deuteronomy.

It is certainly remarkable that in its main points the composition of Exodus 19ff. fully agrees with that of Deuteronomy in this matter. In Exodus 19, as here, we find the historical events of Sinai set out side by side with the hortatory allocution. Do these two elements perhaps derive in the last resort from two integral parts of the ancient cultic rite? We do not regard as of any great moment the circumstance that in Exodus 19 the historical account of the events at Sinai is not portrayed in the form of a speech. In itself the question of the form of the ancient tradition is not, of course, an unimportant one. Which is the nearer to this form, that allocution or the strictly historical narration? We believe that it is the more primitive form that has been preserved in Deuteronomy, and that its transformation into an objective recital of historical events is a relatively late development, subsequent to the ancient cultic tradition. The change would have come about under the influence of the composite form of the hexateuchal tradition, into which, as we saw, the Sinai narrative was incorporated at a later date.

At this point our investigation must go into much greater detail, for even at first sight the historical (Deuteronomy 1–5) and the paraenetic (Deuteronomy 6–11) introductory passages reveal a profound disparity in the matter of form. Although in the former we were concerned with a single unified historical survey, which follows the course of events in logical order, the situation in chapters 6–11 is materially different. One cannot speak here of any inherent development in the thought; there are plenty of signs to indicate that this speech is really built up of very many already extant units, which doubtless at an earlier stage each fulfilled its own independent cultic function. Here, too, Klostermann supplied the correct answer many years ago. After a circumstantial analysis of the paraenetic section he comes to the conclusion that

> In chapters 6 and 7 we have what were originally parallel speeches, and which in the liturgy of the reading of the Law would have preceded or followed the recital of particular passages of an ancient book of the Law, forming either the exordium or the peroration. These passages are here loosely joined together in a manner foreign to their original purpose . . . to form a continuous speech whose pattern follows a homiletic line of thought.[41]

To take one example, Deut 7:1ff. would originally have been a paraenetic allocution of this type:

> [When God has brought Israel into the promised land, no agreement must be made with the Canaanitish peoples;] "For you are a people holy to Yahweh your God; and Yahweh your God has chosen you to be a people for his own possession out of all the peoples that are on the face of the earth." . . . [This was due to Yahweh's love and faithfulness, and for this reason Israel is to recognize Yahweh as the true God, who keeps covenant.] "Therefore keep the commandment and the statutes and the ordinances which I today command you to observe." (Deut 7:1-11)

There is no doubt that the passage properly comes to a conclusion at this point, and taken as a whole it strongly resembles the paraenetic allocution of Exod 19:4-6. The verses immediately following (12-15), however, now promise to reward Israel's obedience with Yahweh's blessing upon man and beast and crops, bringing fruitfulness and warding off evil diseases; and there is every reason to accept Klostermann's suggestion that formerly the reading of the Law itself took place between these two sections (i.e., between vv. 1-11 and vv. 12-15). Equally probable is the suggestion he makes that the people responded to the reading of the Law with a shout of acclamation.[42]

According to this line of reasoning, we should see in Deut 7:1-15 a kind of liturgical formulary for the hortatory allocution and the promise of blessing comparable to Deuteronomy 6–11 and 28, passages which on a larger scale (i.e., in a homiletically greater extended form) equally provide a setting for the reading of the Law. There is unmistakable correspondence between the original form and the developed composition so far as their content is concerned, a correspondence which is particularly striking in the promise of blessing which again in chapter 28 concentrates upon agricultural concerns: fruitfulness, rain, etc.

The part of the paraenetic pronouncement which (like the prophet denunciation) precedes the direct address by the Deity is certainly to be seen in Exod 19:4-6, in the state most nearly approximating to that of its original liturgical form. Evidently this particular element was peculiarly well suited to an increasingly wide variety of adaptations. It is clearly recognizable in Psalm 81, in those verses (7 and 8) that precede the proclamation of the Law. Both Psalm 95 and Mic 6:3-5 should also be considered in this light. It would be unreasonable to expect more than bare indications in such freely adapted compositions; yet it is clear that this pronouncement included as a fixed element an allusion to God's saving acts of power, and had the character of a call to repentance.

Deuteronomy as a unity now reveals itself to us in a new light as a rather baroque agglomeration of cultic materials, which nevertheless reflects throughout one and the same cultic occasion. It is the outcome of a very long process of literary crystallization, which returns in the end to a monumental unity of structure. It is symptomatic of the amazing inherent cohesion of the material that even the smallest liturgical units from which Deuteronomy is built up are all constructed on the same plan, in accordance with the same principles of the cultic pattern, as the book of Deuteronomy as a whole. In its massive final form the book bursts all cultic bounds, and yet retains the pattern of hortatory allocution, reading of the Law, sealing of the covenant, blessing, and curse.

The Festival and Its Earlier History

The last section served to corroborate duly the belief that the Sinai tradition is a cultic tradition. At the same time it has extended our knowledge of the cultic occasion that underlies it, at least with regard to its main features. There can now be no difficulty in answering the question as to which festival it is that we are concerned with. Rather less simple is the question of what the historical antecedents of this festival are. What, so far as we can tell, was its earliest setting in the history of Israel, both in time and place?

In Exodus 19ff. the Sinai tradition actually contains some sort of a date, and the most obvious course to take in investigating the festival underlying the tradition is to make this our starting-point. The relevant text reads:

> In the third month after the exodus of the Israelites from the land of Egypt, on that day they came into the wilderness of Sinai. (Exod 19:1)

It has always been recognized that the verse is textually corrupt, that *bayôm hazzeh* cannot here mean "at this time."[43] For some unknown reason the designation of the day of the month—perhaps *be'ehad lahodeš*—has been omitted. Nevertheless the third month after the exodus, and therefore also after the Passover, can point only to the Feast of Weeks. This dating is that of the priestly writer, and would therefore correspond to the late Jewish dating of the feast; for the Feast of Weeks is the feast of revelation and of giving of the Law, the prescribed lection for which is precisely that of our text, Exod 19:1ff.[44]

Now this Jewish tradition must not be rejected out of hand as a late interpretation, even though we must certainly reckon with the possibility that the text at this point was only at a later date made to harmonize with a quite recent usage. Fundamental considerations based on earlier statements nevertheless arise to contradict this theory.

Let us go back for a moment to the admittedly not very ancient passage at Deut 31:10ff. Here we find a statement which must be regarded as much more reliable, for the very reason that it contradicts the later practice:

> Every seven years at the time of the year of release, at the Feast of Booths, when all Israel comes to appear before Yahweh your God at the place which he chooses, you shall read this Law before all Israel. (Deut 31:10b-11)

This text was at one time distrusted on principle, on the grounds that the reading of a "Book of the Law" must be a very late cultic custom; nowadays we see clearly that, although the reading from a *book* might still indicate a late date, the usage of a proclamation of the divine commandments which underlies it must have been a very ancient cultic practice. Moreover, it is clear that the association of this ceremonial proclamation of the Law with the Feast of Booths is no mere fiction, for in Nehemiah 8, too, the same ceremony is observed at the Feast of Booths, and the later tradition as known to us does not tally with these earlier accounts.

The Feast of Booths was in earlier times pre-eminently the festival to which the community came on pilgrimage. It is therefore inconceivable that the festival of the renewal of the covenant between Yahweh and the people should not be identified with this very same festival.

It may be added that the *šemittah*, the agricultural fallow year that was proclaimed at the Feast of Booths in the seventh year, is, in its theological motivation, closely associated with this festival of renewal of the covenant. The institution of the "fallow year" (*šemittah*) is by no means primarily motivated by social considerations; both Exod 23:11 and Deut 15:1ff. are late rationalizations of the primitive conception. Rather it is an acknowledgement of God's unique overlordship of the soil. At the end of a fixed period the community came together to perform a cultic act the only purpose of which was to proclaim Yahweh's sole title to the land.[45]

Now in the covenantal rite it is this very concept of Yahweh's sole ownership that is brought home to the participants, the cultic assembly gathered together from all districts. Yahweh re-enacts in this ceremony his overlordship over Israel. The assembly acknowledges the title and ownership that God has established in His commandments; they enter into the covenant and thereby become his holy people, God's own possession. It may remain for the present an open question whether this ceremony of sealing the covenant took place, like the "fallow year," only seven years (as Alt would hold on the strength of Deut 31:10) or whether it was repeated annually.

Up to this point the situation is quite clear. But now there arises the question of the origin and development of this festival. Mowinckel, who was actually the first to recognize and to investigate the nature of this covenantal rite at the Feast of Booths, holds that the site of this cultic occasion was the temple of Jerusalem.[46] Building up a picture of this festival as he does from the most varied but sometimes quite late references to it, he finds the assumption fully justified and perhaps even inevitable. For us, looking at the problem from the point of view of a single fixed tradition, any such answer would be mistaken, since we would be making it from a point of view outside this tradition, that is, from a common fund of Israelite cultic history lying outside this tradition.

If the Sinai tradition is the tradition of a sanctuary, then no direct relationship with the temple at Jerusalem can be postulated of it. We must therefore ask whether the Sinai tradition contains in itself elements which connect it with the cultic practice of any particular place in Israel, or which bring it into some relationship with a particular place. In our opinion this question can at once be answered in the affirmative. The climax and essential element of this cultic tradition was the proclamation of God's righteous purpose in a succession of commandments. There is only one ancient Israelite sanctuary at which, according to tradition, this usage was practiced, and that was Shechem. Fortunately there are several pieces of evidence that establish this fact.

We turn first to Joshua 24, the account of the "parliament" at Shechem. The important religious and historical questions that are raised by this account may here be left wholly aside. We confine ourselves to the point already made by Sellin and Noth that we are here concerned not simply with a historical event which happened once and for all in the time of Joshua, but rather with a periodically repeated covenantal rite, "in which the oath of allegiance made by the tribal coalition to the new God and to his purposes was continually renewed."[47] The account makes it quite clear that at the central point of this ceremony came the communication of the divine will and the binding of the people under obedience to it. This is above all to be seen in verse 25, according to which Joshua gave statutes and ordinances (*ḥoq ûmišpat*) at Shechem.

But there is a further tradition, wholly independent of Joshua 24, which points to the same festival and confirms and amplifies the date provided by Joshua 24. We refer to those traditional elements, firmly embedded in the very heart of deuteronomic literature, found in Deuteronomy 27; 11:29ff.; Josh 8:30-35.[48] Here, too, we can leave aside the more detailed questions concerned chiefly with the problem of literary strata; it is sufficient for us to note the existence of a second and evidently very ancient recollection of a cultic ceremony at Shechem. This deuteronomic tradition, which has split into several fragments dependent upon one another to a varying degree, undoubtedly looks back to the selfsame cultic occasion, even though it emphasizes predominantly the rites of blessing and cursing. At all events this does not mean that we must reckon Deuteronomy 27 and the other passages as part of a wholly separate cultic tradition, for we have already seen that the ritual of blessing and cursing is organically bound up with the proclamation of the divine Law and the sealing of the covenant.

Apart from this, Deuteronomy 27 connects with the Shechem ritual a particularly primitive proclamation of the divine commandments to the community, in a context that makes excellent sense despite its lack of literary tidiness. The liturgical apportionment of blessings and curses to two mutually responding choirs must certainly be regarded as the original form of the ritual, whereas the pronouncement of blessing and curse (after the sealing of the covenant) was made, according to Deuteronomy 28, at the mouth of a cultic individual, and therefore reflects a refined, less primitive, and thus somewhat attenuated form of the same cultic occasion.

We can, however, go a step further yet. It was Sellin[49] who realized that there was an obvious correspondence between the individual elements of the covenant ritual at Shechem and those of the Sinai covenant. Even if it could be shown that the method by which Sellin arrived at this conclusion (i.e. by the literary association of Josh 8:30-35 with Joshua 24:1-28) is invalid on the grounds that Josh 8:30-35 is not assignable to the Elohist, it would nevertheless remain true that the Shechemite rituals described in Joshua 8 and 24 respectively belong together on grounds of subject matter. It may be that we have two quite independent traditions, each of which retains its particular character and interests intact, but nevertheless goes back ultimately to one and the same covenant ceremony at Shechem. Yet it will still be permissible to place side by side the various cultic elements suggested by the two traditions. We shall then have the following program for the festival at Shechem:

- Joshua's allocution (Josh 24:14-15).
- The assent of the congregation (Josh 24:16-18, 24).
- The proclamation of the Law (Josh 24:25; Deut 27:15ff.).
- The sealing of the covenant (Josh 24:27).
- Blessings and curses (Deut 27:12-13; Josh 8:34).

Such a synthesis of separate fragments taken from different literary traditions can, of course, be made only with some reservation; but the fact of their common origin does indeed give prior justification for the attempt, and the results subsequently confirm the validity of the process. We have only to compare the separate cultic elements of the Shechem ritual with those of the Sinai narrative as we have found them to be in our study of Exodus 19–20 and Deuteronomy! We would hold that our contention that the Sinai tradition had its cultic setting in the ancient covenantal festival at Shechem is as certain as such matters ever can be.

In recent years we have been presented with rather different accounts of the Israelite Feast of Booths, and it cannot but occur to us that the hypotheses offered go far beyond the theological framework of the cultic occasion, which at present engages our attention.[50] In particular, the Sinai tradition knows nothing of the cosmological elements, the battle against chaos, or the creation of the world; neither does it know of the enthronement of Yahweh, the subjugation of the nations and so on. A fresh investigation is called for into the question of how far these cosmological elements, little concerned as they are with Israel's history of redemption, really belonged to the Feast of Booths.[51] At bottom, there is only one thing to be said here: the material of the covenantal rite at Shechem as we have seen it to be is concerned with the ancient and specifically Yahwistic New Year Festival. It is a recognized fact that, after the settlement in Canaan, ancient Israelite belief and cultus only very slowly and by a process of resorption of its environment became interwoven with elements of Canaanitish religion. In our opinion, at all events, the festival which Mowinckel and Hans Schmidt have so graphically described was observed in Israel only at a time when the Shechem covenant-festival and its cult tradition had already become literature!

If we may regard the Sinai tradition as the material of the ancient Shechem covenant festival, a minor feature of this tradition now appears in a new light, to which we briefly advert in bringing this section to a close. Quite fundamental to Deuteronomy, and centrally situated in the tradition of Exodus 19 (vs. 6), is the conception of the "holy nation." It may, indeed, be said that in Deuteronomy this notion expresses the altogether basic consideration upon which the whole theological interest is focused. Thus, following proclamation of the commandments and the sealing of the covenant, we have the significant pronouncement:

> Keep silence and hear, O Israel. Today you have become the people of Yahweh your God. Hear therefore the voice of Yahweh your God and keep his commandments and statutes which I command you today. (Deut 27:9)

And in the Yahwistic tradition there is the following address to the people:

> You yourselves have seen what I did to the Egyptians . . . and now, therefore, if you will hear my voice and keep my covenant, you shall be my own possession above all people; for all the earth is mine. You shall be to me a kingdom of priests and a holy nation. (Exod 19:4-6)

The literary problem has not so far been fully elucidated. Mowinckel suggested that this was a liturgical formulary.[52] Probably it was a paraenetic homily preceding the proclamation of the Law, such as we have found elsewhere in Deuteronomy and in Psalms 50, 81, and 95.[53] Caspari has made a highly detailed study of the pronouncement.[54] He regards verse 6 as a doublet: you are (a) a hierarchy of priests, and (b) a holy people. He believes that these words reflect an actual institution, and are therefore extremely ancient—a view which accords very happily with our own suggestions. Noth, too, has now shown that the expression "people of God" refers to the ancient amphictyonic tribal federation of Shechem, since this conception is much less well defined after the formative period of the Israelite state than it was in an age in which the sacral, cultic bond was pre-eminently the unifying factor between the tribes.[55] It can therefore hardly be an accident that we find the notion of the people of God, the "holy nation," put forward in just that cultic tradition which on other grounds we believe ought to be ascribed to Shechem.[56]

THE ORIGIN OF THE "SETTLEMENT TRADITION"

In the two traditions of Sinai and of the settlement in Canaan we have what were originally quite separate things. This was the first conclusion to which our enquiry led us, and it has been in no way affected by the further discussion of the nature and origin of the Sinai tradition. Rather it has been corroborated. It can indeed be said that there is simply no communality of interest and no inherent connection between the Settlement tradition and the elements of the Sinai tradition that we have seen to belong to the cultic tradition of the Feast of Booths of the ancient Yahwistic amphictyony.

The tradition of the settlement, too, must of course be classed as a cultic tradition. It presents the redemptive history in a rigidly stereotyped form, stamped out as from a mold with a fixity made possible only by the canonizing authority of the sacral cultus. The differences between the two traditions are so great that they cannot possibly be dealt with in detail. We confine ourselves simply to the one observation concerning the main theme, that the tradition of the Sinai festival celebrates God's coming to his people, whereas the Settlement tradition commemorates his guidance and redemptive activity. The Sinai tradition contains a direct and personal revelation of God, and presents the demands of Yahweh's righteous purpose. The tradition of the settlement takes on accepted historical instance of God's saving purpose and validates it as an article of faith.

If the tradition of the settlement belongs to a particular sanctuary, it ought to be possible to point to some probable place of origin for it. But at this point we encounter considerable difficulty arising at least in part from the simple fact that the tradition of the settlement cannot by its nature be wholly contained in one cultic ceremony. In consequence this tradition provides far less easily recognizable indications by which it might be related to known historical circumstances. It is in itself far simpler, both in form and content, than the Sinai tradition: as we have already observed, it is a sort of creed. Its historical variations, however, are naturally less easy to find than were those of a tradition wholly enshrined in the one cultic occasion.

Fortunately for us, what is probably the earliest version of this creed—that in Deuteronomy 26—reveals an integral relationship between the tradition and a cultic occasion. Thus there can be no doubt that the roots of this tradition are to be sought in the cultus. In handing over the "first fruits" (*re'šît*),[57] the worshiper acknowledges the gift made to him of the promised land and speaks the well-known words. Unfortunately it does not appear from this text at what stage of the year this ritual took place at the sanctuary; indeed, it is not even possible to determine whether it belongs to a single fixed occasion in the religious calendar, or whether it might not rather be part of a cultic act which could be performed at any time the worshiper wished. Actually, this possibility ought not to be taken too seriously. The cult of Yahweh, especially in the earlier period, was most certainly not a personal affair, but expressly an undertaking of the whole community. How could the individual, acting on his own behalf in presenting the tribute of his crops, acknowledge the gift of the promised land? Whether the centralizing tendency of Deuteronomy did not put an end to the older mode of collective cultic worship is, of course, another matter.

Now all the calendars of the Old Testament include a festival which is preeminently the festival at which vegetable produce is offered—the Feast of Harvest or Feast of Weeks, called on one occasion explicitly the "Day of the First Fruits" (*yôm habbikûrîm*).[58] The expressions used of it and the statements made about it in the ancient collections of laws are significant. At Exod

23:16 the feast is designated "the harvest festival of the first fruits which you have made" (*ḥag haqqaṣîr bikûrê ma'aśeka*).

As Lev 23:17 shows, it is the fruit of the land, obviously in the form of wheaten loaves, which is here envisaged.[59] The offering of first ripe figs, too, seems to have been an important part of this festival.[60] One may safely assert that the tribute of agricultural produce envisaged by Deuteronomy 26 corresponds to that of Exod 23:13, 34:22, and Lev 23:17,[61] so that according to the ancient Israelite calendar the ceremony in question was observed at the Feast of Weeks.[62]

Our thesis may therefore now be stated in the following terms: the creed as we have it in Deut 26:5ff. is the cult-legend of the Feast of Weeks—that is, it contains those elements of Yahwistic faith which were celebrated at the Feast of Weeks. It must be borne in mind that Deut 26:5ff. is not a "prayer," to be offered on a particular occasion; nor is it a thanksgiving, except in an indirect sense. It is a statement of quite definite and objective articles of faith. That is, after all, the essential characteristic of a cult-legend: it takes definite, objective basic facts of the common faith and actualizes them to furnish the content and the central feature of a cultic festival. The Feast of Weeks was originally, of course, a non-Israelite harvest festival. The cult-legend provided the historical justification that enabled Israel to adopt as its own the ancient Canaanite festival, and from the standpoint of the old Yahwistic faith, it offered quite the handiest method of appropriating an agricultural festival. By the use of the creed, the congregation acknowledges the redemptive sovereignty of Yahweh, now seen as the giver of the cultivable land.

So far we have said nothing of the date of this formulary by which the past was appropriated to Yahweh. The historical justification may in itself go back to very ancient times, but it may also be of comparatively late date. Actually, if one considers carefully the real underlying interests of the Settlement tradition, taking into account the fact that, as we have seen, it is above all the cult-legend of the Feast of Weeks, it will certainly appear that the *Settlement tradition must have originated and have had its historical setting in a place where the ownership of the land really was a live issue*—this, of course, without prejudice to the residual significance which the tradition must have had for later generations. The tradition must point to a place and a time at which the question of the legality of the settlement was of such pressing concern that the faith itself was under compulsion to give an account of it, both for its own adherents and for those outside, and to give, as it were, a religious assurance in the matter. This means that we are at once obliged to reckon the tradition to be of very great antiquity. At what later stage, once the settlement was an accomplished fact of long standing, would there have been any necessity to make this particular question a matter of religious belief?

There is, however, at least one other possible method of getting at the real origins of the Settlement tradition. It is evidently sound procedure to look more closely at what it has to say about the geographical objective and goal that is named in the tradition itself. It is wholly justifiable to suppose that its particular cultic significance is to be sought in the place to which the story points in its conclusion. For the purposes of this investigation, however, we have at our disposal only the later form of the tradition incorporated in a literary guise into the work of the Yahwist; at the same time we cannot rule out the possibility that this version may yet preserve a solid deposit of the ancient tradition.

Does this tradition then also point to Shechem? There are weighty considerations that militate against this assumption, attractive as it may seem at first sight. So far as the history of the tradition is concerned (i.e., not the literary account) the "parliament" at Shechem (Joshua 24) is certainly not the conclusion of the Settlement narrative. The reasons that lead us to postulate a discrepancy between the genuine Settlement tradition and the account in Joshua 24 have already been set out by Sellin.[63] Was not the apportionment of a town to Joshua, and his settlement in it,[64] intended to be the conclusion of Joshua's public achievement? Has the reader of Josh 19:50 any reason to anticipate that this same Joshua has still before him the greatest task of his life—the uniting of the tribes under a common faith in Yahweh? Furthermore, is it at all intelligible on the basis of the Settlement tradition that the tribes were only now summoned to put away strange gods, and for the first time learn what are the demands of this God of theirs, when they have been miraculously led by him throughout the course of a long history of redemptive acts?

The burial of Joseph's bones, too, is unintelligible at this point within the context of the settlement narrative. "Where, then, had the bones been in the meanwhile?" asks Sellin.[65] Even this objection goes to show clearly that we are here dealing with a tradition which was not originally in accord with the preceding account of the settlement in Canaan, as set out in Joshua 1ff.

Above all, however, what of the place? Has Shechem any real part to play in the preceding account of the settlement? From Joshua 1 onwards the detached traditions persistently move within the confines of Benjamite territory, and it is the sanctuary of Gilgal that must be reckoned the real center of interest of the etiological stories. When events move across to Shechem, we at once find ourselves in a quite different atmosphere, as regards both the secular history and the background of tradition.[66] The history of Joshua's parliament stands apart from the surrounding material, just as, elsewhere, the Sinai narrative is an intrusive secondary element within the Settlement tradition.

If, then, we keep to sound rules of procedure in answering this problem of the locality indicated by the Settlement tradition, basing our conclusion on that which is integral to the tradition itself, then we are led quite unequivo-cally to the sanctuary of Gilgal, near Jericho. This is in fact the objective that the tradition has constantly in view. Both the Yahwistic and the Elohistic accounts are associated with this place, which must therefore have been firmly rooted in the tradition. According to the Yahwistic tradition Israel made its way to Gilgal after the crossing of the Jordan (Joshua 3), a sanctuary was established there (Joshua 4), and there the people were circumcised (Joshua 5). At Gilgal, too, is the site of the "camp" (Josh 9:16, 10:6, 9) to which Israel returns after its exploits (Josh 10:15).

Now, however, we come to the main point: according to the ancient tradi-tion it was at Gilgal near Jericho that Joshua undertook the apportionment of the promised land to the tribes. So much the tradition makes clear, despite the fact that it has been heavily overlaid by later accretions. Apart from the unequivocal passage at Josh 14:6-14, we must also refer to Josh 18:2-10, which has been only very superficially worked over by the priestly writer and was originally attributed not to Shiloh[67] (where the "camp" never was), but to Gil-gal.[68] At the conclusion of the story preserved in the tradition, Israel is once more based on Gilgal: Judges 1 seems to presuppose this (see Judg 1:16),[69] and Gilgal is explicitly named in Judg 2:1.

So much for the present state of the Settlement tradition, which concludes with the events that took place at Gilgal. More precisely it might be said that its real interest lies not so much in the settlement as in the apportionment of the land to the tribes by the will of Yahweh. In the last analysis it is less concerned with the political aspect of the settlement, even to make clear Yahweh's role in this matter, than it is to assure us of the inherent legitimacy of the territorial boundaries of the tribes, depending as they do directly upon the declared will of Yahweh. Unfortunately one cannot say at this stage what kind of historical situation underlies this tradition; but it may be taken as certain that in this connection we should think of a quite concrete sacral procedure concerned with land-tenure. Traditions of this sort, which strive at such cost to legitimate a given situation, do not after all spring up from nowhere! May it not be that the whole remarkable system of tribal boundaries in the book of Joshua belongs here?

Alt has shown that historically the system must have arisen in the period before the formation of the political state, and he has come to regard it as a territorial arrangement drawn up for a wholly practical purpose.[70] This view is strongly supported by the fact that the establishment and confirmation of these claims took place in a recurring cultic and sacral act, performed at the sanctuary at Gilgal itself. The practice of casting lots to which the account in the book of Joshua adverts time and time again (cf. esp. Joshua 18:6, 8, 10) must, in fact, derive from an actual cultic procedure; and it must be supposed that the purpose of the Settlement tradition was to legitimate this process. If, however, the Settlement tradition had its original setting at Gilgal near Jericho, it may be that we should regard it pre-eminently as a specifically Benjamite tradition, which was extended to the whole tribal federation only at a later date.[71]

Our by no means wholly consistent conclusion concerning the cultic origins of the Settlement tradition, that it is the cult-legend of the Feast of Weeks originating from Gilgal, may seem at first sight to have little to commend it. One can but sound a note of warning with regard to all reconstructions that derive from one single line of descent where questions of sacral history are at issue. What do we *really* know—especially in a tradition of such crucial theological significance—of the various stages through which it passed in the history of the cultus? Did it branch off in different directions? If so, how? Was it drawn into the stream of a cultus originally quite foreign to it? And so on. Our materials for the solution of this problem offered two approaches, each of which in the first instance must be followed through to its conclusion regardless of the consequences.

We must now, however, take into consideration a fact that seems to militate against the second of our conclusions—that we know of only one period in the history of Israel at which the sanctuary of Gilgal was of any considerable instance, the age of Samuel and Saul (1 Sam 10:8; 11:14-15; 13:4, 7; 15:12, 21, 33). Yet this shrine is very firmly associated with a tradition that undoubtedly goes back to a much earlier date, and is also the scene of a ritual of great antiquity concerned with sacral rights. Therefore, despite the absence of other confirmatory evidence, we are not entitled to reject such a tradition out of hand. So far as Gilgal is concerned, however, the association that grew up between the Settlement tradition and the Feast of Weeks appears to have been a secondary development of the tradition of the shrine.

FROM TRADITION INTO LITERATURE

The Yahwist depicts a side of Israel's experience which we see continually repeating itself in the spiritual history of many nations: ancient and often very scattered traditions are brought together around one central co-ordinating conception, and by some massive *tour de force* achieve literary status. In Israel, where this applies almost exclusively to religious deposits formerly bound up with the cultus, the process penetrated to an unusual depth. For this to be possible at all, the data must of course have lain to hand in the material available. If ancient traditions were collected and built up into new literary units, as was done by the Yahwist, it could only be because they had already become to a large extent detached from the cultic places in which they had grown up. At all events, when the Yahwist gathered them together, the time was already long past when such materials would have been found meaningless and lifeless outside the spiritual environment of cultic activity. Whatever date we may assign to the Yahwist, he belongs to a much later period than the traditions which he incorporates in his work. Indeed, a mere glance at the state of development of the traditions suffices to show that in attaining literary form they have themselves been ruthlessly cut off.

It would be well to consider which way these traditions would have gone, so far as one can see, if the process had not been brought to a halt by their becoming fixed in a literary mold.[72] Doubtless the fact that the living traditions became detached from the locality with which they had cultic associations caused their content to become highly spiritualized; and it cannot be denied that the opportunity to grow away from the remote, stolid, materialistic cultic background was altogether a happy release, opening up unsuspected possibilities of development for the materials which they contained. But, of course, according to the principles which first gave rise to them, they would in any event have been subject to an ever greater degree of devolution.

Every further spiritualization brings with it a dangerous erosion of the very core of the material, for every spiritualization is also a rationalization. Man is no longer in the position of an awestruck unsophisticated recipient of the material, but begins to take control of it and to shape it according to the needs of his own reason. Let us take in support of our case an example in which this process can be readily observed, the story of the manna in Exodus 16). The Yahwistic version of the matter is still quite intelligible as a story, although full of historical difficulties.

The priestly account is very different. The incident is ostensibly presented as a wholly factual matter, but in such a way that no reader will dwell upon the externals, and all can readily grasp the hidden spiritual import. The miracle, which took place at a particular time and place, has been generalized and has become something of virtually timeless validity. It is not a storyteller who speaks here, but a man who is a theologian through and through, and who has clothed his meditations in a highly transparent garment of historical narrative.[73] But the deuteronomist goes a great deal further than this:

> He troubled you and let you hunger and fed you with manna, which you did not know, nor did your father know; that he might make you know that man does not live by bread alone, but that man lives by everything that proceeds out of the mouth of Yahweh. (Deut 8:3)

The priestly writer still preserved the ancient form of the story in its externals, and his spiritualization is but that which shines out through a translucent mode of narration. The deuteronomist on the other hand wholly abandons the original significance of the story. In prosaic language he tells us what weighty spiritual significance really underlay the outward events even at the time of the occurrence. One may freely admit that this spiritualization has given to the old, simple historical event a wider meaning that is both beautiful and important; but there can be no doubt that at the same time the historical recollection has been seriously eroded, and in a palpably mutilated form has now finally become the vehicle of a completely new idea.[74]

In the light of this, it will be well for us to look for a moment at the whole process by which tradition grows into literature. The Yahwist gathered up the materials that were becoming detached from the cultus, and compacted them firmly together within a literary framework. We can only guess at the kind of process of devolution that he arrested by so doing. If at this point we are thrown back upon mere supposition, we may nevertheless suspect that he seized on the material at a time when a certain degree of spiritualization had already asserted itself against the materialism of the cultus, but when the traditions nevertheless still preserved historical facts in a concrete form, and had not lost sight of their significance as actual and unrepeatable occurrences.

The Yahwist

There is an old question as to whether we are to regard the work of the Yahwist as that of a collector or as that of an author. Gunkel answered the question in one way, and Kittel in the other;[75] but nowadays the problem no longer seems quite so simple.

One of Gunkel's most significant shortcomings is his almost complete failure to take into account the coordinating power of the writer's overall theological purpose, and the gathering of the separate materials around a very small nucleus of basic concepts. These basic concepts that bind together the whole structure are not, of course, the products of the personal theological genius of the Yahwist, nor do they represent one of many possible formative lines that might have been chosen. They are themselves an extremely ancient traditional deposit, and there was no alternative to using them.

We may say at once that the Yahwist's outline plan, the framework of which supports the whole of his work, is the Settlement tradition. If he also incorporated in his plan a very great number of detached traditions of the most diverse origin and of many different kinds, he has nevertheless avoided giving even to the most important among them a place comparable or superior to that occupied by the Settlement tradition. They do not stand here as elements which exist in their own right, but are wholly subordinated to the Settlement tradition in an ancillary capacity. It is remarkable that such a bewildering abundance of traditions as are brought to bear by the Yahwist can be knit into the pattern of the fundamental tradition without themselves being distorted. Yet this is in fact achieved in such a way that the simple and straightforward chain of though of the Settlement tradition remains paramount, and the main lines of its theology are barely affected by the accretions.

On the basis of our knowledge of the ancient Settlement tradition which underlies the Yahwist's work, it might reasonably be asked whether we ought not to abandon the suggestion that it comes from the hand of some great collector and editor, and think rather of a long process of anonymous growth. May it not be that this hexateuchal source developed gradually from that short, ancient creed, through the accretion of layer upon layer of old traditional materials added by the efforts of many generations?

There are serious objections to such a theory. Had the various materials been deposited in successive layers like a sediment, the resultant picture would have been substantially different. We should have been able to establish at some point a stratification of the traditions. In fact, nowhere is it possible to mark a division between the ancient bedrock and the later accretions. On the contrary, what we see is a large quantity of detached materials that have been fused into a single whole according to the pattern of one ancient tradition. The various materials all lie as it were in the same stratum. One plan alone governs the whole, and a gigantic structure such as this, the whole conforming to one single plan, does not grow up naturally of its own accord. How could such heterogeneous materials as those embraced by the Yahwist have cast themselves in this form of their own accord?

It lies outside the scope of this study, however, to indicate or to investigate the origins of all the various traditions that the Yahwist has incorporated in his work. There can be no doubt at all that he found already made for him whole complexes of tradition, themselves the outcome of a long process of development. Pedersen has shown us one instance of this, in demonstrating that the narrative of Exodus 1–14 forms a complete whole, deriving from the Passover ceremony.[76] Exodus 1–14 provides an example of a neatly rounded complex of traditional material; its theme is the exodus from Egypt, and with the portrayal of Yahweh's victory over His enemies it reaches both its climax and its conclusion. Thus we have here a genuine Exodus tradition quite distinct from the Settlement tradition, but readily able to be included in this because of its closely related subject-matter. Yet it would be difficult to find another instance of a formerly independent tradition so neatly and unobtrusively welded into the pattern.

A second major complex of tradition that the Yahwist found more or less ready-made is to be seen in the Balaam story; but the process by which such older material is taken up and fitted into the larger work presents relatively few problems. Of greater interest are those cases in which the Yahwist has included traditions that are less easily harmonized with the scheme of the Settlement tradition. The interpolation of such materials strained the original plan almost to bursting point, and resulted in a forcible broadening of its formerly rather narrow theological basis. There are three points at which this is particularly noticeable: in the interpolation of the Sinai tradition, in the development of the patriarchal tradition, and in the introductory addition of the primeval history.

The Inclusion (der Einbau) of the Sinai Tradition

We have already seen that the Sinai tradition must be regarded as an originally independent sacral tradition,[77] and is in fact the cult-legend of the ancient Yahwistic ceremony of the renewal of the covenants at the Feast of Booths. The ancient form of the creed, as well as the poetical paraphrases of it, showed that it formed no part of the Settlement tradition, a fact that could in any case be demonstrated from the tradition itself.

We have no means of knowing where or in what form the Yahwist found this Sinai tradition. We can say with some certainty only that the incorporation of the Sinai tradition into the Settlement tradition should be attributed to the Yahwist, and that probably the fusion of the two traditions had not been previously attempted. Certainly the Yahwist did not find the pattern ready to hand.

Let us cast a brief glance at the various poetical representations of the redemption story (Psalms 78; 105; 135; 136; Exodus 15; 1 Sam 12:8; and Joshua 24). All of them follow to a greater or lesser extent the canonical outline of the Settlement tradition and thus overlook completely the Sinai episode. This is the more striking in view of the fact that they are otherwise very ready to recount events the significance of which is in no way comparable with that of the events of Sinai. Only in the exilic Psalm 106, and in the prayer of Nehemiah 9, does the Sinai episode appear as an event of the redemption story. It can only be that the association of the two traditions was of recent origin, not something that the Yahwist found ready-made, since even at a time later than that of the Yahwist it had not taken root in the traditional account of the history of redemption. It is in fact to the Yahwist himself that we owe the fusion of the Sinai tradition with the Settlement tradition, and it was a long time before the pattern became fully accepted; only at about the time of the Exile did the association of the two win popular approval. Had this association taken place in the pre-literary phase, should we not have expected the two traditions to be rather more tightly and organically interwoven than they are?

We have already mentioned the serious unevennesses and the breaks in continuity that resulted from the interpolation of the Sinai narrative:[78] the

Kadesh tradition is torn in two by it. Everything goes to show that no properly assimilated, integral harmonization of the materials existed. The fusion was made by a purely literary process, and immediately behind the literary work we can still see the sharp outlines of the self-contained, authoritative Sinai tradition.

Even though the interpenetration of one tradition by the other still fails to achieve complete harmony, the Settlement tradition is theologically enormously enriched by its absorption of the Sinai tradition. The former bears witness to Yahweh's generosity, but over against this, at the very heart of the Sinai tradition, is the demand of Yahweh's righteousness. Thus by its absorption of the Sinai tradition the simple soteriological conception of the Settlement tradition gained new support of a powerful and salutary kind. Everything that the Yahwist tells us, as he unfolds the plan of his tradition, is now colored by the divine self-revelation of Mt. Sinai. This is above all true with regard to the underlying purpose of that tradition, which now becomes the record of the redemptive activity of One who lays upon man the obligation to obey his will, and calls man to account for his actions. The blending of the two traditions gives definition to the two fundamental propositions of the whole message of the Bible: Law and Gospel.

The Development (der Ausbau) of the Patriarchal History

Did the ancient Settlement tradition originally contain, as an integral element, any allusion to the patriarchal period? Or was this motif as foreign to it as the Sinai tradition? One may perhaps begin to answer this question by referring to Psalm 78, for in this psalm the account of the historical events begins with the exodus from Egypt, and there is no reference either to the patriarchal tradition or to the Sinai tradition. There is a precisely similar state of affairs in Psalm 136, where the absence of patriarchal history is the more striking in so far as this psalm begins with the creation of the world.

We must not, however, jump to hasty conclusions by trying to answer the question on the evidence of such free adaptations of the traditional material. If we look at a wider selection of the poems which reflect the Settlement tradition in order to ascertain at what point they take up the story, it becomes evident that the Settlement tradition must have stood in a much closer relationship to the patriarchal tradition than it did to the Sinai tradition. We have a whole series of compositions in which the narrative starts from the patriarchal period, but yet knows nothing of the events of Sinai (Deut 26:5ff.; Josh 24:2ff.; 1 Sam 12:8; Psalm 105). Against these there is only the one late psalm, Psalm 106, which takes as its starting-point the oppression in Egypt and contains an allusion to the events of Sinai. The facts demonstrate clearly that there must have been a much closer relationship between the patriarchal tradition and the Settlement tradition.

It will be profitable to pause a while over the brief, concise clauses of our creed, from which ultimately are doubtless derived the long circumstantial adaptations, with all their manifold contributory traditions and fragments of traditions. It is not to these greatly expanded compositions that we look to discover what is so to speak the minimum content of a creed. For this we turn rather to the simplest possible versions of the creed, since only these versions can properly be expected to tell us what is the historical starting-point of the tradition.

We thus return as a matter of course to the passage with which we began the present study, Deut 26:5. There are, of course, no fixed points of reference which would enable us to say with certainty that this text is prior to all other examples of its *genre;* but both its concise, simple form and its intimate connection with a cultic act of great antiquity justify our belief that it is among the examples of the *genre* which approximate most closely to the original. From its pregnant opening—"A wandering Aramean was my father" (*'aramî 'obed 'abî*)—to its conclusion, everything in this creed is so tightly knit, clause succeeding clause with organic inevitability, that there is no trace whatever of inconsistencies which might indicate the fusion of originally independent traditions. The very opening words, concerning the wandering patriarch who becomes a nation, plays a distinctive and important part in the development of the thought, and in view of their relationship to the subsequent statements of the creed impress one as being integral to the original.

The completely unified form in which this creed comes to us seems to justify the assumption that from the very first the opening reference to the patriarchal period was an indispensable component of the creed. This view is confirmed by the other version in 1 Sam 12:8, which, apart from the deuteronomic digression concerning the Settlement, is equally distinguished by extreme conciseness. This account, too, starts from the same point: "When Jacob and his sons went into Egypt . . . ."

The version in Joshua 24 cannot, of course, be measured against these two accounts without certain reservations. Here the original scheme has been filled out by the inclusion of numerous reminiscences, and represents a highly developed stage in the history of the *genre.* Even so, if we leave out of account the subsidiary embellishments, those elements which we have seen to be fundamental to the creed still stand out: the patriarchal period, Egypt, the Exodus, the Settlement. Even in this instance, the reference to the patriarchal period cannot be dismissed as merely one of the many accretions which embellish the narrative, the less so since it seems that what we are dealing with at this point is not properly the hexateuchal tradition.[79]

We therefore take it as proven that from the earliest times the Settlement tradition took the patriarchal period as its starting-point, and began, in fact—as Deuteronomy 26 and 1 Sam 12:8 clearly show—with a simple reference to Jacob. For the Yahwist, therefore, this was a part of the accepted tradition, a basic element of it which had become canonical and which could be elaborated from other available material. We must now try to see what was the particular contribution of the Yahwist.

The literary process by which the content of the patriarchal sagas was brought together, so far as the Yahwist is concerned, has been made fairly clear in the works of Gunkel.[80] His history of Abraham is in essence built up from two cycles, one concerned with Abraham and the other with Lot, into which he has incorporated various independent materials of a similar kind. There are only two sagas that deal with Isaac (Gen 26:6-11, 12-33), both of which were incorporated into the wider framework of the Jacob sagas. The Yahwist's history of Jacob is composed of four strands—(a) a Jacob-Esau cycle, (b) a Jacob-Laban cycle, (c) some cultic sagas, and (d) some sagas concerning Jacob's children.[81] The most completely self-contained of these is the story of Joseph, although even here it is certain that a multiplicity of traditional material has been brought together.[82] The question now is, how far ought we to regard both the literary form and the theological content as the work of the Yahwist? For an answer, we must dig yet a little deeper.

It was above all Alt's study of the "God of the Patriarchs"[83] which brought us significantly closer to a real understanding of the patriarchal sagas. According to Alt we must think of the patriarchs as the recipients of revelations and founders of the cultus in the period before the settlement of the tribes. After the Settlement both the patriarchal figures themselves, and also the residual elements of their cultus, coalesced with the cultic sagas of the Canaanite sanctuaries, and from this time onwards Isaac is associated with Beersheba, Abraham with Mamre, and Jacob with various shrines which lay in the territory of the Joseph tribes.[84] Only at a comparatively late stage in the cultic history of ancient Israel were the sacral traditions that arose in this way fully integrated with Yahwistic belief, presumably at the central sanctuary of the amphictyony.[85]

Even though the form in which the ancient tradition has been captured for later Yahwism by the writer differs from that known to E,[86] the literary fixity in these sources establishes the fact that the process was already complete. The fact that the ancient material of the sagas is filled out and completely permeated by the Yahwistic faith cannot, therefore, be regarded as a result of the J writer's work. Nor can we reckon as a product of the Yahwist's workshop the genealogy that binds into the well-known triad the recipients of the divine revelations. Originally, of course, they stood side by side, quite unrelated to one another. The creed, which in its most primitive form began simply with Jacob, seems to know nothing of the patriarchal genealogy, although Alt has shown how the three traditions were fused into single genealogical whole.[87]

As the few great sanctuaries became more and more the centers of pilgrimage for several tribes, so there must have been a gradual approximation, a mutual assimilation of their different patriarchal traditions. In this connection Alt thinks especially of Beersheba, which, as a place of pilgrimage for the north (Jacob), south (Isaac), and the neighboring Judahites (Abraham), must have given an impetus to this tendency to mutual interpenetration on the part of the traditions. In arranging the various traditions of the patriarchs to present Abraham, Isaac, and Jacob in genealogical sequence, therefore, the J writer is not an innovator, but relies upon an earlier tradition.

When we turn to the separate collections of sagas we are on firm ground at last. The Yahwist would certainly have known a version in which the Abraham cycle and the Lot cycle were already conflated.[88] In the characteristic central section, however, in which Genesis 15 is now included amongst the Abraham sagas, the theological handiwork of the Yahwist is apparent. On the one hand he has brought in the promise, on the other he has introduced a certain tension arising from human reluctance to accept this promise. The situation is reminiscent of Gen 12:10ff., where the promise is jeopardized by disbelief, and of Gen 16:1ff., where weakness of faith results in an attempt to force its content. The strong theological interest that gives cohesion to the Abraham sagas as we have them is certainly traceable to the Yahwist.

The problem of the Jacob sagas is less easy to elucidate. Here, too, it would of course be erroneous to suppose that the J writer built up the entire structure of this massive composition all by himself. The unification of the Jacob-Esau cycle with the Jacob-Laban cycle was certainly already complete.[89] Equally, the Yahwist may have found ready to hand a good deal of such saga material already integrated with materials from other sources. Obviously here we can hardly hope to give anything more than a conjectural account of the Yahwist's share in the overall work.

Most probably this also applies to the origins of the cultic sagas. How did the Bethel saga on the one hand, and the Penuel saga on the other, come to be the landmarks in the story of the patriarch's relationship with God, as narrated in the composite version of the Jacob sagas? It was not the outcome of a simple process of growth, but reflects a conscious theological pragmatism. At the very nadir of Jacob's life, when humanly speaking all is lost and hopeless, Jacob receives the pledge and confirmation of the promise made to Abraham (Gen 28:13ff.), but only after a long period of service is he inwardly prepared to receive it. The prayer of Gen 32:10-12 is indicative of the whole course of Jacob's life-history.[90] Humbled already by men, it is only when he has also proved himself against the onslaught of God that Jacob becomes Israel—for, of course, the narrative of Gen 32:25ff. leaves no doubt that under cover of the spectral figure it is Yahweh himself who comes to Jacob.

It is generally accepted that in the history of Joseph the Yahwist has incorporated into his work a tale that was in all essentials already a finished and complete work. Every reader is well aware how neatly it fulfills its present function of leading up to Israel's growth to nationhood in Egypt. When we look more closely, however, we cannot fail to see that, despite this, it has a significance of its own. Its transitional function in the history of Israel is wholly secondary to its original purpose. It is a story of divine guidance, a testimony to God's providential care, finding its conclusion in a state of "salvation" in which all the earlier tensions of the narrative are resolved.

At the same time it is more mature than the other sagas in the book of Genesis, showing how the inmost recesses of the human soul are nevertheless the sphere of God's providential activity. The Joseph story thus exemplifies the point that the J writer is not wholly and exclusively concerned to construct his thesis along one single theological line. He is always a collector, and as such allows a certain degree of autonomy to the units that he has brought together. Despite this, we do well to recognize that he has wholly succeeded in giving to his work a cohesion which relates all his material to the one underlying theological concept—that of the ancient Settlement tradition.

Yet there are still further contributions that may with some certainty be attributed to the hand of the Yahwist. Indeed, we have not yet mentioned what is perhaps the most important factor of all—the *integration of the patriarchal history as a whole with the idea of the Settlement.* The promise of the *land* is first mooted in the story of Abraham's going out from his own people (Gen 12:7), a motif in which we ought particularly to see the work of the Yahwist;[91] we find it in the solemn conclusion to the sealing of the covenant (Gen 15:18), and then again and again in the history of the patriarchs right through to the Joseph story (see Gen 13:14ff.; 24:7; 26:2ff.; 28:13), despite the fact that it was certainly not found here originally:

> And Joseph said to his brothers, "I am about to die; but God will visit you and bring you up out of this land to the land which he swore to Abraham, to Isaac, and to Jacob." (Gen 50:24)

This particular passage, undoubtedly an addition made by the Yahwist to give cohesion to his work, is extremely illuminating, for it also contains an allusion to the tradition of the God of the patriarchs, a tradition in which Alt found preserved the last vestiges of the pre-Yahwistic cult of the Israelite tribes. For us it raises the problem whether the idea of the Settlement in the patriarchal sagas may not also derive from the same very ancient sacral tradition. The mention of the promise of the land in Genesis 28 raises the question in an even more acute form, for here too we find the Settlement closely bound up with the God of the patriarchs, in what is evidently a stereotyped context:

> And behold, Yahweh stood beside him and said, "I am Yahweh, the God of Abraham your father and the God of Isaac; the land on which you lie I will give to you and to your descendants." (Gen 28:13)

This particular element cannot have belonged to the ancient Canaanite cultic saga: how could it have formed part of a *hieros logos* tied to a particular place? Here we have a genuine element of that pre-Yahwistic patriarchal religion, which assured the semi-nomadic people, driving forward into civilized territory, that they would achieve the goal of their aspirations.[92] Thus the inclusion of the promise of the land in the patriarchal sagas is in itself by no means a free invention of the J writer. It is not, as one might perhaps be inclined to suppose, a pushing back in time of the interest of the Settlement tradition, but belongs to the most ancient of the traditions of which the J writer takes cognizance.[93] The literary appraisal of this ancient traditional element is, of course, a different matter; and here there is cause to believe that the actual prominence of the promise of the land in the patriarchal sagas in J is attributable to the Yahwist's free treatment of the material; for the original promise—and this is perhaps the most important point of all— is actually broken in a remarkable way by its later inclusion in the Settlement tradition.

It has, of course, always been realized that the promise of the land in the patriarchal sagas must have been originally a quite definite and final one, which did not allow for a subsequent departure from the land before the final settlement.[94] By the incorporation of this patriarchal tradition in the scheme of the Settlement tradition, the whole purpose of the original promise is altered; the reader must now understand it in a mediate sense, referring it to the settlement that became a reality only in the time of Joshua. Thus the relationship of the patriarchs to the land in which they dwell now appears to be merely provisional, and their present situation but a temporary one. The priestly writer is the first to erect this into an intelligible theological conception, by means of his conception of the "land of sojourning" (*'ereṣ megûrîm*; Gen 17:8; 28:4; 36:7; 37:1; 49:9; Exod 6:4).

The factual situation is, of course, precisely as in J. The whole patriarchal period has ceased to be regarded as significant in itself; it is now no more than a time of promise pointing to a fulfillment outside itself, a fulfillment spoken of only at the very end of the Yahwist's work.

If it cannot be denied, however, that the Yahwist removed from the traditional patriarchal narrative an element which was originally inherent in it, he has on the other hand given it something which it previously had not: he has shown the promise to be fulfilled in a way which goes far beyond anything envisaged in the earlier version. It must be recognized that the patriarchal period looks not only to the settlement by *all* the tribes, but that there is also a direct pointer to the covenant at Sinai in the heavy emphasis laid on the patriarchal covenant.[95] In this way the whole relationship between God and the patriarchs is presented as a preparatory stage, which reached its fulfillment only in the divine revelation, and in the appropriation of it by the community descended from the patriarchs.

If therefore we think of the J writer as being by no means wholly dependent upon what had gone before, either with regard to the literary form of his work or to the materials he brought together, we can yet scarcely overestimate his contribution in shaping the material, and in directing the theological motivation which runs right through it. It is a very far cry from the simple opening words of the creed to the fully-fashioned patriarchal histories of the Yahwist.[96]

Let us remind ourselves once more of the contribution of the Yahwist to the patriarchal histories. The following are perhaps the salient points, selected only for the sake of convenience from the organic whole that is the J writer's achievement:

1. The extensive development of the original creedal deposit.
2. An internal ordering and arrangement of the saga material, so that Yahweh's guidance is manifest both in isolated instances and in the work as a whole.
3. The integration of the saga materials into the traditional notion of the God of the patriarchs, and his promise of the land.
4. The reorientation of the patriarchal sagas, which now become the introduction to the Settlement tradition, to which they now stand in the relationship of a promise which it fulfills.
5. The relating of the patriarchal covenant to the Sinai covenant, similarly conceived as promise and fulfillment.

The Addition (der Vorbau) of the Primeval History

It is unnecessary at the present day to enter into any particular discussion of the manner in which the J writer's early history of the world was composed from a series of originally independent cycles of material. Broadly speaking there are nine different elements that Gunkel was able to distinguish as the result of critical study of the sagas:[97]

1. The paradise story
2. The Cain narrative
3. The genealogy of Cain
4. The genealogy of Seth
5. The angel marriages
6. The story of the flood
7. Noah and Canaan
8. National genealogies
9. The building of the tower

The problem of the more or less immediate literary antecedents on which the Yahwist may have drawn must remain at this point altogether an open question. Since the discoveries of Ras Shamra there is less reason than ever to doubt the possibility or indeed the probability that such literary models were available as separate entities. On the other hand all the evidence shows that the composition as a whole, i.e., the drawing together of the separate materials with a single object in view, was the considered work of the Yahwist. What motive would there have been for drawing together such hitherto widely separated elements, other than that which the J writer had in mind?

The only alternative is to suppose that the whole composition of Genesis 2–11 was found ready-made by the Yahwist. The suggestion must be decisively rejected in view of the fact that it was just at this point that the basic tradition followed by the Yahwist failed him. Besides, if some of the materials that lay before him had already been edited together, they would certainly have been more thoroughly adjusted one to another, and more intimately fused together than they are. Gunkel has shown in a detailed study what a high degree of incompatibility actually exists between them.[98] It may well be doubted whether these materials enjoyed the same popularity as the patriarchal sagas and the Moses sagas in the Yahwist's own day. They derive from a totally different sphere of culture and religion.

We can therefore say, with all the certainty that is ever attainable in such matters, that the co-ordination of the various elements of the pre-patriarchal history is to be traced to the hand of the J writer. The conclusion is even more assured here than it is in the case of the patriarchal sagas and the Moses sagas.[99] The one basic notion that the J writer has here taken for his theme—the growing power of sin in the world—needs no elucidation at this juncture. It is necessary only to emphasize the tendentious single-mindedness with which the Yahwist pursues this thought, as compared with the emphasis usually laid on the universal scope of the material. All the materials that he has gathered together, with all their manifold aspects, serve only one purpose, which is to show how all the harm in the world comes from sin. It cannot be said that this is the only possible point of view; on the contrary, the writer is asserting his own particular belief.

It is an equally well-accepted fact that the J writer postulates a hidden growth of grace alongside the ever-widening gulf between God and man. The story of the Fall, the Cain narrative, and the Flood story all show God's redemptive activity, forgiving and sustaining at the same time as he punishes. Only in the story of the building of the tower does the divine judgment appear to be the last word, when the nations are scattered and the unity of the human race is lost.

At this point, however, the pre-patriarchal history keys in with the history of redemption: Abraham is called out of all the nations and he is promised the blessing "that all the races on earth will be blessed in him." Thus the opening words of the story of redemption provide the answer to the problem posed by the early history of the world, that of the relationship of God to the nations as a whole. The beginning of the story of redemption in Gen 12:1-3, however, not only brings to an end the early history, as Budde rightly saw,[100] but actually provides the key to it. To trace the origins of the situation back to the early history of the world, and even to the Creation itself, is no mere embellishment. This is not a mere review that, whilst undoubtedly contributing to the understanding of the whole, could quite well be omitted without seriously impairing the overall picture. Any such view is necessarily precluded by the rigid purposefulness and indeed tendentiousness with which the gradual breaking down of the relationship between man and God is presented in the early history.

On the contrary, the pre-patriarchal history, ending on a note of despair in the Tower story, is inseparably bound up with the opening of the redemptive history with its promise of a blessing for Israel and, through Israel, for "all the races on earth." In thus welding together the early history of the world and the history of redemption, the J writer submits his account of the meaning and purpose of the redemptive relationship that Yahweh has vouchsafed to Israel. *He provides the etiology of all Israelite etiology,* and in so doing becomes the true prophet. He proclaims, in a manner that is neither rationally justifiable nor yet capable of detailed explanation, that the ultimate purpose of the redemption that God will bring about in Israel is that of bridging the gulf between God and the entire human race.[101]

If we take into account the fact that this declaration is in no way a part of the tradition which otherwise directs its course from first to last, the unique stature of the J writer's profession of faith is plainly seen. The Settlement tradition started out from the patriarchal history, and at no time contained a statement of the early history of the world in any form. But precisely at the point where it failed the Yahwist, it set him free to develop his own highly personal presentation on his own terms. It might now be asked whether the Yahwist had not perhaps some precedent for bringing the early history of the world into relationship with the redemption history in this way. There is, of course, no proof that there was none, though it is hard to believe that the J writer is following an earlier tradition here. His presentation of the data is too clearly stamped with his own purpose, and one cannot avoid the feeling that the looseness of the composition as a whole stems from the fact that this is the first trial of a new venture. Accounts such as we find in Psalms 135 and 136, which are the earliest parallels we can adduce, are undoubtedly much later in date.

If we regard Gen 12:1-3 as the real conclusion and explanation of the pre-patriarchal history, we must agree with Gunkel that in Gen 12:1ff. we are not dealing with a saga which already existed, but at best with a free composition of the J writer.[102] Gen 12:1ff., including the migration of Abraham, does not in fact represent a fixed tradition, but is a specially composed link-passage which has become by its very nature a declaration of fundamental beliefs. The passage contains three promises:

> (*a*) Abraham will become a great nation,
> (*b*) Yahweh will give land to Abraham's progeny, and
> (*c*) in Abraham all the races of the earth will be blessed.

The Yahwist found the first two promises in the tradition of the patriarchal sagas; but the third and most important came from none of the more ancient traditions. It has the full authority of a prophetic revelation. It is therefore not surprising that this unique notion finds few echoes in the later parts of the Yahwist's work (Gen 18:18; 27:29; 28:14 [Exod 9:16; Num 14:21]). The tradition that the writer is following was of immense import in its own right, and as a collector the Yahwist enjoyed none of the liberty accorded to a modern author in his treatment of ready-minted materials. The unadaptable nature of the traditions precluded any further infiltration of his own fundamental concept. It sufficed that it was proclaimed at one point of the work in a way that made it normative for the whole. We saw above that the contribution of the J wrier is to be seen primarily in the overall composition, i.e., in the method that governs the arrangement of the materials.

The Theological Problem of the Yahwist

In the preceding sections I have tried to trace the main stages by which traditions originally bound up with the cultus reached the literary form that they have in the work of the Yahwist. There is, however, a latent theological problem involved in this process, by which the ties between the traditions and their cultic matrix were gradually loosened. We must briefly advert to this problem in order to show how this loosening came about.

There is a wealth of ancient cultic material built into the work of the J writer, but it would be true to say that there is not one single instance in which the original cultic interest has been preserved. The many *hieroi logoi* have no longer the function of legitimating and guaranteeing the holiness of an actual site, nor have the cult legends of Exodus 1–14 or Exodus 19ff. and 24 retained their ancient sacral purpose, which was exclusively concerned with providing the basis and shaping the pattern of an ancient Yahwistic festival. The materials have been "historicized": their inner content has actually been removed bodily from its narrow sacral context into the freer atmosphere of common history.

We ought, therefore, to consider whether in consequence it necessarily became subject to a process of secularization, or whether the loss which any tradition suffered immediately by its divorce from the cultus was not perhaps made good, although on a different level, by new theological associations.

This is, in my opinion, the question that constitutes the theological problem of the J writer. The atmosphere which surrounds the Yahwist's declarations of faith is almost wholly devoid of cultic associations, a fact which must cause intense surprise to anyone who has followed our investigation from that extremely close association with the cultus which characterizes most of the materials, to the stage at which they are fused together in the literary work of the Yahwist. We are still obviously dealing with materials the great majority of which derive from the cultus, and which therefore were conceived, molded, and for a long time preserved by the cultus. Certainly there are echoes here and there of cultic notions (for example, Gen 7:2; 32:32 [MT 33]; Exod 5:24), and we hear of cultic occasions to which the Yahwist himself was no stranger (for example Gen 4:3-4; 8:20-21; 12:7; 15:9-10; 31:46).

All this counts for very little, however, in the absence of a really serious regard for what underlay these things in the mind of the unsophisticated believer. Where the cultus is genuine, it is a matter of life and death; but the attitude of the Yahwist towards these saving ordinances is one of tolerance rather than of conviction that they are indispensable. At all events the essential interest of his work is far removed from these cultic matters.

This markedly spiritual manner of speaking that we find in J is redolent of the untrammeled days of Solomon. To say this, however, does not solve our theological problems, the full weight of which is felt only when one banishes from one's mind the rationalized view that cultic associations are of little importance. If we apply even our modern standards of the "outward" and the "inward," we see that wherever there is doubt, religion without cultic observance is in danger of becoming flat and dull. The faith is threatened no less by the danger of a one-sided spirituality than by the danger of a one-sided cultic emphasis. Let us say once again that the spiritual atmosphere in which the Yahwist moves is almost unparalleled in the history of Old Testament religion, and it is this fact which raises the problem of the provenance of his theological attitude.

The problem nevertheless presupposes that we can in fact believe such a theological attitude to be really viable. This is not altogether self-evident, for the J writer was certainly a collector, and as such had an interest in preserving the ancient religious motives of his material.[103] Yet there can be no serious doubt that the Yahwist speaks to his contemporaries out of concern for the real and living faith, not as a more or less detached storyteller committed to nothing more than an ancient fund of traditions.

It might, of course, be said that the purpose of his work is to provide for his contemporaries a more complete and fully developed presentation of the creed, that ancient portrayal of the history of redemption, and so to demonstrate its undiminished validity. But this would still not answer the real theological problem. Once the traditions had outgrown the cultic sphere in which their sacral nature guaranteed their truth, the problem of the validity of these declarations of faith was posed anew for the Yahwist. Where was the incentive, and where was the inner justification for such a reassertion of this very ancient deposit of the faith? If he wished for a hearing on theological grounds as a witness to the faith, and not to be just a religious storyteller of no particular consequence, he must have taken his stand on some fact which would give him an objective right to call God to witness. It is quite inconceivable that the Yahwist should have addressed his nation without some such foundation for his beliefs. The fact upon which he based his entire work seems to me to have been primarily the simple historical assertion that not only had the promise to give Israel the land of Canaan been fulfilled, but that subsequently God visibly continued his providential care for Israel. By so doing God set his seal anew upon the ancient creed.

But we may go yet one stage further. The Yahwist no longer thinks of the Settlement and occupation of the land in the sense of the old creed. A limitation of a very material kind has been removed: the Settlement is now the affair of all twelve tribes, and in showing it to be so the Yahwist has achieved a significant extension of his field. However wide or narrow may have been the application of the Gilgal creed in earlier times, it certainly did not cover originally the full tale of the tribes. It referred at the very most to a group of tribes which kept a festival of land re-distribution (*gēs anadasmos*) or something of a similar nature at the sanctuary. Now, however, we have the conception of the "greater Israel" to which Galling first drew attention.[104]

J's work is permeated throughout by this conception; but for him, never-theless, God's dealings with Israel appear in a very different light. Here we are brought back once again to our problem. The Yahwist is much less concerned with cultus, much more interested in political considerations. For him, God's dealings are not something experienced only intermittently in a holy war through the deeds of a charismatic leader. In a word, *the main emphasis in God's dealings with his people is now to be sought outside the sacral institu-tions.* God's activity is now perhaps less perceptible to the outward sight, but it is actually perceived more fully and more constantly because his guidance is seen to extend equally to every historical occurrence, sacred or profane, up to the time of the Settlement. The Yahwist bears witness to the fact that history is revealed to the eye of faith in every sphere of life, private or public.

This view of the faith did not regard the activity of God as tied to the time-honored sacral institutions of the cultus, holy wars, charismatic leaders, the ark, and so on, but undertook to discover it by looking back on the tangled skein of personal and political destinies. Such a view might well be reckoned revolutionary, but it is not the exclusive possession of the Yahwist: his contri-bution has close contacts with another which, in a strikingly similar manner, "stands, with some reservations, in opposition to the cultus, and recognizes the divine activity in the course of history"[105] (the account of Solomon's acces-sion to the throne of David in 2 Samuel 7, 9–20; 1 Kings 1–11). The relationship of these two works is a very wide subject,[106] but we are here concerned only with a few basic considerations. This new way of seeing God's activity in his-tory was set in train by the figure of David, and the historical experiences of Israel under him as king; consequently we must on literary grounds assign to the Yahwist a date later than that of the account of the succession to the throne of David. It is at once obvious that this new perspective of the faith must be directed first of all to what is most immediate—the historical situa-tion in which Israel found itself at the time.

By contrast with the older perspective, bound up as it was with sacral asso-ciations, this logical view of the sovereignty of God in history can, as we have said, be described as altogether revolutionary; and the similarity of viewpoint in the two works is so striking that there must be some integral connection between them. Is it not then likely that the immense development of the ancient creed effected by the Yahwist is much more directly related to David than has hitherto been supposed?

There is another approach that gives substance to this broad suggestion of an inherent relationship between the Yahwist and the history of the royal suc-cession. We said above that the authenticating fact upon which the Yahwist took his stand was simply the historical truth that Yahweh had continued to care for Israel on the basis established in the Settlement. The most outstanding achievement of David's reign, however, was unquestionably the remarkable expansion of the greater Israelite empire far beyond the boundaries that had enclosed the ancient Israelite amphictyony, or even the empire of Saul. Alt has drawn attention to the connection between the extension and consolidation of the empire under David and the territorial claims of the tribes.[107]

The document in the book of Joshua which lays down the tribal boundaries, and also the list in Judges 1 of territories not yet occupied by the tribes, both show that age-old territorial claims, based on ordinances and appointments which were doubtless of a sacral character, were still a live issue among the tribes. But even if it be thought improbable that any connection exists between David's political affairs and these age-old tribal ordinances, the incontrovertible fact remains that under David the empire grew amazingly, to an extent which went far to meet these ancient claims. Those age-old aspirations were already perhaps in danger of sinking into oblivion; but now, was it not to be expected that they would both be revived and also related in a most vivid manner to newly aroused aspirations? What more obvious course was there than to claim for David's successes the authority of those ancient ordinances? The events of David's reign could forthwith acquire a profound religious significance. Age-old decrees of Yahweh were recalled, and David was seen to be the agent of God's will.

Such would have been the joyful realization that swept over the contemporaries of David and their immediate successors. Doubtless they found it surprising, for the days were long past when Yahweh's deliverance of Israel might still be known in actual experience. In the call of Saul, Yahweh's help had once more been revealed in the ancient manner, in a holy war; but then for several decades the faith of Israel had experienced nothing further of that kind. It seemed that Yahweh had withdrawn from the field of history. Then came David's great feats, and with them, almost overnight, the fulfillment of God's ancient decrees. So Yahweh was still with Israel! He had not allowed his purpose to lapse. Nonetheless, his activity had not been such as had been known formerly in the holy wars of old. It was more secret, unsensational, almost hidden under the cloak of secular affairs, visible only to the eye of faith.

The work of the Yahwist must be interpreted in the light of two basic facts: first the new-found recognition of the hidden activity of God in history, secondly the relevance of the ancient territorial claims to the time of David and later. We have already seen how God's control of history is depicted only in the form of a hidden guidance, a notion totally foreign to cultic thought. If we now read the remarkable conclusion of the Yahwist's work, the lists in Judges 1, we are at once aware of the relevance which these apparently remote memoranda of territorial history must have had for David's contemporaries and their successors.[108]

No one could read these stereotyped descriptions of the as yet unoccupied territories without reflecting that God had not in fact left the matter in this state of semi-fulfillment. He had continued his care for Israel and had kept all his promises, even though it was not in the time of Joshua, but not till in the time of David that this was to be seen. That is what the Yahwist's restrained mode of presentation actually invites us to read between the lines at the end of the work. A deuteronomist later expressed it in memorable terms, and—generalizing somewhat concerning the actual historical state of affairs—summed up the whole Hexateuch at the close of the Settlement in this memorable pronouncement:

> Thus Yahweh gave to Israel all the land which he swore to give to their father . . . and gave them rest on every side . . . *not one of all the good promises which Yahweh had made to the house of Israel had failed; all came to pass.* (Josh 21:43-44)

Concluding Observations

At this point we may break off our discussion of the problem of the form of the Hexateuch. Not that the conflation of E and P with J would now appear to be a simple process, nor one which could be altogether explained to one's satisfaction! The problem of the origin and purpose of these two works, their derivation, and the readers for whom they were destined, is as much an open question now as it was before, and will probably remain so. But these problems are generically different from the ones we have been dealing with in our present study. The process by which E and P are superimposed on J, as well as their relationship to one another, is a purely literary question, which adds nothing essentially new to the discussion so far as form-criticism is concerned. The form of the Hexateuch had already been finally determined by the Yahwist. The Elohist and the priestly writer do not diverge from the pattern in this respect: their writings are no more than variations upon the massive theme of the Yahwist's conception, despite their admittedly great theological originality.

The problem of the Elohist has recently been approached from several different angles. We shall add but a few words to this extensive discussion, and these will be exclusively concerned with our own form-critical standpoint. At one time there was a degree of unanimity regarding the point at which E begins. Quite recently, however, the well-known fact that the primeval history prior to P consists of two separate strands, which are still partially distinguishable, has been explained by Mowinckel as the result of a conflation of J and E.[109] An important factor in this line of argument is the belief that E must have included a primeval history: it is held to be inconceivable that the successor of J and forerunner of P should have differed from both so greatly as not to have begun his work with the creation of the world.[110]

This thesis must be decisively rejected. We have already seen that the expansion of the ancient form of the creed by the preparatory addition of a primeval history was a very great theological liberty taken by the Yahwist. Is it any wonder if a successor of the Yahwist felt himself to be under a greater obligation to the form that had been hammered into the religious consciousness of the nation by centuries of traditions?

Furthermore, it has always been pointed out as a characteristic of the Elohist that he is "bound by tradition." He is "more firmly tied to the traditional material of the ancient sagas than he is to the literary and artistic innovations of his predecessors."[111] The Elohist therefore takes a less sharply differentiated theological line, and presents far fewer theological problems than does the Yahwist. He is more nationalistic, and for this reason his presentation, although later in date from a literary point of view, has always been considered more archaic. It is thus no accident that there is no primeval history in E; the Elohist has preserved the ancient Settlement tradition more faithfully than the theologically bolder J writer, not only in the constituent materials but also with regard to the traditional forms embodied in the main structure of his work.

We agree with Mowinckel that E cannot have begun at Gen 15:1, and that there must have been some sort of account of Abraham's antecedents by way of introduction. We must, in fact, suppose that the Elohistic source was abridged when it was combined with J, J having already given an account of Abraham's migration and of what first befell him in Canaan. Galling has made the illuminating suggestion that a reference to Abraham's migration is still preserved in Gen 15:1ff. He holds that this dialogue originally preceded the migration to Canaan, and records Abraham's complaint that he must set out childless on his way: *we'anokî holek 'erîrî.*[112]

The points put forward by Noth in his commentary on Joshua give rise to another consideration.[113] Noth declares himself very skeptical of the identification of the collector of the Gilgal sagas with the writer of one of the pentateuchal sources; more weight should be given, he feels, to the distinctive character of the material deriving from this cycle of tradition. He therefore urges that the literary problem of the Book of Joshua should so far as possible be dealt with quite apart from the results of pentateuchal source-criticism.[114] But are not the problems of the tradition and of the material too closely interwoven at this point with the literary problem? No one will deny the distinctive character of the material of the Gilgal cycle of sagas; yet in the form in which we have it, its ancient etiological interests are consistently brushed aside. All the sagas are quite simply held together by the one common factor of relationship to the Settlement tradition, and it cannot reasonably be claimed that this literary composition has a separate identity distinct from the pentateuchal sources. Can it be seriously thought that this collection of narratives, built up as it is from ancient saga-material, *began* with the reconnaissance of Jericho?

What we must protest against is the isolation of the literary problems of the Book of Joshua from the overall problem of the Hexateuch, whose sources represent one single whole from the point of view of form. In other words, we must consider not merely the literary problem of J and E, but also (what is much more important) the problem of their *genre* with regard to form. We must then ask what the Elohist meant to show us when he brought his work to a close in the books of Numbers and Deuteronomy. We believe, and Noth does not appear to contest this, that the work of the Elohist can be discerned right through from Genesis to Deuteronomy. If that is so, his Settlement story must have had its own conclusion; otherwise we should prefer to accept Rudolph's theory as being more logically demonstrable.[115]

The point of view that we have taken in the present study shows the priestly writer in a quite distinctive light. If we recall what was said concerning the wholly non-cultic, almost secular manner in which the Yahwist portrayed God's activity in history, we are at once aware of the fundamental difference here. The priestly writer aims at the validation of sacral institutions. He provides the theological guarantee of these institutions, important as they are for his own day; and he does so by making a historical survey, in the course of which he gives an account of those revelations and ordinances connected with the history of redemption which correspond to the rites, usages, and beliefs he wishes to validate. The whole tradition, with all its constituent elements, is thus brought back by P within the ambit of the cultus.

In P, however, there now flourishes a mode of sacerdotal cultic thought that is quite new compared with that which obtained in the ancient cultic traditions before they were appropriated by the Yahwist. To put the matter crudely, the priestly writings are distinguished from the latter by the absence of any kind of religious naiveté. The material has been worked over in the light of a theological conception of truly great proportions, and the whole picture from the creation of the world to the erection of the tabernacle at Shiloh[116] has been included in its purview.

Unlike the older cultic material, the Priestly Code shows an interest in validating sacral institutions that is not confined to the legitimation of any one usage. P, in fact, takes an overall view of history, in which God's redemptive activity is revealed at every stage. This means, however, that the priestly writer must accept fully, in his own way, that decisive recognition of the purposeful activity of God in history that characterizes J, as well as J's arrangement of the materials. Judged by the Yahwist's standards, there is a sense in which both E and P can be said to represent a retrograde movement. J's presentation of the case was altogether necessary to the religious life of the Old Testament, but neither could nor was intended to abrogate the divinely appointed cultic institutions of Israel. The priestly writings are swayed by a quite unmistakable desire to restore, a fact which accords well with the assumption that they arose in the period of restoration between Josiah and Ezra.

The Hexateuch achieved its present form at the hands of *redactors,* who received the testimony to the faith contained in each of the source documents at its own valuation, and held it to be binding. No doubt the Hexateuch in its complete and final form makes great demands upon the understanding of its readers. Many ages, many men, many traditions, and many theologians have contributed to this stupendous work. The Hexateuch will be rightly understood, therefore, not by those who read it superficially, but only by those who study it with a knowledge of its profundities, recognizing that its pages speak of the revelations and religious experiences of many different periods. *None of the stages in the age-long development of this work has been wholly superseded; something has been preserved of each phase, and its influence has persisted right down to the final form of the Hexateuch.* Only a recognition of this fact can prepare one to hear the plenitude of the witness which this work encompasses.

We have seen, however, how the extraordinary complexity of the various elements was time and again rigorously subordinated to the interest of the one simple leading conception of the Settlement in Canaan. The chief purpose of this work, indeed, was to present in all its biblical and theological significance this one leading conception, in relation to which all the other conceptions of the Hexateuch assume an ancillary role.

From the creation of the world onwards, what a remarkable road, what vicissitudes, what a wealth of divine ordinances and plans lead to this one goal—the Settlement! But then the Hexateuch is not solely concerned with the religion of Israel, nor even with claiming for God all human allegiance; it aims to lay a foundation for God's kingdom on earth, and to lay it on the bedrock of all human existence.

2

The Promised Land and Yahweh's Land
in the Hexateuch

In the whole of the Hexateuch there is probably no more important idea than that expressed in terms of the land promised and later granted by Yahweh, an idea found in all the sources, and indeed in every part of each of them. It is the patriarchs who receive this promise. They already dwell in the land, but it is a land in which they are still sojourners. Between the promise and its fulfillment stands the age of Moses, an age in which reassurances are given and threats are made primarily in relation to this great ideal of the promised land. The time of Joshua is the time of fulfillment, when Israel takes possession of the land and divides it among the tribes. Yet an examination of this conception that so evidently dominates the Hexateuch seems, oddly enough, never to have been made. In view of the limited space available, only a quite brief rough survey of the subject can be attempted here. To provide a working basis for our investigation let us try first of all to fix the phraseology and terminology in which the conception is clothed.

First in importance we must place the oath made to the early patriarchs, i.e., the promise of the land, and formal references to this promise of the type: "the land which I swore to give to Abraham, to Isaac, and to Jacob." They are as follows: Genesis 12:1-3 (progeny, blessing); 12:7 (land); 13:14-16 (land, progeny); 15:5 (progeny); 15:7 (land); 15:18 (land); 18:4-8 (progeny, land, new relationship to God); 17:19 (70) (progeny, new relationship to God); 18:10 (progeny); 22:17 (blessing, progeny); 24:7 (land); 26:3 (land); 26:4 (progeny, land); 26:24 (blessing, progeny); 28:3ff. (progeny, land); 28:13-15 (land, progeny, blessing); 32:13 (blessing, progeny); 35:9-12 (progeny, land); 46:3 (progeny); 48:4 (land, progeny); 48:16 (blessing, progeny); 50:24 (land); Exod 6:4-7 (land, new relationship to God); 13:5 (land); 32:13 (land, progeny); 33:1 (land); Num 10:29 (land); 14:23 (land); 32:11 (land).

Deuteronomy understands the oath to the early patriarchs only as a promise of the land: Deut 6:18, 23; 8:1, 18; 9:5, 27; 10:11; 11:8-9, 18-21; 26:3, 15; 28:11; 31:7, 20; 34:4 (JE) (land); Josh 1:6 (land); 5:6 (land); Judg 11:1 (land).

Stylistically the phrase varies considerably. Sometimes it is in the first person, sometimes it is spoken by human beings in the third person; nor is it always described as an oath. For our purpose, however, this is not significant. We shall discuss later the fact that the promise of the land is very often linked with other promises.

The word *'ereṣ* (land) is too lacking in definition for the purpose of our investigation, but among the particularly characteristic terms, there is a word *naḥalah* (possession), which is especially prominent. The occurrences are to some extent ambiguous. In the older sources, J and E, the word first of all describes of course the hereditary land of the clan (Gen 31:14; Num 16:14; Josh 24:28, 30, 32). Besides this, however, J and E evidently use the term of the hereditary possession of a tribe, as at Josh 13:7, 14; 14:9, 13-14; 18:2, 4, 7. The term occurs more frequently in P, but has a basically similar application. It denotes the hereditary possession of a clan at Num 16:14; 27:7; 34:14; 36:2ff.; Josh 19:49.

The headings or conclusions of lists speak of the "inheritance" of members of tribes "according to their families" (Josh 13:23; 16:5; 18:28; 19:1-2; 10:40).[1] This phrase automatically presupposes that there can be an "inheritance" of a tribe, and P uses the word in this sense, too: e.g., Num 18:21, 24; 17:62 (Levi); 26:53-54, 56; 36:3; Josh 14:2; 17:4, 6; 19:51. It is not certain that P also knew of an "inheritance" for Israel. Occasionally he speaks of the Israelites to whom the land will fall "for an inheritance," e.g. Num 34:2; 32:18; but this ought to be interpreted in a different sense.

Joshua 11:23; 13:6; 23:4 are deuteronomic. It is in fact the salient characteristic of the deuteronomist that he speaks almost exclusively of the inheritance of Israel (4:21, 38; 12:9; 15:4; 19:10; 20:16; 21:23; 24:4; 25:19; 26:1). Only in a few particular instances does Deuteronomy use the word *nḥlh* of the hereditary land of a tribe: in the case of Reuben, Gad and the half-tribe of Manasseh at 3:18 and 29:7, and in the case of Levi at 10:9; 12:12; 14:27, 29; 18:1ff.[2] At these points the deuteronomist was evidently tied to fixed terminology, and was obliged to deviate from his own specific use of terms. If we look back, we see what a mass of evidence exists in the texts, apart from Deuteronomy, for the use of the term *nḥlh* in connection with the division of the land.

We must not, of course, lose sight of the difficulties which preclude any clear-cut division between sources, especially in the Book of Joshua; on the other hand we must realize that the fact that an occurrence belongs to a particular source is not of decisive significance for our particular investigation, for the priestly writer was especially concerned to adjust the terminology of the older material. The distinctive force of this evidence is not seen in this matter, but rather in certain theological and dogmatic conceptions which are in themselves comparatively easily demonstrated.

The picture as we have seen it was on the whole a uniform one: the term *nḥlh* applied originally to the hereditary lands of both families and tribes. The usage concerning *tribal* lands is manifestly original, and is not due to an extension of the notion of the *family* inheritance which is equally original. The extra-hexateuchal use of the term provides strong early evidence for the *nḥlh* of a tribe (Judg 18:1; 21:23).

On the negative side, it is striking that neither in ancient texts, nor in archaistic literature such as P, do we hear of a *nḥlh* of Israel as a whole. That is clearly a peculiarity of Deuteronomy.

Finally it is important to observe that there is no instance in the Hexateuch of the notion found often enough elsewhere in the Old Testament (1 Sam 26:19; 2 Sam 14:16; Jer 2:7; 16:18; 50:11; Ps 68:10; 79:1) that the land is Yahweh's "inheritance" (*nḥlh*).[3] This point, too, is one to which we shall have to return later.

There are three further terms, of less importance than the one just mentioned, to which we wish to draw attention:

(1) *gôral*, prominent in the priestly writer's account of the division of the land in the sense of "lot" (Num 26:55ff.; 33:54; 34:13; Josh 14:2; 15:1; 16:1; 17:1; 18:11; 19:1, 10, 17, 24, 32, 40, 51, used of the apportionment of the land to tribes by lot). So, too, in JE (Josh 18:6, 8, 10); only in the chapter concerning the Levites (Joshua 21, P) is apportionment by lot to families spoken of (Josh 21:4, 5, 6, 8, 10, 20). The word is found already in JE in the extended sense of "a share of the land" (Josh 17:14-17; Judg 1:3 (of the portion belonging to a tribe) as also in P (Num 36:3) (of the portion belonging to a family).

(2) *ḥeleq*, used of the portion of land belonging to a tribe in JE (Josh 18:5-6, 7, 9; 19:9) and in P (Josh 14:4; 15:13; Num 18:20 (of Aaron); it is used in D only of the landlessness of Levi (Deut 10:9; 14:27; 18:1; 12:12).

(3) *ḥebel*, used in the sense of "share of the land" belonging to a tribe: Josh 17:14; 19:9 (JE); 17:5 (P).

A few problems are raised by this brief review of the facts to which we must now give our attention.

First, precisely how are we to understand the oath to the early patriarchs, and what is its content? It was evidently the contribution of the Yahwist to fuse the whole complex of the patriarchal sagas together. This time of promise corresponds with the age of Joshua, the time of entry into the promised land, and the division of the land marks the time of fulfillment of the promise. This is the theological pattern decisively stamped upon the whole Hexateuch. All later modifications of the pattern (E, P) are of trifling significance compared with this one basic idea which was retained unaltered.

The cultic creed of Deut 26:5ff., however, according to whose outline of the redemptive history the Yahwist constructed his great work, as yet knows nothing of this great motive with all its tension between promise and fulfillment.[4] The question therefore arises, where did the Yahwist find this new element? How did he come to include the whole mass of patriarchal sagas within the scheme of the promise of land in this way? Alt has given us the answer in his book on the God of the patriarchs: it is because the promise of the land is an original element of the pre-Mosaic cultus of the God of the patriarchs.[5]

Here we are in the presence of very oldest tradition. The God of the patriarchs had already promised possession of the land to the ancestors of Israel when they lived in tents on the edge of the settled territory, a fact which is quite clearly shown by the saga which has come down from that time almost intact (Gen 15:7ff.).

Now it is true that the Yahwist has put this extremely ancient element of patriarchal religion on a much broader basis in his own work, and indeed has introduced it even into sagas in which it originally had no place; but the notion itself is certainly not to be thought of as a new element introduced by the Yahwist. What is new is rather that the ancient promise of the God of the patriarchs is now brought into relationship with the settlement under Joshua; for this promise of the land made by the God of the patriarchs was originally quite direct and simple in its application, and certainly did not envisage a fresh emigration from the land and a second entry into it.[6]

In J, however, the promise of the land made to the patriarchs points towards its fulfillment in the age of Joshua; its direct application is disrupted in a remarkable manner, and thus there arises the peculiar dialectical relationship of the patriarchs to the promised land, i.e., to the fulfillment of the promise they had received. The land was granted to them by virtue of a divine oath, but they do not yet possess it: it is still the land of their sojourning. When the ancient promise is fulfilled by the settlement of the Israelite tribes under Joshua, the notion of the promise is still further extended so as to include the greater Israel; for it applied originally only to the smaller association of worshipers of this patriarchal deity, and not to the whole of Israel.

We are now in a position to assess the order of priority of the various elements within the promise. On the face of the matter our survey showed that the promise of land predominated decisively here; and if this was not altogether the chief constituent it was certainly the most prominent among the various elements which were handed down through the ages. The promise of innumerable progeny may have been in some way co-ordinate with it, but in the hexateuchal documents it not unnaturally lost some of its relevance once an account had been given of the birth of the nation in Egypt. When however the priestly writer now adds to the substance of the promise, "I will be your

God" (Gen 17:7, 8, 19 [LXX]; Exod 6:7), this strongly suggests a projection of the Sinai tradition into the earlier narrative; for the phrase, "I am your God, you are my people," is the exact formula of the Sinai covenant (cf. Deut 26:16-19; 29:11-12; Lev 26:12; Jer 31:33) of which, naturally, only the first half can find a place in patriarchal history.

The most telling account of the promise to the patriarchs is, of course, that of Gen 12:1-3, a text which does not depend upon ancient tradition and which was in fact inserted by the Yahwist himself to explain his point of view.[7] It is a striking fact that in this statement, compounded as it is of so many of the elements of the promise, it is the promise of the land which is missing. We must, however, remember that the Yahwist wished to present the promise as a test of faith for Abraham.[8] Only when he has been tested in blind obedience to God does he receive the promise that he will possess the land (Gen 12:7). The promise of the land is thus to some extent kept apart from the great pronouncement in which God declares His purpose, but by virtue of this special treatment it actually gains in importance.

It must be stressed that it is the linking together of the promise of the land and its ultimate fulfillment, with all the tensions this involves, which gives to the Hexateuch as a whole its distinctive theological character. But is this notion all that the Hexateuch has to say of the promised land, theologically speaking?

"The land is mine; you are only strangers and sojourners with me" (Lev 25:23). This one sentence opens up immense possibilities. What new realm of ideas have we entered here? The saying has evidently nothing in common with that promise of possession of the land which runs right through the Hexateuch from the time of the early patriarchs. In no single instance is the land which is promised to the patriarchs and apportioned by Joshua referred to as "Yahweh's land." On the contrary, it is the land which formerly belonged to other nations, and has now been given by Yahweh to his people in the course of a series of historical events.

Alt has shown that the fundamental notion expressed in Lev 25:23 is very ancient, and had cultic significance in ancient Israel.[9] It was as a primary consequence of this basic conception that the great sacral sabbatic year was appointed. Proclaimed at the Feast of Booths in the seventh year (Exod 23:10-11; Lev 25:1ff.), it was an outward visible sign of Yahweh's real and unique ownership of the land.[10] Earth and soil were not tribal property in our sense of the word, but were granted to the clan by Yahweh as a fief which they were to cultivate. The parcel of land thus let out for the time being for cultivation was apportioned to the individual by lot, and was known as a *nḥlh*, *ḥlq* or, by the extension of linguistic usage, simply as a *gwrl* or *ḥbl*.

We have very little information about the details. Probably, as in present-day Palestine, private freehold existed alongside the common land apportioned by lot.[11] The *nhlh*, in which the family grave was situated, was undoubtedly a hereditary possession of the family from generation to generation, and obviously was not affected by the casting of lots (Josh 24:30, 32). Concerning the technical aspect of the matter, too, the Old Testament gives no precise information. It says only "the lot was cast" (Josh 18:6), "it came out" (e.g., Josh 16:1; 17:1), "the measuring-lines were cast" (Mic 2:5), "they fall" (Josh 17:5; Ps 16:6).[12]

It would be of even greater interest to us to know the significance which *nhlh* came to bear when used of a tribe, and whether the tribe, too, acquired it by virtue of a cultic act.

Alt has given us an insight into the conception of the territorial claims of the tribes—those very ancient and highly theoretical claims of particular tribes to particular areas.[13] Is it not probable that these claims derive from sacral dispositions, which from time to time were revised, and newly promulgated with binding force, from the cultic center of the Yahwistic amphictyony? The manifestly very ancient report of the hardship caused to the Josephites by the apportionment of too circumscribed an area (Josh 17:14-18) at least gives us cause to surmise that there was some such procedure. At all events the usage of terms in the Hexateuch leaves no room for doubt about the existence of a firmly based concept of tribal territory, *nhlh*. Passages such as Num 36:3 or Josh 17:5 show conclusively that the tribe was the trustee of the *nhlh*, and held the ultimate title to the land over and above the family.

We must of course reckon with the possibility of late generalizations on this matter, especially in the case of the priestly writer; nobody would accept as historical the account of the apportionment of tribal territories by a lot at Shiloh. Nevertheless the obstinately persistent use of the term *nhlh* to denote tribal lands must in the last resort derive from quite concrete relationships and conceptions, even though these are no longer intelligible to us.

Returning to the statement that the land is Yahweh's possession, it should now be added that of course all the cultic statements about the harvest which are codified up and down the Hexateuch also belong to the same complex as this conception; for the laws concerning firstlings (Exod 23:19; 34:26; Lev 19:23ff.; 23:10),[14] tenths (Exod 22:28; Num 18:21ff.; Deut 14:22; 26:12ff.), the leaving of gleanings (Lev 19:9ff.; 23:22), and so on, in so far as they fall within the context of Yahwistic religion, are certainly to be interpreted in the light of the belief that Yahweh is the real owner of the land and therefore claims "a recognition of his right of ownership"[15] from human beings.

Here, too, we should mention the proscriptions of any kind of cultic defilement of the land. Foreign territory is not Yahweh's territory, and is therefore unclean: it is the domain of other gods (1 Sam 26:19; Hos 9:3-4; Amos 7:17). Defilement of the land seems only to have been occasioned by sexual offences, and by unburied dead bodies (Lev 18:25-29; 19:29; 20:22-24; Deut 21:22ff.;

24:4)—apart from idolatry, which brings into particular relief the cultic relationship between Yahweh and the land. The conceptions that underlie the narrative of Joshua 22 are especially noteworthy, although it is very difficult to fix the date of the component parts of this narrative. Here the tribes living to the east of the Jordan express the fears that they or their children might be denied their "portion in Yahweh" (*ḥeleq baYahweh*) on the grounds that they live beyond the Jordan. It is even held to be debatable whether this land may not be unclean, in contradistinction to the land west of the Jordan, which is in this context expressly designated "Yahweh's land" (*'aḥuzzath Yhwh*) (v. 19).

One cannot help thinking of the apportionment of the land to the tribes in Ezekiel 48, based as it is on rigidly dogmatic principles, which leaves the land east of the Jordan completely out of account. It must remain an open question whether this passage was governed by late doctrinal considerations, or whether, on the contrary, it preserved recollections of a quite ancient belief that originally the proper area for Israelite tribal settlement was the land west of the Jordan, the land east of the Jordan being by contrast only secondary "colonial" territory.[16]

These considerations will already have given some idea of the far-reaching implications for Hebrew religion of the conception that the land belongs to Yahweh. It is now quite clear that this notion is of a totally different order from that of the promise of the land to the early patriarchs. It is a wholly cultic notion, as compared with the other which may be characterized as the historical conception.[17] Leaving aside Josh 22:19, it can be said that the cultic conception is foreign to the whole atmosphere of the hexateuchal narrative proper, which is governed throughout by the historical outlook (i.e., the promise of the land to the patriarchs, looking forward according to the theological scheme of the creed to the age of Joshua). By contrast, hexateuchal *legislation* is covered by cultic conceptions right down to the latest doctrinal laws such as that of the Jubilee year.

It might be asked at this point whether this cultic complex of ideas may not originally derive from Canaanite sources, as against the historical conception which is undoubtedly an ancient Yahwistic one. If this were so, would it not explain the existence of two different strands in the theological attitude to the land? In the religion of the baalim, Baal is above all the lord of the land and the giver of all blessings.

This line of argument cannot, however, be sustained. The notion that Yahweh is the true owner of the land can be traced back to the very oldest commandments of Yahweh, and was evidently current at a time when syncretism with the features of Canaanite religion had not even begun to appear. It would obviously be wrong to say that Canaanite beliefs exerted no influence at all on the theological conception of the land in the Hexateuch; but this influence was exercised in a different direction. Among Others, it is to be found in the emphatic portrayals of Yahweh's blessing on the land. Even the saying that the land "flows with milk and honey" may be of this kind. Above all, however, there are the descriptions of an almost paradisal blessing on human progeny, on the offspring of the cattle, on basket and kneeding-trough, the fruit of the fields, rain for the earth, peace, deliverance from wild animals, and so on (Lev 26:3-12; Num 13:23, 28; 14:7-8; 24:3ff.; Deut 28:2-7, 11-12); these descriptions would surely seem to have been composed under the influence of Canaanite nature-religion.

There remains yet one further topic to be dealt with. Although we said that the theological statements in the Hexateuch concerning the land derive from two basically quite distinct viewpoints, these two viewpoints did not remain separate. The account of the division of the land among the tribes is expressed in terms of conceptions and attitudes that come from the realm of cultic ideas.

There are two reasons why the historical conception should be overlaid in this way by cultic notions. First it results from taking over ancient documents and texts which themselves originally derive from cultic circles. Secondly, in the course of developing the historical conception the hexateuchal sources have borrowed terminology from the cultic background (cf. the present use of *nḥlh, gwrl, ḥlq*). This is, of course, a fairly superficial phenomenon, which was made possible by the fact that these terms gradually became generalized in meaning and lost their distinctive connotation. The notion that Yahweh owns the land and that Israel is thus Yahweh's vassal nowhere appears in the hexateuchal narrative on anything like an equal footing with the dominating historical conception.

Among the hexateuchal source-documents it is, of course, the great theological compositions of P and D that give the greatest prominence to the land and to the Settlement. The priestly writer has developed the theological outline into a highly complex system. The patriarchal period, as the period in which the promise is made, looks forward to the age of Moses and Sinai as well as to the time of Joshua and the Settlement. The age of Moses is associated with the newly revealed relationship with God, a relationship realized by cultic means; the time of Joshua brings with it the Settlement, as the fulfillment of the oath made to the early patriarchs. The fact that the fulfillment of the divine promises was now divided, however, might have constituted a threat to the very existence of the progeny of Abraham, now grown to nationhood: how could this nation maintain its life when it still had no land of its own?

At this point the story of the manna is introduced. The manna is but a foretaste of the blessing which will sustain the nation after the Settlement, and immediately after the crossing of the Jordan, while Israel is encamped at

Gilgal, the manna ceases and the people eat the produce of the land (Josh 5:10-12).

P has also defined, and in exact terms, the relationship of the patriarchs to the promised land. They already live in the land, but as yet it is only promised to them. They do not possess it: it is the "land of their sojourning" (Gen 17:8; 28:4; 36:7; 37:1; 47:1; Exod 6:4). But are the patriarchs to be thought of as having only this unfulfilled relationship to the land, a relationship that was to be so strangely interrupted? Were they in truth chosen by God to receive the promise, and yet must die before it was fulfilled? In this connection the narrative of Genesis 23 concerning the purchase of the first plot of land is especially significant: the patriarchs did in fact possess a small strip of the land, their burial-place, as an earnest of the remainder. In their death they were no longer sojourners in "Hittite" territory, but had already a share in the fulfillment of the promise.

With regard to Deuteronomy, it must be clearly understood from the outset that by the very nature of its form it presents a quite different picture from those outlines of the history of redemption which grow out of the historical creed. Deuteronomy develops into finished form the tradition of the Shechemite festival of renewal of the covenant, in the course of which the congregation was put under oath to keep the commandments of Yahweh.[18] Accordingly one might expect the notion of the land promised by Yahweh to have no place in Deuteronomy, since it was wholly foreign to the Shechemite tradition.

On the contrary, however, Deuteronomy is dominated from beginning to end by the idea of the land which is to be taken in possession. It forms the theme both of the laws and of the paraenetic discourse; our very first observation was that Deuteronomy has fused together in a most intimate way the promise of the land made to the early patriarchs and the tradition of the commandments given at Mt. Sinai. The deuteronomic commandments have no other purpose in view than that of laying down the new style of cultus and the new way of life for the radically altered circumstances arising from the Settlement. "When you come into the land which Yahweh your God gives to you, then you shall . . ."

Throughout Deuteronomy, commandments are laid down in these or similar terms (Deut 12:1; 17:14; 18:9; 19:1; 21:1; 26:1). It is nevertheless striking that alongside this presentation of the commandments there is another one, in which the commandments are not seen as the norm of the new life in settled territory, but in which compliance with the commandments is the condition on which the land may be received and possessed. Israel is to observe the commandments *in order that* he may enter the good land, or may have long life in the land which Yahweh is going to give him (Deut 4:25-26; 6:18; 8:1; 11:8-9,

18-21; 16:20). Does not the promise of the land in this conditional form pave the way for a declension from grace into law? At all events, Deuteronomy reflects a substantially more advanced situation than that envisaged by the priestly writer, for whom the land remains a pure gift of God.

This marked difference of outlook from the older traditions is also to be seen in the linguistic usage of the term *nhlh*. In this matter, too, Deuteronomy has broken free from the traditional derivation, and has built up a new conception on a broader basis, that of the "inheritance of Israel" (*nhlt yiśrael*).[19] It is clear that this usage of the term to denote Israelite territory as a whole has no foundations whatever in any ancient institution, but must be accounted a late innovation in the interests of a dogmatic theory. Yet it must be emphasized that in making this innovation Deuteronomy is following a course already adumbrated by the older hexateuchal sources. As early as J, the promise of the land made by the God of the patriarchs was associated with the Settlement by all Israel under Joshua. The priestly writer, by imposing his own pattern on the account of the Settlement and the division of the land, gave even weightier expression to this idea of the "greater Israel."[20] But his presentation of the matter was still not thorough enough, as it still speaks only of tribal territories, and regards the whole territory of the "greater Israel," which is really what it has in mind, only as the sum of these tribal territories, *nhlwt*. It is only the deuteronomist, who, by breaking with the older conception and introducing a quite new linguistic usage, gives adequate expression to the notion of the land of Israel as a unified whole.[21]

We do not know whether the remarkable conception of a still greater expansion of this territory (Deut 12:20; 19:8) is related to historical events, or whether it rests on a haggadic, theological exposition of older texts already found in Deuteronomy. Entry into the promised land brings the nation rest (*menûhah*), a benefit first mentioned in this connection in Deuteronomy (Deut 12:9; 15:19; 28:65), which thenceforth assumes considerable significance in the deuteronomic literature.[22] The expression implies above all a quite literal cessation of the tribulations experienced during the desert wanderings, and a condition of peace under Yahweh's protection for the now sedentary people of Israel.

As a literary work, however, Deuteronomy certainly dates from a time subsequent to the Settlement, and it is therefore only by a singular kind of fiction that it takes Israel back to Horeb once again: Israel has in fact long been dwelling in the promised land, and we must therefore see a clear eschatological thread running through the whole work. All the benefits of which it speaks, and in particular the state of "rest" which is the sum of them all, are set before the assembly once again as a promise made to those who decide for Yahweh.

Here we come face to face with one of the most interesting problems of Old Testament theology: promises which have been fulfilled in history are not thereby exhausted of their content, but remain as promises on a different level, although they are to some extent metamorphosed in the process. The promise of the land itself was proclaimed ever anew, even after its fulfillment, as a future benefit of God's redemptive activity; but to demonstrate this fact it would be necessary to adduce extra-hexateuchal evidence, and the problem thus lies outside the scope of the present study.

3

Faith Reckoned as Righteousness

"He believed Yahweh; and he reckoned it to him as righteousness."
(Gen 15:6)

The present study will not be concerned with the solution of the well-known difficulties posed by Genesis 15, which are predominantly prob-lems of literary criticism, but is intended only as a contribution towards the understanding of v. 6 of this chapter. This verse is both the conclusion and the climax of a narrative that can be classed, but only just, as a saga. The dialogue between Yahweh and Abraham is supplied with the bare minimum of back-ground, and certainly owes much more to rigidly theological cogitation than to popular narrative tradition. The outcome of this theological reasoning is summed up in v. 6, which reads like a carefully balanced theological formula.

Here we come to our problem: how precisely ought we to understand what we have referred to as the "theological" element here? Is it conceivable that the statement that faith is reckoned as righteousness arose wholly and solely from the reflections of a theologian? What is the derivation of the terms employed in this notable statement? Such a pronouncement concerning the relationship of man to God, above all so weighty a divine judgment on humanity as this, is inconceivable amongst the peoples of antiquity except on the basis of quite specific sacral traditions. But where are we to look for such traditions?

The verb *ḥšb* has an area of meaning expressed in English by the words "conceive of," "regard as," "reckon."[1] It also designated a process of thought that results in a value-judgment, but in which this value-judgment is related not to the speaker but to the value of an object.[2] The numerous occurrences that appear in more or less everyday speech are not of interest to us here, any more than the few instances taken from the conventional phrases of the cultus.

Leviticus 7:11ff. deals with the ritual minutiae of the offering of so-called "peace offerings" (*zebaḥ ha-šelamîm*). The flesh must be eaten on the day on which the sacrifice is made, and, if need be, on the following day. If, however, any of the flesh is not eaten until the third day,

> he who offers it shall not be accepted,
> neither shall it be reckoned to him,
> it shall be an abomination. (Lev 7:18b)

This is a case of a "reckoning" which is to be pronounced by the priest, rejecting the individual worshiper in circumstances of an exceptional nature, in which the priest is called on to pass a kind of cultic judgment on him; but in so doing he is acting as Yahweh's mouthpiece. In accepting or rejecting the sacrifice he is declaring in categorical terms the will of Yahweh. There is a similar statement in the law of the altar in the Holiness Code:

> If anyone does not bring it [i.e., the animal he has killed] to the door of the tent of meeting . . . blood-guilt shall be reckoned to that man. (*dam yeḥašeb*) (Lev 17:4)

Here, too, the word *ḥšb* denotes a declaratory act that the priest performs on behalf of Yahweh, although in this case it concerns a capital offence with regard to the cultus, for blood-guilt is to Yahweh the most heinous of all sins. Accordingly it attracts the extreme punishment, that of being "cut off from among the people." If at this stage we take a preliminary glance at Gen 15:6 and ask what terminology could be used to express the exact opposite of "blood-guilt" (*dam*), only one word out of the entire cultic and theological vocabulary of Israel seems applicable—the word "righteousness" (*ṣedaqah*).

A third reference to the priestly decision, expressed by the term *ḥšb* in Num 18:27, deals with the "reckoning" of the levitical offering. We pass over this occurrence since it has nothing substantially to add to what has been said.

Now that we have established the nature of the process that results in a cultic judgment, and occupies so important a place in the cultus, our next task must be that of applying our findings more widely by using the methods of form criticism. It must now be asked in what form the priestly decision was communicated to the worshipers. In the case of our first example, Lev 7:18, what did the priest actually say to the cultic worshiper? Anyone who has the slightest knowledge of the language of the linguistic forms of the Priestly Code will at once think of those peculiarly terse declaratory nominal sentences that occur so frequently in P. If, for instance, we take the law of leprosy in Leviticus 13, we see sufficiently clearly how the priest announced his finding in the stereotyped cultic phrase, "he is unclean" (*tame' hû'*) or "he is clean" (*tahôr hû'*). The endings of the various sections are particularly distinctive:

> (If) the priest finds from his examination that the eruption has spread in the skin, then the priest shall pronounce him unclean: It is leprosy (*ṣara'at hû'*). (Lev 13:8)

Many similar declaratory formulae are found in this collection of laws (e.g., Lev 13:17, 25, 28, 37, 44, 46). There is no doubt in these instances that the priest actually uttered these phrases, *ṣarath hû'* or *tahôr hû'*, as an authoritative pronouncement to the person concerned. If we turn from these phrases to the formally very similar pronouncements in the sacrificial law of Leviticus 1–5, we may reasonably regard these latter as the actual formulae with which the various sacrifices were acknowledged: "it is a burnt offering" (*'olah hû'*), "it is a gift-offering" (*minhah hû'*), "it is a sin-offering" (*hattat hû'*).[3]

To acknowledge that a sacrifice has been properly performed, however, is of course nothing more nor less than to "reckon" it to the worshiper. Yahweh has accepted it, and allows it to stand to the credit of the worshiper as a sacrifice. Here then is the answer to our question concerning the form of words which the priest pronounced over the sacrificial flesh in the case envisaged by Lev 7:18. He said, "It is an abomination; it will not be accepted (*piggûl hû' lo' yeraṣeh*), a sentence which is in fact attested word for word in Lev 19:7.

We may, however, approach this problem of cultic "reckoning" from another angle by enquiring into a quite different aspect of the Yahwistic cultus. Let us examine once again[4] the catechetical series of commandments in Ezek 18:5ff. It is certain that Ezekiel did not compile this series of commandments himself: the arrangement of these ten paragraphs is a cultic compilation, and Ezekiel incorporated this formulary into his theological argument.

> If he does not eat [sacrificial flesh] upon the mountains or lift up his eyes to the idols of the house of Israel, does not defile his neighbor's wife, or approach a woman in the time of her impurity, does not oppress anyone, but restores to the debtor his pledge, commits no robbery, gives his bread to the hungry . . .

But it is the conclusion of this text that alone is of interest to us here:

> He is righteous; he shall have his life.
> Ṣaddiq hû' hayoh yihyeh.

Here yet again we have a declaratory formula. It corresponds fairly closely in form with the promise of blessing that comes at the end of the "temple-gate liturgies." The series of commandments in Psalm 15 ends with the promise that "he who does these things shall never be moved" (Ps 15:5b), and that of Psalm 24 with the words: "He will receive blessing from Yahweh, and vindication from the God of his salvation" (Ps 24:5). Even the prophetic liturgy of Isaiah 33 follows the ancient cultic practice by adding a promise of blessing after proclaiming the commandments (Isa 33:16). Here it is of importance only as evidence that the declaratory apodosis of Ezek 18:9ff.: "he is righteous" (*ṣaddiq hû'*) was still a relic of the liturgical usage. It is true that the verb *hšb* (to reckon) does not appear in this text, but it is certainly to be understood. If we rephrased the text, might it not equally well read: It shall be reckoned to him as righteousness (*yeḥašeb lô ṣedaqah*)?

The difference between the declaratory formulae and the occurrences of the cultic term *hšb* is simply that the latter are found in directions to the priests, instructing them in the kind of tests they are to apply. The former prescribe the exact form of words on the declaration to be made to the worshiper.

Now that we have to some extent elucidated the antecedents of Gen 15:6 in Hebrew tradition, the full import of the Elohist's statement at last becomes plain. It is revealed as a polemical and indeed revolutionary declaration. The process of "reckoning" is now transferred to the sphere of a free and wholly personal relationship between God and Abraham. There is no cultic intermediary, no priest to speak as the mouthpiece of Yahweh. It is, indeed, a striking fact that the most important feature of cultic "reckoning"—the declaratory judgment pronounced to the worshiper—has altogether disappeared. The writer tells his reader that Yahweh has made the "reckoning," and in the present context it is evidently quite irrelevant whether or not Abraham was aware of the fact, and if so, how.

The most astonishing difference, however, is that the cultic "reckoning" depended on something done by the human worshiper, by way of sacrifice or specific obedience, and at all events in some active manner. Here, however, in a solemn statement concerning the divine purpose, it is laid down that it is *faith* that sets men on a right footing with God. Yahweh has disclosed his plan for the future, which is to make Abraham a great nation. Abraham has fully accepted this, has put his trust in Yahweh. Thus in Abraham's case faith was the supreme achievement of his whole life, although admittedly the writer does not use the word "faith" to mean "achievement" in the strict, legalistic sense of the word.[5] On the contrary, he says that only faith, which is the wholehearted acceptance of Yahweh's promise, brings man into a right relationship—that Yahweh "reckons" it to him.

As we said, this sounds polemical and revolutionary, and perhaps it was intended to be so. But it is also at least possible that our author lived at a time and place in which ideas and terminology which were formerly tied to the cultus had come to be used more or less unconsciously in such spiritualized contexts; when he coined this statement, therefore, any kind of polemic against cultic "reckoning" may have been far from his mind. If so, what is contrasted in Gen 15:6 with the cultic process of "reckoning" (brought about through a multiplicity of particular acts) is actually the whole process of the relationship between Yahweh and mankind. Above all, this process is subjective and inward-looking, so that the accent is now upon the inward and personal attitude of the worshiper.

There is no doubt that faith, in the Elohist's view, is a quite specific spiritual self-commitment of the human soul. For this reason man's whole inner consciousness, and his commitment to Yahweh, is now included in the process of vindication. The contrast between this and the Yahwistic passage concerning Abraham's covenant is altogether remarkable! Whereas the theophany of Gen 15:7ff. comes upon Abraham almost as a shock, so that even his physical vitality was reduced to its lowest ebb, and all the emphasis falls on the objective reality of the sealing of the covenant, in the Elohist's account everything centers upon the subjective attitude of Abraham to the promises of Yahweh!

4

The Joseph Narrative and Ancient Wisdom

The Joseph story is in every respect distinct from the patriarchal narratives that it follows. Whereas almost all the stories of Abraham and of Jacob are limited in length to twenty or thirty years, the four hundred or so verses of the Joseph narrative patently show it to be a document of quite a different literary form. Quite evidently it is not a "cycle" of sagas, that is, a catena of what were originally self-contained narrative units.[1] If we go on to compare the internal characteristics of the two, the differences become still more marked.

The stories about Abraham, Isaac, and Jacob consist of local, cultic saga-material brought together by the Yahwist or an even earlier writer under the heading of promises made to the forefathers of Israel with regard to the land and to their progeny. The Joseph narrative is a novel through and through, and the material is in no way associated at any point with genuine local traditions.[2] From the point of view of literary technique the Joseph story displays resources far beyond those of the ancient sagas—in the depiction of involved psychological situations, for example, or in the use of telling phrases in the course of action. In this respect it has affinities with the Court History of David (2 Samuel 6 to 1 Kings 2), and for this reason it may be taken for granted that it cannot have been written before the early part of the monarchic period.

There are, however, many factors that link the Joseph narrative even more closely with the spiritual outlook of this period. Gunkel himself remarked upon the delight in all things foreign which characterizes the Joseph story,[3] the enlightened interest in the customs and social structure of a distant nation, the magnificence of Pharaoh's court, the installation of the vizier, the storage of cereal crops, the mummification of dead bodies, and so on. The early monarchic period saw the abandonment of many patriarchal traditions, but it also saw a wholly new departure in spirituality, a kind of "enlightenment," an awakening of spiritual self-consciousness. Men became aware of their own spiritual and rational powers, and whole new dimensions of experience opened up before their eyes, inwardly as well as outwardly. They were dimensions of which the faith of their forefathers had taken no account.[4]

One of these new dimensions with which we have become familiar in the literature of the period is what might be called the anthropological factor, a concentration upon the phenomenon of man in the broadest sense, his potentialities and his limitations, his psychological complexity and profundity. A further step immediately dependent upon this one was the recognition of the fact that this human factor can and must be developed and educated. This was the underlying purpose of the earliest wisdom literature.[5] Such education, however, is impossible unless there exists some guiding patterns of humanity, even though it may not offer a final and definitive ideal of development. Ancient Israelite wisdom had such a pattern, and applied it in no uncertain manner. We shall try to point out some of its characteristics, for it is the purpose of this study to show that the Joseph narrative is closely related to the earlier wisdom writings as a manifestation of this educational ideal.

None would dispute the fact that this early wisdom literature belongs within the context of the royal court, and that its principal aim was to build up a competent body of future administrators. Joseph himself is an administrator, who became one by demonstrating to Pharaoh that he possessed the twin virtues of outspokenness and good counsel—precisely the qualities upon which the wisdom-teachers continually insist. To speak well at the decisive moment, to give sound advice in any and every contingency of state affairs, and so if possible to take his place among the king's entourage—such was the main aim of the education of the scribe.

> Do you see a man skilful in his work?
> He will stand before kings. (Prov 22:29)

As Ben Sira was later to say,

> Neglect not the discourse of the wise . . .
> For of them thou shalt learn instruction
> And how to minister to great men. (Sir 8:8)

It could equally well have been said in the days of Solomon. Let us cite but one out of the multitude of examples available in Egyptian literature:

> If you are a tried counselor who sits in the hall of his lord, gather your wits together right well. When you are silent, it will be better than teftef flowers. When you speak, you must know how to bring the matter

to a conclusion. The one who gives counsel is an accomplished man; to speak is harder than any labor.[6]

It would certainly be a mistake to see in these and many similar exhortations no more than a desire to impart a superficial gloss that would enable a young man to climb rapidly in his profession. If it were so, we could not properly speak of an educational ideal here. Yet the wise men present us with a very imposing and well-found pattern for human living, which in some respects has striking points of contact with the humanistic idea of antiquity.[7] They depict a man who by his upbringing, his modesty, his learning, his courtesy and his self-discipline has acquired true nobility of character. He is, let us say it at once, the image of Joseph! Joseph, as the writer of the narrative draws him, is the very picture of just such a young man at his best, well-bred and finely educated, steadfast in faith and versed in the ways of the world. The foundation on which such a character is built, as Joseph himself recognizes, is "godly fear"; and the fear of Yahweh is quite simply obedience to the divine law (Gen 42:18; Prov 1:7; 15:33).[8]

Theologically speaking this foundation is the most important factor in the whole educational program, for wisdom is not directed *towards* the cultus and *towards* divine revelation, but works outwards from them. Because it knows nothing of man's yearning for salvation, the program has a certain undogmatic flexibility of approach, and shows pronounced realism in its concern for that which is practicable. Concern for the absolute standards of divine law emerges with particular clarity in the story of Joseph's temptation by Potiphar's wife (Genesis 39), which brings to mind a vast area of wisdom-teaching on the subject of "strange women" (*nokrîyoth*).[9]

The narrative of Genesis 39 reads as if it had been devised expressly to illustrate the warnings of the wisdom writers (Prov 22:14; 23:27-28).[10] Another person concerning whom the wise men give a warning is the "hot-tempered man," the uncontrolled, passionate man whose exact opposite is to be seen in the "cool spirited," patient man (*qar rûaḥ*; Prov 17:27; 15:18; 16:32).[11]

> He who is slow to anger has great understanding, but he who has a hasty temper exacts folly. (Prov 14:29)

In his relationship with his brothers, Joseph is the very pattern of the man who can "keep silence," as described in Egyptian wisdom-lore. He is the "prudent man who conceals his knowledge" (Prov 12:23), and who "restrains his lips" (Prov 10:19). Above all, the "patient man" does not give way to his passions, and the writer intends us to be amazed at the extraordinary control that Joseph is able to exercise over his emotions (Gen 42:24; 43:30-31; 45:1). It must not be forgotten that this prohibition of any display of emotion[12] ran counter to the whole instinct of the ancient Hebrew. Israelite wisdom-writers refer to a self-controlled man as *mošel berûḥô,* and a "tranquil mind" such as he has (Prov 14:30) is a constructive force for good in the life of the community: "He who is slow to anger quietens contention" (Prov 15:18). Of whom is this truer than of Joseph? We may go yet further: even Joseph's magnanimity and his general forbearance from any kind of revenge find striking parallels in proverbial wisdom:

> Do not say, "I will do to him as he has done to me;
> I will pay the man back for what he has done." (Prov 24:29)

> Love covers all offences. (Prov 10:12)

To build up the whole man in this way is not the work of a night; such discipline is learned only in the hard school of humility (*'anawah*). That "humility comes before honor" and that "the reward of humility is riches and honor"—these are the lessons so richly illustrated in the first part of the Joseph story.

So much, then, for the educational ideal and the pattern of human living exemplified in the Joseph narrative, as compared with the teaching of early wisdom-literature. Let us now turn to the underlying theological presuppositions. Our case could not be regarded as proven if there were divergences between the Joseph story and the wisdom writings on this fundamental issue.

Early wisdom literature is notoriously sparing of strictly theological pronouncements, but so, too, is the Joseph narrative. There are only two passages which explicitly refer to the purposes of God. The first occurs in the recognition scene, when Joseph makes himself known and ascribes the past events to the guidance of God, who has brought all the vicissitudes they have suffered to a happy conclusion (Gen 45:5ff.). The same thought is still more pointedly expressed in the words, "You meant evil against me, but God meant it for good" (Gen 50:20). Here the problem of the relationship between human intentions and the divine control of events is still more keenly felt: God has all the threads firmly in his hands even when men are least aware of it. But this is a bare statement of fact, and the way in which God's will is related to human purposes remains a mystery. Thus the statements of what "you meant" and what "God meant" are in the last analysis irreconcilable.

Let us, however, compare Joseph's comments, both here and in Gen 45:8, with the dictum of Proverbs that "A man's mind plans his way, but Yahweh directs his steps" (Prov 16:9). Here, too, we have a statement that Yahweh controls all things, and also a sharply drawn contrast between human plans and the divine direction of affairs. The similarity of thought is most striking, and that it is not fortuitous is shown by the aphorism of Prov 19:21: "Many are the plans in the mind of a man, but it is Yahweh's purpose that will be established."

Just as in Joseph's dictum, the purposes of God and man are set over against each other, and the purposes of God prevail. As a final demonstration that this opposition between the divine economy and human intentions is a central issue in the theology of wisdom-writing, I quote the Egyptian Amenemope: "That which men propose is one thing; what God does is another" (*Amenemope* 19:16).[13] In each case the human purpose is expressed in the first sentence, the divine activity in the second, and in view of this similarity of form and content between the proverb of Amenemope and the comment made by Joseph it may well be asked whether the latter is not in fact a wisdom-saying which has been adapted to the purpose of the story: "You meant evil against me, but God meant it for good."

There is a further saying in the Book of Proverbs which is very closely related to this dictum from the Joseph story: "A man's steps are ordered by Yahweh, how then can man understand his way?" (Prov 20:24). The writer's bewilderment here contains an element of resignation that should not be overlooked. There is evidently another side to the wisdom-writers' impressive faith in the overriding providence of God, a side which manifests itself as a frank skepticism with regard to all human activity and purpose. The topic is too wide for discussion at this point. It cannot be denied, however, that even in the Joseph narrative a deep cleavage threatens to arise between divine and human purposes, and that human activity is so heavily fettered by the all-embracing divine control of events that it comes dangerously near to losing all significance whatever.

> No wisdom, no understanding, no counsel, can avail against Yahweh. The horse is made ready for the day of battle, but the victory belongs to Yahweh. (Prov 21:30-31)

In this remarkable passage, the whole doctrine is made explicit: Yahweh is wholly free to dispose of the issue as he will. What then remains for men to do? They can, and indeed must, make decisions and preparations, only to find that all their plans meet with an insuperable obstacle, and that all their wisdom comes to nothing against the will of Yahweh.

According to this doctrine, all early events are subject to a law that is wholly beyond the grasp of the human mind. "God's life is achievement, but man's is a denial," says Amenemope (19:14), expressing an attitude which is common both to the wisdom-sayings quoted above and also to the Joseph story; all of them regard the purposes of God as altogether hidden, incomprehensible and unfathomable. So long as there was present a divinely inspired interpreter, there was no danger in this. When, however, man is left alone with this uncompromising doctrine, we at once discern an undertone of despair in his questioning, "How can a man understand what his purpose is?" This is what has happened in Qoheleth (3:11; 7:24; 8:17), whose skepticism has its roots deep in the past.[14]

What place, then, ought we to assign to the Joseph story, both spiritually and with regard to the ancient traditions? It displays no historico-political interests, nor any cultic, etiological motive. It is equally devoid of any specifically theological interest in redemptive history. We can only say that the Joseph story, with its strong didactic motive, belongs to the category of early wisdom writing. Several consequences follow, which can only be lightly touched upon here.

First, with regard to wisdom writing as a whole, seen not simply as collections or proverbs but as a literary phenomenon, which from the beginning had an extremely wide spiritual scope: If the influence of wisdom was so significant over so wide a field of literature in ancient Egypt,[15] it would be very surprising if a similar state of affairs had not also prevailed in Israel. In that case, however, we must be prepared to reassess the Joseph story in the light of the possibility that it is closely related to contemporary Egyptian literature. There is, of course, no question of its being an Egyptian story, at all events in anything like its present form: it is far too clearly stamped as a story about a non-Egyptian, written for non-Egyptians. On the other hand it must certainly be presumed that Egyptian literary influences and models, even specific literary sources, all played their part in the formation of the Joseph narrative. It cannot be accidental that the Wisdom of Amenemope speaks of that same control of events by "God,"[16] with a similar emphasis on the fact that it is incomprehensible to man, which characterizes the history of Joseph.

The educational ideal of Amenemope, too, is one of discretion, modesty, self-control and deliberation,[17] the very qualities displayed by Joseph. If, further, we look for a close parallel to the narrative technique of the Joseph story, we shall find it pre-eminently in Egyptian stories such as the *Peasant's Lament*,[18] whose psychological realism is of a very similar type.

Finally, the whole question of the mythological background of the Joseph story calls for re-examination if we are to postulate the presence of Egyptian influence,[19] for we cannot exclude the possibility of such a background in the very early stages of the development of the narrative as we have it. It is a remarkable coincidence that the *Tale of the Two Brothers*, which has often been compared with the Joseph story, has recently been convincingly explained as deriving from mythological sources.[20]

In short, then, we may say that the Joseph narrative is a didactic wisdom story which leans heavily upon influences emanating from Egypt, not only with regard to its conception of an educational ideal, but also in its fundamental theological ideas.

5

There Remains Still a Rest
for the People of God

Among the many benefits of redemption offered to man by Holy Scripture, that of "rest" has been almost overlooked in biblical theology, despite the fact that, theologically speaking, it expresses a highly characteristic notion. In various books of the Old Testament, compiled at different periods, the belief is expressed that God will give, or has given, "rest" to his people. Let us first trace the idea in its most clearly defined form, in which God gives rest and his people receive it.

We first meet this promise of rest in Deuteronomy, theologically broadly based, yet expressed in clear, sharp outline:

> . . . you have not as yet come to the rest and to the inheritance which Yahweh your God will give you. (Deut 12:9ff.)

> Therefore when Yahweh your God has given you rest from all your enemies round about, in the land which Yahweh your God gives you for an inheritance to possess, you shall . . . . (Deut 25:19)

It is well known that Deuteronomy is unique in the Old Testament, in that it depicts the nation's situation here and now in the land of Canaan as the state of salvation. Deuteronomy does not turn its gaze to a distant future in which at last Israel may become God's people: at Mt. Horeb Israel is chosen as a complete nation, fully assembled at the time, and receives God's promise of the gift of the "pleasant land." It is emphasized that redemption is a present reality and that all Israel is the chosen people; and it is evident that this notion of the land that Israel is to inhabit, and which matches Israel's nationhood, is a theological conception of the highest order. No one who has read Deuteronomy need have any doubt of this. In this work the land is undeniably the most important factor in the state of redemption to which Israel has been brought, and on this basis the nation is to expect an additional gift from Yahweh—"rest from all enemies round about."

We must not spiritualize any of this: this "rest" (*menûḥah*) is not peace of mind, but the altogether tangible peace granted to a nation plagued by enemies and weary of wandering. It is also a direct gift from the hand of God. Deuteronomy therefore has no eschatological expectation of the kind known to the prophets. The state of salvation has been established by God by means of the covenant, and the characteristic message of Deuteronomy is that it still continues undiminished. The life of the chosen people in the "pleasant land," at rest from all enemies round about, the people owning their love for God and God blessing his people—this is the epitome of the state of the redeemed nation as Deuteronomy sees it.

The question is nevertheless rather more complicated than this, as will appear from what has already been said. In view of all the circumstances, we are bound to assume that Deuteronomy was not written before the Settlement, and probably not in fact until the late monarchic period. If that is so, we cannot avoid the conclusion that it nevertheless contains a latent element of expectation. Anyone who tries to put back the clock as does the deuteronomist, and forces Israel to think back to the time of its first election by God, bears witness in the boldest possible manner to the fact that God's covenant and faithfulness still holds sway over the nation. What is still more to the point, he asserts that even now there is still a promised blessing awaiting the chosen people.

This was indeed the basic premise of the deuteronomic theologians: Israel had indeed entered the promised land, but because they forgot Yahweh and clung to the cult of the baalim[1] the promises have not yet been fulfilled. Nevertheless, Yahweh has not revoked his covenant. Thus before our eyes a miracle of faith is performed: the intervening period, wasted as it has been by sin, is expunged from the record, and Israel is carried back again to the hour of its first election.[2]

This notion of "rest" now comes to occupy an important place in the religious thought of Israel. It is thought of as a rest found by a weary nation through the grace of God in the land he has promised them. In particular its echoes are heard throughout that massive historical work to which we apply the designation "deuteronomic" (from Genesis to 1 Kings),[3] although it certainly should not be attributed to the compilers of Deuteronomy because of important theological differences in its application. A considerable difference is to be seen at once: in this deuteronomic literature the rest which God has promised to his people is often spoken of as something which was accomplished in the past. Yet it is significant that in this great work the beginning of the divinely given rest is not uniformly represented, i.e., there is no one single starting point for it. On one occasion it begins in the time of Joshua, depicted in these beautiful words:

> And Yahweh gave to Israel all the land which he swore to give to their fathers . . . and Yahweh gave them rest on every side just as he had sworn to their fathers; not one of all their enemies had withstood them. . . . Not one of all the good promises which Yahweh had made to the house of Israel had failed; all came to pass. (Josh 21:43-45; compare Josh 1:13, 15; 22:4)

On another occasion it is David of whom it could be said that Yahweh had given him rest on every side (2 Sam 7:1, 11). Actually, the state of rest may be more truly ascribed to the time of Solomon than to any other. In the most solemn hour of Solomon's reign he can come before the people and point to the complete fulfillment of God's promise:

> Blessed be Yahweh, who has given rest to his people Israel, according to all that he promised; not one word has failed of all his good promise which he uttered by Moses his servant. (1 Kgs 8:56)

This uncertainty concerning the time at which the "rest" began is quite remarkable. Joshua, David, Solomon: it can be said of all of them that God gave rest to the nation in their day, and hence the gift of rest can no longer be something which happened once and for all. One gets the impression that someone who knew full well the deuteronomic saying about "rest" hesitated to apply this weighty notion to any one stage of the history to which he looked back. Who shall say that his hesitation was not justified? When in fact he *did* apply the notion to the historical account, it unexpectedly broke into three pieces: one could speak of divinely given rest (*menûḥah*) equally well in the case of Joshua, David, and Solomon. Did that not imply, therefore, that although substantially it was a position taken over from his predecessors, the position taken up by the deuteronomist could no longer be held against assault?

The Chronicler's historical compilation is of late literary date, but leans heavily on Deuteronomy, and at the point under discussion it shows even more clearly how far it has swung away from the real deuteronomic conception of "rest." "Rest from all enemies round about" is now a gift which God grants from time to time to pious kinds. Of course Solomon is a "man of peace" here, too (1 Chron 22:9); but, according to the statement of the Chronicler, God also gave rest to King Asa (2 Chron 15:15) and to Jehoshaphat (2 Chron 20:30). Between whiles, however, the book tells once more of bloodshed and strife and apostasy from Yahweh. The Chronicler has traveled a long way from the deuteronomic understanding of "rest," which was that God need give it once only in order to bring about a final condition of redemption. The deuteronomic witness to this state of salvation soared to the heights, but when it was subsequently applied to the past history of the nation the curve of its flight dipped sharply down to earth once more.

The remarkable thing, however, is that while this decline was taking place, quite a different trend was already gaining momentum unobserved. In this same work, where we cannot miss a feeling of anxiety lest the deuteronomic conception of "rest" should not be maintained in all its purity, Solomon is already being thought of as a "man of peace" ('îš menûhah; 1 Chron 22:9), in a quite new sense, the essential feature of which is not that the nation finds rest, but that God finds rest among his people!

> And now arise, O Yahweh God, and go to your resting place, thou and the ark of your might. Let your priests . . . be clothed with salvation . . . O Yahweh God, do not turn away the face of thy anointed one! Remember your steadfast love for David your servant. (2 Chron 6:41-42)

With this exalted messianic invocation Solomon brings to a close his long prayer at the dedication of the temple. What has happened to cause the Chronicler to modify so profoundly the significance of the Solomonic age in the history of God's dealings with his people?

In facing this problem it must first be said that there is no question whatever of this writer weakening his grasp of the significance of a historical event. He is less concerned than any other historical writer in the Old Testament to establish the facts of past history for their own sake; more than anyone else, when he speaks of sacred history, he speaks of issues that are of burning interest to himself and to his contemporaries. When he adds to the promise that the nation shall find rest, the further expectation that now God too may find rest among his people, it is *his* desire and *his* hope that he expresses.

This expectation, which is so to speak a stabilization of the nation's relationship to God, is taken in the form of a quotation from Psalm 132. In this psalm the thought of the intolerable situation which arises from the want of a permanent home for the ark becomes the material of a theological insight, and is developed into an expectation of a thoroughly eschatological kind, perhaps in the context of a cultic procession. The expectation is that now at last Yahweh will rise up and come to his resting-place amidst his people Israel; and in this passage the Chronicler found in a remarkable way precisely the authority he needed in order to build upon the notion of "rest" for the nation the further hope that Yahweh would come to dwell among his people. There is an excellent example of this combination of the two ideas in 1 Chron 23:25: "David said, 'Yahweh the God of Israel has given peace to his people and he dwells now in Jerusalem forever.'"

We have still to consider the passage from the Psalms on which is based the well-known discussion in the Epistle to the Hebrews. Halfway through Psalm 95 comes the cry:

> If only you would hearken to his voice today! Do not harden your hearts as at Meribah. . . . Your fathers tested me there. . . . I swore in my anger, "They shall not enter my rest." (95:7b-11)

This psalm is worthy of note in many respects, and especially so with regard to this "today," which offers a new hope of salvation set over against the one lost by the folly of those who took part in the desert wanderings. Further, we must notice in what terms the lost salvation is described. Yahweh says, "They shall not enter *my* rest." The saying depends, of course, upon the line of thought expressed in Deuteronomy; but that Israel could have entered *God's* rest—this is no longer deuteronomic! Neither is it the eschatological expectation of God's rest among his people. The subject of this transition from disturbance to rest is still the nation, but the resting place, if we may so call it, is now different: it is God's rest. Surely this does not refer to some eschatological benefit, but to a gift that Israel will find only by a wholly personal entering into its God.

It is in this form that the testimony of the Old Testament is taken over in the New Testament. The author of the Epistle to the Hebrews intends only to supply a commentary on it (Heb 3:7—4:13). He wishes to apply the words of the psalm to his readers' own situation: the "today," in which the psalm renews God's offer of rest, has dawned with the coming of Christ. The promise of entry into God's rest still stands. Needless to say, it is a new interpretation of this "rest" to regard it as an eschatological hope to which the believer attains only after this life.

If we think of the complex of ideas set out above as being the ultimate development of a considered biblical theology, we block up the channels of our own theological understanding of it. Nothing at all has developed—nothing, that is, if by development we mean that each succeeding link in the chain supersedes and exhausts the force of its predecessor. We have in fact seen that at the very point at which one could indicate something like a definite trend in the history of this conception, we could not avoid expressing anxiety lest the fullness of the original statement be lost. Let us rather call this a chain of witness in which both the overall plan and the particular mode of expression are governed pre-eminently by the insight of each living witness.

It is true, of course, that one of the links in this chain has so nearly approached the limit of what can be said under the old covenant that it has a peculiar claim to be regarded as a prooftext. Much as this outward and visible combination of the Old and New Testaments may commend this chain of evidence to the reader of the Bible, nevertheless the "fulfillment" of the Old Testament in the New Testament does not really depend simply on the quotations that are cited as prooftexts by the New Testament. It should in fact be said in this connection that the Old Testament idea of "rest" contains theological elements which are missing from the discussion in Hebrews 3, for it was by no means the intention of this passage to draw together at one focal point all the strands of Old Testament evidence.

The deuteronomist believes in the possibility of rest from adversaries ("Satans," 1 Kgs 5:4 [MT 5:18])[4] even in this present age. He believes in a situation in which the people of God find rest with God, just as a woman finds rest with her husband (Ruth 1:9); and this deuteronomic presentation of "rest" bears witness to the same God whose voice we hear in the New Testament. That other, even bolder presentation which looks to the hope that God will find rest with his people bears perhaps even more eloquent witness to the God of the New Testament, for it speaks of him in the form of a servant. We see in fact something of the reason for his self-concealment, namely that the dwelling so far prepared for him is not yet suitable and that his perfect coming to his own is still to be awaited. Neither of these presentations of the matter is adduced in its real sense as scriptural evidence in the New Testament.

By way of conclusion, however, something must be said of an important characteristic of the argument in the Epistle to the Hebrews. It is not only Psalm 95 which is quoted here, with its typical understanding of the notion of "rest"; the statement that God rested when he had completed the work of creation is also cited (Gen 2:2). Now the content of this chapter concerning the creation of the world is not by any means central to the theological thought of the Old Testament. Israel always kept far more in the forefront of its mind the fact of its election and of the covenant that promised redemption (or condemnation) to the people of God—things that in fact can be discussed only when the first article of the creed is taken for granted. The notion of "rest" in the terms in which we have been discussing it must certainly be classed among the later articles of the creed, since it is part of the promise of redemption.

The singular characteristic of Gen 1:1—2:4a is that it ventures, starting from faith in the God of the covenant, to draw a conclusion with regard to God the Creator of all things, a conclusion which moreover to some extent borders on the purely speculative. This is most plainly seen in the statement that connects God's rest from the work of creation with the institution of a seventh day, a day of rest, which is contrasted with the days of creation. The statement asserts that the world is no longer being created, but that it has already been given rest by God, and that this rest is perceptible to the eye of faith. Above all, however, the sentence makes so bold as to declare that even the living, creative God is at rest!

We shall not expound this further here, but it must at least be said that this conception of Gen 2:2-3 and the idea of salvation outlined above have absolutely nothing whatever in common. The idea of "rest" in Deuteronomy, in Chronicles, and in the two psalms we quoted is by its very nature firmly bound up with the Old Testament notion of the "way." It is a message addressed to the whole human situation, viz., the hardship of human life and the problem of man's relationship to God. This promise of rest can be appreciated only by one who knows, as surely as he knows the passage of time, how Old Testament man finds himself *in via* in a sense which affects him to the very core of his being. In the assertion made in Gen 1:2ff., on the other hand, an article of faith is set up, as it were, in the place of God himself, affirming that there is a "rest" which has no immediate bearing whatever upon human life.[5]

These are the two prooftexts that the author of the Epistle to the Hebrews has welded together! The simple fact that he can do so is an indication of the scope of the promised rest of the New Testament. This rest is an eschatological expectation, a fulfillment of the prophecies of redemption, an entering into that rest which there has always been, from the beginning, with God. In the fulfillment of this hope the whole purpose of creation and the whole purpose of redemption are reunited. Such is the insight vouchsafed to the writer in the simple juxtaposition of these two texts!

6

Ancient Word and Living Word—
Deuteronomy

Research on the Book of Deuteronomy has, in the past few decades, had more success than research into any other book of the Old Testament. With respect both to the whole and to many details, we have learned to regard Deuteronomy quite differently than was the case at the turn of the century.[1] One question, however, has not yet been clearly answered—indeed, it has never even been properly asked. For the Christian theologian it would seem to be the most important question of all: the question of the relationship between law and gospel. To be sure, if the conception were right according to which the Old Testament contains only law and the New Testament only gospel, then we could be spared the effort of a special investigation. But this conception is doubtless too great a simplification. For the very reason that our interpretation of Deuteronomy has been so changed through new exegetical insights, we must examine anew the question whether or not Deuteronomy considered Israel to be under the "law," that is, whether or not it taught Israel to earn its salvation. It is true that even today Deuteronomy is called in almost all scholarly works a "book of the law," or even a "law code." But it is not difficult to show that this designation is not appropriate, and that it misses the essential characteristic of the book completely.

Legal ordinances are found in the Old Testament in two different styles: either as a direct "apodictic" saying of God, or as an impersonal conditional sentence. Deuteronomy, however, is characterized by neither of these styles, for it is conceived as a speech of Moses to Israel, a personal address by one human to other humans. This is something unique in the legal literature of the Old Testament. Since differences of style in the literature of the ancient Near East are never accidental, the fact that Deuteronomy, unlike, for example, the Book of the Covenant (Exod 20:22—23:33), is composed as a speech of Moses must have its special reasons. It has long been seen that the style of

89

Deuteronomy is "parenetic." But what does this mean? The whole framework (Deuteronomy 1–11, 28–31) is exclusively parenetic, that is, it consists of a great many sermons of various lengths. It would hardly be accurate to consider these sermons purely literary products. It is much more probable that they are to be considered the literary deposit of an extensive preaching activity as it had already been developed in the late period of the monarchy, perhaps by the Levites. It would be incorrect, however, to contrast this parenetic framework with the legal part, Deuteronomy 12–26, for the parenetic style by no means ends with Deuteronomy 11. The so-called "legal" part is throughout also characterized by a parenetic formulation. The inner structure of the individual sections is very interesting in this respect.

We shall choose as an example two sections from Deuteronomy 15. At the head of the ordinances about the year of release (15:1-11) stands the sentence: "At the end of every seven years you shall grant a release." According to its style, this sentence is immediately recognizable as an apodictic command, similar to the commands in the Ten Commandments. We have here, therefore, a sentence from the oldest sacral tradition of Israel. As can be seen from Exod 23:10-11, it is a question of leaving the fields fallow in every seventh year, a usage that could easily be carried out during the time of Israel's semi-nomadic existence when the cultivation of the land was, in a pastoral economy, only a supplementary means of subsistence. The original significance of this custom is, of course, not social but sacral: it was an acknowledgment of God as the lord and owner of the cultivated land (see Lev 25:23!). God's right of possession was to be visibly demonstrated every seven years.

After this ancient apodictic commandment, v. 2 is a typical example of the form of a legal interpretation: "And this is the manner of the release." Here we are in a much later stage of the tradition, for the old commandment is suddenly applied to quite new economic conditions, which lay far outside the horizon of that earlier era. A money economy with the concomitant appearance of debt had developed extensively during the monarchy, and so the old law of leaving the fields fallow was reinterpreted as a law about the remission of financial debts after the passage of six years. This is theologically a very interesting occurrence. Israel was flexible enough to be able to drop antiquated religious forms of life; or better, every generation tried to hear the will of God for its own time and its own special conditions of life. Therefore, ancient formulations were under certain circumstances no longer sufficient. Israel had to attempt to hear the word of God ever anew.

We enter into another stage of the tradition, the third, with vv. 4-11, for these verses have no legal character about them at all. We have here, rather, all the characteristics of a sermon: "you shall not harden your heart or shut your hand against your poor brother, but you shall open your hand to him, and lend him sufficient for his need . . . your heart shall not be grudging when you give to him." Whoever speaks in this manner is not so much concerned with legal ordinances as he is with the inner disposition. He wants his hearers to take the commandments very personally into their consciences.

The situation with regard to the law concerning Hebrew slaves, regulating the service and the freeing of a debt slave after six years (Deut 15:12-18), is similar. A comparison with the form of this law in Exod 21:1-11 shows that the formulation of Deuteronomy comes from a much later time. Here too we see the characteristic transition from a legal to a parenetic presentation: "It shall not seem hard to you, when you let him go free from you"; "remember that you were a slave in the land of Egypt," etc. It is here in the preaching parenetic that we see the essential and specific characteristics of Deuteronomy. No, Deuteronomy is not a legal "code," but a collection of widely diverse sermons on old sacral ordinances.

Deuteronomy is not a literary unity, as can be clearly seen by any reader from the repeated superscriptions (1:1; 4:44-45; 6:1; 12:1), or from the constant shifting of the address between the singular and the plural. The observation of the various stages of the literary composition of the book is also important for a theological understanding. We see that Deuteronomy has grown with the generations. It was not stored away in a museum after its first appearance. Israel lived with this book, and it accompanied Israel as a living, that is, as a constantly present word of God. It did not speak to Israel in just one specific historical situation. Even more important, Israel did not limit it just to this one special situation, as if God's word and will could only here be attained. But when we say that the word of God in Deuteronomy accompanied Israel throughout its history, we do not mean that it became thereby a timeless, so to say, philosophical truth. It always remained a concrete word that was spoken within the area of human history. In the literary complexity of Deuteronomy we can perceive something of the complicated path of the word of God through a segment of human history. In that this word speaks to people always in their own times, we can learn something from Deuteronomy of God's condescension to people in their special circumstances.

We still have not answered the question about law and gospel in Deuteronomy. Even when it is not a law code, still it contains "legal," moralistic preaching. On this point we must take the following considerations into account: Deuteronomy is one great unfolding of the revelation on Sinai, of that moment when God stretched out his hand toward Israel to make it his own. Now this election of Israel to be the people of his possession is without any doubt fundamentally prior to any commandment. Never is this election spoken of in a conditional sense—when you obey my commandments, then you shall be my people. When Israel was elected it had not yet had any opportunity of showing its obedience. This is very clearly expressed for example in Deut 27:9-10: "Keep silence and hear, O Israel: this day you have become the people of the Yahweh your God." With this categorical statement the election is accomplished. Only in second place comes the demand for obedience: "You shall therefore obey the voice of Yahweh your God, keeping his commandments and his statutes, which I command you this day." Thus Deuteronomy, like the Heidelberg Cate-chism, thinks of thankfulness as the true motive for obedience. Therefore, God is to be loved (Deut 6:4); and because Israel is "a people holy to Yahweh" (Deut 14:1-2, 21), it must refrain from all heathen customs.

One can, therefore, certainly not say that Deuteronomy is "law" that instructs Israel to earn its salvation through obedience. Yet, on the other hand, we cannot understand Deuteronomy simply as a gospel of salvation. There are, to be sure, many passages where the love of God is spoken to Israel's heart in a fashion that is simply unique in the Old Testament:

> [Y]ou are a people holy to Yahweh your God; Yahweh your God has chosen you to be a people for his own possession, out of all the peo-ples that are on the face of the earth. It was not because you were more in number than any other people that Yahweh set his love upon you and chose you—for you were the fewest of all people; but it is because Yahweh loves you, and is keeping the oath that he swore to your fathers. (Deut 7:6-8)

But seen as a whole, the mode of speech of Deuteronomy is not indicative but imperative, exhorting and warning. Here is a form of theological speech, the peculiarity of which has only in our day been theologically clarified: par-aclesis, a form that is developed extensively in the New Testament epistles.[2] Does it mean a legalization of the message of salvation? But paraclesis is quite different from a moralizing sermon. It does not think of calling into question the indicative of the gospel; it is rather a speech of exhortation directed to those who have already received the word of salvation. It has occasionally been said that paraclesis could be summed up in the phrase "become what you are": "let not your heart faint; . . . for Yahweh your God is with you" (Deut 20:3-4). This is paraclesis, an exhoration in view of the indicative fact of salvation.

We must consider another important point, without which we would understand the paraclesis of Deuteronomy only incompletely; namely, the time in the history of salvation in which the preaching of Deuteronomy is addressed to Israel. Deuteronomy stands in the middle between promise and fulfillment. The election has occurred; God has revealed his saving intention and his readiness to lead the people of Israel into the land of Canaan. The

Israel addressed in Deuteronomy has already stood before Mt. Sinai; but the entry into the promised land is still in the future. Israel is still on the way to the land of salvation, the land of Canaan—"you have not as yet come to the rest and to the inheritance that Yahweh your God gives you" (Deut 12:9; see 25:19). The Israel addressed by Deuteronomy is still waiting for the fulfillment. But in this very condition of "not yet" it is threatened by many dangers. In the situation of Israel between promise and fulfillment much can still happen, even disaster. We can even speak of a deep concern that runs through the deuteronomic paraclesis, that Israel in the last minute before the fulfillment could lose its salvation. There was, in fact, reason enough for such a concern.

It is not difficult to reconstruct from the deuteronomic preaching, as if from a photographic negative, the religious situation of the Israel here addressed, the Israel of the late monarchical period. What did this Israel still know of its God? The symbols of the heathen nature cult had penetrated into its worship. Every sanctuary had its own cultic tradition; the God who was worshiped in Beersheba had different traits from the God of Betheel or Gilgal. Was it still one God that Israel served and not rather a divided God? The deuteronomic paraclesis stood over against a dangerous break in the entire tradition of faith. Already there must have been something like a generation gap. There was a gulf between parents and children, and the children no longer knew what the parents had experienced (Deut 11:2); everything had first to be explained to them (Deut 6:20-25). The temptations of a nature religion threatened to tear families apart (Deut 13:6-11). This heathen nature religion had its own organs and spokesmen (Deut 13:1-5), and it was even within the realm of possibility that whole cities should fall away from the faith of their fathers and go over to the Baal religion (Deut 13:12-18). Even among those who did not go so far, who externally still adhered to the old faith, there was much religious disorder. Apparently they were no longer capable of correctly perceiving their own situation before God, for they had to be exhorted not to forget God's benefactions (Deut 6:10-12). They complacently attributed to their own ability that which they owed to God's blessings and providence (Deut 8:17; 9:4-6). It would be possible to add many further examples, but the total picture would not be changed. It is the picture of a congregation that found themselves in a rather hopeless situation as far as their faith was concerned. The connection with the faith handed down from their fathers was broken, and their faith was exposed to a profound decomposition through the intrusion of conceptions from the heathen nature cult. This was the situation in which Deuteronomy found the people of Israel, and now we come to what is theologically of the greatest importance in the whole book of Deuteronomy.

Would anyone be surprised if Deuteronomy, after such religious decay, had simply considered Israel to be lost and a return to God to be impossible? But the opposite is the case. Deuteronomy erases seven centuries of disobedience and thoughtless ingratitude, places Israel once more in the desert before God, and lets Israel hear again the gracious election to be the people of Yahweh's possession. This Israel experiences with no reduction the same thing now as before in the desert, and yet this Israel was not at all still the same. The Israel that Deuteronomy confronts had superficially hardly a point of resemblance to that people that once stood at the foot of Mt. Sinai. Culturally and economically and politically it lived in very different conditions. But this is what we find so important about Deuteronomy, that it was able to speak the old gospel word of God's election undiminished in a situation that was so very different from that of old Israel. God had stretched out his hand to his people once more at this advanced hour, and therein lies the reason why Deuteronomy had not despaired of Israel. If it had depended on its own initiative, Israel would never have found its way out of the neglect of its faith. But the initiative lay with God.

What can we say to all this from the standpoint of the New Testament faith in Jesus Christ? First of all, we are astonished how similar Israel's situation before God is to that in which the New Testament church found itself. Between the unconditional word of salvation that was addressed to Israel by Deuteronomy and the election that was revealed to the New Testament church as a free gift—"without the works of the law"— there does not seem to be any fundamental theological difference. In any case the difference did not seem very significant to the church; otherwise how could she have expressed her own consciousness of election and the joy of being accepted by God as the people of his possession with the very same words as Deuteronomy: "you are a chosen race, a royal priesthood, a holy nation, God's own people" (1 Pet 2:9). Or with respect to what we have said about the situation in the history of salvation between election and fulfillment, just think of the Epistle to the Hebrews! It sees the distinctiveness of the situation of the church in the fact that she too was still journeying toward the final fulfillment; it retains the conception of the wandering people of God and speaks, too, of the fulfillment of the promises as an entry into rest. But when we speak of the similarities of the New Testament church and the Old Testament people of the covenant with respect to their position before God, we must also recognize the differences. The New Testament church is no earthly people with a king and an army that goes to war; it is not administered by elders, priests, and prophets; and it does not celebrate Passover or the Feast of Tabernacles. In short, we are not the people of Israel addressed by the preaching of Deuteronomy.

In the wide-ranging deuteronomic theology there is one almost uncanny passage where Israel's situation before God seems to become almost identical with that of the New Testament church. In Deuteronomy, too, the word of salvation addressed to Israel stands in relief against the dark background of a mediatory suffering and dying. Deuteronomy sees in Moses the unique prophet; he is the pre-eminent mediator. What God had to say to Israel had to be mediated to the people by Moses, for Israel did not think itself capable of enduring the direct voice of God. For this reason the people begged Moses to expose himself to the voice of God in Israel's place, and then to speak to Israel in God's place: "Go near, and hear all that Yahweh our God will say; and speak to us all that Yahweh our God will speak to you; and we will hear and do it" (Deut 5:27). From this "go near" everything else follows. Moses is assigned the task of vicariously running the risk of a meeting with God for the people. Now it is very interesting how, in the opinion of Deuteronomy, this risk of a meeting with God face to face really includes everything for Moses. After Israel had committed the great sin of the worship of the golden calf, it was Moses who had to intercept the anger of God. For forty days and forty nights he lay prostrate before God with strict fasting. The long intercession that he prayed at that time is set forth verbatim by Deuteronomy (Deut 9:18-21, 26-29). Even the death of Moses occurred vicariously for Israel. Yahweh's grievous anger over Israel struck Moses alone; on account of the sins of his people he was not allowed to enter the promised land (Deut 1:37; 4:21-22). But in spite of all this Moses did not rebel against God. It is true that he prayed that "this cup pass from" him, but God forbade him bluntly any further word on this matter (Deut 3:23-27). Thus Deuteronomy sees in Moses the only one who was really exposed to the wrath of God. For the sake of Israel's salvation, he alone was excluded from salvation. How close Deuteronomy comes here to the New Testament conceptions of the vicarious suffering and death of Jesus Christ! But again we must say: Moses is not Christ.

It must in all truth be confessed that the determination of the relationship of the two testaments has seldom caused so much difficulty as in our own time. We feel ourselves so remote from the marvelous freedom that the evangelists and apostles had in their use of the Old Testament. The Old Testament spoke directly to them, so that wherever they opened it, they found a present witness for their theological, Christological, or ecclesiological argumentation. Still, we are beginning to understand again how the outlines of the New Testament Christ-event are constantly sketched in God's historical acts with Israel. And so we may see in the picture of Moses found in Deuteronomy a shadowy prefiguration of the salvation-event of the New Testament.

Does not everything presented in the Old Testament have a characteristic openness toward the future? And future in the Bible always means a future that God will give from his own hands. With the creation the horizon of history already opens up, and the attention of the reader is accordingly directed forward. The stories of the patriarchs, too, are told with reference to the future, namely, the people that is to come and the fulfillment of the promises. And even more Deuteronomy! Is it not from the first to the last sentence open to the future, to a fulfillment that lies beyond itself? We must also consider the following: If Deuteronomy comes from the late monarchical period (and there is no reason to doubt this), then we see that even the Israel of this late time knew that it had not yet reached the great fulfillments God had promised. It thought of itself as still on the way, still in the expectation of the final rest. Is it any wonder that the early church began to read this Old Testament that was so thoroughly open to the future with a new understanding? The church saw everything in the Old Testament in the light of the appearance of Christ, and in this light the possibility of a new interpretation was indicated. Now, after the appearance of Jesus Christ, the old texts began suddenly to speak anew; now their reference to Christ became at once clear, and there began a marvelous process of reciprocal understanding. The Old Testament became an aid to understanding the Christ-event—one only has to consider how in the gospels the riddle of the Passion is illumined step-by-step by the Old Testament. The Old Testament also helped the church to a new understanding of herself; she began to understand that the existence of the wandering people of God was repeated in her, for she too was in movement from a promise toward the fulfillment, from the grace of election in Jesus Christ to the return of Christ and the consummation of the world. But also the other process was at work: the Christ-event became an aid to understanding the Old Testament. The light reflected from Christ gave a new possibility of understanding the various religious experiences of Israel.

Now to return to the subject of this essay, it is simply a question whether or not Deuteronomy seen in the light of Christ still speaks to us, that is, whether or not a word of God for our time can still be heard here. In view of all the cultic, ritual, and social-legal material in this book, the modern Christian is only all too ready to answer this question with a "No." It would, of course, be a crass "Judaizing" if one were to urge Christians to follow all the laws of sacrifice and purity and all the regulations that are connected with the sacral conceptions of old Israel. But, on the other hand, we must be clear about the fact that it does not lie in our power to determine from which part of the Bible God will speak to us. There can be no limitation of some areas in which the word of God can speak and some in which it cannot speak. Even the old distinction between the ritual law and the moral law cannot be allowed to limit the freedom of God's word. For those who "are in Christ Jesus" only this is valid, that they are freed from the law and from the sentence of death pronounced by the law. But they are not freed from paraclesis.

Let us listen then to a certain tone that is again and again to be heard in the deuteronomic paraclesis and that can even be called constitutive for Deuteronomy—the constant exhortation for the people of Israel not to be afraid in the imminent battle, because God himself will be with them and will overcome all opposition. Deuteronomy does not only contain a whole series of war ordinances, but also its entire paraclesis is characterized by a noticeable war-like mood. When one reads Deuteronomy, one sees a whole people who, with weapons in their hands, are ready under the leadership of their God to take the last step into the promised land. The Christians are no earthly people and they do not fight with weapons in their hands. But when they read all this—these exhortations not to be afraid and not to lose their trust in God—will they not think of their own situation in the world, in which they are still journeying and in which they are still involved in many battles? They will, of course, have to interpret everything anew by the Spirit of Christ—there is no sentence in the Old Testament that we do not have to interpret anew!—but could it not be so, that from this war-like paraclesis, which at first seems abolished and outdated, an unexpected consolation can come to us?

In the deuteronomistic passage, Josh 1:1-9, we see again the great majesty of the divine guidance: "Every place that the sole of your foot will tread upon I have given you. . . . I will not fail you or forsake you." Thus it is said that all obstacles that shall arise before the people of God have already been overcome in God's providence. God has already cleared the way; still more, he has already given us as a possession every foot of land on which we shall tread in the realm of the glorious new life. Is not this a passage for a Christian sermon?

Let us consider another passage in Deuteronomy, the warning against every presumptuous attempt of humanity to make its own way into the transcendental world of God through divination, augury, or necromancy (Deut 18:9-14).[3] With a wave of the hand this whole arsenal of occult practices is dismissed, for this is not the manner in which Israel meets its God. The word of God will always be with Israel, and thereby Israel is granted a much closer communion with God. Or let us consider still another object of Deuteronomy's preaching, the provisions for the cities of refuge (Deut 19:1-13). The very same people that recognized more than any other people the necessity for law and justice knew at the same time that there was with God a sphere in which all human justice was suspended and in which all human claims were no longer valid, in which God's judgment and protection alone counted.

Although we must draw to a close, we realize that we have now arrived at a point where our theme really first begins. Everyone must seek oneself in this wonderful book, and when one reads with attention, one will be able to hear many things that are surprisingly pertinent to our faith and to the life of our congregations in the presence of God. We must just have the courage to speak the old word into a new situation. But has not Deuteronomy already before us done the same thing? Even if one did not know what to make of all the details of this book, still Deuteronomy would remain a model in the wonderful freedom in which it has spoken the traditional word of God into a changed present. This steadfast conviction that God did not merely speak sometime long ago to an ancient people, but that he is ready to speak to people wherever they are, into the very heart of their own times, will remain a challenge to Christians until the end of time.

7

The Tent and the Ark

Throughout the religious history of Israel there is no other institution that remained for so long at the very heart of theological thinking as did the Tent and the Ark. It is typical that the Chronicler countered the priestly writer's Aaronite tradition of the tabernacle with a forthright theology of the ark associated with the Levites.[1] Even at so late a date tent and ark are evidently not fully reconciled in the religious heritage of Israel, but are the rallying-points of quite distinct theological parties. We may reasonably assume, therefore, that in earlier ages, too, the relationship between the two palladia was not without its tensions, and it will be interesting to trace the history of their mutual relations.

Out of the immense wealth of material that is available, we shall not concern ourselves primarily with either the political history of the tent and the ark, nor with the purely archaeological problem. The problem of the tent and the ark can also be discussed purely from the point of view of the history of their traditions, and it would seem that the divergences here are evidence of theological distinctions and compromises that are worthy of attention as a problem in themselves.

Let us begin with the latest accounts and work backwards from them in order to elucidate the problem. It may be possible in this way to disentangle the jumbled strands and so gain an understanding of the complex of religious thought that finally arose from these various elements.

According to the account given in the priestly code, what we have been accustomed to speak of as the Tabernacle is actually a highly composite affair. In a sumptuously ordered tent there is a whole series of cultic objects, of which the most prominent is the Ark of Yahweh. The ark is a chest of acacia wood, about four feet in length, two feet six inches in depth, and the same in breadth, able to be carried by means of poles passed through rings on either side. Both the chest and the poles are overlaid with gold. Inside are the tables of the law.

Thus far the ark presents a single, self-consistent aspect. Moses was commanded, however, to make a "cover" (*kaporeth*) of pure gold, to fix a cherub at each end of it, and to put it on top of the ark. What is the purpose of this cover? As yet etymology has given no help in this matter.[2] According to the account (Exod 25:10ff.), the cover would appear to be nothing much more than a lid, for its width and length tally precisely with those of the ark, whilst its height is not mentioned.

If the ark is a receptacle, the cover still cannot be regarded merely as a necessary finishing touch. A glance at the provisions of the priestly code, moreover, shows that the cover constitutes a very special part of the ark. It is in fact the secret place where Yahweh speaks directly to Moses, the spot where personal contact is maintained between God and his people. The exact point from which God speaks is fixed very precisely: "from between the two cherubim upon the cover." It is clear that here the ark has another quite different function besides that of providing a safe resting-place for the tables of the law, and it may safely be asserted that although the cover is only one part of the ark it is actually of greater significance than the ark itself, both in its own right and also with regard to its function.

A decisive question now arises, however, as to how precisely Yahweh is thought to be associated both with the "cover" and with the tabernacle. Does Yahweh dwell in the tent or not?

The notion that Yahweh dwells in the tent is certainly to be found in P. To take only one important indication, we find an extremely frequent use in a cultic sense of the phrase "before Yahweh" (*lifnê yhwh*). The ceremonies of offering sacrifice, of slaughtering, waving, lifting up, making atonement, and laying out shew-bread, all take place "before" the God who is thought of as being in the tent (for example, Exod 27:21; 28:35; 29:11, 23, 24, 26, 42; 40:23, 25, etc.; Lev 1:5; 4:6; 14:23). From time to time this fairly generalized definition of place is more narrowly defined. According to Lev 4:7 the altar of incense stands before Yahweh; similarly the curtain is before Yahweh, and occasionally, too, the place at the entrance to the tent is described as being "before Yahweh." The Most Holy Place, in fact, is undoubtedly thought of as the particular abode of Yahweh.

A quite superficial reading of the provisions of the priestly code, however, reveals that over against the idea that Yahweh is present in the cultic place there is another view diametrically opposed to this—that Yahweh does not dwell in the tent, but appears there from time to time when he so pleases. When he *does* appear the fact is always announced as a quite special event, and is accompanied by miraculous phenomena. For example, when Moses finished making the tabernacle a cloud covered the tent, and the "glory" (*kabôd*) of Yahweh filled the dwelling.

The text of Exod 16:10 is particularly instructive. The people are quarrelling with Moses and Aaron; as they look in the direction of the desert, the "glory" of Yahweh suddenly appears in the cloud. Numbers 16:42 is very similar: as the congregation are grumbling, the cloud and the "glory" suddenly become visible over the tent. The obvious implications of this and other narratives is that Yahweh normally shuns earthly places, but that from time to time he appears from afar and deals personally with men at the spot which He has chosen (Num 9:15ff.; 10:11; but see also Exod 29:43; Lev 9:6, 23; Num 14:10; 16:19; 20:6).

An illuminating circumstance with regard to this understanding of the matter is to be seen in the use of the verb *ya'ad* in the niph'al (*wenô'adtî* or *'iwwa'ed*) by Yahweh himself: "I will present myself to you, will meet with you."[3] The phrase would be meaningless if Yahweh were thought to be continually present, but makes sense if the tabernacle is understood to be the only place where Yahweh meets with men in order to reveal his will, and without causing their death by so doing.

The attitude of P to the ark thus shows some striking anomalies: the ark is both the chest in which the tables of the law are stored, and also the place where revelations are communicated; Yahweh dwells in the tent and the "glory" of Yahweh appears from time to time in the cloud *over* the tent. One cannot help suspecting that here two streams of thought have flowed together, which were originally separate. It may be possible to disentangle them to some extent by tracing the problem further back, paying special attention to the discrepancies that we have already noticed.

The deuteronomic notions associated with the ark and the tent derive, theologically speaking, from the distinctive basic assumptions of Deuteronomy. For our purposes it is not of importance to distinguish between the various literary strata, since all the statements about the ark depend substantially upon one and the same fundamental view of the matter. At Horeb Yahweh gives Moses the task of making an ark (*'arôn*), of acacia wood, for the purpose of storing the tables of the law (Deut 1:1ff.). A note at Deut 10:8, probably an interpolation, assigns the carrying of the ark to the tribe of Levi. For theologians of deuteronomic persuasion the ark has thus one single purpose—that of acting as a receptacle for the tables. It has no other role, and since in deuteronomic circles the term "covenant" (*berîth*) became the technical expression for "decalogue," "Ark of the Covenant" (*'aron ha-berîth*) became the specifically deuteronomic term for the ark.

The wide divergencies between Deuteronomy and the priestly code need no further explanation. So far as Deuteronomy is concerned the ark has no cultic significance and no relation to sacrificial worship, whilst all reference to the ark as the dwelling place of Yahweh is done away with. Shall God dwell on the earth, when all the heavens cannot contain him? So argues the Deuteronomist (1 Kgs 8:27), and in consequence he strips away from the ark every trace of magical belief, and it becomes what it had certainly never been before—a receptacle for the tables of the Law.

One of the most striking features of the deuteronomic view is the absence of the tent: nowhere is the ark in any way associated with the tent. It is true that there is one mention of the tent (*'ohel mô'ed*) in Deuteronomy, when Moses and Joshua enter it, but the passage is unanimously attributed to the Elohist by all the commentators (Deut 31:14-15).[4] But we have no need to invoke this finding of textual criticism. Even supposing that this verse is of deuteronomic authorship, a suggestion that carries little conviction, the complete absence of any connection between the ark and the tent would be no whit less remarkable.

The differences between the deuteronomic and the priestly conceptions of the ark far outweigh the similarities, a circumstance which in itself compels us to pursue our investigations further into the past. What are the theories associated with the ark in earlier periods of Israelite religion?

The account of the installation of the ark in Solomon's newly built temple offers many valuable points for our consideration (1 Kgs 8:1ff.). Solomon and all the people bring the ark to the temple with immense cultic pomp, and it is then carried by the priests into the Most Holy Place. We have already been told how Solomon had made for the Most Holy Place two cherubim of olive wood, each about fifteen feet high, and about fifteen feet from wing-tip to wing-tip. From the somewhat circumstantial description it appears that these figures stood side by side with wings outstretched, and it is said that the priests set the ark down beneath the wings of the cherubim.

Superficially the most striking fact of all is that here once again we find cherubim, although such beings seem to have been quite unknown to the deuteronomist in connection with the ark. Although in this case they are not so closely linked with the ark as they are in P, who tells us that they were fixed to the top of it, it is nevertheless clear that their function is expressly that of guarding the ark. What function pertains to the ark itself, however, guarded as it is, is not immediately apparent. The account itself tells us nothing; but the whole arrangement of the temple shows it to have been constructed as a dwelling-place for Yahweh, and the undoubtedly genuine consecration formula spoken by Solomon says quite plainly that Yahweh will dwell in the darkness of the temple (1 Kgs 8:12ff.). The ark must therefore bear some relationship to Yahweh's presence. But what relationship?

When King Hezekiah received Sennacherib's arrogant letter, he spread it out in the temple before Yahweh and began to pray: "Yahweh, thou God of Israel, who is enthroned above the cherubim . . . ." (2 Kgs 19:15). This invocation is noteworthy in many respects. It shows clearly that Yahweh is thought of as being present in the temple in a wholly concrete way, enthroned in fact above the cherubim. We here meet for the first time an idea with which we must concern ourselves more closely. At once a difficulty arises. It is utterly impossible to reconcile this conception of the throne with the description of the cherubim in Solomon's temple. Apart from this, the function of the cherubim is expressly of a quite different order. Their task is to protect the ark! Yet it must be admitted that the notion of the ark as a throne is inherently far more probable.

There is a text in the Book of Jeremiah that is of great importance for this problem. Jeremiah, speaking of the eschatological state of salvation, says: "they shall no more say, 'the Ark of Yahweh.' It shall not come to mind. Jerusalem shall be called the throne of Yahweh" (Jer 3:16).

It could not be said more plainly that formerly the ark was regarded as Yahweh's throne. Ezekiel, too, in one place calls the temple the place of Yahweh's throne (Ezek 43:7). If, however, the ark in the temple was Yahweh's throne, the statements concerning the ark and the cherubim in the Most Holy Place now all fall into their proper place. Which is then the original conception—that of the throne, or that of the cherubim as protectors? We have not the slightest hesitation in regarding the idea of the throne as the original conception, and the notion of the cherubim as protectors as a later modification presumably of a rationalizing nature. Yet before we pursue the matter further, let us investigate the indications given in the earliest accounts of the ark.

We shall at once leave out of our reckoning the few scattered references in the Hexateuch, since their date and derivation is by no means established. The history of the ark in 1 and 2 Samuel has the advantage of giving a fairly long, connected account, whilst its great antiquity and its primitive character are both beyond question.

In this account we find the ark in a temple at Shiloh. Here Yahweh reveals himself to Samuel. The ark is taken out to the camp, and falls into the hands of the Philistines, but causes great calamities in the land of the enemy and for this reason is sent back from thence to Kiriath Jearim. From this place King David finally brings it home.

Tricked out as they are in motley colorings, all these stories nevertheless display a fundamentally unified religious approach. In the final analysis, the point of each of these narratives depends on the intimate association of Yahweh with the ark. Where the ark is, there is Yahweh. This view is pressed to the point where at times it almost seems as if Yahweh and the ark are one and the same. Thus in a desperate situation, for example, it seems appropriate to carry out to the camp both the ark and, naturally, the God who is associated with it; and the Philistines accordingly say to one another, "God has come into the camp" (1 Sam 4:7).

We shall mention only one of the many passages which might be called in evidence, that concerning Yahweh's self-revelation to Samuel as he slept beside the ark. A voice calls to Samuel, but nothing whatever is said of Yahweh's coming: it would be superfluous, for Yahweh is already there. All that is said expressly to suggest movement on the part of Yahweh is that he "stood forth" (*wayyityaṣṣeb*, 1 Sam 3:10), but this occurs only *after* Samuel has been called three times. Before that, then, Yahweh was not standing. Is it not self-evident that Yahweh was thought to sit on the ark as on his throne? Now it is in the context of these very same ancient narratives concerning the ark that we find, twice, the phrase: "Yahweh who sits enthroned on the cherubim" (*yhwh yošeb ha-kerûbîm*, 1 Sam 4:4; 2 Sam 6:2).

Critics have regarded this description of Yahweh with suspicion, but a longer view of the matter shows that the notion that Yahweh is enthroned upon the cherubim is most carefully avoided in later literature. There is no evidence for it either in P or in connection with Solomon's temple—understandably, for it is an archaic conception, as we see from the ancient battle-cry in Numbers 10. This cry belongs to the oldest stratum of our information concerning the ark. And since it is certainly out of place in its present context it may best be dealt with at this point.[5] What we have here is a brief invocation that is used whenever the ark moves on or comes to a halt. The text is not in the best of condition, but this does not affect the real issue. "Rise up, Yahweh, that thine enemies may be scattered before thy face, and that their adversaries may flee. Be seated, Yahweh, amidst (?) the ten thousand thousands of Israel" (Num 10:35-36).

Here, too, the notion is presented in the most concrete possible form. When camp is broken, Yahweh rises from his throne; when a halt is made, he seats himself again upon the ark.

If however we wish to arrive at a clear view of the matter, so far as may be possible, we must now call archaeology to our aid. What has archaeology to teach us concerning the thrones of gods, and in particular, what has this to do with cherubim?

Cherubim, winged creatures with the bodies of animals or of human beings, are known to us from all the ancient religions of the Near East. The important fact is that their presence indicates that a god is near at hand or actually present. This is true whether they are there to protect the dwelling-place of the god, as in Assyrian temples (see also Genesis 3), or whether they have the task of carrying the god. The Assyrian rock-relief at Maltaia depicts the gods in procession.[6] The gods are standing on winged creatures, and Ishtar sits on a throne of cherubim borne by other cherubim. It certainly illustrates admirably the biblical conception of "sitting enthroned upon the cherubim" (*yošeb ha-kerûbîm*).

At the same time this brings us only to the beginning of our more perplexing problems. Are we to think of the ark as a throne? And if so, where is the God himself? To speak of an image of the deity is to disregard the unanimous evidence of the entire Old Testament.[7] For this reason the problem of the empty throne has recently been the subject of particularly thoroughgoing investigations.[8] We must certainly be prepared to think in terms of the existence of some such conception, which would correspond most appositely with the Israelite idea of God.

More convincing than the numerous Greek examples,[9] which are too remote for comparison, are two Phoenician thrones of Astarte, the seat of which is supported by winged creatures on either side whilst the back bears a sacred inscription. The throne itself is empty in each case.[10] Here we are much closer to the ark and to the notion of "sitting upon the cherubim" (*yošeb ha-kerûbîm*). But there still remain two important questions. The cherubim depicted in P, and in the account of the arrangement of the temple, are undoubtedly of human form. These so-called "throne cherubim" are quadrupeds, as are also the cherubim which have been found in Israel, both those of the altar of incense at Taanach[11] and those in the Baumwoll grotto at Jerusalem.[12]

We must, however, add that the cherubim described in the Old Testament accounts are no longer the cherubim upon which Yahweh sits enthroned, but creatures whose function has become that of protecting the ark. From this it may be assumed that, in those earlier times, as the ark ceased to be thought of as a throne so the cherubim began to be regarded as human in form. The influence of Egyptian patterns would appear to have been at work here, for it is only in Egypt that the wings have a protective function, and it is this aspect which is emphasized when the significance of the cherubim is modified in Israelite thought.[13]

This raises in an even more pressing form the following question: if the ark was originally a throne, why is it never actually called a throne? There is a wide degree of latitude in the designation of the ark, yet the word *'arôn* (ark), never disappears. There must be some reason for this.

The remarkable thing is that the ark can actually be regarded as a receptacle, although admittedly at a time later than that at which it was thought of as a throne. Nevertheless, even if the deuteronomist does regard the ark as a receptacle, we cannot believe that it was he who changed its function from that of a throne into that of a box, especially as the throne was already known by the name of "ark." There is a clear indication here that the conception of the ark has not by any means developed along one single, straightforward, ascertainable line.

The deuteronomist regards the ark as a chest, and certainly does not intend to perpetuate the view that it is a throne; rather he prefers to link up with another and probably much older tradition according to which the ark was, as its name implies, a box. But the Old Testament gives us no hint as to the provenance of this view, nor of the time or place at which it was current; for, as we saw, the very oldest accounts do not think of the ark as a receptacle. Yet one cannot help feeling that the purpose of an object which is known as a chest must be to contain something.

At the end of a quite admirable study of Amun, Kurt Sethe recently made some suggestions which merit our attention concerning the parallelism between Yahweh and this invisible Egyptian wind-god.[14] In the ogdoad of the original Hermopolitan gods, Amun represents air, the wind which brought movement to the deadness of chaos. Gradually this wind god came to be regarded more and more as a spiritual being. Just as air is everywhere and yet is invisible, so Amun became a mysterious spirit, the breath of which is in all things, which flows through human throats, and, like the air, is omnipresent. By this line of reasoning, in Sethe's opinion, the ark might be intelligible if it were a box which contained nothing but air.

Comparisons have often been made in the past between the ark and the portable processional boats of the Egyptians containing shrines for the gods. Sethe therefore assumes that the shrine on Amun's processional boat actually contained nothing. This conclusion, however, is purely a matter of conjecture, for there is no evidence at all that Amun's invisibility is brought into relationship with an empty shrine. Like all Egyptian gods, Amun can be represented as an image of human shape.

A link in the chain is missing from the other side, too: Yahweh is nowhere associated with the inside of the ark. He sits upon it as on a throne. What is more, we have only to compare the nature of the two gods: what has Yahweh in common with Amun? Yahweh is strictly limited to his own territory; Amun is the air, the breath which is in all things. Amun's character is established in the first instance by a process of painful speculation, and is then developed quite freely. The notion that he "is in all things" is regarded by Sethe as extremely ancient. Amun is and remains a cosmic element.

On the other hand, Yahweh is the God of history,[15] passionately furthering his own purposes and jealously guarding his unique position. For thousands of years Amun tolerated without any objection the presence around him of the related gods of the theogony. What comparison is there between him and

Yahweh?[16] But there are still further considerations. For weighty reasons, we must call seriously in doubt the relationship between the ark and both Moses and the religion of Sinai; and in so doing we finally demolish the artificial connection between Amun and Yahweh at its decisive point. But we must prove our case.

Did the tribes already possess the ark when they came out of the desert? First let us investigate this matter in the ancient sources. We find no mention in them of the making of the ark. On the contrary, it is named in only two places throughout the whole of pre-deuteronomic writings of the Pentateuch, and neither passage can be adduced as proof of the historicity of this tradition.[17] Numbers 10:33ff. merely takes the war-cry of the ark which we have already mentioned, and tricks it out with historical circumstances. Even the Massoretes bracketed the passage, using a particular mark, because it does not properly belong in this place and clearly stands quite apart from its context.[18] The text flows much more smoothly without this verse,[19] and has nothing whatever to do with war. Why, then, this sudden appearance of the battle-cry?

There is still further difficulty in the fact that the ark is introduced here as if it were something well-known to the reader, although the Elohist has so far not mentioned it, and also in the fact that it is spoken of as the "ark of the covenant." The expression is decidedly suspect, even apart from the fact that it assorts very ill with the notion that Yahweh is enthroned on the ark. It is also to be noticed that the passage concerned shows how the people are guided by the cloud (Num 10:34), a conception that simply cannot be reconciled with the theory of the ark, as will later become apparent.

The other passage, Num 14:44, is held by the majority of commentators not to be original. The people take the field against the Amalekites at Hormah contrary to Yahweh's command, "but the ark of Yahweh and Moses did not go out of the camp." Here, too, the ark is introduced without warning, and here again it is referred to as the ark of the covenant. We must now draw attention to a matter which has not been mentioned hitherto: the Elohist knows explicitly only of the tent, which according to his version is pitched outside the camp (Exod 33:7ff.). Yet the ark is in the camp! Is it to be supposed that the Israelites kept the ark in the camp and *outside* the tent? Surely not.

If only there were some light on the main problem as to whether the ark was indeed originally associated with the religion of Yahweh at all, we might still be prepared to suppose that some genuine recollection underlay these two passages we have cited. The suggestion brings us to the most valid objections to the belief that the ark had its origin in the time of the desert wanderings. One of the most important indications is to be found in the name of the ark. In the books of 1 and 2 Samuel the phrase "the ark of God" (*'arôn ha-'elohîm*) occurs twenty times and "the ark of Yahweh" (*'arôn yhwh*) twenty-six times. These combinations, even thus baldly set down, show how tenaciously the term "God" clings to the word "ark."

If one goes through the occurrences in detail, it is true that they do not appear to come from different sources,[20] but it is noticeable that the great majority of the occurrences of the term "ark of Yahweh" arise from the account of the ark's adventures in Philistine territory. When the writer is speaking about the deliberations of the Philistines, about the evils which befell Dagon, the inhabitants of Beth Shemesh and so on (1 Sam 4:6; 5:3-4; 6:1-2, 8, 11, 12, 19, 21; 7:1), the indefinite term "God" would necessarily be avoided, for it was not simply the fact that the ark of *a* god was being held captive which gave rise to all these complications. What needed to be emphasized was the nature of this *particular* God, and the fact that he was on foreign soil. The point of the narrative depends upon this fact, whereas in other narratives (where there is no need to stress the matter) the term "ark of God" is more common.[21]

The term "ark of Yahweh" does not appear throughout the whole history of Samuel's early life. One may therefore feel secure in asserting that the ark was originally designated "the ark of God." We may compare this with the designation of other cultic objects which we know to have been unequivocally referred to Yahweh by name from the outset. Solomon's temple is referred to on countless occasions as "the house of Yahweh" (*bêth yhwh*), just as the tent erected by David was "the tent of Yahweh" (*'ohel yhwh*, 1 Kgs 2:28ff.).

We can but touch on the many indications of Canaanitish religion which we find associated with the ark: the cultic building (1 Sam 1:9; 2 Sam 6:10ff.), the lamps (*ner ha-'elohîm*, 1 Sam 3:3), the oracle by incubation (1 Sam 3:2ff.), David's dancing naked before the ark (2 Sam 6:14, 20), and the connection of the ark with the autumn festival.[22] What, finally, is the import of the ceremonial formula "the ark of God which is called by the name of Yahweh"? A kind of "renaming" seems to have been necessary to validate the particular relationship of Yahweh to this cultic object.[23] But the main proof of our thesis depends upon our showing how fundamentally different was the notion of God which attached to the real palladium of the desert period, and here we come to quite the most important aspect of the problem of the tent and the ark.

Information concerning the sacred tent is even more meager than that concerning the ark. The oldest and most instructive account of the tent is contained in Exodus 33. The problem of the source of the text, whether it be J or JE, remains unsolved, and there are all the signs of a major lacuna in the text at this point; but what can be inferred from the data we have is itself quite sufficiently revealing. We learn that Moses used to pitch the tent outside camp, and called it "the tent of meeting" (*'ohel mô'ed*). When it was necessary to consult Yahweh, Moses went out to the tent, followed by the expectant gaze of the people, and when the pillar of cloud came down upon the door of the tent, all the people prostrated themselves in worship. Meanwhile Yahweh spoke to Moses as one speaks to a friend. Then Moses returned to the camp.

First let us set down the negative aspects of this evidence. Nothing whatever is said of the ark, for obvious reasons. The purpose of the tent is clearly defined in a way which renders it wholly incompatible with the theology of the ark. Yahweh is not in the tent, but always comes down to it from the heaven above, for which reason the tent is correctly known as the "tent of meeting." The tent is thus simply a meeting-point for Yahweh and Moses, and nothing more.

The same view finds expression in the verse from E already quoted (Deut 31:14ff.), in which Moses and Joshua enter the tent and Yahweh appears in the cloud and talks to Moses. This is invariably the view found in the ancient accounts of the desert period, in which the appearance of the cloud ('anan) is the infallible indication of Yahweh's coming. Yahweh can come down to his people only in the cloud: he appears in the cloud to guide them in their wanderings; the cloud throws the Egyptian army into confusion; Yahweh comes down on Sinai in a cloud to show his glory. When Aaron and Miriam murmur, the cloud appears over the tent, as it does when the spirit is conferred upon the seventy elders (Exod 13:21-22; 14:19ff., 24; 19:9, 16; 24:15, 16, 18; 33:9, 10; 34:5; Num 10:34; 11:25; 12:5, 10; 14:14). This is the conception that has been handed down to us from the period of the desert wanderings, and from it arose the notion of the tent of meeting. The very idea of "meeting" is intelligible only if Yahweh is thought to be afar off!

We may now safely assert that where such a view of God prevails, there is no room for the ark or for the theological attitudes that go with it. We have seen from the ancient stories of the ark how inseparably God was thought to be attached to it. Where the ark went, Yahweh went too. This cannot be said of the tent. It is no exaggeration to say that on the original premises there is no way of bridging the gap between the idea that Yahweh came into the camp with the ark (1 Samuel 4) and the belief that he came down from above upon the tent in a cloud. What is the cloud for, if Yahweh is in any case there already? Nowhere in the ancient histories of the ark is there any suggestion of a manifestation which descends in a cloud, despite the continual accounts of Yahweh's deeds which we find in these histories.[24] Indeed, it would be completely nonsensical if there were such a manifestation, for Yahweh sits continually upon his throne. "Arise" (qûmah), they call to him, and when he appears to the sleeping Samuel he has no need to come down from above, but is said only to "stand forth before him" (wayyityaṣṣeb).

We may sum up our conclusion as follows: the notions of "meeting" and of "being enthroned" are mutually exclusive, and this seems to us to be the strongest of all arguments against the possibility that the ark originated in the desert. Undoubtedly a reliable recollection is recorded in the oldest accounts, and these know nothing of any association between tent and ark. Both passages which depict the ark as already extant in these early times mention it along with the tent, but totally unrelated to it—a sure indication of the secondary nature of these texts. Thus the two palladia could not be integrally linked together, as they had been to begin with, but were inevitably mutually repellent by virtue of the radically divergent ideas associated with each of them.

Once we have learned to distinguish between these two mutually exclusive complexes of ideas, we can trace in greater detail the various stages which we have established by looking into their history. We may regard the two conceptions of ark and tent as two currents flowing side by side in a single stream down the ages of Israel's religious history. In the end the idea of the tent drives out completely the notion of the ark as a throne, but has absorbed certain essential elements of this conception.

When David tells us that he has set up a tent for the ark, we still cannot regard this as implying a fusion of the old ideas associated with the tent and the ark, since this makes no provision for the incorporation of the special characteristics of the ancient tent of meeting. David still has no cultic building, and he therefore makes temporary arrangements, a fact which in itself proves that he intends to replace the tent by a temple. Hence David in no way takes into account the ideas connected with the tent of meeting, since the temple is expressly a dwelling for Yahweh (2 Sam 6:17). On the other hand, Nathan's protest against the building of a temple must be understood as a vindication of the tradition of the tent against the parallel tradition of the ark (2 Sam 7:5ff.).

The account of the arrangement of the Most Holy Place is perhaps not wholly original, but precisely for this reason it provides us with a valuable pointer: the cherubim are of set purpose removed from the ark, and their function is changed so that they now protect the ark. By this alteration the notion of the ark as a throne is very greatly weakened. The deuteronomist sets it aside altogether. He achieves this by going back to the much more ancient view that the ark is a receptacle. Modernized and divested of all numinous associations, it now becomes the receptacle for the Law. This is indicative of the tenacity with which traditions are maintained once they have been admitted: the deuteronomist does not make an attack on the idea of the throne in commending the conceptions associated with the tent of meeting. On the contrary, he introduces his own theological notion that it is the *name* of Yahweh which dwells in the cultic place, thus combating the older conception of "indwelling" by producing a new one.

Now at last the time had come when the ideas associated with the ark could be combined with those belonging to the tent. This was the theological achievement of the priestly code, which itself stands firmly in line of tradition of the tent. It would not be true to say that P simply continues the process from the point at which D leaves off. Against this view is the very fact that whereas P stands in the line of tradition of the tent, D follows the tradition of the ark. Nevertheless it would be true to say in general terms that P has progressed beyond the point reached in Deuteronomy. The ark, understood to be the receptacle for the Law, is now installed in the tent.

We found in the highly numinous conception of the "cover" one element which was altogether foreign to the view that the ark was a receptacle. A further contradiction was seen in the juxtaposition of the beliefs that on the one hand Yahweh was always in the tent, and on the other hand that he appeared only from time to time, in the cloud. Now that we understand better the nature of the ark and of the tent we begin to see these contradictions in a wider perspective. The attitude which regards the ark as a receptacle for the Law unquestionably derives from the deuteronomist's reinterpretation; on the other hand we believe it possible now to understand how this is related to the sacral significance of the "cover." This was formerly the most holy place where Yahweh sat enthroned, and since we previously found side by side the ideas of "meeting" and "indwelling," we need not now be surprised even by this fact, for it was as the throne of Yahweh that the ark was installed in the tent.

The combination of such originally heterogeneous conceptions can be illustrated in a particularly striking way from the function of the "cover": here Yahweh had formerly been thought to sit enthroned, and still according to P's teaching Yahweh reveals himself between the cherubim. To this extent everything fits in with the basic conception of the ark; but now this view is directly linked with that of the place of meeting. Yahweh's self-revelation from the cover of the ark is not in any way a communication from one who sits enthroned upon the ark. Yahweh merely appears here and meets with Moses at this spot (*wenô'adti*). It is on these lines that the notion of the appearance of Yahweh is now attached to the ark, even down to the use of the typical word *ya'ad* (Exod 25:22; 29:42-43; 30:6, 36; Num 17:19 [see Lev 16:2]; Num 7:89). Here is undoubtedly a theological combination that goes far beyond the inventive powers of the ancient inhabitants of Beth Shemesh or the sons of Eli.[25]

All this sheds further light on the relationship of the temple to the tabernacle of the priestly writer. Wellhausen's statement that the tabernacle is the temple projected back into the period of the desert wanderings must now be called in question. P stands in the "tent of meeting" tradition, but by contrast the ark was the very heart of the temple, and the whole lay-out of the temple was designed on the understanding that it was a dwelling for Yahweh. The

Chronicler took the ark seriously and consequently regarded the temple as the house of the ark; he was thus more decisively a supporter of the temple than was P, whom we now see to have used the tabernacle tradition as a corrective to the notion of the temple which had developed in his day.

The theology of the tent, originally unrelated to the ark and at times certainly eclipsed by it,[26] ultimately gained the ascendancy. The ark was accepted into the tent only at the cost of surrendering its characteristic associations. We thus arrive at our second conclusion, that Yahwism not only absorbed many other elements which were originally foreign to it, but also absorbed the ark itself, and by virtue of its unique power drew in those elements which were congenial to it whilst rejecting the others.

A problem now arises which is of special interest to the theologian, and which we shall touch on in bringing this study to a close. In what respects was the religion of Yahweh enriched by the theology it took over with the ark?

The ark is a cultic object originating in settled territory. It thus stands in a religious tradition which is concerned to produce and to preserve the benefits of civilized life. The direct relationship between the ark and a sedentary civilization is to be discerned above all in the connection between the ark and that fundamental feature of settled life, the house. The ark stands in a most intimate relationship to the cultic house. We find it initially in a quite ordinary kind of temple at Shiloh; it is installed in the house of Obed Edom, and in Jerusalem it is the nucleus around which the whole design of Solomon's temple is built up. To this the tent is diametrically opposed, and it is most significant that at the decisive moment the claims of the temple are contested in favor of those of the tent.

It must, however, be emphasized that foreign religious elements were not drawn in quite indiscriminately along with the ark. To mention only the most important of such elements, the Yahweh of the ark is not a nature-deity, and nowhere is there any trace of a fertility cult connected with the ark. Three features nevertheless emerge which were not associated with the Yahweh of the desert wanderings, but which found their way into Yahwism through the adoption of the ark.

According to the primitive view, Yahweh was not native to the land; even when the nation was in a settled state it was believed that he appeared from the south in times of great extremity, and we know that this remoteness of Yahweh was consciously felt to be a serious problem.[27] Quite clearly this separation of Israel from its God could not but lead to a crisis in the religion of Yahweh. There were gods in the land who were certainly easier to find, who lived, so to speak, on friendly terms with the inhabitants, and could be called upon for aid at any time. The fact that with the ark Israel received an assurance of the continual presence of Yahweh must therefore have been a matter of inestimable moment.

Now he was there with them; in time of need one could make a pilgrimage to him; he went out to war with Israel, and finally came into the capital city in order to dwell in the midst of his people. Yet, as we are reminded by the temple consecration-prayer, Yahweh's superiority over all creation remained inviolate, in contrast to all the nature-deities of the land. This is the first point.

The second is closely bound up with it. Yahweh had revealed himself to certain of the tribes in the desert, had made a covenant with them and given them ordinances in connection with this covenant. When Israel settled in the promised land this relationship was disturbed. Other tribes which had not been with Israel at Horeb joined themselves to Israel,[28] and Israel now became a nation. A nation, however, has different interests to protect, and self-defense becomes a vital problem of a very different order. For this reason, it is a religious problem. Now that the tribes had developed into a nation, could they still remain under the protection of Yahweh, or had they moved out of the jurisdiction of the God of Sinai? Again, the ark provided the focal point at which Yahweh could be thought of as the nation's divine protector.

Kautsch established the fact that the title "Yahweh of hosts" (*yhwh seba'oth*) originally belonged to the ark, and it is certainly no accident that the politically-minded David became interested in the ark. Only Deuteronomy contains extensive legislation concerning the camp, sieges, military service, and war (Deut 20:10ff.; 23:10ff.; 24:5ff.); and if the chronicler, a pretentious advocate on behalf of the ark, fairly revels in stories of Yahweh's subvention in holy wars, no doubt there was good precedent for it. National religion and the ark are inseparable.

In conclusion we must draw attention to yet one more feature of the theology of the ark. If we look back over the long chain of tradition from Shiloh, through the deuteronomist to the chronicler, we are struck by the characteristically buoyant optimism. Cultic, religious joy is evidently inseparable from the ark. Israel shouts for joy when the ark comes into the camp; we are told of the joy of the inhabitants of Beth Shemesh when they see it, of David's dancing, of playing with harps, drums, and cymbals. The deuteronomist, who stands in the full stream of the tradition of the ark, never tires of promoting cultic rejoicing (*śimḥah*), and at the end of the line stands the chronicler, whose public worship consists almost wholly of praise and thanksgiving, and who specifically entrusts the task of singing to the attendants of the ark. Through the influence of the ark, Yahwism learned to temper the severity of justice with a handsome measure of mercy, and both the deuteronomist and the chronicler sought continually to formulate in theological terms the resultant status of man before God.

These seem to us to be the more important factors by the adoption of which Yahwism gained in breadth and depth, and in which the theology of the ark lived on. For the rest, the theological attitudes connected with the ark were inevitably overlaid by the weightier traditions of the tent. Just how much weightier was this theology of the tent can be seen by looking at the New Testament, in which it could most appositely be rejuvenated. The terms *skēnoun, skēnē, skēnōma* (see esp. John 1:14; also 2 Cor 12:9; Heb 8:2; 9:11; Rev 7:15; 15:5; 21:3) here become once more expressions of the most profound theological insights, whereas the ark is mentioned seldom and only in passing (Heb 9:4; Rev 11:19). The theology of the tent found in the New Testament the fulfillment which was prophesied for it in the earliest times: here God speaks to men "as a man speaks to his friend" (Exod 33:11).

8

The City on the Hill

In our understanding of the prophetic message, we are still in the throes of a conservative reaction against the well-known account of the matter given by such writers as Bernhard Duhm. The case is actually less simple than this, both with regard to the novelty of the prophetic notions, and to the opposition offered to them on the part of the people. We should see the prophets rather as those who hold and proclaim eschatological beliefs that were already extant, and in all essentials fully developed, in the popular tradition. There was no argument as to the validity and rightness of these conceptions, which equally were regarded as axiomatic by the prophets themselves. A much more fruitful cause of dissention was the question of their application and its consequences. There is no doubt that the prophets laid claim to an unprecedented measure of liberty, both in their handling of ancient and accepted religious ideas and, even more particularly, in their application of them to a particular situation and to a particular group of people. It seems, however, that the time has come when we must make a new evaluation of the notion of prophecy, taking into account this dependence on tradition. In the following pages, however, we shall consider only one aspect of these eschatological conceptions—one that was taken up by some of the prophets and was sometimes developed in distinctive directions.

Isaiah's whole prophetic work centers upon the holy city of Zion, the chosen city of Yahweh. So exclusively is this notion pursued that one cannot help asking whether Isaiah was even aware of the covenantal theology that finds its classical formulation in the source documents of the Hexateuch. For him the sole basis of the religious justification, not only for Zion but for Israel itself,[1] lay in the fact that Yahweh had founded it (Isa 14:32), and that a tremendous promise had been made concerning it to the throne of David. Yet this statement of the facts in itself shows that the tradition preserved and expressed by

Isaiah was not a unity, but rather a decidedly complex agglomeration of traditions. Isaiah takes his stand on the sure ground of Nathan's prophecy, that tradition of the Davidic covenant in which Yahweh confers divine sonship upon the Davidic line of kings, and promises that the throne of David shall endure for ever.[2] With this tradition, however, is interwoven a conception which is really independent of it, that of the holy mountain, a notion fairly clearly derived from panoriental mythology and perhaps first associated with the Davidic covenantal tradition by Isaiah itself.[3] It may be remarked in passing that from time to time Isaiah incorporates yet a third conception, that of the holy remnant (Isa 1:9; 14:32; 30:17).

> It shall come to pass in the latter days that the mountain of the house of Yahweh shall be established as the highest of the mountains, and shall be raised above the hills; and all the nations shall flow to it, and many peoples shall come, and say: "Come, let us go up to the mountain of Yahweh, to the house of the God of Jacob; that he may teach us his ways and that we may walk in his paths." For out of Zion shall go forth the law, and the word of Yahweh from Jerusalem. He shall judge between the nations, and shall decide for many peoples; and they shall beat their swords into ploughshares, and their spears into pruning hooks; nation shall not lift up sword against nation, neither shall they learn war any more. (Isa 2:2-4)

This is the first and also the earliest expression of a belief in the eschatological glorification of the holy mountain and of its significance for the redemption of the entire world. It cannot well be doubted that the text is Isaianic in origin, despite the fact that it is, of course, found also in Micah (Mic 4:1-3). It fits perfectly into the overall pattern of Isaianic thought, but one cannot say the same of the occurrence in Micah. The wording of the text is in doubt only in vv. 2 and 3a,[4] and the passage looks forward to a radical reversal in the natural order of the present geographical situation: the hill on which the temple stands will tower above all mountains.[5] The place with which Yahweh has chosen to associate his redemptive purpose will rise up from its inconspicuous and unrecognized position, and will be seen in all its glory by the whole world, with the result that it will be the center of a universal pilgrimage for all nations. We hear them talking on the way there, but only at the end of the oracle do we learn the true purpose of this eschatological migration: the nations are impelled by their own turbulence to seek the holy mountain and so to escape from their unhallowed way of life. There they will receive the divine ordinances, by which they will be enabled to live together in lasting peace.

The prophet evidently envisages the conversion of weapons into tools as taking place only after the peoples have returned to their own lands. The prophecy ends with a strikingly sober and realistic picture, and the scene remains in every sense a historical one wholly devoid of mythological overtones. Nevertheless the ordinances given to the nations are manifestly conceived of as a divine creative fiat: their effectiveness no longer depends upon human, earthly contingencies, but rather the divine word creatively brings about obedience to itself. To receive this instruction is to receive newness of life.

The course of events is rooted in the cultus, and reflects the pilgrimage that Isaiah may well have seen year by year as the pilgrim bands came to the temple at the time of the Feast of Booths. There is, it is true, no mention of sacrifices or oblations, but the divine law itself is received in the cultic place.[6] One might be inclined to regard the whole oracle as a poetic creation of Isaiah's prophetic genius, in which present experience has been universalized and projected into the realm of eschatology. The passage that follows immediately nevertheless shows that Isaiah is here taking up an eschatological conception that was in all essentials already firmly established. If we ask precisely what is the prophet's own contribution, it must be replied that he has dynamically drawn together this already extant material, which we shall see to have had significantly wider application, and has brought it to bear upon what appears throughout his work as a specifically Isaianic concept—that of an eschatological promulgation and fulfillment of the divine law. One may also detect a breath of the Isaianic spirit in the evident desire to get away from the phantasmagoric mythology of the beginning of the oracle to a more soberly historical outline, in which even in the eschaton the nations return to their own lands.

> 1. Arise, shine; for your light has come, and the glory of Yahweh has risen upon you. 2. For behold, darkness covers[7] the earth, and thick darkness the peoples; but Yahweh shines[8] upon you, and his glory appears over you. 3. And nations shall come to your light, and kings to the brightness of your rising. 4. Lift up your eyes round about, and see; they all gather together, they come to you; your sons shall come from far, and your daughters shall be carried in the arms. 5. Then you shall see and be radiant, your heart shall thrill and rejoice; because the abundance of the sea shall be turned to you, the wealth of the nations shall come to you. 6. A multitude of camels shall cover you, the young camels of Midian and Ephah; and those from Sheba shall come. They shall bring gold and frankincense, and shall proclaim the praise of Yahweh. 7. All the flocks of Kedar shall be gathered to you, the rams of Nebaioth shall minister to you; they shall come up with

acceptance on my altar and I will glorify my glorious house. 8. Who are those that fly like a cloud, and like doves to their windows? 9. For the coastlands shall wait for me, the ships of Tarshish first, to bring your sons from far, their silver and gold with them, for the name of Yahweh your God, and for the holy one of Israel, because he has glorified you. 10. Foreigners shall build up your walls, and their kings shall minister to you; for in my wrath I smote you, but in my favor I have had mercy on you. 11. Your gates shall be open continually; day and night they shall not be shut; that men may bring you the wealth of nations, with their kings led in procession. (12. For the nation and kingdom that will not serve you shall perish; those nations shall be utterly laid waste.)[10] 13. The glory of Lebanon shall come to you, the cypress, the plane, and the pine, to beautify the place of my sanctuary; and I will make the place of my feet glorious. 14. The sons of those who oppressed you shall come bending low to you; and all who despised you shall bow down at your feet; they shall call you the City of Yahweh, the Zion of the holy one of Israel. 15. Whereas you have been forsaken and hated, with no one passing through, I will make you majestic forever, a joy from age to age. 16. You shall suck the milk of nations, you shall suck the breast of kings; and you shall know that I, Yahweh, am your saviour and your redeemer, the mighty one of Jacob. 17. Instead of bronze I will bring gold, and instead of iron I will bring silver; instead of wood, bronze, instead of stones, iron. I will make your overseers peace and your taskmasters righteousness. 18. Violence shall no more be heard in your land, devastation or destruction within your borders; you shall call your walls Salvation, and your gates Praise. 19. The sun shall be no more your light by day, nor for brightness shall the moon give light to you by night; but Yahweh will be your everlasting light, and your God will be your glory. 20. Your sun shall no more go down, nor your moon withdraw itself; for Yahweh will be your everlasting light, and your days of mourning shall be ended. 21. Your people shall all be righteous; they shall possess the land forever, the shoot of my planting, the work of my hands, that I might be glorified. 22. The least one shall become a clan, and the smallest one a mighty nation; I am Yahweh; in its time I will hasten it. (Isa 60:1-22)

The much wider scope of this passage from Trito-Isaiah might give us to pause before comparing it with the oracle contained in Isaiah 2; but if we reduce this prophecy to its simplest terms—and they are, indeed, very simple ones—it corresponds closely in outline with the earlier Isaianic prophecy.

The chapter is a self-contained entity, in which Yahweh himself speaks (cf. vv. 7b, 9, 10b, 13, 15a, 17, 21ff.), although the exact form of a divine pronouncement is not consistently maintained. Yahweh is addressing a city, and calls upon it to awake in anticipation of the glorification that his coming will bring to it. A contrast is drawn in the dimension of cosmic reality: impenetrable darkness hangs over the heathen world, but the brightness of Yahweh's own glory has risen over Jerusalem. This phenomenon, manifestly visible to all the nations, has the self-same effect as that described in Isaiah 2: nations and kings come in from all directions, desert nomads from the east and ships of Tarshish from the west, to pay tribute to this divine glory now revealed upon earth. The purpose of their pilgrimage is pre-eminently a cultic one: they are bringing incense (v. 6), innumerable herds of sheep for Yahweh's altar (v. 7), and the finest timbers for the building of the temple (v. 13).

But that is not all. The oracle has an immediate relevancy to the situation of Israel almost two hundred years after the time of Isaiah ben Amoz: a great part of God's chosen people are still in exile and have not yet returned home, and it is the heathen themselves who will bring back the dispersed. "Your daughters shall be carried in the arms," we are told (v. 4). In other respects the post-exilic situation, following the return of the first group of exiles, is made abundantly clear: Zion is still without walls, and lies defenseless at the mercy of her neighbors (v. 14); the land is given over to violence (v. 18); the city is bereft of commerce, avoided by merchants and travelers (v. 15); the people are few in numbers (v. 22).[11]

It is therefore the more striking that in this oracle the tribute that is foretold is not paid exclusively to Yahweh. Israel, too, has a share in it.[12] The erstwhile oppressors will serve Israel, they will help to build the holy city, and the treasures of the world will fill the new Jerusalem. Yet in all this Yahweh himself remains in the center of the picture, and his will and his all-guiding providence "will make Israel majestic" (v. 15). Yahweh, indeed, will be so immediately experienced by Israel that the nation will live by his light and no longer by the light of the sun and moon. They will recognize Yahweh as their savior (v. 16b), and will live in peace, secure from any violence.

It is evident that this oracle follows step by step the same eschatological material used by Isaiah. Especially is this to be observed in the closing verses, where *hamas* (violence) is a highly significant word: it denotes the destruction of due order, and we recall that it was the irruption of violence (*hamas*) that, according to the theology of the priestly code, shattered the primeval orderliness of creation itself (Gen 6:11, 13)! Here, then, we have the eschatological fulfillment of the divine law, the dawn of eternal peace.

Yet the difference between this passage and Isaiah 2 is unmistakable. In the former passage all the interest was concentrated on the heathen nations and on the significance that the transfigured Jerusalem had for them. Now, on the contrary, attention is focused almost exclusively on the holy city, which itself shares in the divinely ordered reign of peace. Mention is made, it is true, of the new acknowledgment of God's sovereignty by the heathen—indeed, they bear witness to the glorious works of God[13]—but this has reference primarily to their eagerness to come and to their willingness to contribute in this way to the glorification of the holy city. The proportions of this migration are suggested by means of the subjective effect of the experience: the oracle gives a foretaste of the events as seen from the point of view of the city itself. Zion will be "radiant," its heart will "thrill" (v. 5), and, as in an altogether analogous situation in Isa 49:18ff., Zion will ask with astonishment, "Who are these that fly like a cloud?" (60:8). It cannot understand the vast fleet of ships bearing in upon it. Indeed, the original summons to the city, calling it to bestir itself in preparation for the great eschatological miracle to come, sketches in subjectively the fact of this migration.

It is very difficult for us properly to evaluate on the one hand the remarkable interdependence of these ancient and well-established eschatological conceptions, and on the other hand the free adaptation of them. One gets the impression that Isaiah has taken material that was originally no doubt of very diverse origin, and has welded it together as tightly as possible into one single basic concept. Yet Isaiah 60 makes it clear that a much wider scope might be allowed to the poetic imagination. We must admit in the fact of this material that our understanding of what constitutes poetic originality and what traditionalism is wholly inadequate. Duhm's destructive criticism in his commentary stands opposed to the equally emphatic judgment of J. Burckhardt; and both are blinded by a romantic, western outlook.[14]

> For thus says Yahweh of hosts: In yet a little while,[15] I will shake the heavens and the earth and the sea, the dry land; and I will shake all nations, so that the treasures[16] of all nations shall come in, and I will fill this house with splendor, says Yahweh of hosts. The silver is mine, and the gold is mine, says Yahweh of hosts. The latter splendor of this house shall be greater than the former, says Yahweh of hosts; and in this place I will give prosperity, says Yahweh of hosts. (Hag 2:6-9)

The prophetic oracles of Haggai are dated by year, month, and day, and this prophecy delivered in the late autumn of the year 520 B.C.E. is thus roughly contemporary with that of Isaiah 60. We learn from the Book of Haggai of the serious problems that confronted the returning exiles, but under the influence of the prophets the rebuilding of the temple nevertheless became for the people the touchstone of faith. A start was made upon the work, evidently at the instigation of the prophets, but the people soon became discouraged when the little they had achieved thus far made it clear what a poor thing the finished product would be: "Is it not in your sight as nothing?" (Hag 2:3). But the prophet takes a very different view, and this is where our present oracle begins.

In a short while God will shake heaven and earth. The prophet seems to expect a radical overturning of the entire cosmic order. Now, despite the fact that Haggai gives only a very brief account of the eschatological events, we see the immediate effect on the heathen world, shaken by the cosmic disturbance: all flow to Jerusalem, now evidently visible from every quarter of the earth. Of the nations themselves Haggai has nothing to say, but rather concerns himself solely with the treasures that will then "come in." A starkly challenging sentence proclaims Yahweh's exclusive right to possess them (v. 8). It is as if they have been hitherto on temporary loan, and are still held back from their true purpose as the property of Yahweh. In the eschaton, however, they will return from this misappropriation into the exclusive control of Yahweh, their rightful owner.

It would seem superfluous to say more concerning this text—i.e., with regard to the supposed materialism and avarice which so many expositors have described as a jarring note both in this oracle and in that of Isaiah 60. There is no question here of greed for gain, but a proclamation by Yahweh which the prophet sets down with uncompromising boldness, and any exegesis which casts doubt upon this mighty purposefulness of Yahweh in the present world-order stands self-condemned in its own supposed spirituality.

Yahweh, then, will glorify by his own eschatological act this temple of the new Jerusalem, which as yet presents to the prophet's contemporaries so discouraging and poverty-stricken a spectacle. The statement that Yahweh will give prosperity to this place[17] comes almost as it were without warning. The prophet has given to the traditional eschatological material so strong a bias that neither the recipients of this prosperity (Israel? or the heathen?) nor the mode of its reception (proclamation of the divine commandments? participation in the cultus?) have been brought within our purview. We nevertheless saw that this expectation of final peace formed an inalienable and most important element of the ancient eschatological concept. Even Haggai could not end his oracle without mentioning it.

In concluding our discussion of these three oracles, stemming as they do from a single stock of tradition, there are two temptations to be resisted. It is scarcely possible to reconstruct on the basis of our study the original conception that is at the root of our texts. For this purpose we should need to adduce still further texts, for not only Psalms 46 and 48, but also Isa 25:6-10a; Zechariah 14; Tob 13:9-17; 14:5-7, all belong within the same general complex as the three prophecies. We therefore refrain from any comparative evaluation of these oracles, or any attempt to play off one against the others. How could we possibly assess whether or not a prophet has properly discharged his task vis à vis his own generation, or whether he has used or abused his liberty of remolding in his own way the traditional materials? To make any such judgment we should need at the very least a precise and detailed knowledge of the historical situation, and of its potentialities as well as its dangers.

Let us then say no more than that Isaiah 60 stands almost exactly half-way between Isaiah 2 and Haggai 2, although not, of course, from the point of view of its value. The version found in Trito-Isaiah has common links with each of the other two, whereas Isaiah 2 and Haggai 2 exemplify opposite extremes. According to Isaiah ben Amoz, Israel is the spectator of something which concerns Yahweh and the heathen nations alone, and Yahweh receives no tribute from the peoples who come to Zion: his presentation is no less one-sided or abbreviated than the opposing one which we found in Haggai, where it is the heathen nations who are almost wholly excluded from the picture, and the reason for their coming is as obscure as their part in the eschatological weal.[18] No more was said than that the treasures would "come in" to the temple of the new Jerusalem. The conclusion would seem to be that Trito-Isaiah, despite what are clearly his own embellishments, has given the fullest expression to the basic conception that underlies all three oracles.

It may be worthwhile, however, in concluding our study, to make a suggestion concerning Matt 5:14. It is most probably that the reference here to the "city set on a hill" is concerned with something more than a simple analogy drawn from everyday experience. The saying about the city which is visible to all is closely bound up with that concerning the light of the world: the eschatological congregation of the faithful is the city set on a hill, and their light will be visible to the whole world. The saying thus takes up an ancient eschatological apocalyptic theme, re-echoing that already sounded by Isaiah in the Old Testament.

Part II

From Samuel to Kings

9

The Beginnings of Historical Writing
in Ancient Israel

In the modern western world we take it altogether for granted that the writing of history is a valid intellectual occupation. It is seen as an indispensable prerequisite for the deeper understanding of our human existence. In this respect western civilization is the heir and also the pupil of both Greek and biblical historical writers. If for a moment we lift our eyes from this great fund of intellectual historical writing, we cannot but agree that what we understand by "historical sense" in the strictest sense is by no means widespread among other nations and civilizations.

A historical sense is a particular form of causational thinking, applied in practice to a broad succession of political events. It therefore involves a particularly acute perception of the realities of a nation's situation. It is not difficult to show that most peoples of antiquity were not impelled to analyze their situation in this way. Their historical existence, that is to say their existence in an irreversible time-sequence, presented no problem to them. They were in no position to see great political events in terms of historical contingency, and did not find it necessary to fit these events into a wider pattern of historical cause and effect. For this reason they produced no historical writing.

Of course these civilizations produced all kinds of historical documents. Court chronicles and annals were compiled, lists of kings were drawn up, civic records were kept; but all this still does not amount to the writing of genuine history. Still less can we allow the name of history to accounts of wars, ceremonial inscriptions, or the records of buildings erected by some ruler. "Bare lists of rulers or their ancestors, however imposing their length, are in themselves no indication of chronological thinking. They are merely evidence of a conservative state of mind, in which laws and customs are carefully preserved by tradition, and there is not continual recourse to first principles."[1]

A striking inability to think historically in the sense defined above is characteristic of the ancient Egyptians. Eminently conservative, eminently literate, they limited their reflections on the past to mere antiquarian details, and were incapable of building up wider pictures.[2] Similarly the civilizations of Mesopotamia, despite the checkered history of this area, built up no ordered conception of history beyond documents of the kind mentioned above. At the most one can speak only of an attempt to establish an intelligible sequence of historical events by means of lists. They lacked the power to meet the task of presenting the history of the nation in a unified and orderly form.[3]

Not until the empires had finally stepped down from the stage of history did Berossus attempt to write their history, and then only under Greek influence. Even then it was not historical writing in the true sense, for "genuinely historical writing that faithfully represents its own era always and invariably grows out of the political life of the day, whatever shape or form that may take."[4] There are only two peoples in antiquity who really wrote history—the Greeks and, long before them, the Israelites. It is the task of this study to analyze the historical writing of the latter only in its early stages.

We cannot trace the origins of ancient Israelite historical writing. At a particular point in time it is there, and already we have it in its fully developed form. We can, however, trace the predisposing factors that made such an achievement possible to this people.

First there was what we earlier described as a "historical sense," that peculiarly characteristic capacity to experience history *consciously*. The intellect is directed almost exclusively towards the historical reference of every phenomenon, and it can therefore properly be said that there is a primacy of the real over the ideal.[5] It would be difficult to find a nation so markedly preoccupied from its earliest days with the question of its own origins. What nation in antiquity was so precisely informed concerning its earlier migrations, or was able to give account of the period in which it became settled by producing reliable documents (compare, for example, the lists in Judg 1:19ff.)? "There is probably no other nation on earth whose genuine historical traditions, established by contemporaries, go back to a time so near to the beginnings of its nationhood."[6]

Historical thinking, in fact, is a part of the nation's consciousness even in its most primitive manifestations. In those remarkable situations and circumstances that surrounded ancient Israel there was already an inescapable compulsion constantly to enquire into the origin and growth of the nation. This fact can perhaps be no more strikingly demonstrated than by pointing to that category of Old Testament narrative which had grown up long before there was any real historical writing—the etiological saga. It may be questioned whether it was found in such profusion and diversity amongst any other people.

The etiological saga may be sparked off by any remarkable or inexplicable fact that attracts man's attention. It undertakes to show why things should be as they are, turning the reader's attention to the past, and describing an event that elucidates the problem. The simplest form of the saga, both with regard to its structure and to its mode of reasoning, is that connected with a particular place. Why is there a heap of stones before the city gate at Ai (Josh 8:29)? What is the significance of the twelve stones at Gilgal (Josh 4:20ff.)? How is it that a Canaanitish family continued to reside in Jericho (Josh 6:25)? Why was the mound of the ancient city of Jericho never resettled (Josh 6:26)?

In these sagas, the connection postulated between the past event and the contemporary state of affairs is still a comparatively loose one. Of much greater relevance to the hearer are the facts that form the material of tribal etiological sagas or ethnographic sagas. Genesis 9:18-27 answers the question of how it came about that the Canaanites had sunk to so abject a condition of slavery. It was, we are told, a result of their immodesty and sexual depravity (cf. Lev 18:22ff.). Why did the Ishmaelites, a tribe closely related to Israel, remain such wild sons of the desert (Genesis 16)? How did the peoples of Ammon and Moab originate, and how were they related to Israel (Gen 19:30ff.)? How did Edom (Esau) and Israel (Jacob) become estranged, although they were brothers, and how did the latter attain to the primacy (Genesis 27)?

Whatever may be our opinion of the answers that the sagas give in certain instances, in every case the questions to which these narratives aim to provide a historical answer are very serious ones. Everywhere there is evidence of an effort to explain the present in terms of the past, and this effort is itself the most explicit expression of historical thinking.[7]

Let us now look at a quite different application of the etiological motive, in order to show how diversely and how vigorously the Hebrew mind carried out this kind of conscious investigation. We refer to the primeval etiologies. How can one explain the painful effort involved in man's tilling of the soil? Whence comes the anguish of a woman in childbirth, in a world that God created free from any jarring note (Gen 3:16ff.)? Why is mankind divided into races that no longer understand one another (Gen 11:1ff.)? The objects of these questions are matters of universal experience, and the fundamental factors of all human existence are deduced from etiological premises. Furthermore—and this is the important point—they are treated as matters of *history*, as belonging to an unrepeatable course of events which humanity has passed through with God.

The second predisposing factor which we must mention is Israel's quite outstanding talent for narrative presentation, about which so much has been written; what we refer to is the ability to depict the characteristic, unique aspect of people and situations with the greatest economy of linguistic apparatus, a feature of Israelite literature which has become the model for all western poetic writing. The style is simple, lucid, and moderate in tone, rigorously avoiding superlatives, even—and indeed especially—at crucial moments. It is in fact this very restraint of presentation which leaves the reader with an impression of forceful writing and momentous subject-matter.

The third predisposing factor we wish to speak of here is of a quite different order. It derives from the unique religious conceptions of this people. From the earliest times Israel had been accustomed to seeing in every unusual event the direct intervention of God. Old Testament man attributed to Yahweh even those occurrences of public or private life that every other religion would have traced to the activity of demons, or other anonymous intermediate beings. The depression that overcame Saul was an evil spirit sent by Yahweh (1 Sam 16:14), and Yahweh decreed the plague in Jerusalem as well (2 Sam 24:1ff.). The conception of God as active in all things was so all-pervasive that faith was left with no alternative explanation: it was inconceivable that there should be any gap in this chain of causality. "Does evil befall a city unless Yahweh has done it?" asks Amos (3:6), demanding of his hearers an answer that will be uncompromising, and also most uncomfortable for people of an unsophisticated religious outlook.

Quite clearly this doctrinal conception cannot fail to give rise to a most powerful organizing principle, that of the inescapable succession of historical events. Indeed we must go further, and say that Israel owes to its unique religious faith a capacity to see and understand as history what is really no more than a succession of isolated occurrences. It is well to bear in mind from the outset this religious basis of the historical thought of the Old Testament, so that we may be in no doubt that it is totally different from the Greek conception of history. *The Israelites came to a historical way of thinking, and then to historical writing, by way of their belief in the sovereignty of God in history.* For them, "History is under God's management. He sets the process in motion by his promise. He sets its limits according to his will, and watches over it. . . . All history has its course in God, and takes place for God."[8]

We are, indeed, in the presence of a unique conception of history, in which the significance of events is not to be sought in what happens here on earth. The real actors in the drama are neither nations nor kings nor celebrated heroes. Yet the whole course of events is pursued with breath-taking interest, and the writer is himself deeply involved in the narrative, precisely because this is the sphere of divine activity.

It is true that Herodotus, too, recognized "metaphysical powers, which operate in the realm of earthly events through a multiplicity of omens, prophecies, and dreams,"[9] but this factor in history is shown only from time to time. It is not applied consistently, nor is it integrally related to the course of events. The subject of history for Herodotus is from first to last the human issue of the struggle between Greek and barbarian, and, as Herodotus explains in his preface, his aim is to save from oblivion the glory of great deeds. Thucydides is, or course, much more explicit than Herodotus, maintaining an "icy skepticism" on the subject of divine intervention.[10] From our point of view, however, the difference between the two authors is of no consequence, for both Herodotus and Thucydides are exclusively concerned in their writings with the history of man.

SAGAS OF HEROES

Before we turn our attention to ancient Israelite historical writing as such, we must first look for a moment at a type of tradition that, although it has not yet developed into historical writing, is nevertheless closely bound up with the historical outlook. We refer to sagas of ancient heroes. A brief comparison of the two may serve to give us a more profound insight into the essential nature and particular features of historical writing.

Of all the types of ancient Israelite sagas, including those to do with places, cultic practices, etymologies, tribal origins and so on, the hero-sagas are unquestionably the most nearly historical. They do not tell of hazy figures from the distant past, as do the patriarchal sagas of Genesis: their heroes stand in the full light of history. Neither their own historicity, nor the scene of their activities, nor the reality of the political conflicts in which they are involved can be impugned. We find hero-sagas in the Book of Joshua, more particularly in Judges, and sporadically in 1 Samuel. We shall take as an example the cycle of tradition concerning Gideon, without however entering into details of its analysis.

On the whole the tradition concerning Gideon presents a fairly rounded picture. It begins with his call, and then goes on to show proof of the charisma that has fallen upon Gideon by recounting a feat of valor performed by stealth. Then comes the account of his mighty deed, the defeat of the Midianites, narrated in all its detail. Finally we are told how Gideon nevertheless succumbed to the temptation to idolatry after his victory. The story thus comes to an effective conclusion: the man who began so brilliantly has readily become involved in grave sin, so that having forfeited his charismatic gift he sinks at the last into the oblivion of anonymity.

Nevertheless, this catena of narrative is not by any means a history; it is a conglomeration of very diverse sagas. The section describing Gideon's call (Judg 6:11-24) was once an etiological cult-saga, and contains all the elements characteristic of such a composition: the appearance of the deity, the first sacrifice offered on a hitherto unhallowed spot, the building of an altar, and finally the observation that this altar has been preserved "to this day." The narrative was a typical *hieros logos*, whose purpose was to guarantee the legitimacy of a cultic shrine by recounting the manner in which the sanctuary was founded and established. The saga has no other purpose than this.

What, then, has the mention of the altar, and the very precise description of the sacrifice, to do with Gideon's call to be a deliverer of his people? Evidently the sense of the old saga has been forcibly twisted and given a new direction. Whether the figure of Gideon was specifically mentioned in the ancient cult-saga one cannot say. It is readily conceivable that the recipient of the revelation in the more ancient version of the saga did not yet bear the name Gideon. Be that as it may, the fact remains that the material of an etiological cult-saga has been subsequently transformed into a hero-saga. The original purpose of validating a shrine has been pushed into the background, and overlaid by Gideon's call to be a charismatic leader.

In this version, of course, the narrative has broken free of its own limitations. It certainly no longer has the shape it had when it stood on its own, since it is no longer a self-contained story, but demands to be completed by an account of the deeds of the one who has been called. The fact that the saga of the call as we now have it leads on to the following saga of Gideon's feats is a strong argument against an early date. Whoever turned it into a hero-saga had the real hero-saga (Judg 7:1-8, 21) in front of him. This would support the conclusion that we should in any case have reached on other grounds—that the story of the hero's call is usually one of the later accretions to any hero-saga.[11]

The saga which now follows, and which deals with the suppression of Baal-worship in Ophrah (Judg 6:25-32), is another instance of an ancient cult-saga, the purpose of which was to explain when and how the cultus of Yahweh superseded the Baal-cultus at this shrine.[12] The content of the narrative, however, is complicated by the fact that the material of an etiological saga concerning the struggle between Jerubbaal and Baal has been woven into it.

Quite a different situation is found in the long central section of the Gideon tradition, which contains the story of Gideon's victory over the Midianites (Judg 7:1—8:3). With a small company Gideon makes a surprise attack on the camp of the Bedouin who have invaded the settled territory, and in the subsequent pursuit the Midianite leaders are killed. This is a typical hero-saga, and was never anything else. Gideon and his deeds form the subject of the saga. Yet even this statement must be qualified, for the deeds were brought about by Yahweh and accomplished in the power of the spirit that came upon Gideon. The real initiative lay not with man but with Yahweh, and the ability to carry out the feat was not human ability but a charisma. Gideon acted as a charismatic leader, a tool in the hand of Yahweh.

It is possible that the section in which the unserviceable troops are sent home was not a part of the saga in its earliest form (Judg 7:2-8). In the present version it enhances the miraculous nature of the events; God did not need a great army, but only a handful of men wholly prepared to be used by him. The saga uses this to further its case even at the climax of the story, showing that at bottom it is Yahweh alone who acts. The men surrounded the camp, swung their torches, smashed their jars, and sounded their horns; but every man remained standing in his place. The destruction of the enemy was the result of a "divine terror" (compare Exod 23:27; Isa 2:10; 2 Chronicles 20), a panic in which the enemy brought about their own downfall. Thus at its climax the narrative illustrates the fact that when God intervenes to act and to deliver, human cooperation is not called for.

This is highly significant. The saga has depicted the hero altogether sympathetically, and it could not possibly be said that in order to heighten God's own stature his human agent had been reduced to a shadow-figure. On the contrary, the account is full of pictorial detail. The reader cannot but feel the suspense as he follows the events. Yet at the very height of the drama the feat of arms is unexpectedly taken out of the hero's hands. God alone has acted, and deliverance has come from him alone.

Later we shall have to recognize that this does not happen in historical writing, where no sensational miracles are produced at the culmination of events, dropping as it were from heaven into a vacuum exhausted of all human activity. On the other hand we shall find there, too, this pursuit of the parallel interests—on the one hand that of the earthly event and its protagonists, on the other that of God and his activity.

How is all this related to history? We cannot fail to recognize the narrative as a saga, yet one has a strong impression that it reveals a very sound knowledge of the historical occurrence. No one would assert that the whole thing is a poetic fiction. "There cannot be the slightest doubt that Gideon defeated the Midianites."[13] The saga is well informed even as to the details. The place names in Judg 7:1, 22 are hardly an invention. The saga also knows exactly the number of troops involved in the operation, and on this showing there had been no more than a local call-up. This, of course, the saga is not prepared to admit, and in the latest version it makes it appear that before he dismissed the useless men Gideon had behind him the whole military potential of Israel, some thirty-two thousand men. The saga also parts company with historical reality in its ending, introducing a play on words ("winepress of Zeeb," "rock of Oreb") with an etymological motive.

If we continue our analysis of the Gideon narratives we next come to the account of the pursuit of the fleeing Bedouin into Transjordania (Judg 8:4-21). The narrative appears as the immediate continuation of what has gone before, but this is simply due to editorial handling and it cannot actually refer to the same events. The names of the enemy leaders are different, and the motive for pursuing them (blood-revenge) is a different one. From a point of view of literary type this narrative, too, is a hero-saga with a good historical foundation, but unfortunately only its second half has been preserved to us.

It is not easy to assess the value of the material contained in the conclusion of the story of Gideon (Judg 8:22-28), concerning the refusal of the proffered kingship and the making of an ephod (a garment-like drapery for an image of a god). It may be that this latter element represents what remains of an etiological cult-saga explaining the provenance of the ephod at Ophrah. The passage concerning Gideon's refusal of the kingship on principle displays a strong theological interest, and must be regarded as late in date, at least in its present form.

Let us review our conclusions. The tradition about Gideon is not a straightforward narrative, but consists of a number of separate stories of very diverse kinds, which have subsequently been arranged in sequence. Some of these stories are to be classed as etiological cult-sagas. These add very little to our understanding of the history of Gideon, since they are not really interested in the events of Gideon's day, but only in cultic matters. They have no reference to the great events in the wider life of the tribes, i.e., to their political history.

The very opposite is true of the narratives which we have designated as hero-sagas. These are much more directly related to historical actuality, since the subject of the narrative is a political event that was already known to history. This class of saga reveals a thorough knowledge both of the whole historical context, and also of a good deal of detail. It may reasonably be questioned whether the designation "hero-saga" really does justice to the true nature of this genre. In truth it is not the "hero" himself whom the saga seeks to glorify. Gideon is called to be no more than God's tool, and is endowed with a charismatic gift of leadership. It is God's miraculous activity in history that is glorified, and this is characteristic of all the hero-sagas throughout the Old Testament.

We might equally well have chosen other examples from the book of Judges. In every case we find narrative units which were formerly independent or are complete in themselves. If now they form a part of larger contexts, this is the result of later editing and is to be explained on literary grounds. It cannot be explained by looking at the wider historical setting. We cannot in any circumstances claim that they constitute historical writing, even though they may provide us with all kinds of reliable historical information, and even though they may move further and further away from what is proper to the saga and correspondingly nearer to the category of historical narrative.

The History of the Succession
to the Throne of David

Let us turn our attention to that narrative sequence which must be regarded as the oldest specimen of ancient Israelite historical writing—the history of the succession to the throne of David. The purely literary problems, especially those concerning the actual limits of the narrative, are nowadays fairly clear. Undoubtedly it is the fulfillment of the "Testament of David" (1 Kings 2) that forms the conclusion, although the beginning is less clearly definable. Rost's penetrating analysis has nevertheless shown with some certainty that the beginning is not to be sought in 2 Samuel 13,[14] but has been ingeniously interwoven with the end of the so-called story of the ark.[15]

This story was originally a complete and independent narrative cycle, which gave an account of the vicissitudes of this renowned palladium on its way from Shiloh, the ancient shrine of the Yahwistic amphictyony, to the new royal city of Jerusalem. In type this extended narrative is a cult-legend, the purpose of which was to show that thenceforth Jerusalem was a legitimate cultic place for Israel. Accordingly its climax falls at the end, with the description of the solemn bringing of the ark into Jerusalem. Amidst the offering of many sacrifices, the sounding of trumpets and cultic dancing, the sacred ark was carried into the tent that had been prepared for it.

This magnificent scene might well have concluded the narrative, but quite remarkably there now follows an incident from David's private life (2 Sam 6:16, 20ff.). Michal has witnessed the dancing of her royal husband from the window with great displeasure, and when he returns to the palace she reproves him severely. David defends his conduct, and the narrator brings this incident to a close with the comment that Michal remained childless to the day of her death. It has been asked, very reasonably, what possible significance this little drama could have within the context of a cult-legend that speaks of public and sacral affairs, more especially since it forms the conclusion of it. What view are we to take of this little biographical tail-piece? Rost has shown, however, it is very far from being an insignificant tail-piece. Rather it is the real starting-point of our historian's thesis. The childlessness of the queen, whose vocation was motherhood above all, introduces for the first time, albeit in negative form, the historian's theme. It is a beginning that leaves us with gloomy forebodings. Now, however, the suspense is heightened for the reader by the interpolation of the section that immediately follows this incident—the passage concerning Nathan's prophecy (2 Samuel 7).

Nathan delivers an oracle to the King, a divine promise that his throne and his dynasty will endure unbroken.[16] This second part of the opening of the story arouses great hopes, for, in its prophecy that the throne now guaranteed by God will last forever, it opens up a prospect which is nothing short of miraculous. The introduction to the narrative work that starts at this point is thus quite singular in that there is the sharpest possible antithesis between the mighty promise of God and the frustration of human potentialities in Michal's sterility. The reader has no idea how the tension can be resolved; he can only suppose that God will miraculously take a hand in the ensuing events. It will be as well to give a brief outline of the course of the narrative, and to elucidate a few points as we do so.

In 2 Sam 9:1-13 David institutes an enquiry into possible survivors of Saul's family. There is, however, only one son of Jonathan, the crippled Meribaal, still alive. David brings him to his court with an old servant of Saul's and allots him a place at the royal table among the princes. Similarly David gives an undertaking to Ziba, one of Saul's old retainers, who has meanwhile become a servant of Meribaal, together with his family. This generous gesture has doubtless commended itself to David for predominantly political reasons, for any descendants of his predecessor who remained unknown to him might easily become a source of danger. There is now nothing to fear from this direction. This section of the narrative, moreover, has yet greater significance for the whole, in that the personages it introduces will appear on two later occasions in the story.

Second Samuel 10 carries us out into the sphere of foreign policy. A new king has ascended the throne of Ammon. The ambassadors sent to wish him well in the name of David are ill received, and war breaks out between the two nations. In the first battle Joab, David's commander-in-chief, is able to defeat the Ammonites and their allies. The enemy succeed in reassembling their forces and reorganize the army with strong reinforcements. David, however, by bringing up the whole of the Israelite forces, succeeds in defeating the allied armies a second time. The Ammonites withdraw into their heavily defended capital city, where they await their opponents. At this point the story of the military operations breaks off, and the reader is suddenly brought back to Jerusalem and into the King's most intimate private affairs. The purpose of this interruption will soon become apparent.

Second Samuel 11 relates that while Joab completed the investiture of Rabbah, David remained in Jerusalem. One day, when he had risen from his couch after the midday siesta, he saw from the roof of his house a woman washing herself in the court of one of the neighboring houses, "and the woman was very beautiful." It was Bathsheba, the wife of the "Hittite" Uriah, who was at this time serving with the army in the field. David has her brought to his palace and commits adultery with her. Bathsheba then returns to her own house. The narrator now unfolds the murky story of the King's scheming attempt to hush the matter up, which comes to nothing because of Uriah's noble bearing, and also, it would seem, Uriah's suspicions. After every effort to bring Uriah and Bathsheba has failed, David changes his tactics. He determines to have Bathsheba for himself, and in order to achieve this does not scruple to sink to the crime of murder. On the strength of a hint given by the King and readily understood by Joab, Uriah falls in battle as if by mischance, and after the due period of mourning David takes Bathsheba for himself. She bears him a son. But "the thing that David had done displeased Yahweh." The way in which Nathan reproaches David for his sin is well known. Of the three prophecies of doom (2 Sam 12:7-10, 11-12, 14) probably only the last is original: God will forgive David his sin, but the child must die.

In the scene that follows the narrator draws an impressive picture of David's independence of outlook over against that of his contemporaries. Whilst the child still lives David lies on the ground, praying and fasting. No one dares tell him of the child's death. When, however, he sees the courtiers whispering among themselves he knows that the child is dead. He gets up, washes and anoints himself, takes off his mourning garments and has a meal served to him. This behavior passes the comprehension of the courtiers, and David tries to explain in answer to their reproachful questioning:

> While the child was still alive, I fasted and wept; for I said, "Who knows whether Yahweh will be gracious to me, that the child may live?" But now he is dead; why should I fast? Can I bring him back again? I shall go to him, but he will not return to me. (2 Sam 12:22-23)

Here is the most complete resignation to the finality of death. David is not so easily consoled as the courtiers have supposed. On the contrary, his words bespeak an agony of grief, but faced with the irrevocable nature of his loss, David is driven to a final acceptance of the fact of death. He makes no further gesture of complaint, but returns to his daily life in utter desperation. We must, of course, bear in mind that for David the death of the child was also a pledge that his sin had been forgiven.[17]

Following this domestic interlude the narrator once more returns us to the theater of the Ammonite war and shows us the final phase of this struggle, the capture of the Ammonite capital.

Here we must pause for a moment. The Bathsheba story has always been a source of wonder to expositors. It displays a quite outstanding artistry in its manner of presentation. The narrator maintains throughout a salutary restraint and delicacy of approach. "He discharged his delicate task with dignity."[18] The story of David's adultery is inextricably bound up with the story of the Ammonite war. This account of the war, however, as Rost has conclusively shown, did not originate from the pen of our historian, but is the official account of the campaign taken from the royal archives and incorporated by the historian into his own work.[19] So that it might be fully integrated with the history of David, it was necessary to divide it in two, and the story of Bathsheba was inserted between the two parts.

On this showing, this story never had an independent existence outside its present setting. Its theme is of great significance in that it introduces into the narrative sequence both the mother of the heir to the throne and the heir himself. Every reader knew of Bathsheba as the mother of Solomon; but it was only after much confusion and conflict that this second son of hers was able to ascend his father's throne. Very significantly, it is said of him as early as in this passage that Yahweh loved him (2 Sam 12:24).

In chapter 13, apparently without any connection with what has gone before, there begins a series of events that is to lead directly to the most involved political situation. The cause of these disturbances, which were to cause so profound an upheaval in the life of the nation, lies in a matter of purely private concern—the infatuation of Prince Amnon for his half-sister Tamar. Amnon frets over it to such an extent that it is finally noticed by his entourage. One of these intriguers whose presence at court never bodes any good advises him to pretend to be ill and to get the princess to nurse him; the rest would follow of its own accord. Amnon takes the advice and quickly achieves his object. There is unconscious pride in the words with which Tamar reminds the passionate Amnon of his duty: "No, my brother, such a thing is not done in Israel." But Amnon is overcome by his own desires and violates the princess. "Then Amnon hated her with very great hatred; so that the hatred with which he hated her was greater than the love with which he had loved her." Tamar goes to the house of her brother Absalom, who tells her that he will deal with the matter.

David was certainly very angry about the occurrence, but took no steps to punish Amnon, whom he loved because "he was his first-born" (2 Sam 3:2). Here suddenly the main theme emerges once more: Amnon was David's eldest son and therefore heir to the throne. The incident was not then a purely private matter, but had a political significance, and we follow with growing tension the ills that gather round the house of David.

Two years pass in which Absalom provides no indication of his intentions. We see here something of that cold calculation which was a pronounced feature of his character. Absalom now arranges a sheep-shearing festival out in the country, and here, when everyone is merry with wine, Absalom has his brother Amnon put to death. For the ambitious Absalom the rape of Tamar was no doubt merely a convenient pretext for the removal of the heir to the throne, for now Absalom became the heir apparent. It is a neat piece of storytelling that describes how the false rumor reaches the court that Absalom has murdered all the princes. Matters were bad enough as it was!

Once again David fails to assert his authority in his own house. He takes no steps against Absalom, who meanwhile has fled to Geshur, and for three years the matter is allowed to remain in the air. Then time takes its revenge. The king thinks less harshly of Absalom, and Joab decides that the time is ripe for him to make a move. He sends a "wise woman" from Tekoa with a trumped-up plea for justice to set before the king. According to the tale she has two sons, one of whom has killed the other, and the clan now demands the death of the former. This, however, would wipe out the male line of the family. David gives judgment that in this particular case the law of blood revenge shall be suspended, but in so doing he has unwittingly pronounced judgment concerning the case of Absalom.

This scene with the suppliant woman is once again a masterpiece of psychology. The conclusion is particularly finely drawn. The king sees through the comedy that has been played out before him, but only at the moment when he must admit that the ruse has succeeded. Even when she is unmasked the cunning old biddy is not at a loss, but quite unabashed seizes the opportunity to indulge in still further flattery: "You have all the wisdom of an angel of God." "The verses present a delightful picture of feminine loquacity and persuasiveness, and of royal forbearance."[20] Joab had gambled on David's weakness where his children were concerned, and had not been correct in his assessment of his royal master. Absalom is allowed to return to Jerusalem, but for two whole years is not received in audience by the King. Then Absalom himself forces the issue. He sees, of course, that the King has dealt only in half-measures, and builds upon the fact with characteristic drive. The prince is now received at court. He pays homage to the King, who kisses him. The reader draws a deep breath: now at last, after seven years, the wretched business seems to be settled. But it is at this very moment that the seeds of deadly conflict are sown.

Absalom goes home a new man. He has ambitious plans, and he furthers them by quite publicly drawing attention to himself, seeking by this means to gain popularity with the people. For four years he continues to work on public opinion. He chooses Hebron as the venue for mustering the conspirators and the outbreak of the rebellion. On the pretext of paying a vow he obtains leave of absence from his father, and only immediately before the beginning of hostilities does the wholly unsuspecting David learn of the *coup d'etat*. The situation in Jerusalem is too unfavorable to David for him to be able to meet the insurgents' attack there—apparently the number who could be safely relied upon in the capital was too small. He therefore quickly leaves the city with his loyal followers in order to gain time to collect an army.

The description of this evacuation of the capital, and of the various important meetings with the King (2 Sam 15:13ff.) is another of the narrator's literary triumphs. The highly diversified conversations provide an excellent medium for depicting the various aspects of the new situation. "The narrator develops his picture of David's situation and personality in a masterly fashion, building it up of reflections from many different facets."[21] The first encounter as David withdraws from the city is with the Philistine Ittai, whose faithfulness despite his foreign origin stands in sharp contrast to the treason of the King's own son. The gain of six hundred troops, of course, provides David with welcome reinforcements.

The King has gone very little farther before he meets priests bearing the ark, just as the people are marching past him. He does not wish to have the ark with him, however, probably because he does not want to see the palladium (which accompanies the army only in a "holy war") involved in internecine strife. In any case there are political as well as religious considerations, since by sending back the ark David assures himself of a situation in Jerusalem that he can turn to account in an emergency. His exit from the city is not depicted as a going forth to battle, but rather as an exceptional kind of procession, an act of penance.[22]

"But David went up the ascent of the Mount of Olives, weeping as he went, barefoot and with his head covered; and all the people who were with him covered their heads, and went up, weeping as they went. And it was told David: 'Ahithophel is among the conspirators with Absalom.' And David said: 'O Yahweh, I pray thee, turn the counsel of Ahithophel into foolishness'" (2 Sam 15:30-31).

The desertion of his trusted adviser to the rebels is a serious blow for David.[23] His authority and his reputation for wise counsel might restrain Absalom from many rash actions that might have been to David's disadvantage. But he has little time to repine over the unfortunate turn of events, for a fresh encounter claims statesmanlike attention.

"When David came to the summit, where God was worshiped, behold, Hushai the Archite came to meet him with his coat rent and earth upon his head" (2 Sam 15:32). David will not take the loyal Hushai with him, but sends him back to Absalom in Jerusalem as a spy, giving him a free hand to work against Ahithophel in his own way. We shall have occasion to return to this little scene later.

Shortly afterwards David meets Ziba, who hopes to gain favor with him by bringing him useful provisions. He further reports that his master, Jonathan's crippled son Meribaal, has taken sides with Absalom, since he has aspirations to the throne of Israel. The King thereupon invests Ziba with all Meribaal's possessions.

The last meeting we are shown is the most humiliating of all for David. Shimei, a Benjamite of Saul's family, follows his procession, cursing and execrating him passionately as he goes. Now at last, he avers, David's blood-guilt for the house of Saul will be avenged. David forbids his followers to retaliate: he will bear the abuse as a humiliation laid on him by God.

At last the exhausted procession reaches the Jordan, where it is able to halt. The narrator utilizes this pause in the events to make us familiar with what has been happening in Jerusalem. Absalom has taken possession of the city, and is deliberating with his advisers what steps to take next. Here we meet once again with Hushai, who has succeeded in insinuating himself into Absalom's confidence. Following a proposal made by Ahithophel, Absalom first takes possession of his father's harem, a symbolic action intended to gain the confidence of the people for Absalom. It is a visible demonstration that he does not contemplate a reconciliation with his father, but has made a definite break with him.[24]

Now comes the real council of war, in which Ahithophel and Hushai make flatly contradictory suggestions. Once again the speeches are admirably turned. They are models of rhetorical refinement, and no doubt highly appetizing morsels to their original readers. Ahithophel advises pressing on immediately, whilst the King is still weary and his forces not yet organized. His purpose is to settle the issue with the least possible bloodshed, and to win over the nation for Absalom with the minimum of violence, as he explains in his apt metaphor of bringing home a not wholly unwilling bride.

The narrator has expended particular care on Hushai's speech. It is made up of two parts—the rebuttal of Ahithophel's argument (2 Sam 17:8-10), and his own counter-proposal (17:11-13). The danger is that it contains a mixture of truth and falsehood. So far as the hearers are concerned he has one great advantage that he skillfully exploits—the fact that he is the one who has seen David most recently. He talks much more grandly than the restrained Ahithophel, and what he finally proposes is evidently less appropriate to the real situation. He describes the King as "enraged, like a bear robbed of his cubs." He must not be allowed to gain an initial advantage in battle. Rather, the whole army "from Dan to Beersheba" must be called out against him, and then he must be taken by surprise "as the dew falls on the ground." If he should entrench himself in a city, then that city must be dragged with ropes into the valley until not a stone is to be found of it. This grandiloquence arouses the enthusiasm of Absalom's men. They decide in favor of Hushai's advice and reject that of Ahithophel. Hushai sends a report of the council of war to the King through the priests, and Ahithophel, realizing that Absalom's case is not quite hopeless, hangs himself.

Meanwhile, David has put to good use the respite gained for him by Hushai (2 Sam 17:24ff.). He has moved into Transjordania, has newly provisioned his army and has organized his forces into three commands. Joab keeps him away from the now inevitable battle, so that the state may not once more be endangered by his love for his children. The King, however, has given strict orders to the three commanders to deal leniently with the crown prince. The battle now ensues, and proves catastrophic to the rebels, owing to the unfavorable terrain. In fleeing from the field Absalom has the misfortune to be unhorsed by the branches of a tree, and is helpless to defend himself when Joab runs him through. David's troops break off the pursuit, and the war is over.

All eyes now turn towards the King. How will he take the dreadful news? The narrator heightens the tension by relating at length how the young and unsuspecting Ahimaaz is eager to carry tidings of the victory to the King. But Joab knows David better: the mission will not be without its dangers, and he therefore sends a Moor.

At this point the scene moves to Mahanaim, the King's headquarters, and the tempo of the narrative is slowed yet further. The sentry sees the messengers coming, Ahimaaz having undertaken the journey after all, and he concludes that the tidings are good. The King sits anxiously waiting in the guardroom below. The two breathless runners arrive almost simultaneously and report the victory; but David asks only after Absalom, and so hears the dreadful news.

> And the king was deeply moved, and went up to the chamber over the gate, and wept; and as he went, he said, "O my son Absalom, my son, my son Absalom! Would I had died instead of you, O Absalom, my son, my son." (2 Sam 18:33)

David is quite beside himself with grief. His dejection communicates itself to his whole army, which drags its way into the city "as an army steals away which has covered itself with shame." Only Joab's extremely harsh words can stir the King to show himself to the people.

After the defeat of the rebellion, however, there remain many tensions to be resolved. The northern Israelites were the first to come to their senses. Matters were more difficult in Judaea, where some degree of pressure and a conciliatory gesture on the part of the King were needed before David could venture to return. The account of his return (2 Sam 19:16ff.) is now so constructed by the narrator as to form an artistic contrast to the description of the humiliating outward journey (2 Sam 15:13ff.). Some of them are the same people whom David has met on the way out, but now the circumstances are quite different, and the noble behavior of the King, purified as he is by his suffering, shines like a brilliant light on all around him.

First comes Shimei. David forgives him and will not be drawn by any of his followers to take just vengeance. Then Meribaal meets him, protesting that he has been slandered by Ziba (see 2 Sam 16:3). The King lets the matter rest, and tells him to share his former possessions with Ziba.

There is a particularly fine scene between the King and the eighty-year-old Barzillai, who wished to escort him back across the Jordan. Barzillai had given his support to the King in a most difficult situation (cf. 2 Sam 17:27). David wished to reward him by taking him into his court, but the old man has no desire to be uprooted. He would not enjoy court-life, he protests, and would prefer to spend the rest of his days at home and to die near the grave of his forebears. He asks only that David will take his son with him, before taking his leave and returning to his own home.

The army's return to Jerusalem is for the most part a rather joyless procedure, however. There are reports of friction between north and south, of deep-seated conflicts which were not the work of Absalom, but which were inherent in the structure of the Davidic empire, and which Absalom had skillfully exploited in furtherance of his plans.[25] The King's victory in battle had done so little to resolve these tensions that the rebellion flared up again even before David had time to return to Jerusalem. Once again it was a Benjamite, a member of the tribe to which Saul had belonged, who sought to re-establish the ancient Israelite empire. Judah and the new Davidic throne in Jerusalem were for the race-conscious Israelites an innovation of doubtful value. The call of this man Sheba seems to have found an echo among many Israelites in the confused situation that still obtained; but this rebellion too was soon put down. Sheba's adherents withdrew to Abel, a city in the extreme north. David's army pursued him thither, and after skillfully conducted negotiations the rebel leader's head was handed over to the besiegers as the price of the city's reprieve. Joab thereupon returned to Jerusalem with the army.

At this point there is doubtless a serious break in the sequence of events reported by our historian. At all events the conclusion of the narrative as a whole is not to be found here. Its theme was not, of course, that of Absalom's revolt, but the problem of the Davidic succession to the throne that Yahweh had promised to uphold, and this question was as much an open one as ever. The immediate continuation of the story is to be found in 1 Kings 1, and here the question of the succession to the throne, which has produced subterranean rumblings throughout the reign of David, comes peremptorily to the surface. Rost has therefore rightly described this chapter as the key to the understanding of the whole narrative.[26]

David has grown old. The lovely Abishag of Shunem is found for him, but he begets no further children by her. This little incident prepares us for the fact that it now remains to be decided among David's surviving sons which of them shall ascend his throne after his death. The eldest of them is Adonijah, who has Joab and the priest Abiathar on his side. His rival is Solomon. He, too, has powerful supporters—the priest Zadok, the prophet Nathan, Queen Bathsheba, and the royal bodyguard. The struggle between the two begins with a feast that Adonijah gives for his adherents.

Whether it had already been planned to proclaim Adonijah the legitimate successor to the throne at this time is not made clear. At all events the opposition party credits Adonijah with this intention, in order to be able to force the issue. Nathan goes to David together with Bathsheba, and the two of them remind him of his promise made at some earlier date that Solomon is to inherit the throne. The aged King becomes the tool of their party, and gives orders to forestall Adonijah by anointing Solomon. They have now attained their object, and the anointing is celebrated with great solemnity. The noise of the festival penetrates to Adonijah's festive board, and in no time at all the guests scatter to the four winds. Adonijah, who is in greater danger than any of them, flees for sanctuary to the altar, but Solomon grants him provisional amnesty.

The "Testament of David" in 1 Kgs 2:1-9 as we have it has undoubtedly been retouched, although it would be a mistake to regard the whole passage as an interpolation. The question of its historical reliability must not be confused with the literary problem. The whole of this historical work looks beyond David to Solomon, and the compiler was writing for Solomon's contemporaries. It is therefore understandable that he excuses certain measures taken by Solomon at the outset of his reign, on the grounds that he was carrying out his father's last wishes. Joab and Shimei are not to escape retribution, and favor is to be shown to the sons of Barzillai. "Then David slept with his fathers, and was buried in the city of David." Solomon ascended his throne.

There now begins a new Israel, the depiction of which lay outside the scope of our historian's brief. He therefore does no more than recount the fortunes of those known to the reader from the story of the contest for the throne. Adonijah, Solomon's unsuccessful rival for the throne, asks to have Abishag. It was a rash request, for a claim to the King's harem in those days looked remarkably like a claim to the throne itself (cf. 2 Sam 16:21ff.). Solomon at all events regarded it as such, and promptly had Adonijah put to death. Abiathar, too, the priest who had been so loyal to David, was removed from the scene by being banished to Anathoth. Joab was put to death in the sanctuary whither he had fled for safety, and an opportunity soon arose to do away with Shimei. By means of these measures, which are still related to the time of David and to the problems of his reign, "the kingdom was assured to Solomon, the problem of the succession to the throne resolved, and the story brought to an end."[27]

The Significance of This Historical Work

In our resume of this great historical work we were obliged to strip it of all its grandeur. This was the more necessary in order that we might examine in detail the forms of this historical composition, its style, its artistic technique, and above all its power of dramatic presentation. The construction is altogether masterly. The reader is transported into the most varied surroundings with kaleidoscopic effect: we move from the clamor and tension of public occasions to the quietness of the inner chamber, or to the secrecy of an intimate conversation.

Yet however engrossed the reader may become in delightfully drawn vignettes, he never loses sight of the main theme of the overall picture. "That which especially evokes our admiration, however, is the multiplicity of the characters who move across this stage, each brought vividly to life before our eyes in all the color and detail of a miniature-painter's masterpiece. In contrast to the saga, there is here a striking capacity for depicting involved psychological situations."[28]

At the very center of events, of course, stands David himself, a far from simple character, whose whole life is a mass of contradictions. Far-sighted as a statesman, as a man he is torn by many passions that drive him even to criminal acts; yet he is always capable of great generosity, and in adversity he shows his true dignity. He must have been possessed of a compelling personal charm, which gave him great power over people. Nevertheless, as he aged his splendor inevitably grew tarnished in the eyes of his people, and he saw himself losing popularity and public esteem in favor of his very attractive sons. As the narrator stresses in view of the struggles that were to come, David was utterly and blindly devoted to these sons. It was a weakness that became a major fault, and brought both throne and empire to the brink of catastrophe.

Around this central character are grouped the many other players in the drama, each sharply outlined, every one distinctively portrayed. There are the princes, Amnon, Absalom, Adonijah; the generals, Joab and Amasa; the counselor Ahithophel; then there are the common people, Ziba and Barzillai; the rebels Shimei and Sheba; and finally there are the women, the princess Tamar, Queen Bathsheba, and the audacious woman of Tekoa. Yet not one of those who has an important part to play in this drama leaves the stage to vanish into obscurity. We are allowed to follow them all right to the time of their death—David, Amnon, Absalom, Adonijah, Joab, Amasa, Shimei, Ahithophel.

This last observation brings us back once more to the question of the overall scope of this composite narrative. The fact that the narrator follows up so many of his characters through the years until the time of their death is a weighty argument against the hypothesis that this is actually one single great narrative. The older exegetes prefer to think of the narrative material as a succession of "short stories" (*Novellen*), but Rost has proved convincingly that the materials are much more closely integrated than this. If we take as a test case the favorite among these "short stories"—the account of Absalom's rebellion—it is soon realized upon close examination that we cannot define its limits in any satisfactory way (2 Samuel 13–20). There are unmistakable threads connecting it with both what precedes it and with that which follows it, so that we are obliged to reckon with a much broader context. The writer has displayed his material as a whole in a succession of separate scenes, and has broken up the narrative in order to maintain a certain perspective; but this should not deceive us into thinking that it can be dismembered to give a series of separate short stories.

Our author shows masterly craftsmanship in the construction of his work, and in the use of dramatic relief at points where the tempo of events slackens, where the tension is released, and the reader is allowed to draw a breath. Nevertheless, these pauses most certainly do not mark the conclusion of individual stories. It seems reasonably certain that this is the new contribution made by the writer to ancient Israelite historical writing—the production of the long narrative compilation that brings together a great many events.

Let us look back for a moment to the Gideon tradition. This too was a narrative-sequence of wide scope, but one that was altogether lacking in literary unity. It consisted of single sagas, each complete in itself, so that the tensions to which it gave rise were in every case resolved in its own conclusion—always the surest sign of the termination of a literary unit. The overriding unity of the whole narrative was attained only by arranging a number of such sagas in order, and then providing link-passages to give cohesion to the whole.

Quite a different state of affairs prevails in our history of the succession to the throne of David. The story in which David brings Meribaal and Ziba to the court, for example (2 Samuel 9), cannot possibly be regarded as a unit that at one time had a separate existence. On the contrary, the purpose of this information remains somewhat obscure to the reader in the first instance, and it is only later that he understands it fully, when Ziba and Meribaal play their undistinguished parts during the rebellion (2 Sam 16:1-4; 19:25-31).

One may choose examples where one will: even those sections of the narrative which appear to be neatly rounded off turn out not to be self-contained units, for not one of the various sections is complete in itself. The problems raised in any section have repercussions far beyond the limits of that section, and this whole narrative runs its course to the end without a break or a join.

Now, this difference in form between the Gideon tradition and the history of the succession to the throne of David results simply from the quite different nature of the material with which we are concerned. Can we really call this material "sagas"? Not only the mass of the material, but also its intrinsic complexity, goes far beyond what may be contained in a saga. Quite apart from this, we have none of the marks of the saga. We can only say that these chapters contain genuine historical writing—the oldest historical writing in the Old Testament. Let us show in more detail that this complex of narrative does in fact merit this description, one that notoriously can seldom be rightly conferred on the literary output of a nation.

"Genuinely historical writing which faithfully represents its own era always and invariably grows out of the political life of the day, whatever shape or form that may take."[29] This dictum also applies to the historical writing with which we are concerned here. Only a political state that makes history can *write* history. The small kingdom of Saul did not provide the necessary conditions, either politically or culturally, for the writing of history is one of the most sophisticated of human cultural activities. It can grow to maturity only on a broad national basis, and in an atmosphere of developed political consciousness. Saul's tiny kingdom, still hovering between the condition of a sacral federation of tribes and genuine nationhood, in no sense afforded an adequately fertile soil for its growth. But after the union between north and south, David's empire became a state capable of great expansion, assured of external security as the result of several successful wars, although internally still a mass of problems.

These were conditions in which historical writing could develop. Admittedly they were no more than minimal conditions, and the fact that such writing did arise at this time is not adequately explained by saying that the conditions existed, nor can it ultimately be explained at all. All at once it is there, mature and artistically fully developed to an extent which makes it impossible to envisage further development in this direction.

This historical work did not aim to deal with all the political complications, external and internal, of the reign of David. Rather it takes as its subject one single topic, doubtless the most interesting and characteristic feature of the period. Following the original pattern of the Israelite state, the kingdom took the form of a charismatic monarchy. By virtue of divine appointment and his own anointing, Saul acquired a charisma that enabled him to emerge victorious, and this proof of his divine election led to the confirmation of his office by acclamation on the part of the people (1 Sam 11:5ff.). It will be seen at once that this is a continuation of the ancient institution of charismatic leadership so clearly depicted in the stories of the "judges."

The tradition attributes to David's kingship this same characteristic which it saw in Saul's, "a military kingship in the national sense, resting in the last resort upon Yahweh's appointment, guaranteed by feats of arms performed as leader of the national army and ratified by the acclamation of the people."[30]

With David, however, the situation is profoundly modified, in that the institution of charismatic kingship is replaced by the principle of a hereditary dynasty. This is the real import of Nathan's prophecy, which stands at the head of the historical work that we have been considering and that gives the divine assurance that the house and throne of David will endure forever (2 Samuel 7). Now at last we are in a position to appreciate the immediacy of the problem of succession to the Davidic throne. It is in fact the first problem raised by a wholly new institution in the history of Israel's political organization: how is the principle of dynastic succession to operate? However necessary this institution may have been in view of the new political structure of the Davidic empire, it certainly contained a latent danger in that it opened the door to bitter rivalries among the princes of the blood. The notion of primogeniture was evidently not regarded as an established principle.[31]

Our historian therefore takes for his theme the question of who shall occupy the throne of David in these changed constitutional circumstances. It is true that with his habitual restraint the writer does not explicitly state his purpose at the outset: he allows it to emerge gradually from the material itself. Only at the end of the work do we find a clear statement of the problem that has actually occupied the reader from the start, in the urgent question, "Who is to sit on the throne of our Lord the King, to reign after him?" (1 Kgs 1:20, 27).

It is, of course, no more than a literary device that this question should be formulated only in the last act of the drama. No explicit formulation could present the problem in a more impressive light than that in which it has already appeared before the reader, forcing itself upon him through the historical events and developments of which he has been reading. We have seen how brilliantly the narrator achieved this effect. He began with the childlessness of the queen. After the removal of Amnon, the eldest son, Absalom became the center of interest, and with his return to the court and his reconciliation with David it looked as if he would be the next to wear the crown. He came to grief because of his own ambitious plans, and the question of the succession is more pressing than ever. Solomon now enters upon the scene. His birth as Bathsheba's child has already been mentioned by the writer, but in such a way that the reader has lost sight of him in the pressure of events. It was in any case not he but his elder brother Adonijah who was the legitimate claimant to the throne. By means of intrigue the old king was successfully persuaded to give an assurance that Solomon should inherit the throne, and thus finally after David's death Solomon becomes king and Adonijah is passed over.

We know nothing of the historian who has described these events for us.[32] He must have been one who had an intimate knowledge of what went on at court. His portrayal of personalities and events breathes an atmosphere that must silence any doubts as to the reliability of his account. He displays a penetrating understanding of human nature, and his characterization of David is particularly impressive. The King is shown consistently in a warmly sympathetic light, and is treated with great respect, although the writer always preserved an unfettered liberty of judgment with regard to him. He never conceals his faults of omission or commission, but at those points where, with a "heroic truthfulness"[33] unique in the East, he has to speak of what is foul and hideous, he never does so with a relish for the unsavory, but always with delicacy and discretion. This brings us to the most important question—that of the theological and interpretative standpoint of the historian.

The most striking feature here is a negative one: the immense restraint that this writer practices. The later deuteronomic historical writer never introduces a king to his readers without first having given an unambiguous judgment on him. Here there is no trace of any such prejudicial statements. On the contrary the narrator is at pains to conceal himself and his evaluations behind the material itself. He does not praise David, nor does he blame Absalom. Events take their course.

The reader is very soon aware, however, that he is not being confronted with a succession of meaningless accidents. Absalom's destiny and David's destiny are being fulfilled. Thus gradually, even though only very indirectly, we are able to perceive a quite definite attitude to the events on the part of the historian. In the strictest sense of the word this is not a destiny that is being worked out, for there is nothing arbitrary or depersonalized about it. It is the expiation of dire guilt. What the reader sees is a tightly drawn chain of causality which links sin with suffering. The insidious allurement of ambition, honor, and achievement enmeshes men in their own guilt and brings them to destruction. Amnon, Absalom, Adonijah, Ahithophel, Sheba, all are at fault, and, over and above the failings of them all, the guilt of the king himself provides "the motivating force of the whole story,"[34] through his licentiousness and still more through his criminal weakness with regard to his children.

In this context the meeting with Nathan is a scene of great importance. The prophet foretells, as the punishment for the shameful outrage against Uriah, that what the King himself has done in secret will be done to him publicly, "before all Israel and in the sight of this sun" (2 Sam 12:11). A few chapters later we see how Absalom takes possession of the King's harem as a ceremonial act in the sight of the entire city (2 Sam 16:22).

The solemn declaration of a prophet has brought into prominence the motive of retribution that pervades unseen the whole work. The *jus talionis*, so often secretly at work in history, is here prophetically revealed as the personal activity of the Lord of History against the adulterer. The whole history of David can, indeed, be in some sense understood as the history of the punishment for this one transgression. "In Amnon's rape of Tamar the libidinous act of the father is repeated. It leads to Absalom's blood-guilt, and sets off the whole train of wrangles and tangles from which in the end Bathsheba and her son Solomon emerge victorious as the ultimate beneficiaries.[35]

We must ask, however, whether our author's theology of history is limited to this one conception of retribution that he shows to be operative in history. If it were, this fundamental conception could hardly be called a theological one, for the notion that this nemesis is God's own way of dealing with men is kept very much in the background. Eduard Meyer, who saw in our text one of the earliest examples of secular historical writing, actually described this historical work as "purely secular." "Any kind of religious coloring, every thought of supernatural intervention, is wholly excluded. The course of this world, and the nemesis which is fulfilled in the chain of events set in motion by one's own guilt, all are portrayed as matters of plain fact seen by the onlooker."[36]

This is true so far as it goes. Seen in the round, the idea of retribution is introduced so impersonally and is so integral to the story that one could not on this account designate the work a "theological" history. It would seem to savor rather of the pessimism of many of those sagas of guilt and fate known to us in antiquity. "Sinister forces embedded in man's own nature strike out at him, drive him back and ensnare him in a mesh of guilt and anguish from which he cannot escape."[37] Our historian would certainly agree with Thucydides that the *orgai*, the inner urges and passions, are at the root of all human activity in history; but in so saying we have not elucidated his attitude concerning the ultimate force which is operative in history. It will become clear that in this matter he does not share the "icy skepticism" of "Thucydides.[38]

We must go on to investigate at what points in this work the author speaks of God. We are not thinking now of the numerous more or less rhetorical appeals to God which are put into the mouths of the protagonists in dramatic situations, for it is by no means certain that we could discover from these the real convictions of the author. The question is rather whether there are passages in this historical work in which the author expresses a positive theological judgment concerning God and his relationship to the events set out.

There are in fact three such passages—2 Sam 11:27; 12:24; 17:14. Considering the scope of the work, this represents a surprising paucity of passages in which the narrator drops his severe reticence with regard to his own viewpoint and takes up a theological attitude on his own account. Precisely for this reason these passages are, of course, especially important, and their significance for the whole work must not be overlooked.

The form of each of these three passages is similar. Each of these theological comments is extremely terse. Still more striking, however, is the abrupt and disjointed manner in which they break into their context: "The thing that

David had done displeased Yahweh"; "and she bore a son, and he called his name Solomon; and Yahweh loved him." In each case these statements stand quite free of their context, for the narrator has kept the reader's mind occupied with everything *but* God's attitude to men. It is as if he were reluctant to interrupt his account of purely historical matters, and so wished to confine his comment only to what is absolutely necessary. He gives a rapid indication of his position, and returns with redoubled concentration to the progress of events, concerning himself exclusively once again with human beings and human affairs. Yet this unusual procedure on the part of the historian must not mislead us into thinking that these passages are unimportant. On the contrary, their very isolation and inconspicuousness in a narrative apparently concerned exclusively with the strictly historical should serve to warn us against too narrow an interpretation of the work as a whole.

The significance of the observation at the end of the story of David's adultery is plain to see. The narrator could not allow his reader to pass on to the next event without some comment. A terrible deed has been committed, the consequences of which cannot possibly be foreseen at this juncture. It is not the historian's purpose to point out here that this crime was to have more dire consequences for David. He prefers rather to encourage the reader to associate God's judgment on David with the developments that now ensue. If he has taken note of the brief and quite unemotional warning at 2 Sam 11:27, and then read of the succession of blows which befall the house of David, the reader will know where to look for the explanation of all this piling up of disasters: God is using them to punish the King's sin.

Equally significant is the pronouncement that God loved Bathsheba's child (2 Sam 12:24). As a theological comment on the history it is if anything even more completely detached from its context than the previous one. It lays a positive emphasis quite unexpectedly on one of the characters in the drama. The statement is sufficiently paradoxical in itself, since the reader is told nothing about the child except that he exists. Who would have foreseen a magnificent future for the child of such a union? Quite evidently the author has something more important to do than write an essay on this newborn infant. Yet here is a note of the quite irrational love of God for this child, and at the end of the long story when Solomon is left in command of the field after untold complications, the reader will recall this sentence and understand that it is not human merit and virtue which have made the throne secure, but a paradoxical act of election on the part of God.

The third of these comments in which the author expresses his mind concerning God's control of history must be dealt with rather more fully. The pronouncement stands at the end of the dramatic account of Absalom's council of war. It is as if the speaker made a brief curtain appearance at the end of an act to give the spectators a further explanation of what they have just seen: "For Yahweh had ordained to defeat the good counsel of Ahithophel, so that Yahweh might bring evil upon Absalom" (2 Sam 17:14).

The text becomes wholly intelligible only if we call to mind an event that was described several scenes earlier than Absalom's council of war—David's withdrawal from the threatened capital. Among the other shattering items of news, the King learned at this time that Ahithophel, a shrewd man who had enjoyed his close confidence, had joined the rebels. After the treason of Absalom himself, the desertion of this man was the hardest blow of all, for Ahithophel's advice was "as if one consulted the oracle of God" (2 Sam 16:23). Now God alone can be of assistance! So in this moment David prays, "Oh Yahweh, I pray thee, turn the counsel of Ahithophel into foolishness."

Events move on; David climbs further up the mount, and when he comes to the place "where prayer was made to God" Hushai meets him, and places himself unconditionally at his service. David sends him back to the city as a spy. Events now develop in the way that we have seen, and reach their first preliminary conclusion when Ahithophel's advice is rejected.

The whole situation is very neatly arranged. Who would have thought that the King's fleeting prayer could have played so important a part in the dramatic sequence of events? The meeting with Hushai claims the whole attention of the reader, but it is noteworthy that this conversation follows at the very place "where prayer was made to God." With his customary restraint the narrator makes the observation by way of pointing out that this is no coincidence, but a dispensation of God.[39] We must also bear in mind that David's withdrawal as a whole has taken the form of a penitential progress. It is, then, at this point that David's fortunes change radically. Hushai's cunning advice was Absalom's undoing. We now understand why the historian should pause at this juncture, when the fate of Absalom is sealed, to point out to the reader the theological significance of the events. This was the turning point in the rebellion, and the change in the situation was the work of God himself, who had heard the prayer of the King in his profound humiliation.

Let us look back over these three texts. Their significance for the evaluation of the whole historical work is plainly to be seen. They cannot be regarded as unimportant comments of a conventional kind: their positions, always at natural pauses in the story, is too prominent for this. These pronouncements, it need hardly be said, express a quite definite view of the relationship of God to history.

At the beginning of this investigation we spoke of the contrast between this historical work and the hero-sagas. There, at the height of the confusion of war, God himself intervened miraculously in earthly events; and this activity of God in human affairs was so conclusive and all-embracing that there was no room left for any human activity. How differently things look in this historical work! There is no miracle, and no charismatic leader appears. Events unwind themselves according to the laws of their own nature. Even those passages in which the historian speaks of God are no exception. Once the writer has given us his highly significant pointer, events move on without our noticing the slightest break in the chain of earthly causality.

How then did our author conceive of the activity of God in history? We should say that he evidently thought of it as something hidden, and certainly not confined to sensational events that stand out from all other occurrences. The comment on the rejection of Ahithophel's advice should certainly not be taken to mean that God intervened only in the course of the discussion, rather in the manner of a "spirit of confusion." The happenings in the council of war are neither more sensational nor more miraculous than any of the other happenings that the historian describes. Rather he depicts a succession of occurrences in which the chain of inherent cause and effect is firmly knit up—so firmly indeed that human eye discerns no point at which God could have put in his hand. Yet secretly it is he who has brought all to pass; all the threads are in his hands; his activity embraces the great political events no less than the hidden counsels of human hearts. All human affairs are the sphere of God's providential working.

It is this conception of the *concursus divinus* that makes it possible for our historian to do justice to human effectiveness in his presentation of human activities. He needed no religious trimmings or moralizing glosses. A completely simple profession of faith underlies this work, and for this reason it must in every sense be reckoned a theological history, however worldly the colors in which it is painted. The actors in this drama are men of flesh and blood, not "religious characters" but men who force events with passion and grim determination. Yet the reader is taught to look on God as the hidden Lord and ruler of history. Men do not sink to the status of puppets, and there is ultimately nothing artificial in the reference to God, so that the reader is kept in a state of tension which no one can help feeling who has any real faith.

That this should be so represents an artistic and theological achievement, whose maturity and sureness of touch cannot be sufficiently praised. It would nevertheless be an inadequate description of this work to say merely that it is a "history of divine guidance," that is, a narrative sequence that aims to show the reader the guiding hand of God and his providence, which in the end brings everything to a right and good conclusion. There is more to it than this. The underlying theme of the whole work is the succession to the throne of David. At the outset we were told of the promise of God that the Davidic throne should endure forever. Then we saw the appalling vicissitudes into which it fell, until at last the divinely appointed heir assumed the crown and the problem of the succession to the throne was solved. If, however, it was the purpose of the historian to show how God preserved the Davidic throne through all the vicissitudes of history, then theologically speaking his theme was a messianic one.

We emphasized above the peculiarly secular mode of presentation adopted by our author, comparing it with the naïve attitude to the miraculous evinced in the hero-sagas. This view of history and of God's activity in history must have been nothing less than revolutionary in its day. God's activity is not experienced now as something miraculous and intermittent, as in the old "holy wars." It is hidden to the natural eye, but is understood to be more continuous and all-embracing. God works in every sphere of life, public as well as private, in profane matters no less than in religious ones. Most important of all, however, the emphasis on the divine activity in history has suddenly shifted from sacral, cultic institutions (the holy war, the charismatic leader, the ark of God, and so on) to the realm of the profane. However highly one may rate the originality and theological genius of our writer, such an outlook must have had its precursors in the history of spirituality, for all historical writing presupposes a "common cultural consciousness."[40]

There is no real difficulty at this stage in relating this particular work to the age of Solomon, in which it undoubtedly took its origin. Only in Solomon's era did the new order, which began in the time of David, develop its cultural potential to touch every facet of human existence. With Saul, Israel ceased to be a tribal federation on a sacral basis (an amphictyony, that is) but political relationships on the whole had still changed very little in Saul's day. They changed only when David brought about a great territorial expansion of the empire. The ancient Yahwistic amphictyony had effectively prevented a mixture with communities committed to different creeds, but its boundaries had now been superseded. Wide tracts of Canaanite territory were incorporated into the kingdom of Israel. A new life opened up, culturally much more broadly based than that which had been possible only a generation earlier. We are told that Solomon entered into commercial relationships on a large scale with distant lands. Wealth flowed into the country, luxury and high living became the order of the day at court, a grand program of building was set in train.

This blossoming of economic life was naturally followed close behind by an intensive interchange of spiritual ideas. At no time in the whole history of this nation were the prohibitions against the importation of spiritual and religious nations so generously interpreted as at this period. The court was a center of international wisdom-lore, as the Egyptian courts had been in an earlier age. The presence of so many foreigners gave rise to obligations that were willingly fulfilled, and shrines were set up for non-Israelite deities. In short, the time of Solomon was a period of "enlightenment," of a sharp break with the ancient patriarchal code of living.

The depth to which these influences penetrated cannot be too profoundly appreciated. The age of the old, simple, sacral statutes was past beyond recall. The archaic institution of the holy war and the simple form of the cultus at the sanctuaries, with all their cult-legends, were undermined by a flood of secular ideas. The cultic legends became detached from their original localities and were turned into literature. May we not discern in the present historical work the effect of the chilly wind of an emancipated spirituality, modernized and freed from the cultus? Yet the author is no exponent of "enlightenment" in the usual sense of the term. Admittedly the conception of Yahweh's activity through the ancient sacral institutions has become obsolete, but the belief that he is active in history most certainly had not. On the contrary, now for the first time it was possible to understand God's activity in an all-embracing sense. It is no longer seen as something that operates from time to time through the charisma of a chosen leader, but as a much more constant, much more widely embracing factor concealed in the whole breadth of secular affairs, and pervading every single sphere of human life.

The real theological significance of this work resides in the very fact that this process is carried through so swiftly and so surely. With this work there begins a wholly new conception of the nature of God's activity in history.[41]

10

The Deuteronomic Theology of History
in 1 and 2 Kings

An exhaustive monograph recently appeared in Noth's collection of studies of the history of traditions, concerning the work of the deuteronomic historian.[1] It has closed a regrettable and indeed shameful gap in present-day Old Testament studies. Noth has subjected the literary problem to a wholly new examination, and has above all shown conclusively that this great work is not the result of literary redaction, but fully deserves without any qualification the rarely merited designation of "historical writing." On the one hand all kinds of ancient historical texts are brought together and welded into a single whole, within the framework of an overriding plan. On the other hand a rigorous selectivity has evidently governed the entire work, and the reader is referred continually to the sources for everything that lies outside the scheme of its theology of history. In both respects the office of the historian in the strictest sense of the world has been faithfully discharged.

No doubt this history has its own highly individual approach, and indeed bears the stamp of a quite distinctive theology, which explains why it was misinterpreted by an age that felt itself obliged always to judge solely by the ideal standard of "objective historicity." We are concerned here only with its particular theological approach. We may take for granted the deuteronomist's well-known literary technique, which welds together all kinds of sources dealing with the reign of a king, so as to make of them a single whole within the framework of a larger work, only occasionally interpolating words of his own to report speeches or to make reflections. We speak of this historical work as deuteronomic, because certain standards of judgment found only in Deuteronomy, or predominantly in Deuteronomy, are accepted as normative for its evaluation of the past.[2]

It is well known that throughout Deuteronomy the question of the purity of the cult of Yahweh in Jerusalem, as opposed to all continuing Canaanite cults at the high places, has become the "article on which the community stands or falls" *(articulus stantis et cadentis ecclesiae).* By this standard, which by this time had become wholly binding, Deuteronomy judges all past events; and it is notorious that on these grounds all the kings of Israel fall under condemnation, because they all "walked in the way of Jeroboam the son of Nebat." Of all the kings of Judah, five receive qualified approval. To the secular historian this type of judgment will seem unreasonable and crude, and it is true that the deuteronomist flatly refuses to assess the kings on the basis of their own particular historical situation and its problems.[3] His assessment of them is not arrived at by weighing up the multifarious pros and cons and by drawing up a kind of balance sheet of achievements and shortcomings.

The fact that the kings are evaluated much more in terms of "either-or" than "both-and," however, derives from the peculiar theological attitude of this work, which boldly undertakes to express the ultimate verdict of God himself. The deuteronomist does not enquire into the manifold doings of the king for better or for worse, but speaks only of the one deciding factor upon which in the last analysis, as he believes, acquittal or condemnation depends. In so doing the deuteronomic historian decisively attributes to the kings the power to choose freely for or against Yahweh, in contrast to the so-called classical historians of Israel, who rather depict humanity as the passive object of God's purpose in history.

It is purely a modern question whether this procedure does the kings an injustice, objectively speaking, in judging them by a standard that was actually irrelevant to their own day. The question of interest to us is rather this: was the standard of mandatory cultic unity laid down by the deuteronomist something altogether new to Israel? Admittedly it was unknown in the monarchic period, but we have seen that the deuteronomist certainly does not regard it as an innovation, and in practice it does no more than bring up to date a heterogeneous mass of ancient values, giving them immediate relevance. The history of the cultus, moreover, shows that at an earlier period, in the age of the ancient Israelite amphictyony, Israel recognized that it was very largely bound by this standard. The deuteronomic canon of judgment thus appears in a rather different light from that in which earlier critics felt themselves obliged to look at it. In this case, we may reasonably make allowance for the fact that in every period of history the past is always to some extent misjudged by the *subjective* application of standards which have become binding on a later age; but this does not mean that there can be any doubt of the *objective* rightness, and indeed the necessity, of making such judgment.

The great events in the shadow of which the deuteronomist wrote were the catastrophes of 721 and 586 B.C.E., which for him were heavy with theological import. They expressed Yahweh's sentence of condemnation upon both kingdoms, following which the redemptive history of Israel had come to a halt. This is the key to the understanding of the deuteronomist's position. He writes from the bewilderment and crying need of an age in which there is no salvation!

We must try to see the obvious deficiencies of his historical writing against the background of this unique situation. Thus placed, the deuteronomist no longer had at his disposal sound standards of judgment for many of the events of the past. Yet he is actually concerned only with the theological significance of the disasters which had befallen the two kingdoms. To this end he had pored over the history of the past page by page, and his conclusion was a very definite one: this was not Yahweh's fault. Generation after generation of Israel had piled up an ever-heavier burden of guilt and perfidy, and in the end Yahweh could not do other than reject his people. The breach of cultic unity is not the only accusation that the deuteronomist brings against the kings. He demands to know whether the kings trusted in Yahweh (*baṭaḥ*, 2 Kgs 18:5) and whether they were "perfect" with Yahweh (*šalem 'im Yhwh*, 1 Kgs 11:4, etc.).

Admittedly the offences that he mentions are preponderantly cultic ones.[4] Very often he is content to record in the form of an unimaginative list of accusations the fact that a king did not keep "the statutes and the commandments and the ordinances of Yahweh." There is a palpable lack of graphic ability here. Evidently what the writer means is that the king in question, and his contemporaries, fall far short of the *total* demand of obedience to God. The deuteronomist judges the kings by the standard of perfect obedience.

This question of obedience is the one fundamental notion underlying deuteronomic historical writing. Alongside this subjective test, however, a second test now appears in the history of Israel—an objective one, which regularly coincides with the first. We meet it as soon as we raise the question as to *how* God acts in history. The deuteronomic view of the matter is evidently that God has revealed his commandments to Israel, and has threatened to deal with disobedience by means of heavy punishments, and even by condemning the nation to extinction. This has now come about. Yahweh's words had fulfilled themselves in history, and had not failed, as the deuteronomist puts it (Josh 21:45; 23:14; 1 Kgs 8:56; 2 Kgs 10:10). The word of Yahweh is thus related to historical events by the fact that once he has spoken, his word always and invariably achieves its purpose in history by virtue of its own inherent power (Deut 23:47).[5]

This conception, however, can be reconstructed in a much clearer form from the work of the deuteronomist. We refer to that system of prophet prediction and of its exactly observed fulfillment that pervades the whole work of this writer. This may be described as the theological plan of the work, parallel to the structural plan, although by its very nature it is handled with greater freedom and elasticity.[6]

1. *The prophecy:*
   2 Sam 7:13: Yahweh guarantees David's kingdom by the mouth of Nathan: his son will build a house for Yahweh.
   The fulfillment:
   1 Kgs 8:20: "Yahweh has fulfilled the promise which he made." Solomon has ascended the throne and built the temple.

2. *The prophecy:*
   1 Kgs 11:29ff.: Ahijah of Shiloh declares that ten tribes will be taken away from Solomon's kingdom, because he has neglected Yahweh, worshiped idols, and has not walked in the way of Yahweh.
   The fulfillment:
   1 Kgs 12:15b: Rehoboam rends the kingdom catastrophically, "for it was a turn of affairs brought about by Yahweh that he might fulfill (*heqîm*) his word, which Yahweh spoke by Ahijah the Shilonite to Jeroboam the son of Nebat."

3. *The prophecy:*
   1 Kings 13: An unknown prophet foretells that Josiah, a descendant of David, will slay the high priests upon the altar and burn men's bones upon it.
   The fulfillment:
   2 Kgs 23:16-18: Josiah defiles the altar at Bethel by burning human bones, "according to the word of Yahweh which the man of God proclaimed."

4. *The prophecy:*
   1 Kgs 14:6ff.: Ahijah of Shiloh declares that Jeroboam, having been made ruler of Israel by Yahweh, has done worse than all his predecessors. His kingdom will therefore be extirpated "as a man burns up dung until it is all gone."
   The fulfillment:
   1 Kgs 15:29: The usurper Baasha makes away with the house of Jeroboam, "according to the word of Yahweh which he spoke by his servant Ahijah the Shilonite."

5. *The prophecy:*
   1 Kgs 16:1ff.: Jehu ben Hanani asserts that Baasha, having been raised by Yahweh to be the ruler of Israel, has gone astray in the same way as Jeroboam, and has led Israel into sin. For this reason the same will befall him and his house which befell the house of Jeroboam.

The fulfillment:

1 Kgs 16:12: "Thus Zimri destroyed all the house of Baasha, according to the work of Yahweh, which he spoke against Baasha by Jehu the prophet."

6. *The prophecy:*

Josh 6:26: Whoever rebuilds Jericho, "at the cost of his first-born shall he lay its foundation, and at the cost of his youngest son shall he set up its gates."

The fulfillment:

1 Kgs 16:34: Hiel builds up Jericho; "he laid its foundation at the cost of Abiram his first-born, and set up its gates at the cost of his youngest son Segub, according to the word of Yahweh which he spoke by Joshua the son of Nun."

7. *The prophecy:*

1 Kgs 22:17: Micaiah ben Imlah foretells that Israel will be scattered and bereft of its shepherd; let each return to his home in peace.

The fulfillment:

1 Kgs 22:35ff.: (not especially indicated as such by deuteronomist) Ahab is mortally wounded. Let each man return to his home!

8. *The prophecy:*

1 Kgs 21:21ff.: Elijah's prophetic threat against Ahab and his house.

The fulfillment:

1 Kgs 21:27-29: Since Ahab has humbled himself on hearing the judgment, the punishment will fall only on his son (cf. 2 Kgs 9:7ff.).

9. *The prophecy:*

2 Kgs 1:6: Elijah prophesies that Ahaziah will not recover from his illness, but will die.

The fulfillment:

2 Kgs 1:17: Ahaziah dies "according to the word of Yahweh which Elijah had spoken."

10. *The prophecy:*

2 Kgs 21:10ff.: Unnamed prophets declare that because of the sins of Manasseh evil will befall Jerusalem, "such that the ears of everyone who hears of it will tingle."

The fulfillment:

2 Kgs 24:2: Yahweh sends the Chaldeans, etc., against Judah, "according to the word of Yahweh which he spoke by his servants the prophets." Also of importance is 2 Kgs 23:26: despite Josiah's reform, Yahweh does not turn from his fierce anger; because of Manasseh's provocations he has determined to destroy Judah, too.

11. *The prophecy:*
2 Kgs 22:15ff.: Hulda prophesies that Josiah will be gathered to his fathers, and will not see the evil which is to befall Jerusalem.
The fulfillment:
2 Kgs 23:30: The body of Josiah, killed in battle at Megiddo, is brought back to Jerusalem and buried there.

This survey can evidently give no more than a broad outline of the theological structure of deuteronomic history in the books of the Kings. Actually in this particular respect, the deuteronomist demands the close attention of his readers and considerable vigilance on their part, if they are to realize that everywhere there is a self-fulfilling relationship between the divinely inspired prophecy and the historical occurrence, even at those points where it is not expressly mentioned. The histories of Elijah and Isaiah are taken up by the historian for this very reason.[7] By and large one can work on the assumption that the deuteronomist makes explicit mention of the fulfillment of a prophecy more particularly in those cases where the fact is not so immediately perceptible to the reader, whilst in those instances where the events speak for themselves he was able to dispense with this.

On the other hand one must bear in mind that from a literary point of view the deuteronomist is working almost exclusively with traditional material, which does not always readily accommodate itself to his basic theological attitude. It contains abundant difficulties of its own, and is on that account even less adaptable to the purposes of the deuteronomic groundplan. We tend habitually to overestimate the degree of literary license exercised by ancient writers with respect to traditional literary material.

Taken one by one, these prophecies raise a good many problems for us. There is no cause to doubt that the quotations given mostly derive from actual prophecies. An indication of this may be seen in the undeuteronomic and highly picturesque language, as well as in the poetic form (*parallelismus membrorum*) in which many of these sayings are preserved (for example, 1 Kgs 14:10, 15; 16:4; 2 Kgs 21:13). It seems, however, that these sources did not provide a very abundant supply of material for our author, or he would not have quoted three times over, and against three different kings, the oracle, "Anyone belonging to X who dies in the city the dogs shall eat; and anyone who dies in the open country the birds shall eat" (1 Kgs 14:11; 16:4; 21:24).

There is too little evidence here for any conclusions to be drawn regarding the nature of these "deuteronomic" prophecies, on the basis of the material content of their oracles. One could hardly mention the prophecies of an Ahujah, a Jehu ben Hanani, or the unknown prophets of 2 Kgs 21:10ff., in the same breath as the so-called writing prophets. They seem to be wholly lacking in a wider historical perspective. Their gaze is fixed exclusively on the history of the Israelite nation, and they therefore speak of the activity of Yahweh in history, punishing or sparing according to the inherent nature of the situation. It might thus well be that, behind this highly schematized presentation of the matter, a prophetic outlook of a rather unusual kind is to be discerned. We see from 2 Kgs 17:13 what is the deuteronomic view of the characteristic function of the prophets: Yahweh testifies by them (*he'îd*) in order to call the nation back to himself and to the keeping of his commandments.

In view of its origin, this deuteronomic theology of history may be said to be that of the early prophets: the oracle is infallibly self-fulfilling, and therefore determines the course of history. It is interesting to notice how the deuteronomic proceeds from the basic assumption that the history of the two kingdoms is nothing more or less than the historical expression of the will and word of Yahweh. This is what makes history intelligible, and one can therefore "read back" this motive into the past. It is apparent, from many different aspects of his presentation of the history of the two kingdoms, that for the deuteronomist the events of past history are the criteria by which theological truth may be known.

The fate of the Northern Kingdom is actually sealed by the first sin, the apostasy of Jeroboam I.[8] The particular sin of all later kings is expressed in the stereotyped comment that they walked in the sin of Jeroboam. Yet the matter was not quite so simple as this for the deuteronomist, in so far as Yahweh actually spared this kingdom for a further two hundred years. This enigmatic situation, which is in fact no more than a postponement of punishment, is explained in terms of the mercy of Yahweh, who does not overlook the comparative goodness found even in reprobate kings. Ahab humbled himself before the sentence of punishment, and for this reason the sentence on his house was not executed in his lifetime (1 Kgs 21:29). Jehu performed certain acts which were pleasing to Yahweh, and thus his descendants were to occupy the throne of Israel for four generations (2 Kgs 10:30; 15:12). At a time of great oppression on the part of the Aramaeans Jehoahaz prayed to Yahweh for aid, and in consequence Yahweh mercifully held his band from punishing the sinful kingdom (2 Kgs 13:23; 14:26).

Then, however, came the bitter end, and the deuteronomist shows in his great epilogue at 2 Kgs 17:7ff. how Israel's transgression of the commandments of Yahweh brought judgment upon itself. There is no doubt of the *theological* sources from which the deuteronomist compiled his account. The premises of his argument are the will of God as set down in the commandments of Deuteronomy, and the course of the history of the Northern Kingdom determined by the word of God which itself creates history.

The situation with regard to the history of the kingdom of Judah is rather different. Here, too, the story is presented primarily as the history of human disobedience, and of steadily mounting divine disapproval. But what has to be explained is the divine restraint, God's patience over a much longer period. We must take into account here an element of the deuteronomic theology of history which so far has been left out of our reckoning:

In 1 Kgs 11:13 Yahweh tells Solomon:

> I will not tear away all the kingdom; but I will give one tribe to your son, for the sake of David my servant and for the sake of Jerusalem which I have chosen.

At 1 Kgs 11:32 Ahijah the Shilonite tells Jeroboam:

> He shall have one tribe, for the sake of my servant David, and for the sake of Jerusalem, the city which I have chosen.

1 Kgs 11:36:

> Yet to his son I will give one tribe, that David my servant may always have a lamp before me in Jerusalem, the city where I have chosen to put my name.

Concerning Abijam, the deuteronomist says in 1 Kgs 15:4:

> Nevertheless for David's sake, Yahweh gave him a lamp in Jerusalem, setting up his son after him and establishing Jerusalem.

Concerning Jehoram, the deuteronomist says at 2 Kgs 8:19:

> Yet Yahweh would not destroy Judah, for the sake of David his servant, since he promised to give a lamp to him (for his sons) forever.

In speaking of the "lamp" which Yahweh promised to David, the deuteronomist is of course referring to Yahweh's promise to establish and uphold the Davidic dynasty, given in the prophecy of Nathan in 2 Samuel 7.[9] It is interesting to observe how this deuteronomic prophetic tradition is welded into the wider scheme of deuteronomic theology, and is associated with the cultic place, so that two traditions of quite different origin have been fused into a single whole (see esp. 1 Kgs 11:36). But it is not only by way of explanation of Yahweh's patient forbearance with the kingdom of Judah that the deuteronomist introduces this "deuteronomized" prophecy of Nathan's. It is a part of a tradition that has a considerably more important function than this.

In 1 Kgs 2:4 David gives his charge to Solomon, so that Yahweh may fulfill his promise that "there shall not fail you a man on the throne of Israel."

In the temple consecration-prayer at 1 Kgs 8:20 Solomon says:

> Now Yahweh has fulfilled his promise which he made; for I have risen in the place of David my father, and sit on the throne of Israel as Yahweh promised, and I have built the house for the name of Yahweh the God of Israel.

In the same passage, at 1 Kgs 8:25:

> Now therefore, O Yahweh, God of Israel, keep with thy servant David my father what thou hast promised him, saying, "There shall never fail you a man before me to sit upon the throne of Israel."

In 1 Kings 9:5 Yahweh tells Solomon:

> Then I will establish your throne over Israel forever, as I promised David your father, saying, "There shall not fail you a man upon the throne of Israel."

From the point of view of literary analysis, all these texts, like the passages quoted above, are part of the particular theological framework which the deuteronomist has given to his work, and for this reason have a special significance for the outlook of the work as a whole. They nevertheless represent an aspect of the traditions that is wholly undeuteronomic, and show a pronounced messianic interest.

This observation leads at once to the question of how the deuteronomic conception of David arose.

The actual historical narrative concerning David is remarkably free from deuteronomic additions. This is surprising, in view of the immense number of references to David contained in the account of subsequent historical events, which show him as the ideal of a king who is pleasing to Yahweh. The reasons for this, however, are purely literary ones. The story of David appears in a self-contained document, of such scope that the deuteronomist was obliged to abandon his usual technique of interpolating theological comment and imposing a theological framework. Apart from the well-known modification of the intention of Nathan's prophecy in 2 Sam 8:13, the deuteronomist hardly speaks before the end of the history of David, although his own picture of David has nevertheless emerged clearly. There is a remarkable shift away from this point of view in the deuteronomic presentation of post-Davidic history.

> In 1 Kgs 3:3 we read that Solomon walked in the statutes of David his father.
>
> 1 Kgs 3:14 tells us that David walked in the statutes and ordinances of Yahweh.
>
> 1 Kgs 5:3 (MT 5:17): David was prevented by his wars from building the temple, but is its real spiritual founder.
>
> 1 Kgs 8:17ff.: David intended to build the temple, and did well in so doing.
>
> 1 Kgs 9:4: David walked before Yahweh "with integrity of heart and uprightness."
>
> 1 Kgs 11:4: David's heart was wholly true to Yahweh.
>
> 1 Kgs 11:6: David followed Yahweh wholly.
>
> 1 Kgs 11:33: David walked in the ways of Yahweh, and did what was right in his sight.
>
> 1 Kgs 11:38: David walked in the ways of Yahweh, did what was right in his eyes and kept his statutes and commandments.
>
> 1 Kgs 14:8: David kept Yahweh's commandments and followed him with all his heart, doing only that which was right in his eyes.
>
> 1 Kgs 15:3: David's heart was wholly true to Yahweh.
>
> 1 Kgs 15:5: David did what was right in the eyes of Yahweh, and did not turn aside from anything that he commanded him all the days of his life except in the matter of Uriah the Hittite.
>
> 1 Kgs 15:11: Asa did what was right in the eyes of Yahweh, as David his father had done.
>
> 2 Kgs 14:3: Amaziah did what was right in the eyes of Yahweh, yet not like David his father.
>
> 2 Kgs 16:2: Ahaz did not do what was right in the eyes of Yahweh, as his father David had done.
>
> 2 Kgs 18:3: Hezekiah did what was right in the eyes of Yahweh, just as David had done.
>
> 2 Kgs 21:7: Yahweh said to David (!) and to Solomon his son: "In this house and in Jerusalem, which I have chosen out of all the tribes of Israel, I will put my name for ever."
>
> 2 Kgs 22:2: Josiah walked in all the way of David his father.

This collection of texts equally contains only deuteronomic statements. The picture is quite unambiguous: it is David who is the king after the deuteronomist's own heart, and not, as has so often been said, Solomon.

David is the prototype of the perfectly obedient anointed one, and thus the pattern for all succeeding kings in Jerusalem. But what kind of a David is this, who walked before Yahweh "with integrity of heart and uprightness," whose heart was wholly true to Yahweh, and who did only (*raq*) that which was right in his eyes? Unquestionably this is not the David we have seen in the history of the succession to the throne, that singularly contradictory character, so tenacious and firm in political matters, yet so dangerously weak in his own house; so deeply involved in guilt, yet in the end so graciously led by Yahweh through all his difficulties.

This altogether human characterization is now overlaid by quite a different and unrelated conception of David as the prototype of a theocratic monarch, and a model of obedience. This deuteronomic conception exemplifies pre-eminently a messianic view of David, which must have been current in his own day. It is difficult to know how and where this picture of David, purged of all dross, took its origin. In Psalm 132 we find this same picture of David as a model of obedience. More particularly, however, Isaiah already seems to take it for granted (for example, Isa 1:21).

Be this as it may, in taking up this strongly established tradition the deuteronomist has moved right away from his native climate of the Book of Deuteronomy, whence his theological viewpoint originates.[10] The wide extent to which the deuteronomist employs this tradition in his work shows that the deuteronomic tradition in its purest form could not hold its ground here. The obviously very powerful messianic conception has broke in upon it, and demanded a hearing. The effort so diligently made to reckon the whole matter of the temple to David's account is quite remarkable. Perhaps it was necessary for the tradition of the temple, and of all the far-reaching cultic associations which went with it, to be brought more closely under the shadow of King David in order to validate them afresh from this source.

In the last analysis, what the deuteronomist has done in this respect arises simply from his faithfulness to the tradition which had been handed down to him. A part of this tradition was that principle of historical causality expressed in the Book of Deuteronomy as Yahweh's curse on those who transgress his commandments. The deuteronomic historian also found there the prophetic declaration of Yahweh's promise under the Davidic covenant. He could not leave these two great principles out of account, and indeed he believes the shape and the course of the whole history of the kingdom of Judah to be determined by the mutual interplay of these forces.

We are thus led to the important conclusion that in the deuteronomic presentation of the matter Yahweh's word determines the history of Judah, and that it does so under two particular forms: first, it is a law which controls and destroys; secondly it is a "gospel," a continually self-fulfilling promise to David, which brings salvation and forgiveness. The promise made through Nathan is a kind of *katechōn*, the restraining force that runs through the history of Judah, warding off the long-deserved judgment from the kingdom "for David's sake."

The question at once arises as to what brought this state of affairs to an end. Was the promise of favor the weaker of the two elements, so that in the end it was overcome by the sentence of punishment and driven from the field of history? The final destruction of the kingdom of Judah seems to point in this direction, as does the fact that in the later days of the monarchy the deuteronomist no longer speaks of the saving efficacy of the promise made by Nathan. It is as if the "sure mercies of David" (*ḥasdê David*) had lost their protective power in the face of a growing weight of human guilt.

It seems that in this lies the resolution of the theological dilemma in which the deuteronomist is caught at the end of his work. On the one hand none was less in a position than he to minimize the terrible severity of the judgment; on the other hand he could not, indeed must not, believe that the promise of Yahweh might fail, and that the lamp of David would be finally extinguished, for no word of Yahweh pronounced over history can ever fall to the ground. For this reason there can be no doubt to our mind that the mention of Jehoiachin's release from prison at the very end of the deuteronomist's work (2 Kgs 25:27-30) must be of particular theological significance.

> In the thirty-seventh year of the exile of Jehoiachin king of Judah, in the twelfth month, on the twenty-seventh day of the month, Evil-merodach King of Babylon, in the year that he began to reign, graciously freed Jehoiachin King of Judah from prison; and he spoke kindly to him, and gave him a seat above the seats of the kings who were with him in Babylon. So Jehoiachin put off his prison garments. And every day of his life he dined regularly at the King's table; and a regular allowance was given him by the King, every day a portion as long as he lived.

Obviously nothing is said here in strictly theological terms, but a carefully measured indication is given: an occurrence is referred to which has immense significance for the deuteronomist, since it provides a basis upon which Yahweh could build further if he so willed. At all events the reader must understand this passage to be an indication of the fact that the line of David has not come to an irrevocable end.[11]

In his study of this topic Noth has already cut away the ground from under the feet of many who make quite unjust criticisms of this piece of historical writing. One cannot well explain the deuteronomist's reluctance to examine the great problems inherent in history on the grounds of his incapacity to do so. What he shows us is the history of Yahweh's creative word, and *it is the very working in history of this divine word which ties his hands.*[12]

There is therefore actually a tremendous assertion implicit in the limitation itself: the decisive factor in the history of Israel is not that which commonly creates the largest stir, nor is it the difficulty of the multifarious problems raised by Israel's own situation. On the contrary, Israel's history depends upon a few quite simple theological and prophetical propositions concerning the nature of the divine word. It is this word of Yahweh, and it alone, which gives to the phenomena of history a purpose and a meaning, so binding together into a single whole in the eyes of God its manifold and diverse elements.

Thus the deuteronomist shows, by a wholly valid process, just what redemptive history is within the context of the Old Testament: it is a course of events shaped by the word of Yahweh, continually intervening to direct and to deliver, and so steadily pressing these events towards their fulfillment in history.

11

The Royal Ritual in Judah

The Old Testament contains only two considerable accounts of royal coronations—those of Solomon and of Joash. According to 1 Kgs 1:33-40,
Solomon rides on the royal mule (*pirdath ha-melek*), led by Zadok the priest,
by Nathan, and by the Cherethites and Pelethites, who bring him to the spring
(Gihon) where he is anointed. He then returns to the palace amid the acclamation of the people and ascends his father's throne.

At 2 Kings 11 two accounts have been conflated, both of which, however,
appear to be equally reliable.[1] Having made the temple forecourt secure
against all surprise, Jehoida the priest, sent by the royal bodyguard, brings out
the prince, Joash, and anoints him. The people shout, "Long live the King";
and the King is led from the temple through the guards' gate into the palace,
where he ascends the royal throne. The parallel account in vv. 13-18 gives
details of the proceedings in the temple. We shall come back later to the statement that the young King stood in a particular place.

Both accounts describe unusual coronations, but it is to this very fact that
we owe them both, since the writer had no cause to describe a normal anointing ceremony. Even Solomon's anointing took place precipitately, and it is particularly noticeable that the rite was not at this time tied down to any
traditional ceremonial. It is highly significant that David has to make the
arrangements ad hoc, and that Benaiah, the commander of the royal bodyguard, is entrusted with the oversight of the whole ceremony (1 Kgs 1:36). The
way in which the royal mule is brought into the story seems to indicate that
this is to some extent a traditional element (see 2 Sam 13:29; 18:9). In pre-
monarchist times the ass had been the mount of prominent people and
princely leaders (Judg 5:10; 10:4; 12:14).[2] One may doubt whether this continued to be so during the monarchy after the introduction of horses into Israel.
In this case it would be significant, and in line with numerous other instances,

that the messianic prophecy of Zech 9:9 should intentionally hark back to what must be an ancient tradition.

It is, however, clear that according to both accounts the coronation ceremony was divided into two parts, the anointing in the sanctuary and the enthronement in the royal palace. It is true that the narrator of 1 Kings 1 does not say that by "Gihon" he means to indicate a sanctuary, but this is self-evident, since this place clearly had sacral associations.[3]

Now from all we know of the matter, conditions in Judah were much more favorable to the development and persistence of a fixed royal ceremonial than in the kingdom of Israel. Kingship in the northern kingdom had never quite lost the character of the ancient Israelite institution of the charismatic leader. The appointment of the king, as well as the act of coronation, followed the dictates of a political situation that at times was extremely fluid.[4] Who was to know when and where Yahweh would appoint a new king? The much more stable situation in Judah offered far greater opportunities for a fixed ceremonial. Here the crown remained for centuries in the same dynasty, and, what is more, there was here the strong contributory factor of a continuing ancient tradition of sacral kingship handed down from the old pre-Davidic city-kingdom. Revitalized by Yahwistic beliefs, this proved to be an important formative element, at all events so far as its outward form is concerned. Samaria was a new foundation made by Omri (1 Kgs 16:24), and from this point of view there is obviously a great contrast between the two cities.

To begin with the externals, the king of Judah had a special place of his own, both at the coronation and also on other solemn occasions. We read at 2 Kgs 11:14 that Athaliah saw the king standing on or by the pillar according to the custom. The parallel account in 2 Chron 23:13 is somewhat more precise: "standing beside (on) his pillar at the entrance." Unfortunately the tradition is rather ambiguous. It is true that 2 Kings also reports that Josiah "stood by (on) the pillar" (2 Kgs 23:3), so that we should evidently translate 'al-ha'ammûd as "by (or "on") the pillar," but at this point the parallel in 2 Chronicles has 'al-'amdô ("in his place") (2 Chron 34:31). It is certainly to be understood in any case that the place where the king stood was a raised one. The king would have had to be visible to the crowd that had gathered for the solemnities, so that one may probably think of some sort of pillar-like platform.

Perhaps we ought even to bring into the discussion the "bowl" (kîyôm)[5] three cubits high and five cubits wide which Solomon had made, and from which he is said to have spoken the great prayer of consecration (2 Chron 6:13). It may well be that in noting this fact the Chronicler is concerned to show that Solomon was standing well away from the position occupied by the chief cultic officials; but there is no reason to suppose that the mention of this platform is a pure fabrication. More important than the archaeological problem is the fact that a special position for the king in the temple is also mentioned in Egyptian sources:

> His Majesty came to the sacred dwelling, to the great gate of the Lord of the Two Lands; this is the place to which the king is escorted in the temple of Amun.[6]

In the main account of the enthronement ceremony in 2 Kings 11, the actual coronation itself is described in these terms: Jehoiada the high priest "brought out the King's son (i.e., into the forecourt of the temple) and invested him with the crown and the testimony." We know fairly well what kind of object the crown was.[7] We have a much less clear idea of the "testimony," *'edûth*.

All the more recent authoritative works (Gesenius, *Biblical Hebraica*, commentaries, etc.) are unanimous in suggesting that the word should be amended to read *ṣe'adôth* ("bracelets"), following 2 Sam 1:10. The reading *'edûth* ("testimony") has been regarded as a tendentious alteration of the original intended to bring it into line with Deut 17:18, but the suggestion is not a helpful one in view of the fact that *'edûth* is not at all a deuteronomic word, and in fact in never occurs in the book of Deuteronomy.

According to Gesenius, *'edûth* means "testimony," "an enactment solemnly delivered and received."[8] In the present context it must refer to an object that can be handed over, probably something written. There is no cause to set aside this definition here, since we know that the royal protocol (*nhb.t*) played a similar part in the enthronement of Egyptian kings.[9] What is this royal protocol (*nhb.t*) if not "an enactment solemnly delivered and received?" It contained in particular the ancient titles and sovereign rights and duties conferred on Pharaoh by the god, in brief, the king's authority to rule as the surrogate of the god. If this is accepted, it at once sheds light on a passage in Psalm 2 that has not hitherto been satisfactorily explained. The Anointed one says, "I will tell of the decree of Yahweh: He said to me, 'You are my son.'"

The use of the preposition *'el* following the verb *sipper* is unusual, but however it be construed it is clear that the king is here proclaiming, on the day of his enthronement, a divine decree which has been made in his favor, that Yahweh had adopted him as his son and has committed to him the lordship over the whole world. The decree (*ḥoq*) is to be understood as the royal protocol, and in this passage is the direct equivalent of the "testimony" (*'edûth*) which we have met in 2 Kgs 11:12. This assumption is corroborated by the fact that in the Egyptian royal protocol the divine sonship of the Pharaoh played an important part. Thus Amun-Re of Karnak says to Hatshepsut: "My beloved daughter . . . I am thy beloved father. I establish thy dignity as Lord of the Two Lands. I write for thee thy protocol."[10]

This formulary evidently corresponds very closely to the declaration made by Yahweh to the king in Ps 2:7, and in the subsequent solemn charge delivered to the queen in this Egyptian text we hear further echoes of v. 8 of the same psalm:

> Thus the Lord of all lays down the protocol of His Majesty as the benevolent king of the whole land of Egypt, who takes possession of the lands and defines their needs. His Majesty spoke, as he wrote the protocol for repetition at the jubilees . . . .[11]

Finally we add a further piece of evidence from a long account of Thutmosis III. The passage deals with his election of Amun, and brings together the crown and the royal protocol in a manner which provides an exact parallel to 2 Kgs 11:12: "He put the crown upon me, and himself wrote for me the protocol."[12]

Despite these striking points of correspondence between the royal ritual of Judah and that of ancient Egypt, there is nevertheless a profound difference between them with regard to the relationship between Yahweh and his anointed one. In Egypt the divine sonship of the pharaoh was conceived in mythological terms, and the deity was regarded as the king's father in a wholly physical sense. Such a conception was quite impossible within the context of Yahwism. Here the king became the son of Yahweh by adoption. On the day of his accession he entered into that filial relationship which had been promised to each succeeding sovereign in the prophecy of Nathan in 2 Samuel 7. But we may pursue yet further this distinction, already widely recognized, between the ancient Egyptian conception and that of the Old Testament.[13]

We take as our starting-point the complaint found in Psalm 89:

> You have renounced the covenant with your servant,
> You have defiled his crown in the dust. (Ps 89:39 [MT 89:40])

The whole context deals with the promise made to David, is an appeal to the "sure mercies of David" (ḥasdê David) couched in the style of an "individual lament." It dates probably from the exilic period. Verses 24-36 [MT 25-37] are a paraphrase of the prophecy of Nathan, although they are evidently not directly dependent upon 2 Samuel 7. A whole series of features that are of great antiquity find no parallels there, a fact that weighs against the likelihood that 2 Samuel 7 was the literary source of our present passage. With the verse quoted above the prayer now turns to complaint and petition; the covenant (*berîth*) mentioned here refers, of course, to the Davidic covenant. It is remarkable that the term "covenant" does not actually occur in Nathan's prophecy in 2 Samuel 7, but the notion itself is certainly not to be dismissed as a late theological interpretation. So much is already clear from the very ancient "last words of David" at 2 Sam 23:5.

Psalm 132:12 too, is manifestly a text of great antiquity. The association here of crown (*nezer*) and covenant (*berîth*) is of interest, since it is reminiscent of the passage which we took as our point of departure (2 Kgs 11:12), it having been long recognized that under certain circumstances "covenant" and "testimony" (*'edûth*) are used as exact synonyms.[14] In 2 Kgs 11:12 the "testimony" is a formal, material object: a *te'ûdah* can be shut up and sealed, as we discover from Isa 8:16, whereas in Ps 89:39, it is thought of rather from the point of view of its content. The promise that the Davidic throne will endure forever (Ps 89:4, 36ff.) provides yet further proof that we were right to think of this passage in connection with the royal protocol, for, as we saw above, such a promise forms an integral part of the phraseology of the Egyptian *nḥb.t*.

We may also refer once again to Psalm 2, for we see from Ps 105:10 that "decree" (*ḥoq*) and "covenant" (*berîth*) are so closely related as to be interchangeable terms:

> He confirmed it to Jacob as a decree
> To Israel as an everlasting covenant

This mention of a divine decree serves to introduce the paraphrase of the covenant itself which now follows in vv. 11ff. Precisely the same thing happens in Psalm 2, where the anointed king announces that he will give an account of a decree of Yahweh (v. 7) and in the second half of the verse there follows a paraphrase of the substance of the Davidic covenant. Thus in the passages cited the terms "decree," "testimony," and "covenant" are all virtually synonyms for one and the same thing, and it is clear that in the royal ritual of Judah the genuinely Israelite conception of Yahweh's covenant with the Davidic line has taken over the place occupied in the Egyptian rite by the notion of the divine sonship of the king, mythologically presented as a physical reality.

At this point, however, according to the documents that we have adduced, the course of the accession ceremony branches off in two different directions. In one the king is invested by the priest with the crown and the testimony, and it would seem that the diadem and the protocol were the two items of sacral and legal insignia, conferment of which constituted the essential act of coronation. In this royal protocol Yahweh addresses the king in direct speech, calls him his son, invests him with sovereign rights, confers upon him his coronation name, and so on. Then, however, in a fresh act of the drama, it is the king himself who speaks. Claiming the authority of a divine revelation made to him, he proclaims to the city and to the world (in a more or less threatening speech) the nature of the overlordship which has been conferred upon him, naturally borrowing from the phraseology of royal protocols for this purpose.[15] This latter procedure, unlike the earlier one, could be repeated from time to time at great festivals, and it is conceivable that this second phase of the ceremony took place in the royal palace and not in the temple.

We must now say a word on the subject of royal titles. These actually formed the principal feature of Egyptian royal protocols, around which all the other elements such as the divine sonship and the investiture with sovereign power fell into place. It is well known that there is but a single example in the Old Testament of a complete list of the royal styles and titles—that found in the messianic prophecy of Isa 9:6b [MT 9:5b]. This one text, nevertheless, proves that the accession ceremony in Judah included the conferment of a coronation name by the deity, for Isaiah is not putting forward anything altogether new in this passage, but relies on tradition at least for the form of his text.[16] It seems to me, however, that there is a further clear allusion to this solemn conferment of the name both at 2 Sam 7:9, and at 1 Kgs 1:47. In each case the statement that Yahweh "has made (or may make) a great name" for the king is so deeply embedded in a pronouncement couched in formal language that it is difficult to regard it as no more than the equivalent of "making a reputation."

Isaiah 9 is a difficult passage to assess from the point of view of form criticism. There is no divine pronouncement here, for every indication of such a pronouncement is lacking, and there seems therefore to be no communication whatever by Yahweh in direct speech. Thus it cannot be held that the section contains any pronouncement that Yahweh has charged the prophet to publish. We notice further that in verse 3 Yahweh is addressed in the second person: "Thou hast increased the rejoicing, thou hast made great the joy."[17] The phenomenon is virtually unique, for here Isaiah is addressing a human oracle to God in a rather different situation from that found for example in Jeremiah.[18]

Here we are concerned only with Isa 9:6-7, which contains the announcement of the birth of the son and the proclamation of his coronation name. We might reasonably expect at this point, if anywhere at all, to find the phraseology of the royal protocols. If this is so, the word "child" here ought not to be construed in the literal sense, but rather by analogy with the words "today I have begotten you" in Ps 2:7. The point at issue is the accession of a descendant of David, who now enters into that filial relationship with Yahweh that he offers to the king.

Who, however, are the "we" to whom the royal heir is given? The commentaries do not ask this question and have always assumed that v. 6 is spoken by the people who hitherto "walked in darkness." This cannot be so. In the Egyptian royal protocols it is always the deity who speaks, and the original first person singular style is abandoned only when the king speaks to a third party concerning the charge that the god has entrusted to him. On this showing the words of verse 6 must correspond exactly with the form of the divine pronouncement in Psalm 2. Furthermore, it would be wholly unnatural for the people to say that a child had been born to *them*. It is clear that there has been a change of speaker between vv. 5 and 6, and that the *kî* ("for") at the beginning of v. 6 must be construed absolutely, with the sense of, "indeed," "truly." The anointed one is a prince (*śar*), a viceroy in Yahweh's kingdom. He is not a king (*melek*), but is responsible to one above him, as Caspari has shown in a little-noticed essay.[19]

If we have rightly understood the passage, Isa 9:6 is the one and only text in which the Messiah is unequivocally designated the Son of Yahweh, although that is admittedly the tacit implication of other messianic passages.

PART III

FROM PSALMS TO CHRONICLES

12

The Theological Problem of the Old Testament Doctrine of Creation

The Yahwistic faith of the Old Testament is a faith based on the notion of election and therefore primarily concerned with redemption. This statement, which requires no justification here, poses simply and precisely the problem with which we are here concerned. How are we to define theologically the relationship between this predominating belief in election and redemption, and that belief in Yahweh as Creator which is also attested by the Old Testament? How far is the idea of Yahweh as Creator a relevant and immediate conception, over against his redemptive function?

This question, of course, is one of theology rather than of the history of religion, so that our task is that of investigating the specifically theological role of the doctrine of creation within the context of Old Testament belief as a whole. To state the matter more precisely, the question we have to answer is whether this doctrine is related to that belief in redemption which dominates the whole of the Old Testament, or whether it is independent of it; and here we meet with problems which are the subject of much controversy today. I will do no more than mention them.

Is the creation of the natural order by God adduced as a motive for faith, either in the prophets or in the psalms? Does the doctrine of redemption presuppose a doctrine of creation as its indispensable theological basis? Lütgert's work on creation and revelation[1] puts the case for this belief, arguing throughout from Old Testament data. In his opinion the pronouncements of the prophets would have carried no conviction but for the self-evident testimony of the created order. In the prophetic proclamation of redemption the hearer recognizes again the Creator who is already known to him. If this is not a tenable view, then how is the doctrine of redemption related to the doctrine of creation, theologically speaking?

177

Before we face up to the immediate problem, let us make one brief prelim-inary observation. The most serious attack which the faith of Israel had to meet with regard to the conception of Nature came from the Canaanite Baal religion. The gravity of this crisis is known to us from Hosea and Deuteron-omy, but evidently it does not occur either to Hosea or to the deuteronomic theologians to oppose the Nature religions on the grounds of the doctrine of creation, by pointing to the fact that Nature and all its forces are the creation of Yahweh. On the contrary, surprisingly enough, the theological objections to Canaanitish aberrations are constantly stated in historical terms, i.e., in terms of Israel's redemptive history. Yahweh both promised and granted the land to Israel, and so became the Giver of the blessings of settled life.

Most surprising of all is the use made of this thought in the prayer for offer-ing first-fruits contained in Deut 26:5ff. The worshiper does not give thanks for the fruits which the Creator has provided for him, but simply acknowledges that he is a member of the nation which God brought into the promised land by a historical saving act, thus making him heir to the blessings of this land.

From the earliest times this was Israel's view of Yahweh's relationship to the land, and to its way of life. This was the blessed plot given to the nation by the saving activity of Yahweh, the mighty Lord of history, and it still remained Yah-weh's land. The statement of Lev 25:23—"The land belongs to me; you are guests and sojourners with me"—is extremely ancient, and underlies the whole law of land tenure in the Old Testament. Nevertheless, it does not depend upon the doctrine of creation, but rests directly on belief in a histori-cal act of grace on God's part. Nor does it lead into a doctrine of creation, since so far as one can see it is quite unrelated to it.

This purely negative conclusion serves as a further pointer to the peculiar-ity of the theological problem to which we now turn. We shall certainly have to correct radically the suspiciously simple picture of this matter which is drawn for us in many theological studies of the Old Testament, and which is particu-larly widespread in the unlearned world as a result of the circumstance that Genesis 1 stands at the beginning of the Bible.

To this end we shall not follow the usual procedure of making the creation narrative of Genesis 1 the center of the discussion. We prefer for our present purpose to start from the evidence for the doctrine of creation contained in the hymns of the Psalter and of Deutero-Isaiah, on the grounds that these hymns give more immediate expression to the religious actualities. They are theologically much less hide-bound than the scholarly priestly code, whose course is dictated by a theological system.

Psalm 136 is a litany in praise of the marvelous acts of Yahweh. Verses 5-9 deal with the creation of the world, and at verse ten the psalm abruptly changes its course in order to recount the mighty deeds of Yahweh in history.

In this psalm, therefore, the doctrine of creation and the doctrine of redemption stand side by side, yet wholly unrelated the one to the other. Because of the rigid form of the litany, nothing of particular interest emerges from this psalm with regard to the relationship between the two doctrines which it embraces. We nevertheless observe that the doctrine of creation does not stand in isolation here; the hymn presses on beyond it to the saving acts of God, and we shall surely not be mistaken if we regard this second part as the climax of the psalm.

A very similar situation appears in Psalm 148. Here, too, the psalmist sings of the creation of the world and of the redemptive activity of Yahweh in two more or less unrelated sections. Psalm 33 must also be classed with these psalms. Once again the events of the creation are depicted, in language of great nobility: "By the word of Yahweh the heavens were made. . . . He commanded and it stood fast." Yet this hymn, like the others, does not linger over the thought, but goes on to sing of Yahweh's saving acts in history: "He has brought the counsel of the nations to nought . . . blessed is the nation whose God is Yahweh." And here the singer comes to his main theme, moving on from God as Creator to God as Savior, from protology to soteriology. (I trust that I may be allowed this rather crude theological terminology here. For the present purpose it serves to designate what are in fact the essential distinctions.)

If we now consider a typical hymn from Second Isaiah, we are at once carried a step further:

> Why do you say, O Jacob, and speak, O Israel: "My way is hid from Yahweh"? . . . Do you not know, have you not heard, that Yahweh is an everlasting God who has made the ends of the earth? He does not faint or grow weary. . . . He gives power to the faint, and to him who has no might he gives great strength. Even youths may faint and be weary . . . (Isa 40:27ff.)

We see at once that the doctrine of creation in verse 28 is not introduced for its own sake: it is not of this that the prophet wishes to speak to his people. The prophet speaks of God's redeeming grace, but he has to struggle against disbelief, and in order to arouse confidence in the unlimited might of his God he adverts to the fact of the creation of the world. He does precisely the same thing in the first Servant Song:

> Thus says Yahweh who created the heavens . . . who spread forth the earth. . . . I, Yahweh, have called you. (Isa 42:5)

The creation of the world is frequently mentioned in Deutero-Isaiah, with this purpose of providing a foundation for faith. How little the prophet is concerned with the doctrine of creation for its own sake is made very evident by the fact that in such texts he happily passes over the particular acts of God in creation and goes on at once to speak of manifestations of God's power in history (Isa 40:21ff.; 44:24ff.; 45:12ff.). Thus we can already at this stage make the important observation that at no point in the whole of Second Isaiah does the doctrine of creation appear in its own right; it never forms the main theme of a pronouncement, nor provides the motive of a prophetic utterance. It is there, but as applied by the prophet in the course of his argument it performs only an ancillary function. It provides a foundation for the message of redemption, in that it stimulates faith. It is but a magnificent foil for the message of salvation, which thus appears the more powerful and the more worthy of confidence. Or is it something quite different?

Before we approach this very important topic, let us take a look at the doxologies in the book of Amos (Amos 4:13; 5:8-9; 9:5-6). Here, too, undoubtedly, the psalmist hymns the power of the Creator with an identical theological purpose in view. The doxologies are theological accretions, arising from the reflections of a later writer. The affirmations made in the course of these doxologies have no specific message of their own which it is essential to include for its own sake, but, like the references in Deutero-Isaiah, perform only an ancillary function. Through them the prophetic pronouncement is universalized and so gains in profundity.

Let us, however, return to Deutero-Isaiah, for we have not yet come to the more fundamental theological aspect of the doctrines of creation and redemption. Let us for a moment consider the juxtaposition of creation and redemption which we find in the opening words of the prophet's oracles, a juxtaposition which has already become conventionalized and almost a formality:

> But now thus has Yahweh spoken, he who created you, O Jacob, and he who formed you, O Israel, "Fear not, I will redeem you." (Isa 43:1)

Or

> Thus has Yahweh said, your Redeemer and the One who formed you from the womb . . . (Isa 44:24; see also Isa 44:21; 46:3; 54:5)

We are struck by the ease with which two doctrines, which to our way of thinking are of very different kinds, are here brought together. It is as if for Deutero-Isaiah the creation of the world and the redemption of Israel both exemplify the same divine dispensation, as if that which happened in the beginning of things, and those "new things" (Isa 42:9, 48:6) which are now about to happen to Israel, both result from one and the same divine purpose of redemption. And so in fact they do. If we read on from the texts quoted above, we shall be astonished to see with what forceful effect the doctrine of creation is here brought into harmony with soteriology:

> I am Yahweh, who made all things, who stretched out the heavens alone, who spread out the earth. Who was with me? . . . Who confirms the word of his servant . . . who tells Jerusalem it shall be inhabited . . . who says to the deep, "Be dry" . . . who says to Cyrus, "My shepherd, he shall fulfill all my purpose." (Isa 44:24-28)

Yahweh the Creator, who raised up the world out of chaos, does not leave Jerusalem in chaos; he who dried up the elemental waters will also raise up Jerusalem anew. Here, obviously, the doctrine of creation has been fully incorporated into the dynamic of the prophet's doctrine of redemption. Let us then come at once to the passage in Second Isaiah which is the most remarkable of all for our theological enquiry:

> Awake, awake, put on strength, O arm of Yahweh, awake, as in the days of old. . . . Was it not thou that didst cut Rahab in pieces, that didst pierce the dragon? Was it not thou that didst dry up the sea, the waters of the great deep? That didst make the depths of the sea *a way for the redeemed to pass over?* (Isa 51:9-10)

What has happened there? Undoubtedly the prophet starts by speaking of the creation of the world by Yahweh, but then by a grotesque foreshortening of time he brings this work of Yahweh into direct contact with that act of deliverance which took place at the Red Sea. He has accomplished what at first sight appears to be an incredible transposition from one category to another. But for Deutero-Isaiah the creation does not belong in a category distinct from that of the deliverance of the Red Sea! The prophet maintains with passionate conviction his belief that what appear theologically to be two distinct acts are in fact one and the same act of the universal redemptive purpose of God. At this point the doctrine of creation has been fully absorbed indeed that the doctrine of creation and the doctrine of redemption are both included in the one picture of the battle with the primeval dragon.

A further, rather different, aspect of the matter now becomes clear. It may have seemed surprising that Deutero-Isaiah should be so ready to show Yahweh as the Creator of Israel, the one who formed Israel from the first, rather than to refer to the motion of Israel's election. By contrast with the earlier prophets, indeed, there has been a complete change of front in Deutero-Isaiah. Instead of harking back in the familiar manner to the divine election of Israel, he prefers to speak of the creation of Israel. When the Second Isaiah says, "Thus has Yahweh said, your Redeemer and the one who formed you from the womb" (Isa 44:24), he really *is* thinking of the miracle of creation, and not of the historical act of election; but to base his argument on the creation instead of on the fact of election does not entail any fundamental theological change of front, for as we have seen, Deutero-Isaiah is not in any way sidetracking the doctrine of redemption in so doing. His thought remains firmly within the sphere of soteriology. A particularly good example of this complete absorption of the doctrine of creation into the prophetic doctrine of salvation can be seen in Isa 54:5:

> Your Husband is your Creator . . . and your Redeemer is the Holy One of Israel.

Nevertheless, it cannot be claimed that this characteristic theological viewpoint is simply an instance of prophetic license which deviates from every allowable norm. If we turn once more to the Psalter in the light of this deeper understanding of the matter, we find the same relationship between the doctrines of creation and redemption, at times in highly significant contexts. Psalm 89 in particular should be mentioned in this connection. Following on a formal introductory passage, the hymn begins with a recital of Yahweh's deeds in the creation of the world:

> You rule the raging of the sea. . . . You crushed Rahab like a carcass . . . the heavens are yours, the earth also is yours; the world and all that is in it, you have founded them. The north and the south, you have created them. . . . You have a mighty arm.

At this point, however, the psalm comes back with a jolt to its main theme, the covenant with David, the terms of which are now brought very insistently to Yahweh's remembrance. In this particular context the poet starts from the creation and reminds Yahweh of the mighty works which he accomplished at that time; but this is certainly not an irrelevant piece of verbiage, for all the facts adduced in the psalm, from the creation to the special promise of blessing on the throne of David, contribute to the one theme which the poet stated at the outset: "I will sing of the manifestations of Yahweh's favor" (89:1). The creation itself, then, is to be accounted as one of the acts of Yahweh's favor, *ḥasdê yhwh*. This somewhat surprising suggestion appears in an unmistakable form in Psalm 74, where we read:

> Yet God my King is from of old, working *salvation* in the midst of the earth. Thou didst divide the sea by thy might; thou didst break the heads of the dragons on the waters . . . thou didst cleave open springs and brooks . . . thine is the day, thine also the night . . . thou hast fixed all the bounds of the earth; thou hast made summer and winter. . . . Arise, O God, plead thy cause!

We need not bother about the details. Here we are interested only in seeing what is comprised in the notion of *yešû'ôth*, a word which one can translate only as "saving acts"—the creation of the world and the ordering of nature.

Let us pause here for a moment. We have found a great deal of evidence for the doctrine that Yahweh created the world, but we have not found the doctrine expressed as a religious actuality, standing on its own, forming the main theme of a passage in its own right. It has always been related to something else, and subordinated to the interests and content of the doctrine of redemption. We were indeed able to show, from passages which are certainly not to be dismissed as either farfetched or insignificant, how the doctrine of the creation is at times altogether swallowed up in the doctrine of redemption. We do not hesitate to say, in fact, that we regard this soteriological interpretation of the work of creation as the most primitive expression of Yahwistic belief concerning Yahweh as Creator of the world. The belief finds expression almost exclusively in the mythological conception of the struggle against the dragon of chaos—a conception which Yahwism accepted at a very early stage, but whose originally independent status as a thing in itself Yahwism abolished.

I shall not deal extensively with the account of the creation in the priestly writings. Genesis 1 is not an independent theological essay, but one component of a great dogmatic treatise which moves in ever-narrowing concentric circles. The writer naturally takes his own theological stand in the innermost circle, representing the redemptive relationship between Yahweh and Israel. In order to justify this relationship theologically, he starts from the creation of the world and shows how at each stage in the course of history new statutes and ordinances are revealed, which increasingly guarantee the redemption of the people of God.[2] Thus here, too, the creation of the world by Yahweh is not being considered for its own sake, nor as of value in itself. On the contrary, P's presentation of it, even in Genesis 1, is wholly motivated by considerations of the divine purpose of redemption.

So far as this particular issue is concerned, there is no deep theological cleavage between the priestly writer and Psalm 89 or Psalm 74. We must nevertheless admit that the drawing of these concentric circles represents a theological achievement of the first order, and the same may be said of the perspicacity of the theological distinctions by which the Noachic cycle is neatly separated from the creation story.

What remains to be said? We have still to discuss those psalms which are generally regarded as the main evidence for the Old Testament doctrine of creation—Psalms 19, 104, and 8. In Psalm 19 we find a quite new phenomenon in the thought that the cosmos itself bears witness to God. It certainly cannot be said that this notion finds any very wide support in the Old Testament. On the contrary, it occurs nowhere else with the same clarity. At the same time there is a striking degree of restraint here, in that the created order is not said to be a revelation of "Elohim," much less of Yahweh, but proclaims "the glory of El" (*kebôd-'El*), the word "El" being here the equivalent of divinity. The most colorless possible word has been chosen.

In Psalm 104 this thought, so foreign to Genesis 1, occurs again. It is, however, much less directly expressed, in the form that by its wonderful nature the whole cosmos compels us to recognize the wisdom and the might of God (compare also Job 12:7-10, and perhaps Isa 40:21). It is particularly necessary, however, to compare Psalm 104 with Psalm 19, if only because in both cases there is real evidence for an unadulterated doctrine of creation that stands on its own ground. In these psalms the creation of the world by Yahweh actually supplies the main theme—a very striking phenomenon, in view of all the other evidence found in Yahwistic faith.

This encourages us to enquire into the origin of these psalms. It has long been accepted that neither Psalm 19 nor Psalm 104 can be regarded as wholly original to Yahwistic belief. It is hardly by accident that the first part of Psalm 19 has been truncated as it has, and it has long been held that here we have a fragment of an ancient Canaanitish hymn subsequently adapted to Yahwistic beliefs. It is equally widely recognized that the *Hymn of Ikhnaton* has at least influenced profoundly the writer of Psalm 104.

I would mention here that unrelated, isolated piece of evidence for the doctrine of creation in Gen 14:19: "Blessed be Abram by El Elyon, Maker of heaven and earth." Here, too, we have nothing more nor less than a theological statement concerning the Creator of the world! Once again it can be shown that this notion stems from a non-Israelite source: in Philo of Byblos we read that heaven and earth were created by *'Elioun kaloumenos Hypsistos*.[3] There is food for thought here. I see no point in questioning the weight of this evidence. Yahwism actually did absorb these elements when it could easily have fended them off, as it fended off so much which was incompatible with itself.

I am concerned, however, to demonstrate that there is another quite different source for this kind of belief. Here we are dealing with conceptions and influences that do not spring in the first place from the heart of Yahwism, but rather come into it from outside. Yet Yahwism found in them an appropriate expression of its own religious belief that Yahweh created the world. Where did this belief originate? To answer this question we must call in evidence the wisdom literature of the Old Testament, for there, too, we find this independent doctrine of creation freely expressed.

As Fichtner has shown,[4] the belief in reward and punishment is based on belief in the Creator, not, as one would have expected, on belief in the righteousness of God of the covenant. "He who mocks the poor insults his Maker" (Prov 17:5). Let us look at the *Wisdom of Amenemope* (chap. 25): "Do not laugh at a blind man, nor jeer at a dwarf. Man is but clay and straw; God is the builder, who destroys and builds every day." There can be no doubt that this freely expressed reference to God as the Creator derives its stimulus from Egyptian thought. Again, in the *Instruction for Merikare* we read:

> Provision is made for man, the flock of God; he made heaven and earth for their pleasure . . . he made the air, . . . herbs and cattle, fowl and fishes, for them.[5]

Or in the great *Hymn of Amun:*

> Amun who made men and created the beasts . . . who makes the fruit tree and the herb, and feeds the cattle . . . etc.[6]

Here we have once again that readily intelligible, nonmythological mode of thought which has nothing whatever in common with stories of the struggle against the primeval dragon. As we shall see, Ps 104:10[7] and Psalm 8 also strongly reflect this outlook, which has as its interest the divine economy in this world. It expresses a rational, intelligible purpose, and is therefore concerned above all with those problems which force themselves upon our understanding and which compel our admiration, things very different from these portentous, bizarre elements which belong to the mythical cosmogony.[8] Are we not right to see here the influence of wisdom literature? In my opinion, what we have here is an Egyptian outlook passed on to Israel by traveling teachers of wisdom.[9]

Psalm 8 also belongs to the same complex of evidence for the doctrine of creation, which stems less from specifically Yahwistic beliefs concerning election and salvation than from a reasoned, reflective theology. The beautiful simplicity and originality of it must not blind us to the fact that the faith of the writer results from hard thinking: when I look at the sky, the moon, and the stars, when I reflect upon the wonder of the created order—how small man is! Yet this is the surprising and glorious thing, that God fences man round with his providential care and bestows on him his salvation. It is this sudden twist in the writer's thoughts about the cosmos that seems to me to be significant: the consideration of creation for its own sake is once again left behind. Here, too, it is no more than a starting-point from which we go on to wonder at the miracle of God's providential care and of his purpose of salvation for mankind.

It is scarcely necessary to pursue the matter further. Our main thesis was that in genuinely Yahwistic belief the doctrine of creation never attained to the stature of a relevant, independent doctrine. We found it invariably related, and indeed subordinated, to soteriological considerations. This is not to say, however, that it is necessarily of later origin. Evidently a doctrine of creation was known in Canaan in extremely early times, and played a large part in the cultus in the pre-Israelite period through mythical representations of the struggle against primeval chaos. Yahwistic faith early absorbed these elements, but because of the exclusive commitment of Israel's faith to historical salvation, the doctrine of creation was never able to attain to independent existence in its own right. Either it remained a cosmic foil against which soteriological pronouncements stood out the more effectively, or it was wholly incorporated into the complex of soteriological thought.

A quite different strand of religious influence entered the Yahwistic faith in the form of wisdom-lore, a highly rationalized mode of speculation concerning the divine economy in this world that we may regard as being of Egyptian origin. At this point we were faced with unequivocal, self-justified statements of belief concerning the creation. That these documents should have been repeatedly cited as expressions of Yahwistic belief concerning the creation of the world by Yahweh does not betray a very profound knowledge of Old Testament religion in those who have cited them. We would not, of course, in any way rob the evidence of its value, but we do maintain that in Israel quite obviously a very great many safeguards had to be established, some of them of primary theological importance, before this liberty of treatment could be achieved for an undiluted doctrine of creation; in other words, the doctrine of redemption had first to be fully safeguarded, in order that the doctrine that nature, too, is a means of divine self-revelation might not encroach upon or distort the doctrine of redemption, but rather broaden and enrich it.

I should like to close with the observation that it is impossible to arrive at an assessment of Old Testament doctrine simply by using the methods of historical religion. We made a great mistake in continuing for so long to judge the really quite slight significance of the doctrine of creation by the standard of importance of its later "development." Nor should our assessment depend on the fact that we now regard this doctrine as very ancient. Rather, what we have to do is to investigate the theological structure of the doctrinal statements of the Old Testament.

13

"Righteousness" and "Life" in the Cultic Language of the Psalms

In the nineteenth century the statements made in the Psalms, and especially in the "laments," were widely regarded as the personal testimonies of worshipers drawn from their own lives. For those who maintained a belief in the Davidic authorship of the Psalms, it was not difficult to explain them biographically as well as psychologically, with reference to some situation in his life.

Gunkel's investigations into the categories of Psalms gave rise to a sharp reaction against this view. It was recognized that the different categories had a cultic background, and it was seen that the language of the Psalms was largely determined by an impersonal cultic tradition, and that their individual themes conformed closely to a pattern. Nevertheless, even though the Psalms are molded by cultic convention, Gunkel still perceives behind them the personality and the individual experience of the poet. He still shows great attachment to a personalized and romantic interpretation of the Psalms. His attitude finds its clearest expression in the frequent evaluation of the aesthetic quality of the Psalms, usually based upon the degree of subjectivity evinced by the psalmist, upon his originality, his perceptivity, and so on. This assessment of the part played by the poet as an individual must not be accepted uncritically. At two important points it leads to serious theological error—in assertions of the psalmist's righteousness, and in statements concerning life and death.

PROTESTATIONS OF INNOCENCE

In many Psalms we find repeated protestations of a moral rectitude, which is represented neither as something comparative nor as having been impugned, but quite categorically as perfect uprightness. Let us try to understand these Psalms, which the simple reader of the Bible cannot but regard as the expression of well-nigh intolerable self-righteousness and lack of contrition. The material, well known as it is to every reader of holy writ, is by no means easy to pinpoint scientifically. We shall have to approach the subject obliquely in order to find a point of entry.

The category of the "confessional list"[1] (*Beichtspiegel*) has long been recognized. It consists of a formula of varying length containing a whole series of protestations of sinlessness, which were spoken to the cultic worshiper or used by him in making his own avowal. At all events he appropriated their content to himself, and thus received the cultic absolution and justification that he needed as a member of the cultic community. Deuteronomy 26:13-14 contains a formula of this type, evidently of very great antiquity, which was prescribed for use at the tithe-offering ceremony:

> I have removed the sacred portion out of my house . . .
> I have not transgressed any of your commandments,
> Neither have I forgotten them,
> I have not eaten of the tithe while I was mourning,
> Nor removed any of it while I was unclean,
> Nor offered any of it to the dead . . .[2]

We need not go into details of exegesis. The extreme antiquity of this cultic practice is self-evident; it belongs to a comparatively specialized occasion, and when the worshiper has made this protestation, his gift is reckoned to be ritually acceptable. He himself is, in cultic terms, "righteous" (*ṣaddiq*), since he has adequately met the demands of Yahweh.

There is a similar sequence in Ezekiel:

> If (a man) does not eat (viz., sacrificial flesh) upon the mountains,
> Nor lift up his eyes to the idols of the house of Israel,
> Does not defile his neighbor's wife,
> Nor approach a woman in her time of impurity,
> Does not oppress anyone . . .
> Commits no robbery . . .
> Does not lend at interest,
> Nor take any increase . . . (Ezek 18:5-7)

This approximates closely to the category of the "gate liturgies" of Pss 15:2-5a and 24:4-6. Once again we leave aside consideration of the details. The formulae are concerned with answering the question, "Who, as a matter of general principle, is 'righteous' (*ṣaddiq*) before Yahweh?"—and various norms of cultic and communal life are listed by way of reply.[2] To regard these as a complete statement of the requirements would be to misunderstand them; on the contrary, it is simply the most ordinary limits that are marked out by a selection of characteristic commandments. Those who submit to these demands are pleasing to God, and are members of the great cultic and social community of Yahweh.

The most comprehensive extant example of a confessional list is to be found in Job's oath of innocence (Job 31), a complex passage that is quoted in an abridged form:

> I have made a covenant with my eyes;
> > how then could I look upon a virgin? . . .
> If I have walked with falsehood, and my foot has
> > hastened to deceit . . .
> If my step has turned aside from the way, and my
> > heart has gone after my eyes . . .
> If my heart has been enticed to a woman, and I have lain
> > wait at my neighbor's door . . .
> If I have rejected the cause of my manservant . . .
> If I have withheld anything that the poor desired,
> > or have caused the eyes of the widow to fail,
> > or have eaten my morsel alone . . .
> If I have seen any one perish for lack of clothing,
> > or a poor man without covering . . .
> If I have raised my hand against the fatherless,
> > because I saw help in the gate;
> If I have made gold my trust, or called fine gold
> > my confidence;
> If I have rejoiced because my wealth was great, or
> > because my hand had gotten much;
> If I have looked at the sun when it shone, or the moon
> > moving in splendor, and my heart has been
> > secretly enticed, and my mouth has kissed my hand;
> If I have rejoiced at the ruin of him that hated me,
> > or exulted when evil overtook him,
> I have not let my mouth sin by asking for his life with
> > a curse . . .
> If I have concealed my transgressions from men,
> > by hiding my iniquity in my bosom . . . .

This passage has always evoked unanimous admiration for the delicacy of its moral feeling, and for its unfailing sureness of touch in social relations, and in the relationship of the sexes one to the other. A mistaken confidence in riches, or the completely secret worship of natural objects, are alike sinful in relation to God.

Let us now, however, examine the *form* of this high-water mark of Old Testament morality. Clearly it still has the form of a "self-anathematization." If Job has looked upon a virgin, has put his trust in riches, has rejoiced at the misfortune of a friend then may such and such a thing befall him! And this brings us back once more to our problem. Both the earlier formulae (Deuteronomy 26 and Ezekiel 18) are such as an Israelite could use in all honesty, since they concerned demands that it was quite possible to meet fully. In Job 31 this is not so; Job's "confessional list" postulated perfection, the absolutely irreproachable conduct of an exemplary character. One wonders which is more remarkable—the fact that the form of the confessional list compelled the Israelite worshiper to make his protestation of innocence, and to curse himself should he prove to be forsworn, or the fact that quite manifestly such professions actually were made in Israel. It cannot be asserted that even Job and his "confessional list" reach the extreme limit in this direction, and if they do, we have many examples in the Psalms of similar protestations made with complete confidence. Let us look at them.

Certain passages in the Psalms actually so far exceed the protestations of Job 31 that it is not simply from a negative point of view that they circumscribe the life and conduct of the worshiper. We turn first to Psalm 1, where the marks of the "righteous" (*ṣaddiq*) are set out in the form of a kind of paradigm. First, in negative form, he takes no advice from the wicked (*rešaʿîm*), he does not tread the path of the sinners, and he does not even it with the impious. On the positive side, he is characterized firstly by the fact that he accepts the revelation of the divine purpose joyfully, secondly, that he maintains uninterrupted contact with this revelation.[4] These are certainly assertions of extreme perfection. In this case they have a didactic form and thus a certain objectivity, but elsewhere they appear in the form of highly personal testimony, and are no less unrestrained in their mode of expression or their use of superlatives. This is especially true of Psalm 119:

> In the way of thy testimonies I delight as much
> as in all riches. (v. 14)
> My soul is consumed with longing for
> thy ordinances at all times. (v. 20)
> This blessing has fallen to me, that I have kept
> thy precepts. (v. 56)
> The law of thy mouth is better to me than thousands
> of gold and silver pieces. (v. 72)

O, how I love thy law! It is my meditation all the day. (v. 97)
I incline my heart to perform thy statutes for ever,
    to the end. (v. 112)
Trouble and anguish have come upon me, but thy
    commandments are my delight. (v. 143)

These professions, too, are protestations of perfection. This intercourse with God, this accord with his will, is the mark of the "righteous man."

Let us put aside for the moment the obvious and pressing question of the subjective rectitude and personal truthfulness of the one who makes these assertions, and first investigate the theological tradition of which they are a part. Old Testament religious assertions are far more closely determined by tradition and more highly stylized according to a fixed convention, especially where they appear to be of a personal nature, than we are generally inclined to suppose today. Now the circumstances of the speaker in Psalm 119 is depicted with striking uniformity, despite the fact that the psalm is widely recognized as a highly composite mosaic of proverbial wisdom-material: he is despised (v. 22), threatened by princes (v. 23), his soul cleaves to the dust (vv. 25, 107), he is downcast (v. 28), he pleads not to be put to shame (v. 31), he is derided (v. 51), slandered (v. 69), oppressed (v. 78), persecuted (vv. 84, 95, 109ff.), disdained (v. 141), and so on. This is precisely the style of the "lament," and in fact the wisdom-writer who composed Psalm 119 is making use of the form of the ancient cultic "lament" in compiling his prayer-like "confession." Here is the answer to the important problem raised by this consciousness, this firm conviction that the writer is "righteous" (ṣaddiq) before God.

We now perceive what is the ultimate source of this remarkable and, humanly speaking, altogether audacious certainty: it derives from the ancient cultus. Just how the declarations of innocence came to be a constant feature of the "lament" Psalms, and also of the "thanksgiving" Psalms, can be studied in the compendious work of Gunkel and Begrich.[5]

"Righteousness" (ṣedaqah) in the Old Testament sense is not the height of virtue: as Cremer has shown, it is a notion concerned with relationship, and the man who meets the demands of a communal relationship is a "righteous" man.[6] This communal relationship may be a civil and social one, but more often in the Old Testament refers to that relationship with Israel, which Yahweh has enshrined in his covenant. When Yahweh is said to be "righteous," it means that he is faithful to this covenant relationship that he has condescended to establish. Israel is "righteous" in so far as the nation assents to this covenant relationship, and submits to its cultic and legal ordinances. The relationship as such as not conditional: Israel *is* within the covenant.

We saw, however, that within the cultus from time to time a kind of declaration of loyalty was called for. For all that, anyone who participated in the cultus was "righteous," and only the "righteous" might pass through the temple gate to pray and to offer sacrifice (Ps 118:20). Psalm 5 puts the matter quite simply: "The boastful may not stand before thy eyes; thou hatest all evildoers. ... But I, through the abundance of thy steadfast love, will enter thy house" (Ps 5:5, 7).

What is more, anyone who spoke at all in the cultus did so only on this basis, whether he wished to complain or to give thanks—and, of course, no sayings of those who were excluded from the cultus have been preserved to us![7] Thus the term "righteous" was scarcely predicable of anyone in ancient Israel apart form cultic considerations. The rectitude of the worshiper at all events proceeds from Yahweh, and is conferred on him by Yahweh (Pss 4:1; 17:1; 35:23; 37:6—cf. 69:28, 29). In one passage, it is expressly stated that "God lets (man) see his face, and restores to man his innocence" (Job 33:26).[8]

We must however bear in mind that actually there were only two alternatives: either a man was "righteous" (ṣaddiq) before Yahweh or he was an evildoer (rašaʻ), one who was at fault and thus had no standing before God. There is no room for any intermediate state, or for any of the finer shades so familiar in human evaluations. Presumably in later times Israel applied the term "righteous" not only in cultic situations but also to spiritual matters. But it is significant that even this later age, whose theological insights had evidently attained to a high degree of subtlety, should still have retained this uncompromising attitude. Both Ezekiel 18 and Psalm 1 provide clear evidence of this, although it makes them oddly doctrinaire, and remote from any serious religious deliberation of moral problems.

This brings us to our final consideration. If a man was "righteous" he was wholly so, and not merely inchoatively or relatively so. We have already shown that this was the basic qualification for participation in the cultus. The worshipers pride themselves on this, and rely upon it in their laments. It is a noteworthy feature of any and every complaint and request that the worshiper's right relationship with God, so far as it concerns him subjectively, is never placed in doubt by so much as a hint of his imperfection or unworthiness. The worshiper always represents himself as one who lives *wholly* with God, who has put his whole trust in him and has always obeyed him implicitly. This is not the result of unbelievably obdurate self-righteousness, but something prescribed by the cultus as a means of obtaining the favor God has offered to Israel. Indeed, in this matter of reliance upon one's own righteousness, we are confronted by a quite astonishing phenomenon: we find in many Psalms an eagerness amounting to temerity on the part of the writer to lay claim to a degree of righteousness to which no mere human being could ever possibly attain. Here once again we are brought up against our original problem.

> Hear a just cause, O Yahweh; attend to my cry! Give ear to my prayer
> from lips free of deceit!
> From you let my vindication come! Let your eyes see the right!
> If you try my heart, if you visit me by night, if you test me, you will
> find no wickedness in me . . .
> My steps have held fast to your paths. . . . (Ps 17:1-5)

> Vindicate me, O Yahweh, for I have walked in my integrity, and I have
> trusted in Yahweh without wavering . . .
> For your steadfast love is before my eyes, and I walk in faithfulness to
> you.
> I do not sit with false men, nor do I consort with dissemblers;
> I hate the company of evil-doers, and I will not sit with the wicked.
> I wash my hands in innocence . . . (Ps 26:1-6)

> I have kept the ways of Yahweh, and have not wickedly departed from
> my God.
> For all his ordinances were before me, and his statutes I did not put
> away from me.
> I was blameless before, and I kept myself from guilt. (Ps 18:21-23)[9]

Obviously these passages do not lay claim to absolutely perfect obedience in the usual sense, but rather present a progressively idealized portrait of the "righteous" man. Indeed we seem to perceive, especially in the wisdom Psalms, a positive desire to work out to the full the implications of such a portrait, although in the execution of his project the writer has been very little influenced by genuine personal experience in the strict sense of the term. Without doubt such statements derive from an accepted idealized conception of righteousness, which the worshiper appropriates to himself as he stands before Yahweh.[10]

A more thoroughgoing investigation of this topic would undoubtedly bring to light some highly significant variants. It would probably reveal that the ancient texts that are directly related to the cultus (e.g., Deut 26:18ff.; Ezek 18:5ff.) confine themselves essentially to a definition of obedience which lies within the bounds of possibility, and that he is "righteous" before Yahweh who has offered sacrifice to Yahweh and to no other gods, who has not been involved in the cult of the dead, who has not infringed particular ritual requirements, and who helps the needy. If, as seems reasonable, the "gate liturgy" of Psalm 15 may be said to contain a development of the portrait of the "righteous" man, it accords well with this suggestion:

> He who walks blamelessly,
> and does what is right,
> and speaks truth from his heart;
> who does not slander with his tongue,
> and does no evil to his friend,
> nor takes up a reproach against his neighbor . . .[11]
> who does not put out his money at interest,
> and does not take a bribe against the innocent . . .

It is easy to see how this portrait of the exemplary "righteous man," which the worshiper applies to himself, goes on growing to ever more fantastic proportions as it becomes detached from the actual cultic situation. It may now be freely adapted to suit new insights, and in the wisdom tradition in particular it is used for doctrinal purposes. The ancient soteriological purpose remains intact, and confidence that man may be "righteous" before God remains unshaken.

Looking back on the Psalter as a whole, one is struck by the fact that no doubts assail the worshipers, even where moral scruples would seem most appropriate: am I in fact "righteous"? Have I fulfilled the conditions? Have I performed those obligations to God and my neighbor that justify my confidence that I am pleasing to God? Nowhere do we find this need for reassurance developed to any great extent.[12] The Psalms presuppose a quite different kind of question: seeing that we are righteous, how is it that God acts thus and thus? This consideration may at least serve as a warning against regarding the post-exilic period as a time in which legalism is the prevailing force in Israel.

We must look elsewhere for any condemnation of this usurpation of authority over the saving relationship on the part of the cultus. Such a protest is found but once in the Psalter, and is aimed at just such an unreflective and self-justificatory declamation of a list of divine commandments as we have discovered above:

> What right have you to recite my statutes,
>> or take my covenant on your lips?
> For you hate discipline,
>> and you cast my words behind you. (Ps 50:16-17)

This protest undoubtedly rests upon the condemnation voiced by the great prophets. At no point does the Old Testament close the immense gap that divides their proclamation of future judgment from the assurances of redemption expressed in the cultus.

SETTING IN LIFE

We now turn to a particular body of evidence concerning the communal life of Israel and its relationship to God. At once the inevitable question arises as to where it was that Israel received the word of life from Yahweh, the one who gives or withholds life. This word of life was certainly not just an eternal truth, nor yet primarily a matter of dogma, but arose from an actual decision in a concrete situation, and there can thus be no question but that it was communicated to Israel through the cultus. It is also quite obvious that this promise of life stood in the closest possible relationship to the proclamation of the commandments:

> See, I have set before you this day life and good, death and evil. If you obey the commandments of Yahweh your God which I command you this day . . . I call heaven and earth to witness against you this day, that I have set before you life and death, blessing and curse; therefore choose life. (Deut 30:15, 19)

In form, this passage is an exhortation, very closely bound up with a proclamation of the Law, such as formed the climax of certain great cultic occasions.[13] The participants in the cultus are addressed here not as those who already have life, but as those who have joined in the cultus or have come to hear the commandments of God, at the very moment when the decision between life and death is to be made. We may also call attention to the frequently quoted passage in Ezekiel 18, whose form and ideas both breathe the atmosphere of the cultus. Here, too, there is a series of commandments followed by the stereotyped pronouncements, "he shall live," "he shall die."

There is a very similar situation in the Holiness Code, where a summary of the commandments is followed by the words: "You shall therefore keep my statutes and my ordinances, by doing which a man shall live: I am Yahweh" (Lev 18:5).

Here, too, the liturgical cultic form is clearly discernible, and further evidence could be adduced from the paraenetic material of Deuteronomy. Even if all these texts are comparatively late in date, they nevertheless enable us to reach the firm conclusion that the connection between the proclamation of the commandments and the promise of life was an integral feature of Yahwistic belief.

The ultimate decision between life and death was thus for Israel a cultic matter, and only within the cultus did the individual receive assurance that he would have life. Naturally this assurance was not confined to the festival of the renewal of the covenant when the commandments were recited. The cultus provided many channels by which this assurance might be mediated. Begrich's valuable study of the priestly oracle has shown how the certainty of help and consolation might be given to the individual who in sickness or persecution came before God with his complaint.[14]

Thus in our interpretation of the passages quoted from the Psalms, we must be on our guard against a personal, biographical exegesis. In the controversy between Gunkel and Mowinckel I side with the latter, who severely criticized the view that they are personal compositions.[15] To know the forms of cultic address, to be familiar with sacral traditions, and to be able to adapt and modify them was a task for the professional, an authorized official and a member of the guild, and it was not simply left in each case to the free choice of the layman to improvise as he would. Had the "individual laments" in sickness, for example, been composed by the sufferer, they would not have contained so little concrete information concerning the patient's actual condition.

It is the experience of every commentator, however, that any exegesis that attempts to deal with the specific situation of a particular worshiper rapidly comes to a dead-end. The sufferings of the worshiper are always schematized and magnified, and in many of the Psalms a multiplicity of ills is ascribed to the worshiper (illness, poverty, hostility, scorn, slander, and so on) so that he takes on the character of an archetypal sufferer before God. We thus have the same situation that we found in the protestation of righteousness. In both cases we ought to see a stylized cultic form, and very probably the assertions made by the sufferer go far beyond what he actually experiences and suffers, in order to bring him into line with a hypothetical prototype.[16]

There is a further respect in which the traditional interpretation of the lament Psalms must be revised. In his excellent monograph on redemption from death, Christoph Barth makes a detailed examination of those curiously extreme statements that the worshiper is already in She'ol, that he lies in the dust of death, and so on. Are they to be taken literally or not? What does "death" mean? His conclusion, based upon suggestions made by the Danish orientalist Pedersen, is that these assertions are not to be thought of as figurative exaggerations, nor as figments of the imagination, but as something quite real. The sick man really *has* fallen into the power of death, for illness and death are alike a privation of strength, and the one shades into the other.[17]

Everyone who suffers from sin and its consequences is brought into contact with death and She'ol.[18] Rightly do we dismiss as inconclusive all attempts to localize She'ol in ancient cosmogony, for in reality the conception has many diverse aspects. The Old Testament associates not only the great deep, the grave, or the desert with the realm of the dead, but also sickness and persecution, in a way which precludes any localization. It would be better to speak of the realm of death.[19]

Barth goes on to draw the inevitable conclusions from this modified conception of death: none of the statements that God has saved a man from death, or the prayers that he *may* save him, actually involves either a resurrection or a future life. All are concerned with this present world. "To save from death means 'to save from an evil death.'" But is this really so?

In a matter of such difficulty it would hardly be profitable to dissect yet again, one by one, the highly problematical relevant passages. Equally it is unlikely that any result would ensure from a statistical analysis of the material. In the second part of his book Barth threatens to succumb to the dangers of this method, but even the weight of one hundred and eighty assertions that there is a "redemption from death" cannot really decide the issue whether certain Psalms may not presuppose something in the nature of a future life. If we are to make any progress here we must leave aside the isolated texts, and attempt to shed some light on the particular cultic traditions which underlie the various statements, trying to assess them from the point of view of their historical setting. In this respect we can make only one small contribution at this stage.

In Psalm 84, a pilgrim song, we read: "Blessed are those who dwell in thy house, ever singing thy praise" (Ps 84:4). The pilgrim will have to leave the holy city again, and he regards as blessed those who always dwell there. Who are these people who dwell in Yahweh's house, and of what does their blessedness consist? A similar cry in another psalm provides the answer:

> Blessed is he whom you choose and bring hear, to dwell in your courts.
> We shall be satisfied with the goodness of your house . . . . (Ps 65:4)

There can be no doubt that those who dwell in Yahweh's courts are the cultic ministers, "bring near" being a technical term in the language of the cultus, whilst to "be satisfied" could well refer to a wholly material participation in the sacrificial offerings. Yet, as we shall see, there is another possible interpretation. These two passages alone, however, tell us very little about a class of persons who, standing apart from the well-known hierarchy of the temple, are also obviously to be distinguished from the wider circle of worshipers in some important theological sense. This is evidently the import of Psalm 27, in which the speaker desires some special privilege, wishing to be enrolled in some inner circle of worshipers of Yahweh:

> One thing have I asked of Yahweh,
> > that will I seek after;
> that I may dwell in the house of Yahweh . . .
> > to behold the beauty of Yahweh
> > and to inquire in his temple. (Ps 27:4)

In this passage we have an explicit statement of what is involved in dwelling in Yahweh's house: it carries with it the privilege of seeing God! Unfortunately we have very little precise information on this delicate matter. Are we to regard "beholding the beauty" and "inquiring" as two different things?[20] In itself the "beauty of Yahweh" (*no'am yhwh*) is more or less synonymous with the "glory of Yahweh" (*kebod yhwh*), although perhaps somewhat more intimate.

For a clearer notion of this vision of God of which the worshiper speaks we must go to Exod 33:18ff., where there is an account of the appearance of Yahweh's goodness (*ṭûb yhwh*). Undoubtedly the "goodness" and the "beauty" of Yahweh are one and the same thing, since a few verses later on (Ps 27:13) the psalm speaks of seeing the "goodness" of Yahweh. It seems to me certain, therefore, that the passage at Exod 33:18ff., as well as the other pericope in this chapter, formerly performed a function in the etiology of the cultus, providing the justification for a ritual which was understood as a theophany, or perhaps even as a substitute for a theophany. The congregation would call upon Yahweh, Yahweh would pass by and declare his name and his attributes, and the congregation would prostrate themselves. Evidently it was only the cultic ministers, and perhaps only certain groups of them, who were privileged to take part in these cultic occasions.[21]

As to the mode of procedure of these rites, we have already seen from the texts quoted that there was in the temple an inner circle of rites and ceremonies, which many would have been glad to witness. Psalm 63 takes us a step further:

> So have I looked upon you in the sanctuary,
> > beholding your power and glory.
> Because thy steadfast love is better than life,
> > my lips will praise you . . .
> My soul is feasted as with marrow and fat. (Ps 63:2-5)

Here again there is a reference to the vision of God, and this singular experience is now closely linked with feasting on the part of the worshiper. We have already come across this feature, and it is made clear in this text that the feasting is to be understood in a spiritual sense as an inward refreshment, "as with marrow and fat." We are thus concerned here with a spiritualization of a cultic practice—of a sacrificial feast. The extent to which this worshiper is concerned with the spiritual aspect is borne out by his reflection on the subject of "life" (*ḥayyîm*). Whereas every other strand of tradition in the Old Testament is in agreement that life, and physical life at that, is the greatest good of all, this psalm alone in the Old Testament gives a different evaluation: "Your steadfast love is better than life." "To be satisfied" and "to live," which between them comprise the whole of human existence, are here removed from the sphere of material life into that of God's steadfast love (*ḥesed*). We are brought very close to the atmosphere of Psalm 36, whose thought borders close on the mystical, and which in this respect stands virtually alone in the whole of the Old Testament.

> How precious is your steadfast love, O God!
>> The children of men take refuge in the shadow of thy wings.
> They feast on the abundance of thy house,
>> and you give them drink from the river of your delights.
> For with you is the fountain of life;
>> in your light do we see light. (Ps 36:7-9)

Here, evidently, is the same mystical life, once again brought into relationship with a cultic feast, and, as in Psalm 63, described in terms of taking refuge with Yahweh. Here, too, the cultic institution is spiritualized, this time with reference to the sanctuary that the temple afforded from the earliest times to the fugitive. Just as the man-slayer claimed the protection of the sacred precincts as being the extra-territorial domain of God, so, by analogy, the sphere in which God himself lives becomes the refuge to which man may fly.

We shall meet this conception again at a later stage. First, however, we must mention the *locus classicus* of this notion of safe shelter with God—Psalm 23. As we read its sublime assurance of participation at God's table, and the words that speak of dwelling in the house of Yahweh, we are convinced that it is one of that group of Psalms whose writers belong to the inner circle of those who have found consolation in the lofty mystical experience of the cultus.

This testimony of an inward and wholly spiritualized life in faith has become so completely the possession of the Christian believer, that the simple Bible-reader might be forgiven for regarding it as characteristic of the psalmists' "piety." But this would be a mistake. If we come to these Psalms from the overwhelming eschatological ethos of the enthronement Psalms, or from the robust conception of the royal Psalms, or from the dramatic turbulence of the "laments," then the quiet reflectiveness and withdrawn peacefulness of these Psalms seems like another world. *We are in the presence of a particular group of spiritual writers* who are to be found among the cultic personnel, as the frequent references to their dwelling in the temple clearly show:

> I cry to you, O Yahweh;
>> I say, you are my refuge,
>> my portion (*ḥelqî*) in the land of the living. (Ps 142:5)

With this assertion we come to a specialized group of avowals of confidence in Yahweh. The spiritualized notion of "sanctuary" is, of course, already known to us, but what underlies the statement that Yahweh is the "portion" of this particular worshiper? The concept is much more fully developed in Psalm 16,

> Yahweh is my portion (*ḥelqî*) and my cup.
>> You enlarge my lot.[22]
> The lines have fallen for me in pleasant places;
>> yea, I have a goodly heritage. (Ps 16:5-6)

The "portion" obviously refers initially to the portion of land which was allotted to the individual in the cultic distribution of territory. Recent investigations have shown that such an *anadasmos gēs* was the regular practice in ancient times in Israel.[23] "The land must not be alienated; you are guests and strangers with me." So ran the ancient principle of traditional Israelite land tenure. The prophet Micah, as well as the account of the division of the land in the Book of Joshua, gives details of the procedure by which this allotment of territory was carried out by the cultic community.[24] Psalm 16 adds a further contribution to our knowledge. We see how tensely the man watches the fall of the measuring-line, and his relief as he sees that he has drawn a favorable portion of land. But this is taken up as a spiritual concept: it is not merely a question of a plot of land, for Yahweh himself is the "portion" (*ḥeleq*).

It is easy to see how this spiritualization comes about. The unanimous tradition of the Old Testament is that every tribe of Israel received an allotted inheritance from Yahweh; Levi alone remained without such a tribal inheritance. Whatever the custom may have been in the oldest histories of the tribe of Levi, this latter tradition, enshrined in Deuteronomy and in the priestly writings, is undoubtedly ancient, since it speaks of Levi as the priestly tribe. It recognizes, too, that the tribe was duly compensated for its landlessness in another direction. "Yahweh is his inheritance" (Deut 10:9), says the deuteronomist "I am your portion (*ḥeleq*) and your inheritance (*naḥalah*)," says the priestly writer (Num 18:20). This statement, standing as it does in the context of practical provisions for the maintenance of the Levites, must be understood in a purely material sense, for they obtain their living from a share in sacrifices and cultic offerings, not by agricultural work.

Yet it would be a mistake to limit the application of the statement to material goods. The very existence of such a Levitical name as Hilkiah (*Ḥilqîyahû*) might serve as a warning here, for when a newborn infant is given the name "Yahweh is my portion," the appellation certainly contains more than a bare reminder of material sustenance. Notice, too, that this is a pre-exilic name! It raises a problem that has far-reaching implications: are we right always to interpret such cultic statements in their most primitive sense? From the very first they were no doubt used in a very wide sense, and the example we took from Psalm 16 shows how wide a range of meaning they can accommodate, without undergoing any radical alteration. In the phrase "Yahweh is my portion" the tribe of Levi, or more probably a particular group within the cultic personnel, saw the promise of a special relationship with God. The guarantees that this relationship carried with it are enumerated in the later verses of the psalm:

> Therefore my heart is glad, and my soul rejoices;
>> my body also dwells secure.
> For thou dost not give me up to Sheol,
>> or let thy godly one see the Pit.
> Thou dost show me the path of life;
>> in thy presence there is fulness of joy. (Ps 16:9-11)

In this passage we find ourselves once more in that strangely mystical atmosphere of which we have already spoken. Here those features that characterized the earlier part of the psalm appear again in a more developed form: life, protection from death, "fulness" in the presence of Yahweh. The blessings enumerated in these verses (vv. 9-11) are all very vaguely described. What is this "path of life," and this "fulness in thy presence"? At all events, what the writer chiefly has in mind is simply protection from an evil death.

The first part of Psalm 73 is the expression of a profound desire for religious understanding. In v. 17 this passionate yearning for enlightenment gives place to a very different attitude, the transition being bridged by an experience in the temple.[25] The psalm continues:

> Nevertheless I am continually with you;
>> You hold my right hand.
> You guide me with your counsel,
>> and afterward you will receive me to glory.

Whom have I in heaven but you?
> And there is nothing upon earth that I desire besides you.

My flesh and my heart may fail,
> but God is the strength of my heart
> and my portion forever.

For lo, those who are far from thee shall perish; . . .

But for me it is good to be near God;
> I have made Yahweh my refuge. (Ps 73:23-28)

The first sentence is a statement of fact, "I am continually with you," and does not indicate any activity on the part of the worshiper. From the second half of the verse onwards there is activity, but all on the part of God, rising to a remarkable climax: "hold," "guide," "receive." The verb "to receive" (*laqaḥ*), with God as its subject and a human being as its object, is a technical term (cf. Gen 5:24; 2 Kgs 2:3, 5), and there is no reason to doubt it is used as such both here (Ps 73:24) and in Ps 49:15, as the great majority of critical commentators agree. The text in Psalm 73 is not difficult to translate, therefore; the worshiper is so certain of being under the protection of Yahweh, the fountain of life, that he finds in the traditional Old Testament conception of the "portion" (*ḥeleq*) a full and complete expression of all that his relationship with God guarantees to him. It is not unusual for such a conception, borrowed from Israel's ancient past, to be taken up and infused with new life in the late post-exilic period from which Psalm 73 obviously originates.[26]

It is, however, of the greatest importance to notice that the radical change of attitude in v. 17 arises from the fact that the worshiper has learned to understand individual human life in eschatological terms (vv. 17-19). He has come to realize that the life of the wicked must be seen from the point of view of its end, and in consequence he now sees his own in the same way. Verses 17-24 thus express a single, self-contained train of thought.

Finally, may we say that this certainty is a very great advance on what we have already seen elsewhere with respect to spiritual fulness and an intimate relationship with God? I believe that we overburden the evidence if we try to find here anything in the nature of a "break through," blazing the trail of a wholly new and revolutionary understanding. To ask baldly whether we are here concerned with life in this world, or with a future life, is to misunderstand this psalm completely.[27] It is not a matter of either. If this psalm speaks more clearly than others of the immense scope of Yahweh's life-giving grace, it nevertheless works from precisely the same presuppositions as Psalm 16. The kernel of the whole complex of thought lies in the notion that "God is my portion" (*ḥeleq*, v. 26b). This is, as we saw, none other than that ancient levitical privilege to which the worshiper clung, upon which he relied, and whose spiritual content is so wonderfully interpreted in Psalm 73 in vindication of the divine providence faced with the problem of evil.

Thus there is here a future hope. It has long been recognized that such a hope is found at least sporadically in Canaanite mythology, and was therefore also known to Israel.[28] We may cite Hos 6:1-3 or Ezekiel 37 as secondary manifestations of an earlier mythological complex of ideas. It is to Israel's credit that this mythological conception of resurrection was rejected in Israel. But among these spiritually alert psalmists quite different forces were at work. Wholly apart from magic and mythology there grew up a confidence based simply and solely upon the certainty of an irrefrangible relationship with God. It is not to be wondered at that this certainty is nowhere expressed throughout the whole range of "laments" and "thanksgiving" Psalms: it grew up only in a small circle of cultic persons, and became established in this way.

Let us not, however, allow the whole burden of proof to rest upon these few spiritually aware and yet fragile passages from the Psalms. Rather, the result of our investigation should be to enable us to distinguish, at least in theory, between the cultic expression and the insight to which that expression gives rise, an insight which in turn takes possession of the cultic expression itself. The one is constant, the other is not; the one is of immense antiquity, the other arises only when the worshipers have achieved a certain degree of subjective maturity; the one is universal and all embracing, the other is particular, appearing as a transient phenomenon of the individual mind.

That Yahweh is the giver of life, that Yahweh saves from death, that Yahweh is Levi's portion: all this and much more was made explicit in the cultus from the earliest times, and still provided a sufficient assurance even in the latest days of the Old Testament. No one expected any modification or wider extension of these cultic declarations. It would be quite erroneous to think of the Israelite of the Old Testament as one who questioned, who was aware to a greater or less extent of the deficiencies inherent in the cultic assurances of "life," or who Prometheus-like battered against locked doors. The cultic assurance given by Yahweh as giver of life and savior from death met every demand, not only as one would expect in patriarchal times, but also in the latest and most sophisticated period. Psalm 73 itself demonstrates that there was always a wealth of new meaning to be drawn from the old formulae, just as they stood.

It is not a question of struggling to gain new insights, as is so often suggested: the new insights are simply received and accepted. Certainly they differ at different periods, and in this respect it is a misapplication of research to bring everything down to a hypothetical level of normality. Our understanding of the cultic life of Israel suffers from an exaggerated tendency to impose uniformity on what must actually have been highly diversified, not only in the course of its historical development, but also in cross-section at any given time. Just what could be made out of the material of cultic pronouncements, and when, where, and by whom it could be made as these pronouncements came to life in the context of the cultus, all depended upon a great many varying factors. It depended not only upon the vitality of a generation as a whole, but also upon the theological reflection and insight of particular groups and movements within the cultic community. One can at least say with considerable confidence that the Psalter reveals the existence within the post-exilic community of a group of spiritually alert Levites who interpreted the promise of Yahweh's gift of life in a sense that is wholly sublime.

14

Some Aspects of the
Old Testament Worldview

All modern commentators are agreed that it was above all in the realm of political history that the Hebrew of Old Testament times became aware of the sovereignty of God. This is, indeed, the characteristic note of Old Testament assertions about God. The faith of Israel is invariably related to an event, a divine self-declaration in history: it originated in a response to divine acts and looked forward to divine acts. Whenever Israel felt the urge to probe more deeply, theologically speaking, into her own situation with relation to God and to the world, she found herself under the compulsion of rewriting her history; and we must learn to see these ever more penetrating historical essays both as Israel's confessions of faith and as her efforts to comprehend the course of a history molded by her God.

Israel had indeed a phenomenal sense of history, and her historical grasp manifested itself in innumerable ways that are often irreconcilable. For us today this is the most striking fact of all, and it is undoubtedly extremely difficult for us to grasp the real import of these amazingly diversified fresh footholds that Hebrew religion continually establishes for itself in history, gaining at each step as it were a new purchase.

For a long time, however, no adequate attempt was made to reconcile this fact that the Old Testament relates everything to history with the general worldview of ancient Israel. The greater part of what the Old Testament has to say about what we call Nature has simply never been considered. If I am right, we are nowadays in serious danger of looking at the theological problems of the Old Testament far too much from the one-sided standpoint of an historically conditioning theology. Indeed, until quite recently no one recognized the existence of any problem at all in the relationship between the religion and the worldview of ancient Israel, using the term "worldview" for the purpose of this essay in a sense which does not include a view of history. So far as her worldview is concerned, it was alleged, Israel simply accepted the assumptions common to the ancient Near East, and in this respect had no distinctive view of her own except in the field of "religion," i.e., in the dimension of relationships between God and man. Theologically, therefore, scholars drew a sharp line of division between Old Testament statements of the worldview of the ancient Near East, which was said to be of no theological interest, and "religious" assertions which concerned Israel's faith. As scientific knowledge the former was simply cast aside, whilst the latter was held to be of profound significance even for Christian purposes.

The consequences of this in innumerable studies of the first chapter of Genesis from the standpoint of practical theology are well known: the worldview of ancient Israel was regarded as already antiquated and superseded, whereas its dogmatic understanding of creation was seen as something still vital and alive. Thus the theologically complex and conflicting statements of Genesis 1 were reduced to a simple doctrine of creation. Yet such a doctrine mighty surely have been expressed with the expenditure of much less mental effort! Genesis 1 contains vastly more than a testimony to belief in God as creator, a conception which in itself could find no place for what is actually the real theological achievement of this chapter, namely the mustering of every available notion in order to set out in the most pregnant terms all that Israel had to say about the creation of the world. Hence our present problem: can one so easily distinguish between the faith of Israel and her worldview? Is it really the case that Israel's doctrine of creation is no more than a device intended to give cohesion to a religiously neutral body of scientific knowledge? Does not the text much rather convey the impression that here faith and worldview interpenetrate each other quite inextricably?

It is common knowledge that at the present day, not only in the realm of philosophy but even in the field of natural science, grave doubts have been voiced against the making of any such division between our beliefs and our worldview. Is it not illusory to suppose that our perceptive faculties can function quite independent of any preconceived beliefs we may hold? Knowledge of the world cannot be attained simply by the perception of the multifarious knowable isolated phenomena that it contains; an attempt must be made to grasp it as a whole. Yet how can we grasp as a whole that which is seen as no more than the sum of its parts?

Certainly the faith of Israel did not regard the structure of the universe as a matter of indifference. It is quite unthinkable that Yahwistic belief could have been linked equally well with some other worldview. It follows as a matter of course that the Yahwism of the Old Testament forms part and parcel with Israel's understanding of the world.

How are we to resolve this obstinate problem? It is tempting to hinge every-thing on the evidence we have of a belief in Yahweh as Creator; and hitherto this is what scholars have mostly done. This course, however, is open to the objection that it takes for granted from the outset that which is in fact the sub-stance of our problem. It is pointless to go on interminably ordering the texts to suit our own preconceived notions; what we have to do is to understand more clearly, if possible, the ontological reality of *Israel's* notion of creation. For in fact *all* religions have something to say about creation, even those Canaanite religions that Israel so bitterly opposed. In Ugarit, for example, El is the creator-god. If we speak simply of a belief in God as Creator, we fail to define the distinctively Israelite notion of creation.

Let us then try in this essay to approach the problem of the Old Testament worldview from a quite different angle, that suggested by the commandment prohibiting the making of images. We must first, however, dispel the erroneous interpretation of this commandment that mistakes its consequence for its pur-pose. The fact that it is forbidden to worship Yahweh under the form of a cultic image is not intended to encourage spiritual worship, nor is it a protest against a merely outward piety too narrowly bound up with material objects. Any sus-picion that materialism may be to the detriment of spiritual religion is wholly foreign to the thought of ancient Israel. A contempt for outward, material forms is, moreover, a blow directed at empty air, for there are very few instances of idolatrous religions in which the image is identified with the god. Even these religions recognize that deity is spiritual and belongs to a higher order of existence than that bounded by the earthly and the material; but recognition of this fact did not restrain the worshipers from setting up idols.

Must we not indeed admit that many of these cultic images do in fact most powerfully portray the spiritual nature of the god? We shall make no progress with our problem along these lines, and a consideration of the relationship between the deity and the image leads us into still deeper spiritual considera-tions.[1] We approach the crucial issue much more nearly if we regard the image as in some sense or other a revelation of the deity. Something takes place between the image and the worshiper; the worshiper receives something that the cult-image expresses, for in some way the deity communicates himself to the worshiper by means of the image. Through it he answers questions and grants or withholds his saving power; in other words, by means of the cultic image there is encounter between God and man. Without the gods, and with-out concrete representations of them, man would be lost in the world! Yet the mystery of godhead bursts out all around him. From it he may gain a blessing and bring order and purpose into his life; apart from it he could not exist. In the sphere of human life there is an infinite variety of points at which divinity shines through, and every point in man's world is at least potentially a point of divine intrusion, and expression of deity, and to this extent a means of communication between God and man. It is this understanding of the situation which makes possible the extraordinary tolerance which idol-cults extend to one another.

Against this cultic pattern Israel set its face as decisively as it did against murder and adultery. To make an image of a calf, even as a plinth for purely ornamental purposes, was uncompromisingly forbidden. The prohibition appears many times in the text of the Old Testament, but it is never explained or justified in so many words—an omission which causes great difficulty to the exegete, for the provisions of divine law in the Old Testament defy our human attempts to see behind them. One can say no more than that the prohibition of images is not aimed simply at bringing about a more spiritual form of worship. If it were, it would be inexplicable that such a moderate, common-sense counsel could lead time and again to those dire conflicts that are recorded from the age of Moses to the time of the Maccabaeans.

The issue is evidently not one of a general basic religious truth that should be clear to any serious-minded human being, and to which sooner or later all religions must come. The worship of a deity by means of an image is not a piece of religious infantilism. From the point of view of a particular complex of religious premises, it is indeed a highly logical mode of worship, capable, as Goethe has shown, of the highest degree of spiritualization.[2] To those of this persuasion the Old Testament attitude is totally incomprehensible, and indeed must seem a scandalous and even intolerable want of *pietas* and godly reverence. "Everything that is profane to them is sacred to us" *(Profana illis omnia quae apud nos sacra)*, says Tacitus bitterly, speaking of the Jews. Indeed, had Israel yielded on this point, had she not maintained her proscription of images, all the other peculiarities of her religion would have been overlooked. This was the crucial point of difference that to the foreigner set Israel enigmatically apart from all other nations and all other religions, and which in the Graeco-Roman period brought upon her the fearful reproach of *amixia*.[3] This it was that the world of classical antiquity saw as the uniquely distinctive feature of Israel's faith, and according to its own lights very rightly condemned.

The prohibition of idols is, indeed, one of the most fundamental tenets of Yahwism, a living principle apart from which Yahwism would not have been what it was; it is not a late, theologically self-conscious accretion, as is clearly shown by its appearance in the most ancient, pre-Settlement period of Yahwistic belief.

If, as we have seen to be the case, "idolatrous" religions understood the world to be the *mise-en-scène* of innumerable divine manifestations, at least the path by which these deities entered upon the stage was a relatively straightforward one of unbroken lineal descent. In this connection many writers have spoken significantly of an "emanation of deity" into the world. But in Hebrew thought, Yahweh was not conceived of as the manifestation of either a cosmic or pre-cosmic event. Yahweh's revelation of himself to Israel could never have been defined in such narrowly static terms as those which are implicit in a cultic image, which is at once the guarantee of the presence of the deity and the focal point from which his powers radiate. Yahweh was present to Israel in a far more personal sense, speaking the living word and performing the historic act. As a recent writer has impressively demonstrated, such a conception of the encounter between God and man, however, makes the use of anthropomorphic language concerning God quite inevitable,[4] and indeed an indispensable expedient. The Old Testament teems with anthropomorphisms. The enigma of the divine revelation to Israel lies in the antinomy between the startling grandeur of its anthropomorphisms and the uncompromising strictness of its prohibition of cultic images.

What concerns us here, however, is not so much the theological as the cosmological implications of the prohibition of images. The fact that Israel contended that Yahweh could not be represented in any earthly form can only be attributed to a fundamentally different understanding not only of God but also of the world. The Hebrews expressed themselves in extreme terms concerning the world as a reflection of the deity: the world declares and proclaims the majesty of the godhead (Pss 19:2; 89:5; 145:10; Isa 6:3; 42:10-12). But beyond this point they never go, and the world is never thought of as a direct manifestation of the mystery of the godhead, nor as an emanation or self-revelation of deity. In prohibiting images Israel drew the line of division between God and the world both more sharply and in a different place from religions that made use of images. Yahweh was not one of the sustaining forces of the universe, nor was he even the totality of them. He was their creator.

Is it not clear from such considerations that the prohibition of images actually gives typical expression to the Old Testament worldview as a whole? The commandment is manifestly much more than a specimen of the kind of cultic bric-a-brac of which innumerable examples are known to any student of the history of religions. Rather it is an element of the faith that must have been implicit in and normative for Israel's very earliest experiences of Yahweh, an element upon which Israel based her deepest understanding of God and the world.

If this is so, however, it can only mean that this unique worldview which the commandment against images has helped us to see must in some way be taken into account in every single expression of Yahwistic belief, not least in connection with the different conceptions of the doctrine of creation. The temporal application of the doctrine will not be affected, but the question of the origin and date of the concept of creation in Hebrew thought may perhaps appear in a different light when brought into relationship with the worldview which had already found expression in the prohibition of images. The prohibition, surely, enshrines a decisive and fundamental recognition of the fact that God is theologically transcendent relative to the world, so that the creation narratives must be understood in a certain sense as the immensely diversified exposition of a theological datum which was already embedded in the most ancient form of Yahwism.

May we then say that this digression on the prohibition of images has indeed helped us to see more clearly what the notion of creation meant to the Hebrew mind? It implied a radical purging of both the divine and the demonic from the material universe; the world is seen as a single entity, complete and undivided (Gen 1:31). The world is neither a *mise-en-scène* nor a participant in the drama of a creation-struggle, even in the most attenuated allegorical sense. Throughout the length and breadth of the created order, even where it is waste and void, the praises of God are heard.

Where else in the Old Testament does the world appear thus unified in offering praise? The Hebrews knew of no such thing as that numinous primordial matter, the seat of immense and mighty powers, personified in Greek mythology by the Titans.[5] Nor did they scour the heavens in a search for stellar deities, a point firmly established in the passage that describes the creation of the stars and emphatically assigns them to an ancillary function (Gen 1:14ff.). The prayers of Israel are brimful of complaints, but they are not complaints about the world and its construction, not about evil spirits that cause diseases and into whose power man is delivered; they are complaints about men and about God himself.

All this is doubtless very surprising, for of course the Hebrews had experience of terrifying and indeed shattering natural events; but they were quite incapable of regarding them as in any way self-subsistent or as having an independent origin apart from or opposed to Yahweh, or as being an inherent part of the material order at best restrained by Yahweh. On the contrary, they were a part of Yahweh's own direct action in the world.

If one may so say, Israel paid a high price for her refusal to accept any form of metaphysical dualism, for by excluding from the world all traces of any theomachic dualism, she was compelled to face the problem in her religious thought of accepting and explaining the dualism as a fact within the godhead itself. Frankly, the Old Testament uses language in this context that often strains the reader's powers of comprehension to the very limit. Every kind of political folly, military catastrophe, disease, earthquake, famine, drought, or locust plague was seen by Israel as a visitation from Yahweh. On the part of the sufferers there was grief, terror, and angry remonstrance (for the accepted explanation made the hardship yet harder to bear), but still the psalm rode roughshod over the sufferers' bewilderment: "it is Yahweh and none other who forms light and creates darkness, makes weal and creates woe. I am Yahweh, who do all these things" (Isa 45:7).

Even if it were true that this particular passage went beyond the mere underlining of a key-feature of Hebrew thought, we should nevertheless be obliged to admit that Israel failed, logically, either to meet or to avoid the problem of metaphysical dualism; and this very illogicality, shown above all in borrowing the motif of the battle with the dragon of primordial chaos, must therefore claim our particular attention (Pss 74:13; 89:10; Job 3:8; 7:12; Isa 51:9). We need not discuss here the question whether this tension arises from unexpurgated traces of an outlook that is in essence foreign to Yahwistic belief, or whether it represents rather a limit beyond which even Yahwism cannot go. But as we contemplate these frontiers of Israel's faith, we are entitled at least to observe that the worldview of ancient Israel bears the decisive stamp of a belief that Yahweh is the one cause of all things.

This assertion, however, carries with it the implication that Israel did not think of the world as a "cosmos" at all; that is to say, she did not see it as a self-contained structure ordered by eternal laws. Certainly Israel was aware of laws of nature, and even made her own particular contribution to the elucidation and definition of these laws, as we now know; but the laws were seen only as the relative principles of a world embraced and held, at times disturbed, but always and unceasingly controlled by God. It was in this divine control, for weal or woe, that Israel found beauty in its most exalted degree.

Since for the Hebrews the world was a created order, held and governed by God, it could never be regarded as self-existent, nor could it for one moment be understood apart from God. If we allow our own notion of Nature to intrude at this point, we run a serious risk of distorting the Israelite conception into the static one of a world which exists and functions only in and for itself. We must try to forget our own idea of Nature if we are to see the world as Psalm 104 sees it, a world continually dependent upon God to sustain and maintain it. If we were to ask ourselves what kind of a world it was which the author of Job 28 saw, we should think twice before applying to it the term "Nature." His world was surely far more abyssal than the one that shelters under our term "Nature," and only he who kept his eyes upon its Maker and Ruler could either comprehend it or endure it. It was only Israel's faith that made it possible for her to understand the world as a world at all. It would be unthinkable to regard Israel's worldview as a matter of indifference, theologically speaking.

As we have seen, those characteristic features of this worldview that have furthered our understanding of the prohibition of images are in fact to be found throughout the Old Testament, and in a wide variety of forms. Here and here alone was it possible for this incredibly realistic view to flourish in human minds. Here alone could this incomparably magnificent freedom of conception develop. Here alone, in his encounter with God, does mankind become great and interesting, breaking through the enigma of his humanity to discover all the inherent potentialities of his self-conscious existence. He becomes, in the final analysis, a man taken over by God,[6] one who must surrender to God all his rights over his own history and who by the very fact of so doing is led to new and unsuspected horizons of freedom. He attains to participation in God, not only by a cultic myth in which he enters upon the divine mysteries through some kind of *hieros gamos*, but by hearing God's word and accepting his historical dispensations. But let none imagine that man is able at will to understand himself in this way, merely at the cost of a little reflection!

I spoke in an earlier paragraph of freedom from the fear of demons. It was a freedom that compelled Israel to re-think the whole fact of sickness. The Old Testament actually contains a wealth of material that enables us to investigate the strong position taken up by Yahwism on this aspect of her overall worldview.[7] There remains the phenomenon of death itself. It is an outstanding achievement of Israelite religion to have removed from the sphere of the cultic and the mythical this, the most highly-charged of topics for religions of every age and clime. Neither the dead nor death itself were invested with sacral powers in Israel's faith, which indeed withstood with remarkable trenchancy every attempt to draw them into the realm of the cultic. Death was nothing in its own right; it possessed no sovereignty, and was no more than a part of God's dealings with man. "You prevail forever against man, and he passes; you change his countenance, and send him away" (Job 14:20). Even in death the hand of Yahweh is to be seen!

What strikes one even more is the fact that the Hebrews were so little interested in death, sharing hardly at all our modern interest in it. Death for them might mean many things: separation from the cultus, exclusion from worship, the silence of God, refusal of divine grace; and it was only over such points as these that the Hebrew began to be interested in the matter. Israel did not objectivize death in accordance with either the ancient mythological view or the modern biological one.

If it is true that our modern, popularized view of Nature has taken the place of the essential Old Testament understanding of the world, namely that the world lies open to God and is wholly within his grasp, then this is equally true of our view of history; and in this, our modern attempt to short-circuit the argument is particularly misleading. The moment we use the word "history," we have imparted an element of abstraction that begs the question. All these notions—Nature, sickness, death, history, and so on—are merely vast ciphers, so many images projected as it were upon a cinema-screen which separates God from man. Anyone who wishes to see the world in some measure as Israel saw it must first rid his mind of both mythical and philosophical ways of thinking. It is much easier said than done!

Nevertheless, the religion of Israel was intensely interested in the world, which it saw in direct and immediate relation to God. It was no less fascinated by the phenomena of the world than by the phenomena of a "history" wholly directed by God. Are we not then confronted at this point with an exegetical task similar to that which we have already in part performed in respect of the Old Testament theology of history?[8] We have yet to discover whether this unique attitude of Yahwism towards the world around it was maintained equally in every direction. Probably Israel was subjected to peculiar temptations on this account. Perhaps even Israel's worldview became hardened as a result of "dogmatic" considerations. And even in Israel there was more than one tenable worldview! Israel was involved in continual dialogue with Yahweh concerning the world, and her worldview was in consequence continually in a state of flux. She was called upon ever and again to rescue the world from becoming a stage for the presentation of divine mysteries and pictorially expressed theophanies, and thus to free it for those who would look upon it with secular eyes as a created thing. It is surprising to see that in the course of this process there is evidence of great concern to maintain a rational and scholarly view of the world.

In the wider field of the history of human thought the Hebrew contribution to our own worldview has hitherto been regarded as slight, if not wholly insignificant. Such a view must surely be revised, for in this very field what Israel had to say had immensely far-reaching consequences that must be evaluated anew. It was something very different from the pre-Socratic notion of *archē*.

UNIVERSALITY AND PARTICULARITY

Of all the problems which are suggested by these considerations, I propose to investigate only one, although it is frankly one of the more perplexing, namely the relationship between the overall worldview of the Hebrews with its tendency to universalize and their understanding of history tending to particularization. We must, of course, bear in mind the fact that this statement of the problem is essentially one made from our own modern point of view, for the Old Testament draws no such distinction between Nature and history, regarding them as one single area of reality under the control of God. At the same time Israel could not altogether ignore the existence of a very real tension between its views of God's handling of the world as a whole, in which the emphasis tends strongly to universalism, and the equally emphatic tendency to look at the particular case in God's dealings with man in history. Let us consider one or two specific texts in which, in very diverse ways, this difficulty that Israel certainly felt finds concrete expression, and in which an attempt is made to resolve it.

Looking from this point of view at the so-called Priestly Code, that monumental account of a history which starts with the creation of the world and ends with the setting up of the tabernacle, one might at first glance gain the impression that the writer was totally unconscious of the existence of any such problem as the one I have set out.

The work opens in Genesis 1 with an account of the Creation seen as history, and pursues its course to the Flood-narrative and to the list of the nations, maintaining a universalistic outlook and developing its theme with an unparalleled breadth of vision. But then the writer leads us rapidly through a genealogy to the situation in which he sees salvation as something simply for Israel, i.e., to the setting up of the tabernacle and the establishment of a cultus that may not be practiced elsewhere. The transition from the universal to the particular is effected without hiatus, and without any explicit recognition of the problem that this involves.

To some extent this may be explained on the grounds that the theological standpoint from which this whole tract of history has been surveyed lies at the end of the road, not at the beginning: the writer's faith is grounded in the tabernacle, within the pale surroundings of those to whom the saving dispensation applies; but in order adequately to emphasize the immensity of his theme of salvation, he reaches out and traces the historical line of descent from the creation of the world down to himself. The chapters concerning the creation of the world and the genealogy of the nations are thus included less in the interests of an all-embracing understanding of the world than in the interests of Israel's own theological self-knowledge. The universalistic part of the primeval history makes a tremendous claim: in order properly to understand Israel and her relationship to God, we must start our historical thinking at the creation itself, for Israel has its own peculiar place in the thought of God himself. It is a claim to which we shall have cause to return later.

In the J strand of the narrative, the relationship between the universal primeval history and the particularized history of redemption is more clearly stated. The Yahwist, of course, depicts the history of God's relationship with humans in terms of humanity's successive widening of the breach between itself and God. Then, with the beginning of the story of Abraham, he indicates that the story of God's dealings with Israel from this point on will lead to a blessing for all nations (Gen 12:20). "The blessing contained in the person of Abraham has a scope as wide as the misery of all the nations of the earth," says

Procksch.[9] In this prophetic expectation there is to be seen a resolution of the tension between the universalist and the particularist view.

Psalm 19

> The heavens are telling the glory of God;
>> and the firmament proclaims his handiwork.
> Day to day pours forth speech,
>> and night to night declares knowledge. (Ps 19:1-2)

This extremely ancient poem begins with the statement that a paean of praise ascends unremittingly not only from heaven, but from the whole creation. The universe glories in its creatureliness; it tells it out and proclaims it. And unbroken tradition, handed on by each day and each night to the next from the beginning of time until now, vouches for the truth of what the created order has to tell. The poem goes on to speak of the sun, which goes forth as a bridegroom in the morning and joyfully pursues its course into the sky, and then at this point what is manifestly a literary fragment suddenly breaks off. In later ages it found a continuation:

> The law of Yahweh is perfect,
>> reviving the soul;
> The testimony of Yahweh is sure,
>> making wise the simple. (Ps 19:7)

A whole world separates the ancient hymn from this new psalm in praise of the Torah. The change of style is unmistakable, for this psalm in praise of the Torah is calm, learned, artless. But this continuation that has been added to the older hymn is by no means an unintelligible editorial lapse. Rather it is a profoundly conceived theological addition. The old hymn spoke of a proclamation made by the whole universe. Does mankind hear it? Is it perhaps something he cannot possibly hear? At least there is good cause for him to tell of the revelation that *is* open to him. He has encountered it in history, and "the word is very near you; it is in your mouth and in your heart" (Deut 30:14). But if we spoke of a proclamation, we must also speak of a revelation that Israel met with in history. Here, once again, there is a certain lowering of the tension between the universal and the particular, even though it be at the cost of what is theologically and stylistically a harsh break in the poem.

Job 28

We now go on to a very remarkable poem found in the book of Job, a poem which nevertheless can be interpreted quite apart from its context:

> Surely there is a mine for silver,
>> and a place for gold which they refine.
> Iron is taken out of the earth,
>> and copper is smelted from the ore.
> Men put an end to darkness,
>> and search out to the farthest bound
>> the ore in gloom and deep darkness.
> They open shafts in a valley away from where men live;
>> they are forgotten by travelers,
>> they hang afar from men, they swing to and fro. . . .
> Man puts his hand to the flinty rock,
>> and overturns mountains by the roots.
>> He cuts out channels in the rocks,
>> and his eye sees every precious thing.
> He binds up the streams so that they do not trickle,
>> and the thing that is hid he brings forth to light.
> But where shall wisdom be found?
>> And where is the place of understanding?
> Man does not know the way to it,
>> and it is not found in the land of the living. . . . (Job 28:1-13)

The poem opens with a picture, unique in the literature of antiquity, of a primitive mine, using it as an illustration of the apparently unlimited technical potential of the human race. Yet at the same time it expresses profound resignation: all the control over nature of which man is capable cannot conceal the fact that the most important thing of all lies beyond his power. He can have no real comprehension of what ultimately holds all things together. In the poem this impenetrable area of knowledge is called "wisdom," "understanding" (*ḥokmah, bînah*), and the writer evidently regards it not only as present in the world but inherent in it, "built-in" to it, yet inaccessible to man. The passage is important to our understanding of the problem in that it presupposes in mankind a desire to know and to dominate, a desire which functions in isolation from and independently of his religious grasp. Yet the secret of creation has receded still further from man by reason of his technological capacity. The glory of the universe now begins to oppress man, to terrify him and to reveal to him the poverty of his resources.

God understands the way to it,
    and he knows its place. . . .
When he gave to the wind its weight,
    and meted out the waters by measure. . . .
Then he saw it and declared it;
    he established it and searched it out.
[And he said to men, "Behold, the fear of the Lord,
    that is wisdom: and to depart from evil is understanding."]
        (Job 28:23-28)

The conclusion of the poem (i.e., the lines placed in brackets above) calls for particular comment. Its purpose is quite clear: it leads our thoughts away from the hopelessness of the question as man poses it and shows the way by which we too may share in this wisdom. For mankind, to be wise is to reverence God. The sentence cannot have formed a part of the original poem. Not only is it in prose, but its presentation as a divine pronouncement is stylistically foreign to the context. Above all it goes over to a wholly different conception of wisdom, no longer using the word to denote the inherent rational purpose of the world, its divinely ordered principle, but rather that wisdom which mankind ought to practice. Here again, then, we have a theological addition and, as before, a somewhat crude break in the style.

Opinions will differ as to the theological value of this addition, although it is difficult to suppress a feeling of regret that so majestic a poem should now come to such an ending; but we recognize here an instance of that perpetual, most earnest, theological concern to show us a way out from the hopeless gloom of the universalist view of the world.

Proverbs 8

There is a long, extended poem on Wisdom in Proverbs 8:

Does not wisdom call,
    does not understanding raise her voice? . . .
To you, O men, I call,
    and my cry is to the sons of men. . . .
I have counsel and sound wisdom,
    I have insight, I have strength.
By me kings reign,
    and rulers decree what is just:
By me princes rule,
    and nobles govern the earth. . . .

> Yahweh created me at the beginning of his work,
>> the first of his acts of old.
> Ages ago I was set up,
>> at the first, before the beginning of the earth. . . .
> When he marked out the foundations of the earth,
>> then was I beside him, like a master workman;
> And I was daily his delight,
>> rejoicing before him always,
> Rejoicing in his inhabited world
>> and delighting in the sons of men.
> And now, my sons, listen to me. . . . (Prov 8:1-32)

The cry of Wisdom as we see her here makes an ultimate appeal: the issues of life and death for mankind depend upon hearing it. Who is this Wisdom? She makes the greatest claim of all, for as has rightly been said,[10] she is of such greatness that God himself wills to be sought and loved in her. In this call of hers, indeed, the whole knowledge of truth possessed by all the nations is summed up. "By me kings reign, and rulers decree what is just; by me princes rule." A truly colossal claim to make! The Wisdom who here reveals herself is none other than that secret of creation, instinct in the universe itself, of which the poem in Job 28 speaks. This is the point of the rather obscure passage at Prov 8:22-31.

There is supreme poetic feeling in these verses, and therefore a distinct limit to what can be done by intellectual analysis of them; yet it is clear that this secret of creation has from the very outset played about the world and mankind in disinterested delight. If we try to disentangle what is said from the near-mythological imagery in which it is couched, the sense is surely this: all creation rises above itself towards God; it contains within itself the secret of its being, a secret which bears witness to its own existence; creation is enveloped in a glory which reflects the glory of God. Profound as are the perspectives which this insight opens up, we must not lose sight of man's capacity to share in this wisdom as the poem sees it: he cannot attain to wisdom by speculation, but only by indirect means.

The passage in the poem identifies the Wisdom who calls to men with that wisdom which is implicit in creation as its inmost secret; but the purpose of the passage is simply to proclaim this convincingly to a generation whose worldview has become overweeningly presumptuous. "Understand this, you men: I who call you to judgment, I whose cry confronts you with the ultimate issues, I am the self-same one who from the very beginning has unremittingly embraced the entire universe, for I am the very secret of the created order. You can have no part in this infinitely profound secret except by your obedience to my call, by your discipleship."

If this interpretation approximates at all to the fundamental thought of Proverbs 8, then it does not differ greatly from Job 28. Certainly there is a wide difference in tone, for Job 28 is gloomy and resigned: man's questioning strikes up against the impenetrable barrier of the secret and is thrown back. In Proverbs 8, on the contrary, the poem is a proclamation made by the secret of itself; and in this the two poems are markedly different. Yet in their basic attitude they are very similar. Wisdom, and with it participation in the secret of creation, comes to man only through obedience to the voice which ever calls him, in his actual historical situation, to decide for God.

So far as we know from the Old Testament, Hebrew thought nowhere else provides so clear and rational a statement of the tension between God's universal control of the created order and his self-revelation in history. The fact that the theologians who produced the wisdom literature were not greatly concerned with the history of redemption naturally tended to preclude this. It must be admitted that even Proverbs 8 does not arrive at a genuine solution of the problem, or why should wisdom need to reveal itself anew if indeed it plays about man and all creation from the very beginning?

Ben Sira 24

In conclusion, we must touch on one further poem in which once again Wisdom speaks concerning herself, here as before making immense claims and directing our gaze back to the foundation of the world:

> I came forth from the mouth of the Most High,
>> and covered the earth as a mist.
> I dwelt in high places,
>> and my throne is in the pillar of the cloud.
> Alone I compassed the circuit of heaven,
>> and walked in the depth of the abyss.
>> . . . in every people and nation, I got a possession.
> With all these I sought rest;
>> and in whose inheritance shall I lodge?
> Then the Creator of all things gave me a commandment;
>> and he that created me made my tabernacle to rest,
> And he said: Let your tabernacle be in Jacob,
>> and your inheritance in Israel. . . .
> In the holy tabernacle I ministered before him;
>> and so was I established in Zion. (Sir 24:3-10)

According to her own statement, Wisdom comes from God; she controls all creation and here once more is regarded as the source of truth as it is known to all nations. But—and this is the key to the whole situation—a new thought now appears. Wisdom has *sought* for a dwelling, and among all nations she has sought in vain for someone truly to receive her, truly to comprehend her. (The same thought will later find expression in the Fourth Gospel: the Word came to his own home and his own people did not received him. [John 1:11]) Our pre-Christian text points to a calamity that has befallen God's revelation to the world: men have shut out from themselves this divine revelation that controls the whole universe. These few sentences depict a decisive step in the history of God's dealings with man. In some sense this catastrophic event might be regarded as a parallel account of the story of the Fall, which equally tells of man's refusal of God, of a turning away from God that was to have an incalculable effect on man's knowledge of truth and of God. Then, however, as the present text asserts, when Wisdom had sought in vain for a dwelling-place among men, God conceived a new plan, and directed this divine revelation to a dwelling-place in Israel. Thus magisterially the poem explains Israel's unique claim to possession of the truth, and the plenitude of her knowledge of God.

What, then, is the common ground among the three wisdom passages that we have considered (Job 28, Proverbs 8, Ben Sira 24)? All three presuppose a desire to understand the universe, and make some claim to have done so. The person who in Job 28 is denied an answer is undoubtedly one who has thus far pressed his inquiry most urgently. The attitude expressed in this passage presupposes a determined striving after knowledge by many thinkers of many generations; it represents a disillusionment with the outcome of a long and highly specialized study of nature. Never before had Israel's faith been called upon to face up to this intensive, wholly unmythological, materialistic analysis of the created order; and, as we have seen, it is still an open question whether we can keep pace with this radical demythologizing of the universe.

A more important question, however, is raised by the fact that all three passages evince a concern to bring the secret of the purpose of creation—a secret whose existence none would deny—into relationship with the historical revelation experienced by Israel. Furthermore, these passages are concerned to show that these two manifestations of deity, in creation and in history, are identical. In the addition to the poem in Job 28 this was done with very little theological discrimination, even perhaps rather crudely; in the poems of Proverbs 8 and Ben Sira 24 it was achieved with profundity and after much reflection. Let us now consider, however, the immense distance that separates this from the historical outlook of the Priestly Code as adumbrated in Genesis 1.

We have already seen that the theological assumption that underlies this presentation of the matter is an integral part of Israel's understanding of the economy of salvation, and that it is from this point of vantage that the writer plots a theologico-historical line leading from the creation of the world to his own position. Indeed, one cannot rightly understand the Hebrew attitude unless one *does* start from the creation of the world. Over against this, the theological problem in the three wisdom passages we have examined has shifted through an angle of a hundred and eighty degrees: here the problem is no longer one of understanding Israel, but of understanding the world; and, accordingly, the solution too has been turned round to face the other way. The man who wishes to understand the world as a created order must align himself with the people of God, and there is, in fact, no direct road leading from the secret of the created order to God.

Religiously speaking, this reorientation of the problem can have arisen only in a radically altered situation, a situation above all in which vastly greater intellectual claims were being made and in which a new urge to understand the world around had freshly erupted—a phenomenon with which we are familiar at the present day. If on the one hand the three passages in question aim to meet those new intellectual demands, accepting the challenge of the question as it was posed, they nevertheless remain quite inflexible in the answer they give: the resigned but firm refusal of Job 28.

Of course, the passages differ a good deal in detail. What Job 28 regards as the allotted bound of human knowledge, Ben Sira 24 sees as the consequence of guilt; but in one way or another, the divine secret of the created order remains beyond the grasp of man to know or to master. Hence in each case we find the problem brought into the context of God's self-revelation to Israel. This is why there is the peculiar lacuna in these passages, that break in the thought that is so characteristic of them. Israel claimed no especially profound insight into the depths of those secrets which God alone held in his power, but she boasted of an understanding of the world as a created order and as a realm whose true glory is visible only to the heavenly. The trisagion of the seraphim in Isa 6:3 reflects very precisely this essentially superhuman view of creation: "The fullness of the whole earth is his glory."[11] To heavenly creatures, but not to humankind, the glory of the world as a creation lies revealed.

As the Hebrews saw it, a person's situation in the world is thus a quite remarkable one: he lives within a created order from which ascends an unending hymn of praise (Psalm 19),[12] yet he himself hears nothing of it. He is rather in the position of Job, reasoning with God and at odds with him, yet needing only to be told that already at the time when God set about creating the world, the heavenly beings shouted for joy (Job 38:7). He must be taught, as if he were blind and deaf, that he lives in a world that could be revealed to him, a world indeed in which, according to the remarkable teaching of Proverbs 8, he is himself enfolded in the self-revealing secret of the created order.

Having reached this point, it remains only for us to cite a sentence of St. Paul that gathers up into one single, extraordinarily profound statement precisely those insights with which we have been concerned in this essay: "Because the world, set amidst the divine wisdom, did not recognize God by means of wisdom, God resolved to save them that believe by the foolishness of the *kerygma*" (1 Cor 1:21).[13]

We are now aware how far into the past the antecedents of this statement reach. Whole new horizons are opened up to us by the recognition that Paul is here setting the deep insights of Israel in the light of the Christian revelation. But this is not the place to probe the matter further.

15

Job 38 and Ancient Egyptian Wisdom

Commentators have always agreed that Yahweh's speech in Job 38 is a superb poem. No progress has, however, been made on the form-category of the speech since Gunkel first initiated the form-critical method. In subject matter, this account of the wonders of creation clearly has much in common with hymns. It has also been thought that there might be some connection between the interrogative form of Job 38 and the rhetorical questions often found in hymns.[1] The interrogative style used in hymns is nevertheless quite distinct from the style of the present passage. It is admittedly a rhetorical device in both cases, but in hymns it is the human worshiper who asks the questions, whereas here he is the person to whom they are put. Furthermore, the fact that Job 38–39 consists entirely of questions from beginning to end precludes us from regarding it as a hymn. We must attempt to approach the problem from a different angle.

The *Onomasticon of Amenemope* (edited with a commentary by Sir Alan Gardiner), is recognized as an encyclopedic scientific work, a "compendium concerning all that Ptah created, the heavens and their appurtenances, the earth and all that is in it." The work mentions other objects, persons, offices, professions, tribes, Egyptian cities, and so on, simply listing a series of nouns or short phrases in each case. The work as preserved to us enumerates six hundred and ten items.[2] It is only the beginning of the list that interests us here, and it might well be useful to compare the list of cosmological and meteorological items in Amenemope with that in Yahweh's speech in Job 38.

1.	Heaven	12.	Morning	1.	Firmament
2.	Sun	13.	Dawn		Heaven
3.	Moon	16.	Sea	2.	Sun
4.	Star		Primeval ocean	6.	Moon
5.	Orion	17.	Underworld	9.	Stars
6.	Great Bear		Darkness	11.	Rainbow
7.	Pavian	18.	Earth	13.	Lightning
8.	"The strong one"	19.	Light	14.	Clouds
9.	Boar		Darkness	15.	Cloud
10.	Storm	22.	Snow		Hail
11.	Orcanus		Hail	16.	South wind
12.	Dawn	24.	"Wind"	17.	Thunderstorm
13.	Darkness		East Wind		Whirlwind
14.	Sun	25.	Torrential rain		Snow
15.	Shade		Thundercloud	19.	Hoarfrost
16	Sunlight	28.	Rain	20.	Ice
17.	Sun's rays		Dewdrops	22.	Dew
18.	Dew	29.	Ice	23.	Rahab
19.	?		Hoarfrost	25.	Sea monsters
20.	Snow (?)	31.	Pleiades		
21.	Rainstorm (?)		Orion		
22.	Primeval ocean	32.	Mazzaroth		
23.	"Flood" (Nile)		Bear		
24.	Rivers	34.	Clouds		
25.	Sea		Waterfloods		
26.	Waves	35.	Lightning		
27.	Great Sea	36.	Ibis		
28.	Lake		Cock		
29.	Spring	37.	Clouds		
30.	Pool (?)		Heavenly water-skins		
31.	Delta	39.	Lion		
32.	Water		Young lion		
33.	Pond	41.	Raven		
34.	Front				
35.	Rear	**Job 39**			
36.	Well	1.	Mountain goat		
37.	Fount		Hind		
38.	?	5.	Zebra		
39.	Riverbank	9.	Wild ox		
40.	?	19.	Horse		
41.	Current	26.	Hawk		
42.	Fountain				
43.	Streams				
44.	Flood				
45.	?				
46.	Currents				
47.	Water-hole				
48.	?				
49.	Banks				
50.	?				

Psalm 148	Song of the Three Young Men
1. Heaven	36. Heaven
3. Sun	37. (Angels)
Moon	38. Heavenly ocean
Stars	40. Sun
4. Heaven	Moon
Heavenly ocean	41. Stars
7. Sea monsters	42. Showers
Primeval ocean	Dew
8. Fire	43. Winds
(? lightning)	44. Fire
Hail	Heat
"Ice" (70)	47. Nights
Stormy wind	Days
9. Mountains	48. Night
Hills	Darkness
Fruit-trees	49. Cold
Cedars	Heat
10. Wild beasts	50. Frost
Cattle	Snow
Reptiles	51. Lightnings
Birds	Clouds
11. Kings	52. Earth
Peoples	53. Mountains
Rulers	Hills
Judges	54. Vegetation
12. Young men	55. Fountains
Maidens	56. Sea
Old men	Rivers
Children	57. Whales
	Sea monsters
	58. Birds
	59. Wild beasts
	Cattle
	60. Men
	61. Israel

Comparison is actually possible only from Job 38:12 onwards, since vv. 4-11 deal with the creation of the world by Yahweh and with the battle against chaos which is wholly foreign to Egyptian thought. The *Onomasticon,* on the contrary, contains no theological or mythological introduction, but confines its attention to the bare enumeration of cosmographical data. Thus there is nothing in Amenemope corresponding to the first part of Yahweh's speech.

What then are we to think of the series of phenomena depicted by Amenemope and by Job 38:12ff. respectively? We certainly cannot claim any precise parallelism. The correspondences begin only with *Amenemope* 12, and even these are far from exact. Nevertheless, the two texts approximate very closely at those points where they enumerate meteorological phenomena: snow, hail, wind, and so on.[3] This is also true of the constellations, although in Amenemope they are significantly listed at the beginning, whereas in Job they interrupt the enumeration of meteorological phenomena almost as if these had been an interpolation in the text at this point (Job 38:31-32). Certainly we are not in a position to say that Job 38 shows literary dependence on Amenemope, although there is undoubtedly some connection between the two texts.

It may be that there existed some other *Onomasticon* that was used by the composer of Yahweh's speech in Job. The *Rameses Onomasticon,* for example, contains lists of plants, minerals, birds, fishes, and animals.[4] In contrast to this, Job 38–39 confines itself to the enumeration of heavenly phenomena, and then suddenly switches to a list of animals from 38:39 to 39:26. That this list is itself not original is clearly indicated by the interpolation here of birds; but doubtless this is to be expected in a poetic work. The fact that in Job we have a free poetic composition naturally means that the original material has been thoroughly worked over stylistically. The poet was thus at liberty to follow up the associations which arose continually in his mind as he worked. The wonder is rather that the technique of enumeration should have been so firmly maintained in the poem. It is only in the second half of Yahweh's speech that the poet gives free rein to his descriptive imagination.

Since we are doubtless still far from having proved our case, we plead in aid a further passage, the "Creation Hymn" in Sir 43:1-33. Compared with the unrelieved interrogative style of Job 38, the form of the sentences in this passage is freer and more varied. Nonetheless, there can be no doubt that this poem, too, follows a pattern that was already laid down. The pattern begins with the heavenly bodies and works its way around to the various natural climatic phenomena, the underlying scheme being rather more easily discerned than it is in Job 38. Yet once again we must not deceive ourselves regarding the extent to which this example depends upon an Egyptian model.

There can, of course, be no question of either of our Hebrew texts depending in any direct, literary sense upon an Egyptian *Onomasticon.* We may nevertheless assert that such encyclopedic works found their way into Israel, and that Israel also learned to compile scientific lists of cosmic and meteorological phenomena as well as of the animal kingdom. In compiling their instructional poems, therefore, the wisdom-writers, well-versed in all kinds of learned literature, had the comparatively easy task of going through this long-established scheme of current scientific learning, and of putting into poetry the somewhat prosaic tabulations. The procedure in Sir 43:1-33 is thus basically the same as that in the "Hymn to the Ancestors" (*paterōn hymnos*) of Sir 44–49. One is a learned account of ethnic history, the other a scholarly natural history—both in poetic form.

As our next example let us consider Psalm 148. This begins with an exhortation to praise Yahweh. The first creatures bidden to praise him are the heavenly ones. They are, of course, outside the scope of the onomastic encyclopedia. Yet when the hymn moves on from the heavenly beings to cosmological and meteorological phenomena, it falls almost at once into the traditional learned pattern, and, as in the *Onomasticon of Amenemope*, leads on from the heavenly bodies to the meteorological occurrences of the earth below.

This section is of particular interest to us at this point, because it goes much further than either Job 38–39 or Ben Sira 43 in the material it uses. The section as a whole is much less full, and, as in the meteorological section, enumerates fewer instances. At the same time it includes more categories: fruit-trees, wild and domestic animals, reptiles, and birds. This series is reminiscent of the *Rameses Onomasticon,* which begins with an almost completely unreadable list of plants and liquids before going on to birds, fishes, and animals.[5]

By contrast, Ps 148:11-12 corresponds almost exactly with the arrangement of the *Amenemope Onomasticon,* which starts with the heavens and goes on to the weather, the earth and thence to the king, to officials, and to various professions. In v. 12 we come to a section concerning young men, maidens, old men, and children which Gardiner classes under the heading "types of human being," and at this point the affinity with the *Onomasticon* is particularly striking. The corresponding passage from Amenemope reads as follows:

> 295. Man
> 296. Youth
> 297. Old man
> 298. Woman
> 299. Young woman
> 300. Various persons

301. Boy
302. Child
303. Lad
304. Girl

For our last example it will be well worthwhile to consider the Song of the Three Young Men 35-68.[6] It is difficult to fix the date of this passage, which was undoubtedly in origin an independent poem, and not a composition expressly written for interpolation into the Book of Daniel. It could well be of the same period as Psalm 148, which it closely resembles but to which it certainly owes nothing, maintaining its own distinctive characteristics throughout as against this psalm. It is therefore interesting to see that here the weather, the mountains, and the hills are followed by a short list of terrestrial water-formations, the foundations, seas, and rivers of vv. 55-56. There is nothing especially striking about the passage itself, except that the *Onomasticon of Amenemope* contains a similar but much more detailed list of terrestrial water-formations in which, among others, seas, rivers, and springs are mentioned. On the other hand the Song of the Three Young Men contains features which could find no place in the Egyptian list, such as angels (v. 37) and sea monsters (v. 57).[7]

The problems thus opened up have numerous ramifications. We ought no doubt to start with the details in order to ascertain in what respects the pattern which was taken over in Israel was modified or extended as a consequence of topographical or climatic conditions. We ought also to establish the extent to which the pattern has influenced Old Testament hymnody as a whole. Above all we ought to consider the theological implications of the fact that Israel adapted this somewhat arid scientific material to the purposes of the worship of Yahweh.[8]

Let us, however, go back to our starting-point in Job 38–39, for we have still reached no conclusions with regard to the form-category of Yahweh's speech itself. The further problems that this raises cannot be solved by regarding the passage as a hymn, for we know of no hymns that consist wholly of rhetorical questions. Could this curious form, which seems to be unique in Israel's literature, be in some sense a derivative of ancient Egyptian wisdom literature?

Let us turn our attention to the well-known polemical writing in which the scribe Hori makes a literary onslaught upon his colleague, called Amenemope. This document, usually known as *Papyrus Anastasi I,* after the only complete extant manuscript, dates from the time of Rameses II (1301–1234 B.C.E.), the time of that Indian summer of Egyptian wisdom writing in which it made its mark upon Israel. Only one section of this extensive document is of interest to us here—the well-known passage on Syria, so valuable for our understanding of the historical geography of pre-Israelite Palestine. Here, in this one single instance (18.9—28.1), we find precisely similar rhetorical questions, and in such profusion that the whole passage forms an almost unbroken succession of such questions. "Hast thou not gone to the land of the Khatti, and has thou not seen the land of Upe?" So the series begins. "Come teach me about Berytus"; "Where is the road to Aksaph?" "Pray instruct me as to the mountain of User. What is its peak like?" "Has thou not gone to the land of Takhsi?"[9]

These are but a few examples. There are in all about fifty such questions. Let us compare these with the questions in Job 38–39: "Where were you? . . . Tell me" (38:4); "Surely you know!" (v. 5); "Have you commanded?" (v. 12); "Have you entered?" (vv. 16, 22); "Have the gates . . . been revealed to you?" (v. 17); "Have you seen?" (vv. 17, 22); "Have you comprehended?" (v. 18); "Where is the way?" (vv. 19, 24), and so on.

No further demonstration is needed to show that the form is identical in both cases. The close relationship of the *form* of the two texts is to be clearly seen in the phrase "Tell me," used once in Job (v. 4) and three times in *Anastasi I*, and even more particularly in the questions "Hast thou not gone?" "Where is the road?" These two questions are, of course, meant to be taken literally in the papyrus, whereas in Job they refer to the "storehouses of the snow" (v. 22) or the "gates of darkness" (v. 17), and can be understood only figuratively.[10]

The stylistic form of these ironical questions in the papyrus, as well as in Yahweh's speech in Job, is doubtless purely a literary device, but we may reasonably ask whether this was always so. Is it not conceivable, indeed probable, that this form of rhetorical question (or, more exactly, catechetical question) originally had its own actual situation in life, and only subsequently acquired literary status? Wisdom teaching belongs to the world of education, and is part of the learned instruction given to those destined for high office.

Let us look once again at the questions of *Papyrus Anastasi I:*

> Pray instruct me as to the mountain of User. What is its peak like?
> How is Byblos built?
> Where is the river Litani?
> How does one cross the Jordan?
> How does one by-pass Megiddo?
> Put me on the road to Hamath.
> When one goes to Adummim, in which direction does one turn?
> How many miles is it from Raphia to Gaza?

Can there be any doubt that these were at one time questions actually asked in the schools? Was not this the method by which young scribes, the future governors of provinces, were taught and examined in the geography of Egypt's neighbors?[11] One has only to look at the opening sentence of the passage, "Come here to be questioned," or the closing words "Answer me now!" Naturally this does not apply to the questions in Yahweh's speech, which are couched in a more literary and poetical form.

Looking back over our findings, however, we find that our conclusions on Job 38 still pose a disturbing problem. We saw that in listing the phenomena of the cosmos and of nature, Job 38–39 follows an established pattern, which derives ultimately from Egyptian wisdom literature as exemplified in the *Onomastica*. We also saw that the catena of questions in Yahweh's speech corresponds very closely with the ironical questions of *Papyrus Anastasi I*, which itself goes back to the catechetical mode of instruction in ancient Egyptian scribal schools. How does it come about, however, that the form of Job 38–39 reflects at the same time two quite distinct form-categories, as if the composer of the speech were dependent upon both the pattern of the *Onomastica*, and the interrogative style of satirical works? What has a learned onomasticon in common with a polemical satire? Perhaps a very great deal!

We need only ask where Hori acquired all this knowledge with which he now bullies his colleague, to his pedantic self-satisfaction. What textbooks would the wisdom-teachers have taken as the basis of their instruction, other than their own learned works—in this case, their onomastica? The *Onomasticon of Amenemope* contains in one particular passage (nos. 250-70) a whole list of Palestinian names, and gives a very fair impression of what the original of *Papyrus Anastasi I* must have looked like.[12]

There is nothing to be said for the view that the outstanding knowledge of Palestinian geography displayed by the writer of the papyrus is based on personal experience, unless, that is, we regard both the style and the content as exclusive and peculiar to Hori himself. If, however, we accept that he is copying and parodying the instructional method of the classroom and catechizing his opponent like a schoolboy, it becomes much more probable that he is simply going through the lists of a textbook.

In the nature of things it would be difficult to prove this conclusively from the text, although Gardiner has in fact made a comparison between the onomastica and this part of the papyrus.[13] An exact investigation of this text from all extant copies with regard to the grouping of localities lies beyond the scope of our present study, but such an analysis would add greatly to the probability that an earlier list had been used as copy, since it would reveal gaps and omissions in the lists of names. Ought we not, however, to regard this type of literature much more as a conventional form based upon an established text? If we do, the personal contribution of the writer would be much less considerable, as regards both style and material, than it is usually thought to be. If the author of the Egyptian polemical work had catechized his colleague not on his geography but on his cosmological and meteorological knowledge, we should have had an exact parallel to Job 38.[14]

16

The Levitical Sermon in 1 and 2 Chronicles

It was Ludwig Köhler who first raised the question of the form-critical category of the exhortations in the Book of Deuteronomy. He pointed to the passage in Deut 4:1, 6-8, and asked:

> Who can speak like this? He who has ears to hear, let him hear the style of this passage. Who can speak like this, so forcefully yet so lovingly, admonishing and making promises, taking for granted the goodwill of his hearers, repeating what is already well known, giving at the same time both moral and spiritual instruction? The prophet does not speak in this way. His sayings are more concise, more definite, more peremptory, fresher and broader both in form and content. Nor is this the language of the popular speaker. His oration is less spiritual, more vivacious, less clerical, more worldly, less patient. This is the style of the preacher. It is in the seventh century that the preacher comes to the fore. The sermon, the greatest and best form of human instruction, begins at this time.[1]

Köhler's definition is wholly convincing. Deuteronomy is motivated by a desire to instruct such as we find in no other book of the Old Testament. It is as if this writer feels himself driven by the problem of passing generations: how can later generations be kept loyal to Yahweh, and how can the link with his mighty acts in history be maintained (Deut 4:9ff.; 6:7, 20ff.; 11:19; 32:46)? The deuteronomic sermon arose in response to this urgent need.[2] The report of the solemn reading of the law by Ezra (Neh 8:7ff.) provides an example of this kind of preaching, albeit in somewhat exceptional circumstance. The text is not altogether clear, but evidently implies that after Ezra had read the law the Levites went among the people and gave them instruction in it. The Chronicler depicts a similar activity on the part of the Levites at Josiah's passover (2 Chron 35:3): it is their duty to give religious instruction to the people, in this instance concerning the ritual of the Passover and its significance.

The priestly code evinces no interest whatever in instructing the people, but I have shown elsewhere that the historical writings of the Chronicler stand essentially in the mainstream of the deuteronomic-levitical tradition, and it is wholly in accord with this that religious instruction in the form of interpolated speeches should play a large part in the Books of Chronicles.[3] It is this fact that calls forth the present investigation. Not only is a very great deal of Chronicles written in this hortatory, sermonic style already so familiar to us from Deuteronomy; the Levitical writer has actually inserted genuine sermons into his text wherever possible. Of set purpose, and with considerable skill, the most diverse situations are so handled by the narrator as to provide the occasion for a religious homily either as their climax, or as a decisive turning-point in the narrative.

Let us look first of all at a straightforward example. King Amaziah of Judah is on the point of going to war. He has, however, enlisted a considerable number of troops from the kingdom of Israel in addition to the Judahites and Benjaminites. At this stage a man of God arrives, and says:

> "O King, do not let the army of Israel go with you, for Yahweh is not with Israel, with all these Ephraimites. But if you suppose that in this way you will be strong for war,[4] God will cast you down before the enemy; for God has power to help or to cast down." (2 Chron 25:7ff.)

This can undoubtedly be classed as a sermon: it seizes upon an actual situation as the occasion for instruction, but does not become involved in the inherent pragmatic considerations; it goes straight to the heart of the doctrinal problem. The King is faced with a grave dilemma; it is not human might, but faith in God that is decisive. Victory and defeat depend upon God, not upon the size of the army. The speech made by the man of God is not in the strict sense of the term "Prophetic," as is made abundantly clear by the prose style in which it is couched, but is rather the application to a specific situation of a doctrine long since established by the prophets.

A second example makes it still more clear how little such speeches are prompted by prophetic inspiration and how little original material they contain. King Asa has become involved in hostilities with Baasha of Israel, and in consequence has been driven into an alliance with Aram. A seer is moved by the events to upbraid the King in the following terms:

> Because you relied on the King of Syria, and did not rely on Yahweh
> your God, the army of the King of Syria has escaped you. Were not the
> Ethiopians and the Libyans a huge army with exceedingly many
> chariots and horsemen? Yet because you relied on Yahweh, he gave
> them into your hand. *For the eyes of Yahweh run to and fro through-*
> *out the whole earth,* to show his might in behalf of those whose heart
> is blameless towards him. You have done foolishly in this; for from
> now on you will have wars. (2 Chron 16:7-9).

As in the previous example, this sermon is a protest against reliance upon earthly might, but this time the theme, so beloved of the Chronicler in his homilies, is not very happily expounded. Had the man of God asserted that the war against Israel had been a failure because of the Syrian alliance, we should have found the argument clear and straightforward; but it is no punishment that the King of Aram, who was in fact Asa's ally, should have escaped from Asa's hand! The distortion of the argument was made necessary by the fact that the ancient account of the matter told of the complete success of Asa's enterprise against Israel.

Of greater importance here, however, is the preacher's quotation of an ancient written source. One might go so far as to say that he is preaching on a prophetic text, for there is no doubt that verse 9a is a quotation from Zech 4:10b. It is most significant that the original context of the saying is completely ignored by the Chronicler. The statement that "Yahweh's eyes range throughout the whole earth" is torn from its context and applied, albeit most effectively, according to its natural meaning. With this quotation the preacher reaches a climax, drawing a contrast between the man who constantly trusts in himself and does not see God, and God who sees all and helps or punishes accordingly. Apart from this quotation from Zechariah, the comment "You have done foolishly" (*niskalta*, v. 9b) recalls very strongly the same word used by Samuel to Saul (1 Sam 13:13).

It may perhaps be thought that we exaggerate the significance of this tendency to quote texts; perhaps we may find it instructive to look at some of the other sermons in Chronicles. Following his victory over Zerah the Ethiopian, King Asa is met by one Azariah, who, inspired by the spirit of God, delivers the following homily:

> Hear me, Asa, and all Judah and Benjamin: Yahweh is with you, while
>   you are with him.
> *If you seek him, he will be found by you,* but if you forsake him, he will
>   forsake you.
> For a long time Israel was without the true God, and without a teach-
>   ing priest, and without law;

> But when in their distress they turned to Yahweh, the God of Israel,
>> and sought him, he was found by them.
> In those times there was no peace to him who went out or to him
>> who came in, for great disturbances afflicted all the inhabi-
>> tants of the lands.
> They were broken in pieces, nation against nation and city against
>> city, for God troubled them with every sort of distress.
> But you, take courage! Do not let your hands be weak, *for your work
>> shall be rewarded.* (2 Chron 15:2-7)

The passage is unmistakably poetical in style, and even if we do not place a very high estimate upon its value as poetry we are aware that an effort has been made to assimilate the style of this passage to that of inspired prophetic utterance. Now, however, we notice once again the peculiar harking back to ancient prophetic pronouncements that gives this speech its characteristic flavor. This time it is from the prophet Jeremiah that the preacher takes the basic idea for his sermon, having on this occasion found two texts to suit his theme, one from Jeremiah's well-known letter and the other from the message of consolation in reply to Rachel's lament.[5]

It cannot be said that the thought contained in these passages sheds any great illumination on the situation arising from Asa's victory, or has even any serious bearing upon it. The statements that God is found by those who seek him, and that the people of God will in due course be rewarded can, in fact, hardly be reconciled with the Chronicler's own way of showing that Israel's victories are due to Yahweh's help, and are meant to instruct the people; nor is it at all clear what purpose is served by a historical and theological retrospect into the distresses of the time of the Judges.

Doubtless any such criticism is misplaced, however, for the homily must be interpreted on its own terms. Evidently it reflects standard Levitical homiletic practice in its quotation of prophetic sayings and in its theological retrospect into national history. We must not assess this sermon on the basis of its present context, and, more important still, we must try to look beyond the artificialities of the particular instance. Once we are able to see this passage as an example of Levitical homiletic practice—abridged, needless to say, for literary reasons—we shall be in a position properly to evaluate it. We might almost claim a classical outline for it. The first part sets out clearly and precisely the conditions on which God is prepared to give his help—i.e., the doctrine. The second part looks back into history, showing that God's nearness is not to be taken for granted, and that there are whole periods of history in which he was far removed—i.e., the application. The third part is a call to faith with the promise of a reward—i.e., the exhortation.

King Jehoshaphat, to whom the Chronicler attributes a notable religious reformation, addresses the judges of Judah in the following terms:

> Consider what you do, for you judge not for man but for Yahweh; he is with you in giving judgment. Now then, let the fear of Yahweh be upon you; take heed what you do, for *there is no perversion of justice with Yahweh our God, or partiality, or taking bribes.* (2 Chron 19:6ff.)

Here the words of a sermon are put into the mouth of the King himself. Accordingly the writer has not troubled to compose the speech in the form of parallel statements, and there are other respects, too, in which this homily is simpler than the foregoing example. Basically, however, there is no difference of method. The King becomes a preacher, and he sets out the theological background of the justice which a judge in Israel must know how to administer. God is the source of all earthly justice, and it must be administered in a way that intimately reflects his being, his purity, and his integrity.

This homily is a sermon, however, in a still more precise sense of the word than that with which we have so far been concerned, for despite its immediate relevance to the contemporary situation it takes its stand upon ancient scriptural texts of acknowledged authority, and justifies its own demands by reference to them. The statement that with Yahweh there is no perversion of justice or partiality derives from the passage in Deuteronomy which enjoins just judgment: Yahweh is the great and terrible God who is not partial and takes no bribe (Deut 10:17). We may also take it as certain that the unusual phrase "There is no perversion of justice with Yahweh" refers to Zeph 3:5: "Yahweh does not pervert justice." The quotation of the phrase from Deuteronomy, which the Chronicler uses in precisely the right context, is apt and makes an effective ending to this sermon on the divine justice.

Another sermon which makes equally apposite use of an ancient text is to be found in 2 Chron 20:15-17. Threatened by a large hostile army, King Jehoshaphat proclaims a fast throughout Judah and offers a solemn prayer in the temple. A Levite now steps forward, moved by the spirit of Yahweh, and speaks as follows:

> Hearken, all Judah and the inhabitants of Jerusalem, and King Jehoshaphat: Thus says Yahweh to you, "Fear not, and be not dismayed at this great multitude; for *the battle is* not yours but *God's.* Tomorrow go down against them; behold, they will come up by the ascent of Ziz; you will find them at the end of the valley, east of the wilderness of Jeruel. You will not need to fight in this battle; *take your position,* stand still, *and see the victory of Yahweh* on your behalf, O

Judah and Jerusalem. Fear not, and be not dismayed, tomorrow go out against them, and Yahweh will be with you."

This speech is more than usually tailored to fit the specific historical situation, but despite the topographical details in v. 16 we must not be misled into thinking of this as anything other than a sermon. The paradox that the battle is Yahweh's, and not theirs, is presented to the people in strictly homiletic fashion, and the underlying thought is not prophetic but instructional, depending upon 1 Sam 17:47: "the battle is Yahweh's." The particularly important quotation in this passage, however, is taken from Moses's speech at the crossing of the Red Sea, where we find the exact words, "take your position and see the victory of Yahweh" (Exod 14:13), to which the Chronicler has added simply "stand still." This time the quotation matches the situation admirably, for shortly afterwards we have an account of Yahweh's miraculous deliverance of Israel.

On the same occasion the Chronicler ascribes a short sermon to King Jehoshaphat himself, immediately following the Levitical homily that we have been discussing. The people break camp the next morning, and move off to join battle at their designated spot, where the King addresses them in order to stir up the faith of the army:

> Hear me, Judah and inhabitants of Jerusalem! *Believe in* Yahweh, your God, and *you will be established;* believe his prophets, and you will succeed. (2 Chron 20:20)

In present-day Old Testament studies we tend to minimize the direct influence of the great prophets upon their contemporaries and their successors, and to urge that we should approach this matter with greater caution. Yet here, at all events, we have proof that one of Isaiah's forceful pronouncements (Isa 7:9) had not failed to make its effect, even though the Chronicler obviously knew of it only in written form. Here, too, the quotation is undeniably appropriate, for the situation in which the Chronicler depicts King Jehoshaphat is very similar to that in which Ahaz is shown in the Book of Isaiah. In both instances there is an explicit test of faith.

Nonetheless, one is very conscious of a decadent and wholly unprophetic element in this speech of Jehoshaphat's. To set Yahweh and his prophets side by side as objects worthy of faith cuts clean across the whole message of the Isaianic oracle. We cannot rightly equate faith in God with faith in his commandments, and then attribute redemptive power to both. Anyone who tries to do so doubtless shows great reverence for holy writ and for the earthly agents of Yahweh, but also displays a singular lack of insight into the real import of the prophetic oracle he quotes.

A very similar speech is put into the mouth of King Hezekiah, who calls together the captains and the people in the square by the city gate, and encourages them with the following oration:

> *Be strong and of good courage. Do not be afraid or dismayed* before the King of Assyria and all the horde that is with him; for there is One greater with us than with him. With him is *an arm of flesh;* but with us is Yahweh our God, to help us and to fight our battles. (2 Chron 32:7-8a)

The words, "Be strong and of good courage; do not be afraid or dismayed," are deuteronomic and are quoted from Josh 10:25, where we have the same succession of four imperatives. Equally, the contrast between Yahweh and an "arm of flesh" is not the Chronicler's own original idea, but depends unmistakably on Jer 17:5, where, after the manner of wisdom literature, a curse is laid upon the man who "makes flesh his arm" and does not trust in Yahweh.

We could adduce many more instances of quotations from earlier writings in such sermons. As we have seen, the quotations are not always correct, nor are they always in line with the thought of the sermon itself. In 2 Chron 29:5-11 there is a speech made by Hezekiah, solemnly calling on the priests and Levites to institute a reform of the cultus. The address contains a historical retrospect, which includes a passing quotation from the prophet Jeremiah (v. 8): at all events it is only in Jeremiah (29:18) that we find the complete form of this ponderous statement that Yahweh has made (or will make) his people "an object of horror, of astonishment, and of hissing."[6]

Another speech that contains no actual quotations, but is full of allusive expression, is ascribed to the messengers whom Hezekiah sent throughout Israel to call the people to the Passover (2 Chron 30:6-9). There are numerous expressions to be found here which belong to the traditional stock-in-trade of the preacher: "those who have escaped," "made desolate," "be stiff-necked," "be faithless to Yahweh," "Yahweh is gracious and merciful," and so on. A remarkable feature of this speech is the notion that the penitence of those who still remain in the land may move Yahweh to bring back from exile their brethren of the Northern Kingdom.

Finally I would draw attention to David's great speech in which he presents his son Solomon to the council, and explains his plans for the building of the temple:

> Hear me, my brethren and my people. I had it in my heart to build *a house of rest* for the ark of the covenant of Yahweh and for *the footstool* of our God; and I made preparations for building. But God said

to me, "You may not build a house for my name, for you are a war-
rior and have shed blood! Yet Yahweh the God of Israel chose me
from all my father's house to be king over Israel for ever; for he chose
Judah as leader. . . . Now therefore in the sight of all Israel, the
assembly of Yahweh, and in the hearing of our God, observe and seek
out all the commandments of Yahweh your God; that you may possess this good land, and leave it for an inheritance to your children
after you for ever. And you, Solomon my son, know the God of your
father, and serve him with a whole heart and with a willing mind; for
Yahweh searches all hearts, and understands *every plan and thought.*
If you seek him, he will be found by you. . . ." (1 Chron 28:2-10)

Once again this speech illustrates the diversity of the traditional material
used by the preacher. The designation of the ark as God's footstool is elsewhere found only in Ps 132:7, from which it has been borrowed in the present instance.[7] This assumption is supported by the fact of the Chronicler's
regard for this psalm in view of its doctrinal content,[8] and there is yet a further indication that the quotation is taken from this psalm. The conception
of "rest" (*menûhah*) after the desert wanderings and the confusion of the
period of the Judges is, of course, unique to Deuteronomy; here, however, it
undergoes a theological transformation. It is not Israel that is to find rest,
but God who will find rest among his people, and this is precisely the sense
in which the notion of "rest" is used in Psalm 132! There is thus a twofold
indication that the speaker is paraphrasing this psalm. Rothstein comments
that v. 4 alludes to the blessing of Jacob (Gen 49:8ff.).[9] Verse 8 is particularly
interesting, since at this point the sermon is out of character, the exhortation being "irrelevant to the interest which dominates the rest of David's
speech."[10] Evidently the Chronicler has lost sight of the particular situation,
and has fallen into the common homiletic style! The notion that God understands every plan and thought (v. 9b) derives, of course, from the Yahwistic
writer (Gen 6:5; 8:21), and the end of this verse once more quotes Jer 29:14,
as does 2 Chron 15:2.

So far we have assumed that the speeches in Chronicles are to be regarded
as sermons, and have collected and explained our material on this understanding. The assumption calls for justification and, indeed, a certain degree
of limitation. If these speeches are free compositions interpolated by the
Chronicler, evidently they will have been shaped to a great extent by his own
presuppositions, and cannot therefore be regarded as the unplanned product
of current homiletic practice.

We may take it for granted that these speeches are intended pre-eminently
to support the prophetic claims of the Levites as conceived by the Chronicler,
that institutional and political interests predominate in them, and that the

choice of quotations cannot fail to be influenced by such considerations. Yet there is a further characteristic which lends considerable interest to the form and content of these passages: the Chronicler is using a form which he finds particularly well suited to his purpose, in the light of his own admittedly limited literary capacity.[11]

It is quite evident that he is following an established pattern, since there is no difference between the speeches made by prophets and those declaimed by kings. If these speeches and, even more particularly, these quotations from ancient writers were found only in passages to which the Chronicler wished to ascribe prophetic inspiration and authority, we might well hesitate to pursue the matter further. But this is not so, and we must therefore go on to ask whether it is likely that the Chronicler himself invented this mode of instruction, expressly for the purpose of putting over his own point of view. But he really is quite the last person whom we should credit with the creation of anything, let alone a new literary form! We are thus driven back to the position of assuming that he relies upon a model, that is to say, upon forms which were well known and in common use in that Levitical tradition in which he himself was at home.

We may therefore recognize in the Chronicler's speeches a distinct form-category, of late origin—that of the Levitical sermon.[12] Since we can distinguish this category only by the indirect evidence of the Chronicler's examples, to define its characteristics is a somewhat unrewarding task.

Stylistically the sermon is, of course, a prose-form, although there appears to have been a predilection for high-sounding elevated vocabulary, and solemn formal phraseology. When the writer wishes to present such sermons as prophetic pronouncements he will occasionally employ a style akin to poetic parallelism, although we are always conscious that prose is the essential medium of this form-category. Further, the use of quotations from ancient authoritative texts is a particular characteristic of these sermons. Telling phrases which seem to lend weight to the theme of the homily are quarried wherever they may be found in earlier literature, and incorporated into the sermon. There is no question of preaching to a text in the modern sense, if only because the text usually stands at the end by way of climax, as a kind of final trump card with which the speaker takes the decisive trick against his hearers (1 Chron 28:9; 2 Chron 15:7; 19:7; 20:17).

It is now easy to see, however, how little the writer is restricted in his choice of quotations by his own particular religious viewpoint and interests. This fact provides us with yet another substantial indication of the existence of the sermon as a distinct form-category. The Chronicler belongs to a very definite religious tradition with its own distinctive outlook, yet his quotations and borrowing from earlier writers belong to no particular tradition and are wholly eclectic in nature. We have seen how varied are the fundamental notions underlying the passages cited—Yahweh's omniscience, his grace which is not withheld from those who seek it, his justice, human faith in him, and so on—a fact which makes it difficult to suppose that the Chronicler himself invented this literary form of the sermon with its interwoven quotations. It is not an accident, therefore, that the content of the sermons is frequently less relevant to its historical setting than one might have wished.

Understandably, there is very little which can be said about the "situation in life" of these sermons, for the Chronicler imports them into all kinds of historical settings which yield no information on this matter. We may nevertheless properly ask whether there is not some practice in real life corresponding to the picture drawn from time to time by the Chronicler, in which messengers are said to be sent round the country to deliver such sermons (2 Chron 30:6-10). It would certainly be conceivable that the Levites, who had been deprived of office through the centralization of the cultus, found a new sphere of activity in religious instruction, and that from time to time preachers went out from Jerusalem, the center of the Levitical organization, into the surrounding countryside.

What were the forces that sustained the religious life of the nation in the post-exilic period, and where are they to be located? The question cannot be evaded. The cultus with all its vivifying power was to be found only in one single place, and the people as a whole certainly came into contact with it on particular occasions. It may well be that letters on spiritual matters such as the Chronicler mentions played a more important part than would at first appear (2 Chron 21:12-15; 30:1).

It remains now to point one or two conclusions that follow from our investigation. There is no doubt that the tendency that we have noticed to quote from earlier written sources is indicative of a declension in religious vigor and spontaneity. The preacher no longer feels himself to be God's plenipotentiary when he makes his pronouncements, which is why he falls back on the old established stock of written material, borrowing from the great writings of the past the authority which he himself lacks. In saying this, however, we must not forget that these sermons do not deal in quotations in the strictest sense of the term: the borrowed phrases are not marked out from their context as especially authoritative ones. The speaker makes no suggestion that the phrases in question are of outstanding significance, and there is never any formula to indicate that a phrase is actually a quotation.

In view of the Chronicler's fondness for quotation that is most surprising. We know, for example, how he will draw attention to a passage which contains laws or ordinances which he regards as important, by the use of some such formula as "as it is written" (*kakathûb*; 2 Chron 23:18; 25:4; 30:5, 18; 31:3, etc.).

No one is at greater pains than he to justify opinions, pronouncements, and regulations by continual reference to their origins or to written sources. If, then, the Chronicler makes such free use of passages from the prophets or the Psalms, it can only be that he does not regard these traditional works as being in the strict sense canonical. We have to reckon with the fact that, when the congregation heard such pregnant phrases taken from the fund of religious tradition, they would recognize them at once; the almost incredible verbal memory for traditional literature, which is characteristic of later Judaism, was undoubtedly already a feature of this earlier period. Nevertheless the absence of any specific reference to the source of quotations bears witness to the fact that the speaker does not hold them in the reverence and esteem which would have been called for if they had been canonical works. Since, however, even pentateuchal passages are adduced in this informal manner, it may be questioned whether our author even knew of the complete Torah *as a canonical work*. The Chronicler's canon seems to have contained no more than a collection of laws and ordinances governing institutional matters, somewhat on the lines of the "Ezra Code" which demonstrably was not identical with either the priestly code or the Pentateuch.[13]

Finally it is important to notice the breadth of the religious interests spanned by these preachers. The pre-exilic and the earlier post-exilic writings have received literary recognition, and, what is more important, they are deeply cherished. The quotations presuppose a lively interest in ancient writings and exemplify the keen desire to make their contents known to the people so far as is humanly possible. It is widely accepted that in the post-exilic period a concern for the Law became predominant, and that legal instruction took pride of place in the congregation. Such a view is barely tenable. The Chronicler's sermons at least to some extent call in question the popular notion that this period is one of "narrow legalism," for the teaching of these sermons embraces the pivotal conception of Israel's faith in her greatest days—and flows from the pen of her post-exilic cultic officials!

Notes

Editor's Foreword

1. Walter Brueggemann, "Biblical Faith as Narrative, Recital, Confession: An Introduction to von Rad's *Old Testament Theology*," in idem, *The Book that Breathes New Life: Scriptural Authority and Biblical Theology*, ed. Patrick D. Miller (Minneapolis: Fortress Press, 2005), 65 [60–82].

2. James L. Crenshaw, "Von Rad, Gerhard (1901–1971)," in *Historical Handbook of Major Biblical Interpreters*, ed. Donald K. McKim (Downer's Grove, Ill.: InterVarsity, 1998), 530 [526–30].

1. The Form-Critical Problem of the Hexateuch

[1.] The Hexateuch refers to the first six books of the Hebrew Bible: Genesis—Joshua.

2. Since writing the above, I see that this question has already been raised by Franz Dornseiff, "Exodos," *ZAW* 53 (1935) 153 [153–71]; but his answer, which relates only to the Pentateuch, is by no means satisfactory.

3. The second of these prayers in particular shows what trifling modifications to the original form can be expected. This prayer is to be said at the handing over of the tithes in the so-called year of tithing, but does not accord at all well with the specifically deuteronomic regulations. There the whole emphasis is laid on the charitable use of the tithes, whereas this prayer insists primarily on the cultic offering of that which is holy. The prayer concerns the cultic integrity of the one who offers the tithes, whereas the whole interest of the deuteronomist concerning the year of tithing is centered upon the recipient of the tithes.

4. The rhythmical and alliterative character of the opening phrases in particular reveals its antiquity.

5. Anton Jirku, *Die älteste Geschichte Israels im Rahmen lehrhafter Darstellungen* (Leipzig: Deichert, 1917), 49.

6. For what follows cf. Jirku, *Die älteste Geschichte*.

7. Hans Schmidt, "Das Schilfmeerlied: Ex xv, 2-19," *ZAW* 49 (1931) 59–66. [Tr.] On the basis of Jer 33:11ff., Psalms 107, 118, etc., Schmidt postulates the existence of a festival at which individual vows were repaid, probably in the course of the autumnal festival. He holds that the Red Sea Song formed a part of the liturgy of this festival.

[8.] RSV: "the deeps congealed in the heart of the sea."—Tr.

[9.] RSV: "till Thy people, O Yahweh, pass by, till the people pass by whom Thou hast purchased."—Tr.

10. Cf. Ps 83:12.

11. Julius Wellhausen, *Prolegomena zur Geschichte Israels* (Berlin: Reimer, 1883), 347ff. [Ed.] See Wellhausen, *Prolegomena to the History of Ancient Israel*, trans. J. S. Black and A. Menzies (Edinburgh: A. and C. Black, 1885); reprinted with foreword by Douglas A. Knight, Scholars Press Reprints and Translations Series (Atlanta: Scholars, 1994).

12. For a fuller account of this matter, cf. Eduard Meyer, *Die Israeliten und ihre Nachbarstämme* (Halle: Niemeyer, 1906), 60ff.

13. Hugo Gressmann, *Mose und seine Zeit: Ein Kommentar zu den Mose-Sagen*, FRLANT 18 (Göttingen: Vandenhoeck & Ruprecht, 1913).

14. Wellhausen, *Prolegomena*, 349; Gressmann, *Mose*, 164ff.

15. Gressmann, *Mose*, 234ff.

16. The sentence is not integrally linked to its context. Neither the subject nor the object has an antecedent, and the identity of both must be inferred from the general sense.

17. Moses gives decisions to those who enquire of him (vv. 13, 15); he makes known the "statutes of God" (*huqqê ha-'elohim*; v. 16); he teaches the people the "statutes" (*huqqîm*) and the "instructions" (*tôrôth*; v. 20).

18. Verses 1 and 4 are later additions, intended as a link with the preceding story of the golden calf: cf. Otto Eissfeldt, *Hexateuch-Synopse* (Leipzig: Hinrichs, 1922), 55–56.

19. Albrecht Alt, *Die Ursprünge des israelitischen Rechts* (Leipzig: Hirzel, 1934), 52 (=*KS* 1:317). "The Origin of Israelite Law," in *EOTHR*, 118.

20. So far as this theologically significant event is concerned, the Yahwist's account is superseded by E; here, too, however, we hear of a sacrificial meal which brings the entire proceedings to a close (Exod 24:11).

21. This does not preclude the possibility that we have a Sinai tradition also in Exodus 32. We would maintain only that, as between the material of Exodus 32 and the tradition dealing with the theophany and the sealing of the covenant, there is not that integral connection which the literary account attempts to display.

22. It can no longer be held, therefore, that the main objection to the original unity of the tradition is overcome by postulating that Sinai was only a short distance from Kadesh. Cf. Rudolf Kittel, *Geschichte des Volkes Israel*, Handbücher der alten Geschichte 1/3 (Gotha: Perthes, 1925), vol. 1.

23. Gressmann, *Mose*, 390.

[24.] Not so RSV.—Tr.

25. Meyer, *Israeliten*, 62.

26. Cf. Johannes Hempel, *Die althebräische Literatur* (Potsdam: Athenaion, 1930), 16.

27. Sigmund Mowinckel, *Le Décalogue*, Etudes d'histoire et de philosophie religieuses 16 (Paris: Alcan, 1927), 129.

28. Cf. Richard M. Meyer, *Mythologische Studien aus der neuesten Zeit*, AR 13 (Halle: Teubner, 1910), 270ff.

29. The facts cannot be adequately explained by the fashionable notion that there has been a process of "historification" (*Historisierung*) at work here, i.e., that extant sacral traditions were subsequently put into a historical setting in the interests of Yahwistic belief. The present literary form of the Sinai tradition certainly derives from the culture form, but the tradition itself must obviously be held to be prior to the cultic elaboration that is based upon it.

30. Cf. Hans Schmidt, *Die Psalmen*, HAT 1/15 (Tübingen: Mohr/Siebeck, 1934), 155.

31. Cf. Mowinckel, *Décalogue*, 154.

32. In Psalm 81 it should be seriously considered whether v. 10a (MT 11a) ought not to stand before v. 9 (MT 10).

33. Mowinckel, *Le Décalogue*, 108; Alt, *Ursprünge*, 64 (*KS* 1:326). *EOTHR*, 127.

[34.] Isa. 2:2ff.—Tr.

35. Alt, *Ursprünge*, 57 (*KS* 1:321); *EOTHR*, 122.

36. Ludwig Köhler, *Die hebräische Rechtsgemeinde (Jahresbericht der Universität Zürich* 1930/1), 17ff. (Reprinted in *Der hebräische Mensch* [Zürich 1933], 163ff.). [Ed.] See Köhler, *Hebrew Man*, trans. Peter R. Ackroyd (Nashville: Abingdon, 1956).

37. Sigmund Mowinckel, *Psalmenstudien* 5: *Segen und Fluch in Israels Kult und Psalmdichtung* (Christiana: Dybwad, 1921), 97ff.

38. August Heinrich Klostermann, *Der Pentateuch* (Leipzig: Deichert, 1907), 348.

39. Ibid., 344.

40. Ibid., 347.

41. Ibid., 246.

42. Ibid., 273.

43. So both Keil and Knobel *ad loc.*

44. I. Elbogen, *Der jüdische Gottesdienst in seiner geschichtlicher Entwicklung*, Grundriss der Gesamtwissenschaft des Judentums (Leipzig: Fock, 1913), 165. [Ed.] See Elbogen, *Jewish Liturgy: A Comprehensive History*, trans. Raymond P. Scheindlin (Philadelphia: Jewish Publication Society, 1993).

45. Alt, *Ursprünge*, 65 (*KS* 1:327); *EOTHR*, 128.

46. Mowinckel, *Décalogue*, 119ff.

47. Ernst Sellin, *Geschichte des israelitisch-jüdischen Volkes*, 2d ed. (Leipzig: Quelle & Meyer, 1935), 1:101.

48. Cf. Martin Noth, *Das System der zwölf Stämme Israels*, BWANT 53 (Stuttgart: Kohlhammer, 1930), 140ff. Reprinted Darmstadt: Wissenschaftliche Buchgesellschaft, 1966.

49. Ernst Sellin, *Gilgal: Ein Beitrag zur Geschichte der Einwanderung Israels in Palästina* (Leipzig: Deichert, 1917), 52ff.

50. Paul Volz, *Das Neujahrsfest Jahwes*, Sammlung gemeinveständlicher Vorträge und Schriften aus dem Gebiet der Theologie und Religionsgeschichte 67 (Tübingen: Mohr/Siebeck, 1912); Mowinckel, *Psalmenstudien* 2: *Das Thronbesteigungsfest Jahwes und der Ursprung der Eschatologie* (Christiana: Dybwad, 1922); Hans Schmidt, *Die Thronfahrt Jahwes am Fest der Jahreswende im Alten Israel*, SGVSGTR 122 (Tübingen: Mohr/Siebeck, 1927). [Ed.] See also John Gray, *The Biblical Doctrine of the Reign of God* (Edinburgh: T. & T. Clark, 1979); and Allan Rosengren Petersen, *The Royal God:*

Enthronement Festivals in Ancient Israel and Ugarit? JSOTSup 249 (Sheffield: Sheffield Academic, 1998).

51. Compare the doubts expressed by Martin Buber, *Königtum Gottes* (Berlin: Schocken, 1936), 121. [Ed.] See Buber, *The Kingship of God,* trans. Richard Scheimann (New York: Harper, 1967).

52. Mowinckel, *Décalogue,* 128ff.

53. I cannot agree that the passage is deuteronomic. The expression "holy people" (*goy qadôš*) is not a phrase used by the deuteronomist, who always uses the word "people" (*'am*). Equally foreign to his work is both the notion and the wording of the phrase, "a kingdom of priests" (*mameleketh kohanîm*). The literary dating of these expressions cannot be regarded as conclusive evidence: even if the wording is not ancient, the theological notion that underlies it certainly is.

54. Caspari, "Das priesterliche Königreich," *TBl* 8 (1929) 105–10.

55. Noth, *Das System,* 121.

56. In this connection, cf. also the stylized form of address used by God: "my people" (Ps 50:7; 81:8 [MT 9], and the secondary usage at Mic 6:3, 5).

57. See Gustaf Dalman, *Arbeit und Sitte in Palästina* (Gütersloh: Bertelsmann, 1905), 1:420.

58. Num 28:26.

59. Dalman, *Arbeit und Sitte,* 1:464.

60. Ibid., 420.

61. So I. Benzinger, *Hebräische Archäologie* (Leipzig: Pfeiffer, 1927), 374ff. Cf. Dalman, *Arbeit und Sitte,* 1:420, 464. The text of Deuteronomy as we have it admittedly does not contain the catchword *bikkûrîm*; it speaks only of *re'šîth*. But as Eissfeldt has shown *re'šîth* in Deuteronomy 26 (unlike the occurrence in Deut 18:4, where it denotes "the best") refers to the "first ripe fruits" and "has the same meaning as *bikkûrîm* in the Yahwistic collection of laws; Otto Eissfeldt, *Erstlinge und Zehnten,* BWAT 22 (Leipzig: Hinrichs, 1917), 43. It should be added that the common tradition of later Judaism links Deut 26:5ff. and its ritual with the offering of the *bikkûrîm*. The wheel thus comes full cycle of its own accord.

62. The Mishnaic tradition allows greater latitude here, in that the first fruits (*bikkûrîm*) may be offered between the Feast of Weeks and the autumnal festival (*m. Bik.* 1:10). It may be that this trend was set in motion by Deuteronomy, with its desire to centralize the cultus, and that the absence of a precise date for the ritual is to be explained on this basis. Since we are here concerned only with the *ancient* tradition preserved in Deuteronomy 26, this does not affect our position. Exodus 23:16 and 34:22 both clearly state that in ancient times the handing over of the first fruits (*bikkûrîm*) took place at the Feast of Weeks.

63. Sellin, *Gilgal,* 50ff.

64. Joshua 19:49-50.

65. Sellin, *Gilgal,* 51.

66. The attempts made to transfer these events from Shechem to Gilgal show how very conscious scholars have been of the hiatus at this point. Compare Rudolf Smend, *Die Erzählung des Hexateuch: Auf ihre Quellen Untersucht* (Berlin: Reimer, 1912), 336; and Eissfeldt, *Hexateuchsynopse,* 81.

67. The priestly tradition that the apportionment of the land took place in Shiloh cannot possibly be reconciled with the earlier tradition. Evidently what we have here is the theory of an age that knew only of the fact that Shiloh was the central sanctuary of Israel before Jerusalem came to occupy that position.

68. Smend adduces the further argument that only in Gilgal is it possible for Joshua to speak of Judah being to the south, and the Joseph tribes to the north: *Komposition,* 320. Cf. also Sellin, *Gilgal,* 49–50, and Noth, *Das Buch Josua,* 2d ed., HAT 1/7 (Tübingen: Mohr/Siebeck, 1953), 108.

69. Smend, *Komposition,* 339.

70. Alt, "Das System der Stammesgrenzen im Buche Joshua," in *Sellin-Festschrift* (Leipzig: Deichert, 1927), 13–24 (*KS* 1:193–202); and idem, *Die Staatenbildung der Israeliten in Palästina* (Leipzig: Edelmann, 1930), 61 (*KS* 2:51); "The Formation of the Israelite State in Palestine," in *EOTHR,* 233 [171–237].

71. For an account of the history of the tribe of Benjamin apart from the Joseph tribes, cf. Noth, *Das System,* 81, 37 and Appendix II.

72. Cf. Johannes Hempel, *Gott und Mensch im Alten Testament,* BWANT 38 (Stuttgart: Kohlhammer, 1936), 46ff.

73. Gerhard von Rad, *Die Priesterschrift im Hexateuch,* BWANT 65 (Stuttgart: Kohlhammer, 1934), 56. This becomes especially clear in the statements that everyone collected what manna he needed, neither more nor less, and that the manna could not be stored up.

74. A similar instance is to be seen in the story of the quails, later understood to be the gift of the Spirit (Num 9:20). Eissfeldt, *Hexateuchsynopse,* 41.

75. Gunkel, *Genesis,* HAT (Göttingen: Vandenhoeck & Ruprecht, 1901), sec. 1-5; ET = *Genesis,* trans. Mark E. Biddle, MLBS (Macon, Ga.: Mercer Univ. Press, 1997), vii–lxxix. Kittel, *Geschichte,* 1:302ff. (omitted in later editions: cf. 6th ed., 2:290 n.3. [Eng. trans. exists only of the later, amended editions.—*Tr.*]).

76. Johannes Pedersen, "Passaḥfest und Passaḥlegende," *ZAW* 11 (1934) 161–75.

77. See pp. 16–20 above.

78. See pp. 10–16 above.

79. Jirku, *Die älteste Geschichte,* 31.

80. Gunkel, *Genesis,* 159ff. ET *Genesis,* 158ff.

81. Ibid., 291ff. ET 285ff.

82. Gressmann, *Eucharisterion: Studien zur Religion und Literatur des Alten und Neuen Testaments,* FRLANT 36 (Göttingen: Vandenhoeck & Ruprecht, 1923), 1:1ff.

[83.] See esp. A. Alt, *Der Gott der Väter* (Stuttgart: Kohlhammer, 1929) (*KS* 1:1–78).— Tr.; "The God of the Fathers," in *EOTHR,* 3–77.

84. Ibid., 56ff. (*KS* 1:52–67); *EOTHR,* 52–66.

85. For an account of the separation of the "national religion of Yahweh" from the cultus of the patriarchal gods at the various sanctuaries cf. also Steuernagel, *Georg Beer-Festschrift* (Stuttgart 1935), 68ff.

86. Alt, "Das System," 24–25 (*KS* 1:23–24).

87. Ibid., 60–61 (*KS* 1:56ff.).

88. Gunkel, *Genesis,* 161.; ET *Genesis,* 161.

89. Ibid., 292; ET *Genesis,* 286.

90. Hempel, *Die althebräische Literatur,* 114; cf. Kittel, *Geschichte,* 1:376: "the binding link is Yahweh's gracious providence, despite human folly and unrighteousness. It is to this that the Yahwist wishes to point."

91. Gunkel, *Genesis,* 167; ET *Genesis,* 167. On Gen 12:1-3, see pp. 49ff. above.

92. Alt, *Der Gott,* 71 (*KS* 1:66); *EOTHR,* 64–65.

93. On the particular part played by the tradition of the God of the patriarchs in J, cf. ibid., 24–25 (*KS* 1:22–23); *EOTHR,* 23–24.

94. Bernhard Luther in Meyer's *Die Israeliten,* 108; Eissfeldt, *Hexateuchsynopse,* 30.

95. There is obviously a certain degree of incompatibility between the two goals set before the patriarchs—the Settlement on the one hand and the covenant of Sinai on the other. It arises from the fact that the traditions were originally independent, and that the tension between the Sinai tradition and the Settlement tradition was not capable of being fully resolved.

96. The inclusion of the cultic sagas especially must be regarded as a major innovation by contrast with the original, simple creed, for the sacral traditions were wholly foreign to the nature of the ancient Settlement tradition.

97. Gunkel, *Genesis,* 1; ET *Genesis,* 1.

98. Ibid., 2; ET *Genesis,* 2.

99. It is quite certain that the individual components derive from Canaanite religion, but it seems to us by no means so certain that the composite whole looks back to a non-Israelite model. Cf. Hempel, *Die althebräische Literatur,* 14–15, 115.

100. Karl Budde, *Die biblische Urgeschichte (Gen. 1—12,5)* (Giessen: Ricker, 1883), 409.

101. It has been suggested that the statement in Gen 12:3b ("in you shall all the families of the earth be blessed") ought not to be understood in this universalist sense. It is said to imply no more than that the name of Abraham will become a token used by non-Israelites with which to bless themselves, wishing for themselves the good fortune and blessing possessed by Abraham [so *RSV—Tr.*]. On the grounds of linguistic considerations alone, it is impossible to say what weight should be given to the occurrence here of a unique niph'al form of the verb, and whether it indicates that the verb is to be taken in a special sense; see Otto Procksch, *Die Genesis,* KAT 1 (Leipzig: Deichert, 1913), 97.

The main objection to so limited an interpretation of this text arises from the fact that it breaks the continuity between the primeval history, especially with regard to Genesis 11, and the promise of redemption. The entire primaeval history would at once sink to the level of a purely decorative addition to the work, ending in a picture of the condemnation of the nations by God. Against this interpretation, detracting as it does from the whole point of the work, we have also the fact that this statement (i.e., Gen 12:3b) at the end of the divine promise stands at a point of the narrative which marks it out as the climax of the whole section. If we allow it only the pale, attenuated meaning suggested, it is completely overshadowed in importance by what has gone before.

Advocates of this view might reasonably be asked whether their exegesis is not based upon a modern misunderstanding of the nature of a blessing. If the nations of the earth wish for themselves the blessing of Abraham, they are wishing to benefit from that power to bless which ultimately belongs to God (Mowinckel, *Psalmenstudien* 5, 6ff.), in which case the suggested interpretation would in effect differ little from our own.

102. Gunkel, *Genesis*, 161, 163; ET *Genesis*, 162–63.

103. We have already seen from the way in which the Joseph story has been incorporated into the Settlement tradition that the interests of the Yahwist are not confined to one single line of motivation. Cf. pp. 45–46 above.

104. Kurt Galling, *Die Erwählungstradition Israels*, BZAW 48 (Giessen: Töpelmann, 1928), 68ff.

105. Leonhard Rost, *Die Überlieferung von der Thronnachfolge Davids*, BWANT 42 (Stuttgart: Kohlhammer, 1926), 139. [Ed.] See Rost, *The Succession to the Throne of David*, trans. Michael D. Rutter and David Gunn, HTIBS 1 (Sheffield: Almond, 1982).

106. Cf. Hempel, *Die althebräische Literatur*, 116ff.

107. Alt, *Staatenbildung*, 65 (*KS* 2:54); *EOTHR*, 225–26.

108. Even if the materials incorporated into Judges 1 are of pre-Yahwistic origin (cf. Wilhelm Rudolph, *Der "Elohist" von Exodus bis Josua*, BZAW 68 [Berlin: Töpelmann, 1938], 272), this does not affect the literary use that is made of them in J. For that matter, it can be shown that a great deal of the material in J is of pre-Yahwistic origin.

109. Sigmund Mowinckel, *The Two Sources of the Predeuteronomic Primaeval History (JE) in Gen I–XI*, ANVAO 1937, 2 (Oslo: Dybwad, 1937).

110. Ibid., 44ff.

111. Hempel, *Die althebräische Literatur*, 125.

112. Galling, *Erwählungstradition*, 45–46.

113. Noth, *Josua*.

114. Ibid., xiiff. (cf. 2d ed. [1953], 7ff.).

115. Rudolph, *Der Elohist*.

[116.] Josh 18:1.—Tr.

2. THE PROMISED LAND AND YAHWEH'S LAND IN THE HEXATEUCH

1. Despite the contrary opinion of Noth, the lists contained in Joshua must be assigned to P; see Martin Noth, *Das Buch Josua*, 2d ed., HAT 1/7 (Tübingen: Mohr/Siebeck, 1953),13ff. The formula, "the lot came out for . . ." is closely linked with Josh 14:1b, 2; 19:51, and these texts in turn are linked with Num 32:18; 34:17 (P). There is also the problem whether P[B] contained the conflated list of places and boundaries, whilst P[A] gave only a summary account of the partition of the land; compare Gerhard von Rad, *Die Priesterschrift im Hexateuch: Literarisch Untersucht und theologisch Gewertet*, BWANT 65 (Stuttgart: Kohlhammer, 1934).

2. Only in one instance is the word *nḥlh* used of the hereditary land of a clan, in the context of a legal provision codified but not actually composed by the deuteronomist (Deut 19:14a).

3. On the question of Lev 25:23 see p. 63 above.

4. Cf. pp. 38–50 above.

5. Albrecht Alt, *Der Gott der Väter* (Stuttgart: Kohlhammer, 1929), 71 (*KS* 1:66); "The God of the Fathers," in *EOTHR*, 63–64 [3–77].

6. Cf. Bernhard Luther in Eduard Meyer, *Die Israeliten und ihre Nachbarstaemme: Alttestamentliche Untersuchungen* (Halle: Niemeyer, 1906), 108; Otto Eissfeldt, *Hexateuchsynopse* (Leipzig: Hinrichs, 1922), 30.

7. Compare Alt, *Der Gott der Väter*, 72 n.1 (*KS* 1:67 n.1); *EOTHR*, 65 n.176.

8. Gunkel, *Genesis*, 164; ET *Genesis*, 163.

9. Alt, *Ursprünge*, 65–66. (*KS* 1:327–28); "The Origins of Israelite Law," in *EOTHR*, 128–29 [79–132].

10. Alt, *Ursprünge*, 65 (*KS* 1:327); *EOTHR*, 128.

11. Cf. J. Kohler, "Gemeinschaft und Familiengut im israelitischen Recht," *Zeitschrift für vergleichende Rechtswissenschaft* (1905) 217.

12. Ludwig Köhler holds that the partition of the land by lot is not to be thought of as a cultic act, but as a wholly secular proceeding ("Alttestamentliche Theologie III," *TRu* 8 [1936] 252–53 [248–84]). We beg leave to doubt, however, whether it is true that "the notion of the 'lot' need not necessarily point to a personal act of a deity." Surely what we have here is a quite fundamental notion, for the Hexateuch knows of no other kind of notion. The land was always of vital concern to Yahwistic belief, and in dividing it by lot the people of God, the *qhl Yhwh*, understood themselves to be the agent of the divine will.

13. Alt, "Erwägungen über die Landnahme der Israeliten in Palästina," *KS* 1:171, 121 [126–75]; "The Settlement of the Israelites in Palestine," in *EOTHR*, 166–67 [133–69]; "Staatenbildung," 61 (*KS* 2:51); "The Formation of the Israelite State in Palestine," in *EOTHR*, 222–23 [171–237].

14. Quite exceptionally, in Deut 26:1ff., the obligation of offering the first-fruits is related to Yahweh's redemptive activity as expressed in the short historical creed which follows.

15. Walther Eichrodt, *Theologie des Alten Testaments* (Leipzig: Hinrichs, 1933), 71 (5th ed., 1957, 92). Eng. trans. by John Baker, 1961.

16. Alt, "Israels Gaue unter Salomo," in *Alttestamentliche Studien für R. Kittel*, (Leipzig: Hinrichs, 1913), 16 [1–19] (*KS* 2:87 [76–89]).

17. An example of the historical conception outside the hexateuchal tradition is to be seen at Judg 11:24: "All that Yahweh our God has dispossessed before us, we will possess."

18. See pp. 27–31 above.

19. The idea that Israel *as a whole* has a *nḥlh* is not found in pre-deuteronomic writings, except in one single instance at Judg 20:6. The notion that Israel is Yahweh's *nḥlh*, however, was certainly current at an earlier date: cf. 2 Sam 20:9; 21:3.

20. Cf. Kurt Galling, *Die Erwählungstradition Israels*, BZAW 48 (Giessen: Töpelmann, 1928), 68ff.

21. It may be shown statistically that the deuteronomist departs from this linguistic usage only when he is compelled to do so by the usage fixed at an earlier date, as in Levi, Gad, Reuben, and the half-tribe of Manasseh.

22. Cf. pp. 82–88 below.

3. FAITH RECKONED AS RIGHTEOUSNESS

1. Cf. Hans-Wolfgang Heidland, *Die Anrechnung des Glaubens zur Gerechtigkeit*, BWANT 71 (Stuttgart: Kohlhammer, 1936), 4.

2. Ibid., 2–13.

3. For a fuller account of these declaratory formulae see Rolf Rendtorff, *Die Gesetze in der Priesterschrift: Eine gattungsgeschichtliche Untersuchung*, FRLANT 62 (Göttingen: Vandenhoeck & Ruprecht, 1954). [Ed.] See also Rodney R. Hutton, "Declaratory Formulae: Forms of Authoritative Pronouncement in Ancient Israel," Ph.D. dissertation, Claremont Graduate School, 1983.

4. See p. 188 below.

5. Rudolf Smend, *Lehrbuch der alttestamentlichen Religionsgeschichte*, Sammlung theologischer Lehrbücher: Alttestamentliche Theologie (Freiburg: Mohr, 1893), 393.

4. THE JOSEPH NARRATIVE AND ANCIENT WISDOM

1. This despite Gunkel, who leaned far too heavily on the assumption that the Joseph story was in origin a saga in making his analysis of it.

2. The writer was able to establish only a quite marginal contact between the Joseph narrative and the promise made to the patriarchs, i.e., at Gen 50:24. So far as the history of the tradition itself is concerned (although not from a literary point of view) this is a quite secondary reference, unknown to the original, independent Joseph narrative.

3. Hermann Gunkel, *Genesis*, 397; ET *Genesis*, 383.

4. There is also a newly awakened interest in scientific natural history at this time: A. Alt, "Die Weisheit Salomos," *TLZ* 76 (1951) 139–44 (*KS* 2:90–99).

5. To this early wisdom literature we assign the collections of proverbs, dating from the monarchic period: Prov 10:1—22:16; 22:17—24:22, 25-29.

6. *Ptahhotep* 24, from the translation by H. Kees. [Ed.] See *ANET*, 412–14.

7. Hermann Kees, *Kulturgeschichte des alten Orients*, Vol. 1: *Abschnitt-Ägypten*, Handbuch der Altertumswissenschaft, 3.1.3 (Munich: Beck, 1933), 268, 283.

8. Ludwig Köhler, *Old Testament Theology*, trans. A. S. Todd (London: Lutterworth, 1957), 110.

9. Gustav Boström, *Proverbiastudien: Die Weisheit und das fremde Weib in Spr. 1–9*, Lunds universitets årsskrift 30.3 (Lund: Gleerup, 1935), 15ff.

10. Compare "The Wisdom of Ani": "A woman who is far from her husband says to you every day, 'I am beautiful,' when there is no one to see." Erman, *The Literature of the Ancient Egyptians*, 240. [Ed.] See *ANET*, 420–21.

11. On the ideal of the taciturn man, see H. O. Lange, *Die Weisheit des Amenemope* (Copenhagen, 1925).

12. H. Kees, *Aegypten*, 284.

13. From the translation by H. Kees, *Lesebuch (Aegypten)* (Tübingen: Mohr/Siebeck, 1928), 46; cf. Kurt Sethe, *"Der Mensch denkt, Gott lenkt" bei den alten Aegyptern*, (Göttingen: n.p., 1925), 141ff. [Ed.] See *ANET*, 423 [421–24].

14. This intrusive skepticism is easily illustrated from the work of Amenemope. The faith that "puts itself into God's arms" (22:7) is closely akin to an embittered resignation: there is no success to be found at God's hands, and yet there is no opposing him. The man who strives to succeed is brought to nothing the very next moment (19:22—20:2).

15. H. Brunner, *Aegyptologie, Handbuch der Orientalistik*, 109.

16. H. Brunner, *Aegyptologie*, 107–8.

17. H. O. Lange, *Die Weisheit des Amenemope*, 21.

18. J. Spiegel, *Aegyptologie*, 117, 131.

19. B. Reicke, "Analogier mellan Josefsberättelsen I Genesis och Ras Shamra-Texterna," *SEÅ* 10 (1945) 5–30.

20. Helmuth Jacobsohn, *Die dogmatische Stellung des Königs in der Theologie der alten Aegypter*, Ägyptologische Forschungen 8 (Glückstadt: Augustin, 1939), 13ff.

5. THERE REMAINS STILL A REST FOR THE PEOPLE OF GOD

1. Deuteronomy is passionately opposed to all forms of Canaanite religion.

2. There is no need to enter into a discussion at this point as to whether this ought to be regarded historically as a direct concomitant of King Josiah's covenant.

3. Since this was written, it has been seriously questioned whether this is a correct delimitation of the deuteronomic work: cf. Martin Noth, *Überlieferungsgeschictliche Studien*, 2d ed. (Tübingen: Niemeyer, 1957), 1ff.

4. "Satan" is here the divinely ordered adversary.

5. The boldness of the statement at Gen 2:2 resides in the fact that the divine rest is not at this point made normative for the rhythm of human life, but is mentioned simply as a fact in its own right. Nothing is said here of the Sabbath law, and Israel learns of it only at Mt. Sinai.

6. THE ANCIENT WORD AND LIVING WORD—DEUTERONOMY

[1.] Note especially von Rad's own *Studies in Deuteronomy*, trans. David Stalker, SBT 1/9 (Chicago: Regenery, 1953); idem, *Deuteronomy*, trans. Dorthea Barton, OTL (Philadelphia: Westminster, 1966). But more recently Robert Polzin, *Moses and the Deuteronomist: A Literary Study of the Deuteronomic History* (New York: Seabury, 1980); Duane L. Christensen, editor, *A Song of Power and the Power of Song: Essays on the Book of Deuteronomy*, SBTS 3 (Winona Lake, Ind.: Eisenbrauns, 1993); Norbert Lohfink, *Theology of the Pentateuch: Themes of the Priestly Narrative and Deuteronomy* (Minneapolis: Fortress Press, 1994); S. Dean McBride, "Deuteronomy," in *DBI* 1:273–94; Alexander Rofé, *Deuteronomy: Issues and Interpretation*, OTS (London: T. & T. Clark, 2002); and James E. Brenneman, *On Jordan's Stormy Banks: Lessons from the Book of Deuteronomy* (Scottdale, Pa.: Herald, 2004).

2. Compare most recently, Edmund Schlink, "Gesetz und Paraklese," in *Antwort: Karl Barth zum siebstigen Geburtstag am 10. Mai 1956*, ed. Ernst Wolf, Charlotte von Kirschbaum, and Rudolf Frey (Zollikon: Evangelischer, 1956), 326–27.

[3.] Compare Frederick J. Cryer, *Divination in Ancient Israel and Its Near Eastern Environment: A Socio-historical Investigation*, JSOTSup 142 (Sheffield: JSOT Press, 1994); Lester L. Grabbe, *Priests, Prophets, Diviners, Sages: A Socio-historical Study of Religious Specialists in Ancient Israel* (Valley Forge, Pa.: Trinity, 1995); Ann Jeffers, *Magic and Divination in Ancient Palestine and Syria*, SHCANE 8 (Leiden: Brill, 1996).

7. THE TENT AND THE ARK

1. Compare Gerhard von Rad, *Das Geschichtsbild des chronistischen Werkes*, BWANT 54 (Stuttgart: Kohlhammer, 1930), 98ff.

2. Martin Dibelius, *Die Lade Jahwes: Eine religionsgeschichtliche Untersuchung*, FRLANT 7 (Göttingen: Vandenhoeck & Ruprecht, 1906), 38; Schmidt, "Cherubthron und Lade," in *Eucharisterion: Studien zur Religion und Literatur des Alten und Neuen Testaments*, FRLANT 36 (Göttingen: Vandenhoeck & Ruprecht, 1923), 137; and see esp. Johannes Hermann, *Die Idee der Sühne im Alten Testament* (Leipzig: Hinrichs, 1905), 32ff.

3. Cf. R. Hartmann, "Zelt und Lade," *ZAW* 37 (1917) 213; Exod 25:22; 29:42ff.; 30:6, 36; Num 17:19.

4. See, for example, Steuernagel *ad loc.*

5. See pp. 109ff. below.

6. Gressmann, *Altorientalische Bilder* (Berlin: de Gruyter, 1909), cxxxv.

7. I disagree here with Gressmann, who holds that the ark was provided with an image of a bull, or even two such images—a view that I find wholly untenable; Hugo Gressmann, *Die Lade Jahves* (Berlin: Kohlhammer, 1920).

8. Dibelius, *Lade*, 64ff.; Hartmann, "Zelt und Lade," 232ff.; cf. Reichel, *Die vorhellenischen Götterkulte* (Vienna, 1897).

9. Dibelius, *Lade Jahwes*, 65ff.

10. Clément-Ganneau, *Comptes rendus de l'académie des inscriptions* (Paris 1907); Ronzevalle, *Mélanges de la faculté orientale*, 3.2:753ff. contains various illustrations; cf. Vol. 5, (1924), Pl. XXXII for a further empty throne of Astarte in Syria. I have to thank Professor Alt for kindly bringing this archaeological material to my notice.

11. Gressmann, *Altorientalische Bilder*, 396–97.

12. P. Dhorme and L. H. Vincent, "Les Chérubins," *RB* 35 (1926) 489 [481–95].

13. We cannot accept the method by which H. Schmidt attempts to reconstruct the cherub-throne in the temple from the indications contained in Ezekiel 1 and 1 Chron 28:18 (*Cherubthron und Lade*). Ezekiel 1 leads to no valid inference: nothing is said of either the ark or the "cover" *kapporet*. What we have here is a vision in which the cherubim are not once mentioned by their usual name, and everything is expressed in visionary, transcendental terms. Where does it lead us? Schmidt makes the two cherubim spoken of in the description of the temple into four, changes the position of their wings, and fills out the picture into a war-chariot. If we compare this with the Chronicler's account, we are reminded that he has his own views on the position of the wings of the cherubim (2 Chron 3:13), which accord even less well with the conception of the four-wheeled chariot. Schmidt's reconstruction forces us to the conclusion that the reference to the ark is to be regarded as a secondary interpolation at 1 Chron 28:18, and that originally the ark bore no representations of cherubim at all.

14. Kurt Sethe, *Amun und die acht Urgötter von Hermopolis* (Berlin: de Gruyter, 1929), No. 4.

15. Kurt Galling, "Amun und der Gott des Alten Testaments," *TBl* 9 (1930) 105 [103–5].

16. It is worth mentioning that shortly *after* the time at which the conception associated with Amun would have had to be "taken over," there was a temple of Amun in Palestine which contained a large image of that deity! (Gressmann, *Altorientalische Bilder*, 98.)

17. Compare Gustav Westphal, *Jahwes Wohnstätten: nach den Anschauungen der alten Hebräer: eine alttestamentliche Untersuchung*, BZAW 15 (Giessen: Töpelmann, 1908), 55ff.

18. Dibelius, *Lade Jahwes*, 8–9.

19. In Num 10:29-32, the people gain a new leader; yet in spite of this, in Num 11:1ff. the people are grumbling again. Both before and after the passage in question the circumstances are those of peacetime.

20. Henry Preserved Smith, *The Books of Samuel*, ICC (Edinburgh: T. & T. Clark, 1899), 33.

21. The term "ark of God" (*'arôn haelohîm*) is used several times in 1 Samuel 4.

22. Mowinckel, *Psalmenstudien* 2, 109ff.

23. Dibelius, *Lade*, 116.

24. Only in one instance do we find an exception to this otherwise firmly maintained view—when the ark is installed in the temple. The cloud is mentioned in this connection at 1 Kgs 8:11. This is, however, pre-eminently a passage in which we cannot be sure that the purity of the original tradition has been maintained, for at this important point no less than three different conceptions have been brought together in the literary account. The actual indwelling of Yahweh in the Most Holy Place (v. 12), the appearance of Yahweh in the cloud (v. 11), and the belief that Yahweh is beyond heaven itself (v. 27) all find a place here.

25. Tur-Sinai, too, regards the ark as a throne, but fails to appreciate that the various statements about it must be differentiated historically; Naphtali H. Tur-Sinai, *Die Bundeslade und die Anfänge der Religion Israels*, 2d ed. (Berlin: n.p., 1930). He puts together all the relevant texts, and produces a description of a cultic object such as could never possibly have existed in view of all the anomalies involved. He regards the ark as a vehicle, symbolizing the storm-cloud; the "cover" (*kaporeth*) is that which conceals the deity; He is enthroned above the wings of the cherubim, who use these wings both to fly and to shelter Yahweh; and the throne itself supports a chest containing the tables of the Law. Apart from any other consideration, however, it must be said that there is no evidence whatever that the ark could be regarded both as a throne and as a receptacle *at the same time*.

26. In pre-exile times the ark was thought of almost exclusively as a throne: cf. Isa 6:1; 2 Kgs 19:14ff.; Jer 3:16ff.; 17:12.

27. Westphal, *Jahwes Wohnstätten*, 46ff.

28. Cf. Martin Noth, *Das System der zwölf Stämme Israels*, BWANT 52 (Darmstadt: Wissenschaftliche Buchgesellschaft), 66ff., 95; reprinted 1980.

8. The City on the Hill

1. On the subject of Israel in the Book of Isaiah, see Leonhard Rost, *Israel bei den Propheten,* BWANT 19 (Stuttgart: Kohlhammer, 1937), 32ff.

2. See Henri van den Bussche, *Le Texte de la prophétie de Nathan sur la dynastie davidique* (Louvain: Nauwelaerts, 1948).

3. Johannes Jeremias, *Der Gottesberg: Ein Beitrag zum Verständnis der biblischen Symbolsprache* (Gütersloh: Bertelsmann, 1919); Hugo Gressmann, *Der Messais,* FRLANT 43 (Göttingen: Vandenhoeck & Ruprecht, 1929), 164ff.

4. The text given here is a translation of the MT. The word "house" in v. 2 is missing in LXX. According to Mic 4:1, the word *nakôn* should stand immediately before *berô'š.* In the text of the Isaiah Scroll found in 1948, dating from the first or second century B.C.E., the words *'el har Yhwh* are missing (*BASOR* [Oct. 1948] 17).

5. To remove this "trait of nature mythology" from the Isaianic oracle is a completely arbitrary proceeding. Whenever it mentions the mountain of Yahweh, the prophetic tradition always regards it as a mountain which towers above all others: Ezek 17:20-24; 20:40; 40:2; Zech 14:10.

6. The proclamation of the divine Law, notably the Decalog, took place at the climax of the Feast of Booths. Cf. Albrecht Alt, *Ursprünge,* 63ff. (*KS* 1:325ff.), *EOTHR* 126–32.

[7.] RSV: "shall cover."—Tr.

[8.] RSV: "will arise."—Tr.

[9.] RSV: "will be seen upon you."—Tr.

10. Verse 12 is a later addition, in prose.

11. Karl Elliger, *Die Einheit des Tritojesaja, Jesaia 56–66,* BWANT 45 (Stuttgart: Kohlhammer, 1928), 87. Anton Causse has also shown in a most evocative manner how the common fund of material drawn from the history of oriental civilization may be brought to bear upon such texts. Cf. *Le Mythe de la nouvelle Jerusalem* (Paris: Alcan, 1938), 8ff. At the great pilgrim festivals people of all kinds came together, fairs were held, games were arranged, justice was administered, and even bitter enmities and feuds were set aside. "Under the protection of the *pax divina* tribes and races came together who otherwise lived apart, and knew peace and security only within their own borders" (Julius Wellhausen, *Skizzen und Vorarbeiten,* vol. 3: *Reste arabischen Heidentums* [Berlin: Reimer, 1887], 84).

12. The use of the term *šereth* (serve, minister to) in v. 10 is probably significant in this respect. The word is used in the later period almost exclusively of cultic service. Israel is the holy people, and the kings of the heathen will at that time serve Israel in much the same way as the Levites now serve the priests (Num 3:6; 18:2).

13. The verb used here is highly significant: *yebaśśerû.* [RSV: "proclaim" (v. 6).—Tr.]

14. *Weltgeschichtliche Betrachtungen,* 170.

15. In v. 6, *'aḥath* should not be taken to mean, "once again," but is to be understood as a variant of *'ôd me'at* (so Wellhausen).

16. Perhaps we ought rather to point thus: *hamudoth.*

17. LXX has a fuller text at v. 9: ". . . and peace of soul, to renew the whole foundation,

to repair this temple." Wellhausen and Budde both regard this as original; but since the passage follows the closing formula, "says Yahweh of hosts," it must certainly be an addition.

18. It has long been recognized as a deficiency in Isaiah's presentation of the matter that Israel itself has no part in the eschatological program. The addition of Isa 2:5 to the original oracle ("O house of Jacob, come, let us walk in the light of Yahweh") is evidently intended to make good this omission.

9. The Beginnings of Historical Writing in Ancient Israel

1. Eduard Schwartz, *Gesammelte Schriften* (Berlin: de Gruyter), 1:54.

2. As an example of this failure to think historically, one may cite Herodotus (2:142), who tells us that Egyptian priests gave him a brief account of the whole immense span of Egyptian history, and goes on to say, "During this period (equal to three hundred and forty-one generations) the sun had behaved exceptionally on four occasions. Twice it had risen where it usually sets, and twice it had set where it usually rises. Yet throughout this period nothing had changed in Egypt with regard either to the produce of the land or of the river, or to sickness or to the number of deaths."

3. Hermann Schneider, *Die Kulturleistungen der Menschheit* (Leipzig: Weber, 1907), 1:138ff.

4. Schwartz, *Gesammelte Schriften,* 1:56.

5. Johannes Hessen, *Platonismus und Prophetismus,* 2d ed. (Munich: Reinhardt, 1955), 19.

6. Elias Auerbach, *Wüste und gelobtes Land* (Berlin: Wolff, 1936), 1:42ff.

7. It should be remarked, however, that in their present form these narratives have almost always lost their original etiological purpose. They have been incorporated into new theological context of overriding significance, and in the process their essential meaning has often been completely overlaid.

8. Ludwig Köhler, *Old Testament Theology,* trans. A. S. Todd (London 1957), 93.

9. Otto Regenbogen, "Thukydides als politischer Denker," *Das humanistische Gymnasium* (Heidelberg 1933), 17.

10. Regenbogen, "Thukydides," 21ff.

11. Hugo Gressmann, *Die Schriften des Alten Testaments,* 2d ed. (Göttingen: Vandenhoeck & Ruprecht, 1922), 2:203.

12. Gressmann, *Schriften,* 2:204.

13. Ibid., 208.

14. Leonhard Rost, *The Succession to the Throne of David,* trans. Michael D. Rutter and David M. Gunn, HTIBS 1 (Sheffield: Almond, 1982).

15. The story of the ark in its present form has been broken up into several pieces, *inter alia* 1 Sam 4; 5; 6:1—7:1; 2 Sam 6:1-20a.

16. The literary analysis of 2 Samuel 7 presents great difficulty. Two points may nevertheless be made with certainty: first, that this narrative was originally a self-contained,

independent story known as such to the historian and incorporated by him into the introductory part of his work; secondly, that the section at that time was not, of course, in its present heavily edited form, but belonged to an earlier stratum of which we may perhaps discern traces in vv. 11b and 16. Cf. Rost, *Succession*, 35–56.

17. Rost, *Succession*, 78–79.

18. Caspari, *Die Samuelbücher*, KAT 7 (Leipzig: Deichert, 1926), 524. "The narrator's technique is nothing short of brilliant. In both parts of the story he keeps the reader in breathless suspense. Delicate matters are dealt with so tactfully that no one can take offence, and indeed these matters are scarcely noticed. The smooth manner in which evil designs are stealthily carried out is inimitably presented both in the letter given to Uriah and in Joab's report." Gressmann, *Schriften*, 2:79.

19. Rost, *Succession*, 61.

20. Karl Budde, *The Books of Samuel*, trans. B. W. Bacon (Baltimore: Johns Hopkins Univ. Press, 1894).

21. Ibid.

22. So, rightly, Gressmann, *Schriften*, 2:17; Caspari, *Die Samuelbücher*, 579.

23. Ahithophel was, of course, Bathsheba's grandfather—2 Sam 11:3; 23:24.

24. A similar procedure was known among the ancient Egyptians. One of the first actions of a new king was to take possession of his predecessor's harem, in order to have the royal wives under his own hand.

25. Concerning this divisive political situation, cf. Alt, *Staatenbildung* (*KS* 2:1–65); *EOTHR*, 171–265.

26. Rost, *Succession*, 67–69. Rost also shows here that 1 Kings 1 never existed as an independent narrative. No one, indeed, who has made a study of the historical work as a whole, will fail to recognize in 1 Kings 1 the handiwork of the same narrator.

27. Rost, *Succession*, 101.

28. Hans Schmidt, *Die Geschichtsschreibung im Alten Testament*, Religionsgeschichtliche Volksbücher 2/16 (Tübingen: Mohr/Siebeck, 1911), 20.

29. Schwartz, *Gesammelte Schriften*, 1:56.

30. Albrecht Alt, *Staatenbildung*, (*KS* 2:47); *EOTHR* 218–19.

31. For the reasons that necessitated these constitutional changes, see Alt, *Staatenbildung*, *KS* 2:44ff., 54ff., 61ff., 74ff.; *EOTHR* 214ff., 223ff., 228ff., 236–37.

32. All efforts to identify the narrator with one of the characters mentioned in the account result in nothing more than vague conjectures. Following Duhm, it has become fashionable to ascribe the account to the priest Abiathar, one of David's most faithful supporters. Cf. 1 Sam 22:22-23; 23:6; 30:7; 2 Sam 15:24; 17:15; 19:12; 1 Kgs 1:7, 19, 25; 2:22, 26ff. But the author may very well have been a member of the court who is completely unknown to us.

33. Artur Weiser, "Die theologische Aufgabe der alttestamentlichen Wissenschaft," in *Werden und Wesen des Alten Testaments*, BZAW 66 (Berlin: Töpelmann, 1936), 213.

34. H. Schmidt, *Geschichtsschreibung*, 21.

35. Johannes Hempel, *Das Ethos des Alten Testaments*, BZAW 67 (Berlin: Topelmann, 1938), 51. Even if 2 Sam 12:11-12 is a later addition to Nathan's prophetic denunciation,

this would not affect the present issue, for the editorial addition would be wholly in keeping with the spirit of the original. The editor has simply underlined one of the less prominent ideas implicit in the story by formulating it as a prophetic pronouncement.

36. Eduard Meyer, *Geschichte des Altertums*, 3d ed. (Stuttgart: Cotta, 1953), 2:285–86: "Thus the golden age of the Hebrew monarchy produced genuinely historical writing. No other civilization of the ancient East was able to do so. Even the Greeks achieved it only at the height of their development in the fifth century, and then as quickly fell away again. Here, on the contrary, we are dealing with a nation that had only just become civilized. The factors which were conducive to this, including the possession of an easily learned script, came to them as to the Greeks from the former occupants of their land; but this only makes their achievement the more astonishing. Here, as in all historical situations, we have the insoluble problem of innate ability. By virtue of their achievement in historical writing, realized independently and fully-grown from the start, the civilization of Israel must be ranged alongside that which was achieved on the soil of Greece to a richer and fuller degree some centuries later.

37. Regenbogen, "Thukydides," 17–18.

38. Ibid., 21–22.

39. "It is at the sanctuary itself that the prayer begins to be fulfilled, and there is no doubt that the narrator sees in this circumstance a sign that the hand of God is working for David's salvation." H. Schmidt, *Geschichtsschreibung*, 24.

40. Schwartz, *Gesammelte Schriften*, 1:41ff.

41. So far as foreign affairs were concerned, the reign of Solomon was very peaceful. No burning issues of a strategic or political nature arose at all. It may be to this that we should attribute one of the more obvious shortcomings of this historical work—that it regards personal and family relationships as the exclusive source of all political conflicts. It should doubtless rather have drawn a distinction between purely adventitious causes and the more deeply rooted issues inherent in the situation. The age of Solomon, however, was less a time of great political consciousness than it was of outstanding cultural achievement. We must also take into account the fact that the writer is not sufficiently far removed from the events themselves to be able to diagnose the faults and weaknesses inherent in the structure of the state. To the observer who stands in close relationship to the situation, the personal factors always loom larger than the objective ones.

10. THE DEUTERONOMIC THEOLOGY OF HISTORY IN 1 AND 2 KINGS

1. Martin Noth, *Überlieferungsgeschichtliche Studien*, 2d ed. (Darmstadt: Wissenschaftliche Buchgesellschaft, 1957).

2. We have limited our present study to 1 and 2 Kings on the grounds that for the deuteronomist the reign of Solomon marks a new departure in every sense, and it is only at this point that he broaches what is really his main theme.

3. His method is thus very different from that of the writer of the history of the

succession to the throne of David. This earlier writer shows his reader the problem of the human and political entanglements in which the king is involved, and presents it as a succession of inescapable consequences. See Gerhard von Rad, *Archiv für Kulturgeschichte* (Berlin: Duncker, 1944), 33ff. Cf. pp. 133–42 above.

4. This is especially true of the great epilogue to the fall of the Northern Kingdom (2 Kgs 17:7ff.).

5. Yahweh's word is not "empty," *req.*

6. The following list should be preceded by the important prophecy in 1 Sam 2:27-36 and its fulfillment in 1 Kgs 2:27 [viz., that the house of Eli should be cut off.—Tr.].

7. It seems very doubtful whether a history of the prophet Ahijah of Shiloh, comparable to the histories of Elijah, Elisha, and Isaiah, ever existed as a complete and independent entity, as Noth asserts (*Überlieferungsgeschichtliche Studien*, 121). If it had, we should at least be obliged to recognize that the literary problems raised by this assumption are of quite a different order from those implicit in the histories of the other prophets. A much greater degree of manipulation must be postulated on the part of the deuteronomist, since Ahijah's utterances are fully integrated with the unmistakable deuteronomic purpose of this work, which is to show the working out of Yahweh's plans for the heirs to David's throne and empire.

8. "(Yahweh) will give Israel up because of the sins of Jeroboam, which he sinned and which he made Israel to sin" (1 Kgs 14:16).

9. Pre-deuteronomic occurrences of this expression are found at 2 Sam 21:17; Ps 132:17; and compare 2 Sam 14:17.

10. In the view of the deuteronomist, it is the responsibility of the King to maintain vicariously the due relationship between God and the people (so Noth, *Überlieferungsgeschichtliche Studien*, 137)—a wholly "undeuteronomic" attitude!

11. The verses bring the work to "an ending that speaks of hope in the grace of God"; Ludwig Köhler, *Old Testament Theology*, trans. A. S. Todd (London: Lutterworth, 1957), 93.

12. The deuteronomist makes Solomon give very clear expression to his correspondence which exists between God's word and the course of history: "Thou didst speak with thy *mouth* and with thy *hand* hast fulfilled it this day" (1 Kgs 8:24).

11. THE ROYAL RITUAL IN JUDAH

1. Bernhard Stade, "Anmerkungen zu 2 Kö. 10–14," *ZAW* 5 (1885) 280ff. [275–97].

2. Judges 10:4 and 12:14 speak of a male ass, *'ayir*. Cf. Ludwig Köhler, *Kleine Lichter*, (Zurich: Zwingli, 1945), 52ff.

3. Solomon must therefore have been led back into the city through the Water Gate (cf. Neh 3:26; 12:37).

4. Cf. Albrecht Alt, *Staatenbildung*, 16ff. (*KS* 2:11ff.); *EOTHR*, 183ff.

[5.] RSV: "platform".—Tr.

6. From an unpublished text of the Eighteenth Dynasty (Hatshepsut). I have to thank Professor H. Kees for his advice in matters of Egyptology as well as for the translations

of the texts. It should be mentioned that Legrain claims to have found the actual spot, marked by an alabaster plaque let into the floor near the eastern entrance (cf. 2 Chron 23:13!) of the great colonnaded hall.

7. Cf. Hermann Kees, *Kulturgeschichte des alten Orients (Aegypten)* (Munich: Beck, 1933), 173. Cf. also Hans Bonnet, *Bilderatlas zur Religionsgeschichte (Aegyptische Religion)* (Leipzig: Deichert, 1934), Plates 63, 65.

[8.] BDB: "testimony of the Ten Words on the tables as a solemn divine charge."—Tr.

9. Sethos I has left an account in the necropolis at Karnak of the words addressed to him by Thoth: "I have written your protocol with my own fingers," "I ascribe to you a hundred thousand years"; C. R. Lepsius, *Denkmäler aus Aegypten* (Berlin: Nicolaische, 1849), 3:151.

10. Lepsius, *Denkmäler*, 4:285. [Queen Hatshepsut is regularly represented in monuments as a man, and is addressed as if she were a king, whence the apparent confusion of genders in the passages cited.—Tr.]

11. Ibid.

12. Lepsius, *Denkmäler*, 4:160.

13. Compare, for example, Hermann Gunkel, *Die Psalmen* HAT (Göttingen: Vandenhoeck & Ruprecht, 1925); Rudolf Kittel, *Die Psalmen* (Leipzig: Deichert, 1914) (on Psalm 2).

14. Richard Krätzschmar, *Die Bundesvorstellung im Alten Testament* (Marburg: Elwert'sche, 1896).

15. For an example of such a speech, see Lepsius, *Denkmäler*, 4:80.

16. H. Gressmann, *Der Messias*, FRLANT 43 (Göttingen: Vandenhoeck & Ruprecht, 1929), 244.

[17.] A conjectural emendation of the unintelligible *hirbîta haggôy lo'* to read: *hirbîta haggîla*—Tr.

18. Isaiah 9:3 is the only example in Proto-Isaiah, since the case is rather different in Isa 6:8, 11, and the "psalm" at Isa 12:1ff. can scarcely be regarded as Isaianic.

19. Wilhelm Caspari, *Echtheit und Hauptbegriff der messianischen Weissagung in Jesaia IX,1-6*, BFCT 12 (Gütersloh: Bertelsmann, 1908).

12. THE THEOLOGICAL PROBLEM OF THE OLD TESTAMENT DOCTRINE OF CREATION

1. Wilhelm Lütgert, *Schöpfung und Offenbarung: Eine Theologie des ersten Artikels*, BFCT 2/34 (Gütersloh: Bertelsmann, 1934), 52, 56, 358, etc. Reprinted Giessen: Brunnen, 1984.

2. Compare Gerhard von Rad, *Die Priesterschrift im Hexateuch: Literarisch Untersucht und theologisch Gewertet*, BWANT 65 (Stuttgart: Kohlhammer, 1934), 188.

3. Karl Müller, *Fragmenta Historicorum Graecorum*, 5 vols. (Paris: Didot, 1841), 3:111ff. Reprinted Frankfurt: Minerva, 1975.

4. Johannes Fichtner, *Die altorientalische Weisheit in ihrer israelitisch-jüdischen Ausprägung*, BZAW 62 (Giessen: Töpelmann, 1933).

5. Hermann Ranke in *AOT*, 35–36. [Ed.] See *ANET*, 417 [414–18].

6. Adolf Erman, *The Literature of Ancient Egyptians,* trans. A. M. Blackman (London: 1927), 283. [Ed.] See *ANET,* 365 [365–67].

7. Psalm 104 even contains an echo of the battle with the primeval dragon, a feature not found of course in the Egyptian version. The fact is an indication of the manner in which in later times the small coin of the conception of creation could be admitted into almost any appropriate context.

8. There is a strong element of awe, therefore, at the very heart of what is actually a purely technical problem.

9. A similar process is at work in Prov 8:22-31.

13. "Righteousness" and "Life" in the Cultic Language of the Psalms

1. Kurt Galling, *ZAW* (1929), 125.

2. Henri Cazelles's essay, "Sur un rituel du Deuteronome: Deut xxvi, 14," *RB* 55 (1948), was not available to me at the time of writing. Deuteronomy provides a rather compli-cated set of regulations on this matter. In certain instances the tithe is paid locally as a sort of "poor-law rate" (Deut 14:28), but a declaration had also to be made at the central sanc-tuary to the effect that ritual demands have been met. Doubtless this is an attempt to accommodate an ancient practice to the law of the central sanctuary. The assertion in the passage quoted was originally made when the tithes were handed over in the sanctuary.

3. In its present form the list contains a few affirmative statements interspersed among the negative ones. In its original form as part of a liturgical rite it certainly con-sisted of negative statements throughout. This list was not, of course, composed by Ezekiel himself, but was an extant composition he incorporated into his own work. Ezekiel is evidently quite intentionally using ancient cultic material as a means of pre-senting his own theological case.

4. In recent exegesis it has become almost standard practice to regard statements made in this psalm somewhat patronizingly as a wistful delineation of the ideals of a scholar poring over the books of the Law. The peculiarly trite diction of the wisdom writ-ers has often led to a serious failure on the part of exegetes to recognize the intensely concentrated nature of their theology.

5. Hermann Gunkel and Joachim Begrich, *Introduction to Psalms,* trans. James D. Nogalski, MLBS (Macon, Ga.: Mercer Univ. Press, 1998).

6. H. Cremer, *Biblisches Theologisches Wörterbuch* (see under *dikaios*). Cf. K. H. Fahlgren, *Ṣedaka: Nahestehende und entgegengesetzte Begriffe im Alten Testament* (Uppsala: Almqvist & Wiksell, 1932).

7. A considerable number of psalms seem not to spring directly from situations of cultic life, but traces of their form-categories and the typical modes of expression remain to betray their former cultic purpose.

8. The text is uncertain at this point. [RV: "he seeth his face with joy: and he restoreth unto man his righteousness." RSV gives a quite different rendering.—Tr.]

9. Cf. also Psalm 110.

10. It might also be said that these declarations often go beyond the limits of what is psychologically possible, e.g., "Trouble and anguish have come upon me, but thy commandments are my delight" (Ps 119:143). If the "laments" allow of such protestations of righteousness on the one hand, and of such abject confession of sin on the other, this is not to be attributed either to the individual temperament or to the personal experience of the worshiper. These extremes are rather to be attributed to the power of the cultus to objectify and to depict typical situations.

11. The text is uncertain at this point (v. 5).

12. This despite Fahlgren, *Sedaka,* 111.

13. Concerning the proclamation of the Law at the Feast of Booths, cf. Alt, *Ursprünge,* p. 65. For the deuteronomic exhortation, cf. pp. 20ff. above.

14. Joachim Begrich, "Das priestherliche Heilsorakel," *ZAW* 52 (1934) 81–92.

15. Sigmund Mowinckel, *Psalmenstudien* 6: *Die Psalmdichter* (Christiania: Dybwad, 1924), 8ff.

16. On Psalm 22, Delitzsch makes the perspicacious observation that "In this psalm David reaches a depth in his complaint which goes far beyond the depth of his suffering, and he attains to a height in his hopes which surpasses the height of any possible reward for his sufferings."

17. "The sufferer is neither dead nor yet in a full sense alive. He is somewhere in between. The decisive factor for him, however, is not that he is still alive, but that he is near to the realm of death." Christoph Barth, *Die Errettung vom Tode in den individuellen Klage- und Dankliedern des Alten Testaments* (Zollikon: Evangelischer, 1947), 117.

18. Ibid., 145.

19. Ibid., 152.

20. We cannot be content to translate the much-debated verb *bqr* simply by "to search" to "to consider closely." The very context in which it stands in Psalm 27 demands that we should think of a more particular, cultic activity. The same is true of the occurrence at 2 Kgs 16:15, although we cannot here examine this text in detail. In the Nabataean language the term *mubaqqiru* is occasionally found as the designation of a cultic official (*CIS,* 2:2118, 2593, 2661, 2667–69), perhaps one who watches the sacrifice. It is not surprising that the verb has a more general connotation in the later parts of the Old Testament, e.g., Ezra 4:15, 19; 6:1, 7, 14. Even Mowinckel regards the occurrences in Ps 27:4, etc., as connected with the watching of a sacrifice. (Mowinckel, *Psalmenstudien* 1:146.) Compare in a contrary sense Hugo Gressmann, *TLZ* (1917) 154.

21. It is difficult to say how we ought to image the cultic process by which Yahweh "passed by." Wolfram von Soden has drawn my attention to a passage in an Assyrian law which seems to refer to a ritual of this kind: ". . . as for the residue (of an inheritance), let the gods pass by" (*Altassyrisches Gesetz,* 25:91). Here is seems that the passing by of the gods (*etequ*) is regarded as a kind of ordeal, in which presumably cultic emblems were carried past.

22. The inexplicable form *tômîk* is commonly read as *tômek.* The text however still remains suspect, for the meaning "hold" does not fit at all well. It has long been thought likely that the word derives from a verbal stem that is otherwise unknown to us, perhaps

with the meaning "to make wide."

23. Albrecht Alt, *Ursprünge*, 65ff. (=*KS* 1:327–28); *EOTHR*, 127–28. Cf. also *Palästina-jahrbuch* 35 (1939) 36–37 (=*KS* 1:150–51).

24. Cf. pp. 85ff. above.

25. It would be very satisfying, and more consonant with our own position, if we could render *miqdešê 'el* by "mysteries," by analogy with Wis 2:22 (so Duhm, Sellin, etc.). But this will not do. *Miqdaš* is always used of the sanctuary as an actual building, and LXX renders it *hagiastērion*, not "mystery." It is difficult to say what kind of experience is referred to here. Since it is found in the same context as the destruction of the wicked, it might perhaps be a divine judgment. Cf. 1 Kgs 8:31ff.

26. This revival of an ancient element of the faith was achieved in this case, as always, only at the expense of some modification of its significance. The old notion of redemption as a physical act is stripped of its ancient, half-mythological dress, and is here certainly thought of as something done by God *after* death.

27. Barth's attitude in this matter is surprising. He has interpreted brilliantly the Old Testament notion of death as found in the Psalms, but he does not draw the obvious inferences concerning the notion of life!

28. Ezekiel 8:14 mentions the cult of a dying and rising god (Tammuz) in the temple at Jerusalem!

14. Some Aspects of the Old Testament Worldview

1. So far as the sources are at all explicit on the matter, the relationship of the deity to the image is determined by sacral (and also anthropological) concepts of a far from simple order. Cf. Karl-Heinz Bernhardt, *Gott und Bild: Ein Beitrag zur Begründung und Deutung des Bilderverbotes im Alten Testament*, Theologische Arbeiten 2 (Berlin: Evangelische, 1956), *passim*.

2.   "As far as ear can hear, as eye can see,

      Thou find'st but known things to compare him with;

      And still the highest flight of thy soul's fire

      May be content with that which represents. . . ." (Goethe, *Proömion*)

3. *Amixia* or *epimixia* is a notion of ancient civic law. Others besides the Jews were reproached with shunning intercourse (*commercium, connubium?*) with other nations.

4. Helmut Gollwitzer, *Die Existenz Gottes im Bekenntnis des Glaubens*, 2d ed., BET 34 (Munich: Kaiser, 1963), 113ff.

5. Georg Picht, "Die Musen," *Merkur* (1963) 627.

6. Hans Urs von Balthasar, *Herrlichkeit: Eine theologische Ästhetik* (Einsiedeln: Johannes, 1961), 1:33. [Ed.] See the English edition, *The Glory of the Lord: A Theological Aesthetics*, vol. 1: *Seeing the Form*, ed. Joseph Fessio and John Riches (New York: Crossroad, 1983).

7. Johannes Hempel, "Ich bin der Herr, dein Arzt," *TLZ* (1957) 809ff.

[8.] Compare chapters 9 and 10 in this volume.—Tr.

9. Otto Procksch, *Die Genesis*, 3d ed., KAT 1 (Leipzig: Deichert, 1924), 97.

10. Hans-Joachim Kraus, *Die Verkündigung der Weisheit: Eine Auslegung des Kapitels Sprüche 8*, Biblische Studien 2 (Neukirchen: Buchhandlung des Erziehungsvereins, 1951), 31.

[11.] Cf. RSV: "the whole earth is full of his glory."—Tr.]

12. Psalm 19.

[13.] Following the translation of Heinrich Schlier.—Tr.

15. Job 38 and Ancient Egyptian Wisdom

1. Hermann Gunkel and Joachim Begrich, *Introduction to Psalms: The Genres of the Religious Lyric of Israel*, trans. James D. Nogalski, MLBS (Macon, Ga.: Mercer Univ. Press, 1998), 54ff.

2. Alan H. Gardiner, *Ancient Egyptian Onomastica*, 2 vols. (London: Oxford Univ. Press, 1947).

3. Amenemope 12-23; Job 38:22-29.

4. Gardiner, *Onomastica*, 7ff.

5. Ibid., 37.

6. Cf. the form-critical analysis made by Curt Kuhl, *Die drei Männer im Feuer (Daniel, Kapitel 3 und seine Zusätze): Ein Beitrag zur israelitisch-jüdischen Literaturgeschichte*, BZAW 55 (Giessen: Töpelmann, 1930), 90–100.

[7.] The original German uses throughout the text of the Benedicite found in the edition of Rahlfs, which includes interpolated verses omitted in RV. The author dismisses these verses as spurious, on the authority of Rothstein, in Emil Kautzsch, *Die Apokryphen und Pseudepigraphen des Alten Testaments*, 2 vols. (Tübingen: Mohr/Siebeck, 1900), 1:182; the text and numbering of verses in the present translation is therefore that of RV.—Tr.

8. Since this was written, my assistant, Klaus Baltzer, has drawn my attention to a list in 2 Esdras 7:39-42: "neither sun, nor moon, nor stars, nor clouds, nor thunder, nor lightning, nor wind, nor rainstorm, nor fog, nor darkness, nor evening, nor morning, nor summer, nor spring, nor heat, nor winter, nor ice, nor frost, nor hail, nor storm, nor dew, nor noonday, nor night, nor shining, nor twilight, nor light . . . ." The series is interesting in that it shows that such compilations existed in Israel in non-poetical material. The question as to whether this list is related to Genesis 1 calls for a separate study.

9. Erman, *The Literature of the Ancient Egyptians*, trans. A. M. Blackman (London 1927), 228ff.; cf. *ANET*, 477–78.

10. The authors of Job and *Papyrus Anastasi I* are, or course, widely removed from one another in chronology, but this form-category used in wisdom literature shows a quite extraordinary persistence. The "professional satire," fashionable in Egypt in the time of the Middle Kingdom, is still found in Ben Sira (38:24-34).

11. A special problem arises with regard to the questions, "Have you gone?" "Have you not been?" and the like. Were these in fact school questions? Did the teacher seek to make his instruction vivid by the pretence that his pupils had actually seen the places concerned? It may perhaps rather be that such questions represent a literary development of this form-category.

12. Albrecht Alt., "Syrien und Palästina im Onomastikon des Amenope," in *KS* 1:231ff.

13. Gardiner, *Onomastica*, 4n.1.

14. It is unnecessary to cite in this connection the Babylonian and Assyrian lists (cf. Lubor Matouš, *Die lexicalischen Tafelserien der Babylonier und Assyrer in den Berliner Museen,* 2 vols. [Berlin: Staatlichen Museen 1933]), since the order of the items in these lists is quite different. The characteristic arrangement, passing on from the heavens and heavenly bodies to meteorological phenomena and then to the earth itself, is known only in Egyptian texts and in Israelite material derived from them. Even the Ras Shamra lists offer no comparable parallels.

An understanding of these correspondences may help in assessing the onomastica and their purpose. We underestimate the learned character of these compilations if we think of them only as spelling books for use in scribal schools (cf. Erman, *Literature,* 190ff.). It is highly improbable that the wisdom writers of Israel based their poetical instructional compositions on spelling books!

16. The Levitical Sermon in 1 and 2 Chronicles

1. Ludwig Köhler, *Hebrew Man,* trans. Peter R. Ackroyd (New York: Abingdon, 1956).

2. We need not discuss here the question as to how far Köhler is right in thinking that the deuteronomic sermon derives from the prophetic pronouncements of an Amos, Hosea, Micah, or Isaiah.

3. Gerhard von Rad, *Das Geschichtsbild des chronistischen Werkes,* BWANT 54 (Stuttgart: Kohlhammer, 1930).

4. Following LXX; the MT is corrupt and gives no good sense.

5. Jer 29:14 = 2 Chron 15:2b; Jer 31:15 = 2 Chron 15:7b.

6. Without the word *zewa'ah,* also at Mic 6:16.

7. So J. Wilhelm Rothstein in *Das erste Buch der Chronik,* KAT 18 (Leipzig: Deichert, 1927), ad loc.

8. Compare 2 Chron 6:41-42, which cites verses from Psalm 132; cf. also von Rad, *Geschichtsbild,* 127.

9. Rothstein, *Die heilige Schrift des Alten Testaments,* ad loc.

10. Ibid., 500.

11. We must not be misled by the fact that the Chronicler presents many of these sermons in the guise of inspired utterances, and that occasionally even the style and form of prophetic oracles are found in them (e.g., the phrase, "Thus says Yahweh," *koh 'amar Yhwh*). These are secondary features, to be explained on the grounds of the general character of the work as a whole.

12. We need not consider at this point how far it is possible to apply the term "sermon" as the designation of a form-category to other literary units. Cf. Konrad Beyer, in his dissertation, *Spruch und Predigt bei den vorexilischen propheten: Eine Untersuchung der Gestalt der Prophetischen mündlichen Verkündigung* (Erlangen: Gutenberg,1933).

13. von Rad, *Geschichtsbild,* 40–41.

Bibliography

Gerhard von Rad's Works in English

Books

1953 *Studies in Deuteronomy.* Translated by David Stalker. SBT 1/9. London: SCM. German ed. 1947.

1960 *Moses.* World Christian Books 32. New York: Association. German ed. 1940.

1961 *Genesis.* Translated by John H. Marks. OTL. Philadelphia: Westminster. German ed. 1958.

1962 *Old Testament Theology.* Vol. 1: *The Theology of the Historical Traditions.* Translated by D. M. G. Stalker. New York: Harper. German ed. 1957.

1965 *Old Testament Theology.* Vol. 2: *The Theology of the Prophetic Traditions.* Translated by D. M. G. Stalker. New York: Harper & Row. German ed. 1960.

1966 *Deuteronomy: A Commentary.* Translated by Dorthea Barton. OTL. Philadelphia: Westminster. German ed. 1964.

1966 *The Problem of the Hexateuch and Other Essays.* Translated by E. W. Trueman Dicken. New York: McGraw-Hill. German ed. 1965.

1968 *The Message of the Prophets.* Translated by D. M. G. Stalker. New York: Harper & Row. Abridged edition of *Old Testament Theology,* vol. 2.

1972 *Wisdom in Israel.* Translated by James D. Martin. Nashville: Abingdon. German ed. 1970.

1976 *Genesis.* Translated by John H. Marks. 2d ed. OTL. Philadelphia: Westminster. German ed. 1972.

1977 *Biblical Interpretation in Preaching.* Edited by Ursula von Rad. Translated by John E. Steely. Nashville: Abingdon. German ed. 1972.

1980 *God at Work in Israel.* Translated by John H. Marks. Nashville: Abingdon. German ed. 1974.

1991 *Holy War in Ancient Israel.* Translated and edited by Marva Dawn. Grand Rapids: Eerdmans, 1991. German 4th ed. 1965.

Articles

1951   "Man and the Guidance of the Hidden God in the Old Testament." *The Student World* 44:140–47.

1959   "The Origin of the Concept of the Day of Yahweh." *JSS* 4:97–108.

1961   "Ancient Word and Living Word: The Preaching of Deuteronomy and Our Preaching." *Int* 15 (1961) 3–13. Translated by Lloyd Gaston.

1961   "History and the Patriarchs." *ExpT* 72:213–16.

1961   "Typological Interpretation of the Old Testament." *Int* 15:174–92. Translated by John Bright. Reprinted in *Essays on Old Testament Hermeneutics*, edited by Claus Westermann, 17–39. Richmond, Va.: John Knox, 1963.

Major Works in German

1929   *Das Gottesvolk im Deuteronomium.* BWANT 47. Stuttgart: Kohlhammer.

1930   *Das Geschichtsbild des chronistischen Werkes.* BWANT 54. Stuttgart: Kohlhammer.

1934   *Die Priesterschrift im Hexateuch.* BWANT 65. Stuttgart: Kohlhammer.

1938   *Das formgeschichtliche Problem des Hexateuch.* BWANT 78. Stuttgart: Kohlhammer.

1940   *Mose.* Wege in der Bibel 3. Göttingen: Vandenhoeck & Ruprecht.

1948   *Deuteronomium-Studien.* FRLANT 58. Göttingen: Vandenhoeck & Ruprecht.

1949–53   *Das erste Buch Mose: Genesis.* ATD. Göttingen: Vandenhoeck & Ruprecht.

1951   *Der heilige Krieg im alten Israel.* ATANT 20. Zurich: Zwingli.

1957   *Theologie des Alten Testaments.* Vol. 1: *Die Theologie der geschichtlichen Überlieferungen.* Munich: Kaiser.

1958   *Gesammelte Studien zum Alten Testament.* ThBü 8. Munich: Kaiser. Expanded ed. 1965.

1958   *Der heilige Krieg im alten Israel.* Rev. ed. Göttingen: Vandenhoeck & Ruprecht.

1960   *Theologie des Alten Testaments.* Vol. 2: *Die Theologie der prophetischen Überlieferungen.* Munich: Kaiser.

1964   *Das fünfte Buch Mose: Deuteronomium.* ATD 8. Göttingen: Vandenhoeck & Ruprecht.

1965   *Gesammelte Studien zum Alten Testament.* Expanded ed. ThBü 8. Munich: Kaiser.

1965   *Gesammelte Studien zum Alten Testament 2.* Edited by Rudolf Smend. ThBü 48. Munich: Kaiser.

1967   *Die Botschaft der Propheten.* Munich: Siebenstern Taschenbuch.

1970   *Weisheit in Israel.* Neukirchen-Vluyn: Neukirchener.

1971   *Das Opfer des Abraham.* Kaiser Traktate 6. Munich: Kaiser.

1972   *Predigten.* Edited by Ursula von Rad. Munich: Kaiser.

1974   *Gottes Wirken in Israel: Vorträge zum Alten Testament.* Edited by Odil Hannes Steck. Neukirchen-Vluyn: Neukirchener.

1976   *Erinnerungen aus der Kriegsgefangenschaft, Frühjahr 1945.* Neukirchen-Vluyn: Neukirchener.

Assessments of von Rad and His Work

Andrew, M. E. "Gerhard von Rad—A Personal Memoir." *ExpT* 81 (1972) 296–300.

Baumgärtel, Friedrich. "Gerhard von Rad's *Theologie des Alten Testaments.*" *TLZ* 86 (1961) 801–16.

Brueggemann, Walter. "Foreword." In Gerhard von Rad, *Old Testament Theology*, translated by D. M. G. Stalker. OTL. Louisville: Westminster John Knox, 2001. Reprinted in *idem, The Book that Breathes New Life,* edited by P. D. Miller, 60–82. Minneapolis: Fortress Press, 2004.

Crenshaw, James L. *Gerhard von Rad.* Makers of the Modern Theological Mind. Waco, Tex.: Word, 1978. Reprinted, Peabody, Mass.: Hendrickson, 1991.

———. "von Rad, Gerhard (1901–1971)." In *Historical Handbook of Major Biblical Interpreters,* edited by Donald K. McKim, 526–31. Downers Grove, Ill.: InterVarsity, 1998.

———. "*Wisdom in Israel,* by Gerhard von Rad." *RSR* 2.2 (1976) 6–12.

Davies, G. Henton. "Gerhard von Rad, *Old Testament Theology.*" In *Contemporary Old Testament Theologians,* edited by R. R. Laurin, 63–89. Valley Forge, Pa.: Judson, 1970.

Groves, Joseph W. *Actualization and Interpretation in the Old Testament.* SBLDS 86. Atlanta: Scholars, 1987.

Honecker, Martin. "Zum Verständnis der Geschichte in Gerhard von Rad's *Theologie des Alten Testaments.*" *EvTh* 23 (1963) 143–68.

Knight, Douglas A. *Rediscovering the Traditions of Israel: The Development of the Traditio-historical Research of the Old Testament, with Special Consideration of Scandinavian Contributions.* SBLDS 9. Missoula, Mont.: Scholars, 1973.

Koch, Klaus. "Gerhard von Rad." In *Tendenzen der Theologie in 20 Jahrhundert: Eine Geschichte in Porträts,* edited by Hans Jürgen Schultz, 483–87. Stuttgart: Kreuz, 1966.

Rad, Gerhard von. "Gerhard von Rad über Gerhard von Rad." In *Probleme biblischer Theologie: Gerhard von Rad zum 70. Geburtstag,* edited by Hans Walter Wolff, 659–61. Munich: Kaiser, 1971.

Rahner, Karl. "Gerhard von Rad." *Das Parlament* 35 (August 26, 1972) 10.

Schmidt, Werner H. "'Theologie des Alten Testaments' vor und nach Gerhard von Rad." *VF* 17 (1972) 1–25.

Smend, Rudolf. "Gerhard von Rad." In idem, *Deutsche Alttestamentler in Drei Jahrhunderten,* 226–54. Göttingen: Vandenhoeck & Ruprecht, 1989.

———. "Rad, Gerhard von (1901–71)." In *DBI* 2:364–65.

Spriggs, D. G. *Two Old Testament Theologies: A Comparative Evaluation of the Contributions of Eichrodt and von Rad to Our Understanding of the Nature of Old Testament Theology.* SBT 2/30. Naperville: Allenson, 1974.

Wolff, Hans Walter. "Gespräch mit Gerhard von Rad." In *Probleme biblischer Theologie: Gerhard von Rad zum 70. Geburtstag,* edited by Hans Walter Wolff, 648–58. Munich: Kaiser, 1971.

———, Rolf Rendtorff, and Wolfhart Pannenberg. *Gerhard von Rad: Seine Bedeutung für die Theologie.* Munich: Kaiser, 1973.

Zimmerli, Walther. "Gerhard von Rad, *Theologie des Alten Testaments.*" *VT* 13 (1963) 100–111.

FESTSCHRIFTEN IN HONOR OF VON RAD

Alston, Wallace J., Christian Möller, and Helmut Schwier, editors. *Die Predigt des Alten Testaments: Beiträge des Symposiums "Das Alte Testament und die Kultur der Moderne"—Anlässlich des 100. Geburtstags Gerhard von Rad (1901–1971), Heidelberg, 18.-21. Oktober 2001.* Altes Testament und Moderne 16. Münster: Lit, 2003.

Clines, David J. A., Hermann Lichtenberger, and Hans-Peter Müller, editors. *Weisheit in Israel: Beiträge des Symposiums "Das Alte Testament und die Kultur der Moderne"—Anlässlich des 100. Geburtstags Gerhard von Rad (1901–1971), Heidelberg, 18.-21. Oktober 2001.* Altes Testament und Moderne 12. Münster: Lit, 2003.

Rendtorff, Rolf, and Klaus Koch, editors. *Studien zur Theologie der alttestamentliche Überlieferungen.* Neukirchen: Neukirchener, 1961.

Wolff, Hans Walter, editor. *Probleme biblischer Theologie: Gerhard von Rad zum 70. Geburtstag.* Munich: Kaiser, 1971.

Select Bibliography on
Old Testament Theology and
the History of Israelite Religion

Albertz, Rainer. *A History of Israelite Religion in the Old Testament Period*. 2 vols. Translated by J. Bowden. OTL. Louisville: Westminster John Knox, 1994.

Anderson, Bernhard W. *The Contours of Old Testament Theology*. Minneapolis: Fortress Press, 1999.

Barr, James. *The Concept of Biblical Theology: An Old Testament Perspective*. Minneapolis: Fortress Press, 1999.

Barton, John. *Understanding Old Testament Ethics: Approaches and Explorations*. Louisville: Westminster John Knox, 2003.

Bellis, Alice Ogden, and Joel S. Kaminsky, editors. *Jews, Christians, and the Theology of the Hebrew Bible*. SBLSymSer. Atlanta: Society of Biblical Literature, 2000.

Brueggemann, Walter. *Old Testament Theology: Essays on Structure, Theme, and Text*. Edited by Patrick D. Miller. Minneapolis: Fortress Press, 1992.

———. *Reverberations of Faith: A Theological Handbook of Old Testament Themes*. Louisville: Westminster John Knox, 2002.

———. *Theology of the Old Testament: Testimony, Dispute, Advocacy*. Minneapolis: Fortress Press, 1997.

Childs, Brevard S. *Biblical Theology of the Old and New Testaments: Theological Reflection on the Christian Bible*. Minneapolis: Fortress Press, 1993.

———. *Introduction to the Old Testament as Scripture*. Philadelphia: Fortress Press, 1979.

———. *Old Testament Theology in a Canonical Context*. Philadelphia: Fortress Press, 1986.

Cross, Frank Moore. *Canaanite Myth and Hebrew Epic: Essays in the History of the Religion of Israel*. Cambridge: Harvard Univ. Press, 1973.

Dietrich, Walter. *Theopolitik: Studien zur Theologie und Ethik des Alten Testaments*. Neukirchen-Vluyn: Neukirchener, 2002.

———, and Martin A. Klopfenstein, editors. *Ein Gott allein? JHWH-Verehrung und biblischer Monotheismus im Kontext der israelitischen und altorientalischen Religionsgeschichte*. OBO 139. Göttingen: Vandenhoeck & Ruprecht, 1994.

Edelman, Diana Vikander, editor. *The Triumph of Elohim: From Yahwisms to Judaisms*. CBET 13. Kampen: Kok Pharos, 1995.

Gerstenberger, Erhard S. *Theologies in the Old Testament*. Translated by John Bowden. Minneapolis: Fortress Press, 2002.

————. *Yahweh the Patriarch: Ancient Images of God and Feminist Theology.* Translated by Frederick J. Gaiser. Minneapolis: Fortress Press, 1996.

Gnuse, Robert. *No Other Gods: Emergent Monotheism in Israel.* JSOTSup 241. Sheffield: Sheffield Academic, 1997.

Gunneweg, Antonius H. J. *Biblische Theologie des Alten Testaments: Eine Religionsgeschichte Israels in biblisch-theologischer Sicht.* Stuttgart: Kohlhammer, 1993.

Hanson, Paul D. *The People Called: The Growth of Community in the Bible, with a New Introduction.* Louisville: Westminster John Knox, 2001.

Hasel, Gerhard F. *Old Testament Theology: Basic Issues in the Current Debate.* 4th ed. Grand Rapids: Eerdmans, 1991.

Hermisson, Hans-Jürgen. *Alttestamentliche Theologie und Religionsgeschichte Israel.* Forum Theologische Literaturzeitung 3. Leipzig: Evangelische, 2000.

Hubbard, Robert L., Robert K. Johnston, and Robert P. Meye, editors. *Studies in Old Testament Theology.* Dallas: Word, 1992.

Janowski, Bernd. *Gottes Gegenwart in Israel: Beiträge zur Theologie des Alten Testaments.* Neukirken-Vluyn: Neukirchener, 1993.

Kaiser, Otto. *Der Gott des Alten Testaments: Theologie des Alten Testaments.* 3 vols. UTB. Göttingen: Vandenhoeck & Ruprecht, 1993–2003.

Keel, Othmar, and Christoph Ühlinger. *Gods, Goddesses, and Images of God in Ancient Israel.* Translated by Thomas H. Trapp. Minneapolis: Fortress Press, 1997.

Kim, Wonil, editor. *Reading the Hebrew Bible for a New Millennium: Form, Concept, and Theological Perspective.* 2 vols. Studies in Antiquity and Christianity. Harrisburg, Pa.: Trinity, 2000.

Knierim, Rolf P. *The Task of Old Testament Theology: Substance, Methods, and Cases.* Grand Rapids: Eerdmans, 1995.

Knohl, Israel. *The Divine Symphony: The Bible's Many Voices.* Philadelphia: Jewish Publication Society, 2003.

Kottsieper, Ingo et al., editors. *Wer ist wie du, Herr, unter den Göttern? Studien zur Theologie und Religionsgeschichte Israels: Für Otto Kaiser zum 70. Geburtstag.* Göttingen: Vandenhoeck & Ruprecht, 1994.

Kugel, James L. *The God of Old: Inside the Lost World of the Bible.* New York: Free Press, 2003.

Levenson, Jon D. *Sinai and Zion: An Entry into the Jewish Bible.* Minneapolis: Winston, 1985.

Linafelt, Tod, and Timothy K. Beal, editors. *God in the Fray: A Tribute to Walter Brueggemann.* Minneapolis: Fortress Press, 1998.

Metzger, Martin. *Schöpfung, Thron und Heiligtum: Beiträge zur Theologie des Alten Testaments.* Biblisch-theologische Studien 57. Neukirchen-Vluyn: Neukirchener, 2003.

Miller, Patrick D. *Israelite Religion and Biblical Theology: Collected Essays.* JSOTSup 267. Sheffield: Sheffield Academic, 2000.

————. *The Religion of Ancient Israel.* LAI. Louisville: Westminster John Knox, 2000.

————. *The Way of the Lord: Essays in Old Testament Theology.* FAT 39. Tübingen: Mohr/Siebeck, 2004.

————, Paul D. Hanson, and S. Dean McBride, editors. *Ancient Israelite Religion: Essays in Honor of Frank Moore Cross.* Philadelphia: Fortress Press, 1987.

Niditch, Susan. *Ancient Israelite Religion.* New York: Oxford Univ. Press, 1997.

Oeming, Manfred. *Verstehen und Glauben: Exegetische Bausteine zu einer Theologie des Alten Testaments.* BBB 142. Berlin: Philo, 2003.

Ollenburger, Ben C., editor. *Old Testament Theology: Flowering and Future.* Rev. ed. SBTS 1. Winona Lake, Ind.: Eisenbrauns, 2004.

Otto, Eckart. *Theologische Ethik des Alten Testaments.* Theologische Wissenschaft. Stuttgart: Kohlhammer, 1994.

Penchansky, David. *What Rough Beast? Images of God in the Hebrew Bible.* Louisville: Westminster John Knox, 1999.

Perdue, Leo G. *The Collapse of History: Reconstructing Old Testament Theology.* OBT. Minneapolis: Fortress Press, 1994.

———. *Reconstructing Old Testament Theology: After the Collapse of History.* OBT. Minneapolis: Fortress Press, 2005.

Preuss, Horst Dietrich. *Old Testament Theology.* OTL. Louisville: Westminster John Knox, 1995–96.

Rad, Gerhard von. *Old Testament Theology.* Translated by D. M. G. Stalker. 2 vols. New York: Harper & Row, 1962–65. Reprinted in OTL. Louisville: Westminster John Knox, 2001.

Rendtorff, Rolf. *Canon and Theology: Overtures to an Old Testament Theology.* Translated by Margaret Kohl. OBT. Minneapolis: Fortress Press, 1993.

———. *Theologie des Alten Testaments: Ein kanonischer Entwurf.* 2 vols. Neukirchen-Vluyn: Neukirchener, 1999–2001.

Religionsgeschichte Israels oder Theologie des Alten Testaments? Jahrbuch für biblische Theologie 10. Neukirchen-Vluyn: Neukirchener, 1995.

Schedl, Claus. *Zur Theologie des Alten Testaments: Der göttliche Sprachvorgang.* Vienna: Herder, 1986.

Schmidt, Werner H. *The Faith of the Old Testament: A History.* Translated by John Sturdy. Philadelphia: Westminster, 1983.

Smith, Mark S. *The Early History of God: Yahweh and the Other Deities in Ancient Israel.* 2d ed. Grand Rapids: Eerdmans, 2002.

———. *The Memoirs of God: History, Memory, and the Experience of the Divine in Ancient Israel.* Minneapolis: Fortress Press, 2004.

———. *The Origins of Biblical Monotheism: Israel's Polytheistic Background and the Ugaritic Texts.* New York: Oxford Univ. Press, 2001.

Smith-Christopher, Daniel L. *A Biblical Theology of Exile.* OBT. Minneapolis: Fortress, 2002.

Spieckermann, Hermann. *Gottes Liebe zu Israel: Studien zur Theologie des Alten Testaments.* FAT 33. Tübingen: Mohr/Siebeck, 2001.

Sun, Henry T. C., and Keith L. Eades, editors. *Problems in Biblical Theology: Essays in Honor of Rolf Knierim.* Grand Rapids: Eerdmans, 1997.

Tigay, Jeffrey H. *You Shall Have No Other Gods: Israelite Religion in the Light of Hebrew Inscriptions.* HSS 31. Atlanta: Scholars, 1986.

Toorn, Karel van der. *Family Religion in Babylonia, Syria and Israel: Continuity and Changes in the Forms of Religious Life.* SHCANE 7. Leiden: Brill, 1996.

———, Bob Becking, and Pieter W. van der Horst, editors. *Dictionary of Deities and Demons in the Bible.* 2d ed. Leiden: Brill, 1999.

Westermann, Claus. *Elements of Old Testament Theology.* Translated by Douglas W. Stott. Atlanta: John Knox, 1982.

Zevit, Ziony. *The Religions of Ancient Israel: A Synthesis of Parallactic Approaches.* New York: Continuum, 2001.

Zimmerli, Walther. *Old Testament Theology in Outline.* Translated by David E. Green. Atlanta: John Knox, 1978.

Index of Authors

Editor's Note: Dates (whenever available) have been supplied for
authors of earlier generations in order to provide historical context.

Index of Ancient Sources

279

FORTRESS CLASSICS *in* BIBLICAL STUDIES

K. C. Hanson, Series Editor

The Quest of the Historical Jesus
First Complete Edition
Albert Schweitzer
edited by John Bowden

Water for a Thirsty Land
Israelite Literature and Religion
Hermann Gunkel

Jesus and the Message of the New Testament
Joachim Jeremias

The Spirit and the Word
Prophecy and Tradition in Ancient Israel
Sigmund Mowinckel

The Fiery Throne
The Prophets and Old Testament Theology
Walther Zimmerli

The Book of Acts
Form, Style, and Theology
Martin Dibelius

From Genesis to Chronicles
Explorations in Old Testament Theology
Gerhard von Rad